William Bollaert

Antiquarian, Ehnological and other Researches in New Granada, Equador, Peru and Chili

with observations on the pre-Incarial, Incarial and other monuments of Peruvian nations

William Bollaert

Antiquarian, Ehnological and other Researches in New Granada, Equador, Peru and Chili
with observations on the pre-Incarial, Incarial and other monuments of Peruvian nations

ISBN/EAN: 9783742883834

Manufactured in Europe, USA, Canada, Australia, Japa

Cover: Foto ©ninafisch / pixelio.de

Manufactured and distributed by brebook publishing software (www.brebook.com)

William Bollaert

Antiquarian, Ehnological and other Researches in New Granada, Equador, Peru and Chili

ANTIQUARIAN,

ETHNOLOGICAL AND OTHER RESEARCHES

IN

NEW GRANADA,

EQUADOR, PERU AND CHILE,

WITH OBSERVATIONS ON THE

PRE-INCARIAL, INCARIAL, AND OTHER MONUMENTS OF

PERUVIAN NATIONS.

By WILLIAM BOLLAERT, F.R.G.S.

CORR. MEM. OF THE UNIV. OF CHILE, ETC. ETC.

WITH PLATES.

LONDON:
TRÜBNER & CO., PATERNOSTER ROW.
1860.

[The Right of translation is reserved.]

DEDICATION.

To SIR RODERICK IMPEY MURCHISON, G. C. St. S., M.A., D.C.L., V.P.R.S., Director-General of the Geological Survey of Great Britain and Ireland, Trust. Brit. Mus., Corr. Ins. Fr., etc. etc. etc.

Dear Sir,—

The distinction to which you have attained in the scientific world, and the interest you have ever evinced in all matters any way appertaining to geological, geographical and kindred pursuits, prove that I could not dedicate this volume to one more worthy of honor and respect than yourself.

Proud of the permission, and sincerely wishing the present work were more worthy of your acceptance,

I remain, Dear Sir,

Your obliged and faithful servant,

W. BOLLAERT.

ANTIQUARIAN, ETHNOLOGICAL,

AND OTHER RESEARCHES IN

NEW GRANADA, EQUADOR, PERU, & CHILE.

NEW GRANADA.

West Indies—New Granada—Santa Marta—History of Chibchas, or Muiscas—Emeralds—Carthagena—Isthmus of Darien—Panamá—Antiquities of New Granada—Chibcha Calendar—Chibcha language and vocabularies.

THE publication of the "Manual of Ethnological Inquiry," by the British Association, in 1852, gave me methodical instruction on the subject of ethnology in particular, and was of great use to me during my second visit to the New World, in 1853-4. The following passage —" Any amount of knowledge, however trifling it may appear in itself, may be of great value in connexion with other knowledge, and, therefore, will be welcomed"—leads me to hope that my researches and observations on some of the South American races, and their peculiar civilization, may not prove uninteresting.[1]

At present, one gets to the West Indies from Europe by steamer, in about twelve days, and to the shores of Terra Firma in three or four more.

We look about and inquire for the aboriginal race of the Antilles, once so populous. We are told that none are left—that they have long since been exterminated by the ruthless Spanish invader. We make some research and find that of the millions who at the discovery of America peopled Santo Domingo, not one pure descendant now exists; that there are only a few Carib families in the islands of St. Vincent and Trinidad,—that they are an indolent and harmless race, fast verging on extinction—intermarrying with Negroes and producing the Zambo, or with the Whites giving rise to the Mustee.

---

[1] Abstract of these observations read at the Dublin meeting of the British Association, 1857.—See Transactions of sections 121.

Schomburgh thinks that some of the monuments in Santo Domingo are the work of an earlier race than those discovered by the Spaniards.

Having sailed over the Caribbean Sea, we alight upon the bold shores of Colombia, covered with dense tropical vegetation. In the back ground are seen the icy peaks of the Sierras of Santa Marta, 20,000 feet or more above the ocean, and, amongst other great rivers, the Magdalena, where the magnificent Victoria Regia is found in such abundance as to be a troublesome weed.[1]

The first point I visited was Santa Marta, 11° 15' N., one of the principal ports of New Granada. Near to the town are a few Tanganga Indians, who are fishermen. At the period of the conquest this district was called Citarme, and with the Tangangas were other tribes, particularly the Gairas and Dorsinos.

Acosta[2] mentions that the Indians of this district had much gold and copper, also *gilt* copper—and the copper was gilt by the use of the juice of a plant rubbed over it, then put into the fire, when it took the gold colour. This author gives a drawing of an altar (destroyed by a Romish priest) of the Arauco Indians who inhabited the mountains of Santa Marta; also a curious terra cotta figure, the work of the ancient inhabitants of this part of the country.

New Granada produces cocoa, tobacco, cotton, indigo, rice, and sugar, in its fruitful vallies or savannas; also timber, dye woods, and cinchonas. There are pearl fisheries on its coasts. Its mountains and streams yield gold, silver, platina, and other metals; the mines of rock salt, coal, and emeralds are important.

The natives of the coast of the Atlantic, from Chiriqui to Goajira are of the Carib race,[3] and very like the Brasilo-Guarani; so are the Mocoas, Seboudoyes, Pastuzos, and others. Those of the country of Tuqueres correspond to the Ando-Peruvian race. The tribes of Chocó,[4] Antioquia,[5] Cauca, Popayan,[5] and Neiva have rather an

---

[1] Down the Paraná drift *Camilotes*, or large water lilies, and in the lagoons are anchored islands of the Victoria Regia, or Maiz del Agua (corn of the water); for its seeds are powdered into meal, from which is made excellent and nutritious bread.—La Plata, &c., by Page, U.S. Navy.

[2] Compendio Historico de la Nueva Granada, por J. Acosta, Paris, 1 vol. 8vo. —Resumen de la Historia de N. Granada, por C. Lopez, Bogotá.

[3] Memoria de la Nueva Granada, por Mosquera, New York, 1852.

[4] Chocó or Cholo, Indians of N. Granada, from the gulf of San Miguel to the Bay of Chocó, and thence, with a few interruptions, to the northern parts of Equador.—" Literature of the American Aboriginal Languages," by Herman E. Ludewig, Trübner, London.

[5] Some gold ornaments from Antioquia, 6° 50 N., are described further on as having something of an Aztec or Toltec character.

Aztec character.[1] The Chibchas or Muiscas have analogies with the Ando-Peruvians.

Some nations are still in a savage state, as the Mesayos, Caquetes, Choques, Mocoas, Omaguas, Goajiras, and others. Those on the Rio Hacha are stubborn, have long faces, their noses rising in the centre, gives them a stern look.

Many of the wild tribes preserve their languages, but the Chibchas and allied nations have nearly lost theirs and now speak Spanish. The Mesayos and some others are said to be cannibals and hardly recognise a Supreme Being; good and evil they attribute to the sun and moon; their ideas as to the immortality of the soul are very imperfect, and they believe in transmigration.

The Pubenanos and Coconucos were ruled, at the time of the conquest, by the chief Payan, and the Paeses and Pijaos by Calambas. In early times these tribes were united with those of Pasto, 1° 15′ N., to defend themselves against the nations of Quito; with the latter were those Peruvians brought in by Huayna-Capac, and who, after his death remained with Atahualpa.

The Coconucos cultivated maize, also other plants, including the potato, (Turma)[2] and patatá (sweet potato). The potato grows wild in the mountains of Paleterá. They counted by sevens, and as well as the Chibchas used and still use the Quipo or knotted coloured strings Mosquera says, there is no evidence to show that the *Chibchas* had the Quipu[3] from the Peruvians.

---

[1] Velasco, His. del reyno de Quito III, 38.—The Indians of Popayan are descendants of the Caribs of the Antilles. J. Acosta, 164, speaks of the powerful chief of Popayan—of a fortress capable of holding 3000 men—a city, the houses of which were large and covered with straw—and of a temple consecrated to their Bacchus.

[2] There is a valley in the interior once called Turmas, where the potato grew in abundance. In the Chibcha language the potato is Yomi; in Peru this root is known as Papa. Tschudi says, there is no word in Quichua for potato, but in the Chinchaysuyo it is Acsu. The patatá is called *camote* in Peru, but its Quichua name is Apichu.

[3] Humboldt observes: That before the introduction of hieroglyphical painting the Mexicans used the Quipu (this Prescott doubts) and which is not only found among the Canadians, but in remote times amongst the Chinese. A.D. 554, the ruin of the Tsin dynasty occasioned great disturbances in Eastern Asia, and about this period the Toltecs were coming south; A.D. 648 is given as the change from the Quipu to painting in Mexico. The Scyris, or kings of Quito, were between the Chibchas and Peruvians, and the Quipu does not appear to have been known to the Scyris. It seems to me that the Chibchas obtained the Quipu at the time of the conquest of Quito by the Peruvians. The leaves of the Ki is used among the women of the Sandwich islands as the Quipu.

They had stone instruments for tilling the land; they masticated the narcotic hayo (the coca of the Peruvians) with Pic or Mambi (an alcaline ash). Inde, a word of affirmation, was similar to the English word indeed.

The Coconucos still believe in evil spirits. Evil is Puil, likewise the name of the moon. Pansig, another term for the devil. Good they expect from Puitcher, also the name for the sun; the stars Sil, the pleiades site-silg; the word site may come from the Spanish word siete; the planets, Silg or Sull; the month Canapuil, or a moon.

The wild Indians are generally polygamists, and some—as the Goijeros—have a wife for household affairs: another, who is the superior, for hunting and war.

The fierce and unsubdued Goajiros[1] inhabit the base of the mountains of Santa Marta. When arms have failed against the savages, the Spaniards have resorted to missionaries to subjugate them. Even these have failed with the Goajiros, who would make a priest load his own shoulders with the things his peons had brought, and thus conduct him to their borders.

Amongst the Goajiros a maternal uncle was counted a nearer relative than the father, "the child of a man's wife may be his, or it may not; but beyond a peradventure the son of the daughter of his mother must be his nephew."

For interesting statistics[2] of New Granada I refer to G. Mollien,[3] who observes, that documents of every kind are scarce; the journals, the memoirs of the viceroys, in which such valuable materials for American Statistics were to be found, have all been carried off or burnt; the members of the government (the Republican) are themselves in a great degree ignorant of the details of administration. In 1817,[3] the Spanish General, Murillo, was successful against the Republicans. His entry into Bogotá was the signal for the most sanguinary executions; he immolated more than 600 persons, including the men of talent: he caused their books and manuscripts to be brought to the public square and burnt. When the botanist, Caldas, was called upon to deliver up his precious papers, he exclaimed: "Take my life, but leave the manuscripts, they are treasures indeed; they have been the work of my entire life; there are things there, discoveries, never to be found again if you destroy my writings. For the love of God, save those papers! take them—if you like—to the King of Spain, for they belong to my country; better that this treasure should be in the

---

[1] Holton's N. Granada, 27.
[2] Colombia, in 1822-3.
[3] La Creation et ses Mystères Dévoilés, par A. Snider, 401.—Paris, 8vo, 1858.

hands of an enemy, than destroyed; posterity will bless you." Murillo ordered the execution of Caldas, and burnt twelve cart-loads of his manuscripts and books! Caldas was born in Popayan, 1771. Shot in 1816.[1]

There was published in Bogotá, the " Papal Periodico de Santa Fé de Bogotá,"[2] and alluded to by the "Mercurio Peruano," in its first number, of 1791. The " Mercurio" hoped, that before 1800 similar journals would appear in Buenos Ayres and Chile. The " Mercurio" went on for a few years, but was stopped by order of the Spanish government. However such periodical works gave much information relative to the ancient and modern history of the country and were important movers in the revolution which caused the colonies to separate from the mother country.

Before entering into details of the history of the Chibchas, I may mention that the principal city of that nation was Santa Fé de Bogotá, then called Theusaquillo, in 4° 36' N., 74° 14' W. Its mean temperature is 58° Fahr., is 8650 feet above the sea. Present population, 50,000 souls; and, situated on a plateau surrounded by mountains, the country is subject to frequent earthquakes.

The present population of the Republic is as follows:

Whites		450,000	} Intelligent and active.
Whites, as Quaterones and Mestizos		1,029,000	
Indians, civilized	310,000	421,000	} Patient, suspicious, frugal.
Indians, uncivilized	120,000		
Mulattos and Zambos		383,000	Strong, intelligent, brave.
Negroes, Ethiopic race		80,000	Patient, distrustful.
In 1843.—The census gave a population of		1,932,279	
" 1851.— Ditto ditto		2,243,730	
" 1858.—Estimated at		2,500,000	

M. Reclus[3] states, that before the Conquest, N. Granada had a population of eight millions.[4]

---

[1] Holton 265. Biography of Caldas,

[2] See Seminario Granadino, Paris edition, 1859—was commenced in 1808 by Caldas, called by Holton the Granadan Franklin.

[3] Bulletin de la Soc : de Geographie de Paris, Jan. et Fev., 1859.

[4] See Chronological Table of N. Granada, Holton 593.

HISTORY OF THE CHIBCHAS OR MUISCAS.[1]

The country of the Chibchas[2] comprehended the table-lands of Bogotá and Tunja, the vallies of Fusagasuga, Pacho, Caqueza, and Tensa, the territories of Ubate, Chiquinquirá, Moniquirá, and Leyva, and then by Santa Rosa and Sogomoso to the highest part of the Cordillera, from whence are seen the plains of Casanare. Its most extreme point to the N. is about Serinza in 6° N., and in the S. Suma Paz in 4°. Its length is near 45 leagues, the width from 12 to 15.

The greater portion of the population living in a cold climate without cattle, had to be careful and industrious, and had such abundance, that they sent to neighbouring districts gold in barter for fish and fruits of the hot countries.

The Chibchas were bounded on the W. by the Musos, Colimas, and Panches, warrior and ferocious tribes, with whom they were in continual hostility. On the N. were the Laches, Agataes, and Guanes, and on the E. by small tribes, who inhabited the country towards the plains, or in the slopes of the eastern cordillera.

Three principal chiefs governed the Chibchas with absolute power, and were blindly obeyed. The Zipa lived at Muequetá (Funza); the country then was surrounded by lakes and arms of the river that watered the beautiful plain, in the centre of which was the city. The Zaque first resided at Ramiriqui,[3] afterwards at Hunsa or Tunja; lastly, the chief of Iraca, who represented the theocratic element, as the successor of Nemterequetaba, the first civiliser of these regions, and who came to them from the East, by Pasca, and disappeared at Suamos or Sogomoso; from which point, towards the plains, the natives made a broad road, which was to be seen at the end of the 17th century.

The Usaques, or chiefs of the towns of Ebaque, Guasca, Guatavitá, Zipiquirá, Fusagasugá, and Ebaté, had only, in later times, lost their independence. The Zipa subjected them, but they preserved their jurisdiction and succession to the caciqueship, reserving to himself the power of nomination when there was no heir, in which case he generally chose from amongst the Guechas or military chiefs who commanded on his frontiers.

---

[1] Translated from "Compendio Historico del Descubrimiento y Colonization de la Nueva Granada, por el Coronel Joaquin Acosta, 8o. Paris, 1848.

[2] Sometimes called Muiscas, and was, after the Mexican and Peruvian nations, the next or third group of aborigines, who had claims to civilization.

[3] See Velez further on, for Pre-Chibcha remains. The country of the Zaque was called Quimi-Zaque, *Hervas*.—Stevenson I., 399. Hunca or Hunsa may mean, *holy city*.—Funza, said to have been the Capital of the Muiscas, the most powerful of the Chibcha nations in N. Granada.—Holton, 202.

The Zaque of Hunsa had likewise some tributary chiefs, but the Zipa continued to enlarge his dominions to the N. at the expense of his neighbour. Had the Spaniards not arrived when they did it is probable that the Zipa of Bogotá would have been the master of the whole of the Chibcha[1] territory, if we may judge from the rapid conquests he had made.

The Zipa we have some notice of was Saguanmachica, who began to govern about 1470. He conquered the Sutagaos, and their chief, Usathama, who, assisted by the cacique Tibacui, came to defend the valley of Fusagasugá near Pazca, where the open country commences.

The Sutagaos made but little resistance, and Tibacui being wounded, advised Usathana to submit to the Zipa, so as to preserve his state from devastation.

Saguanmachica descended with his army from the paramo or elevated plains of Fusinga to Pasca, which had then a well-beaten road to the valley of the Magdalena, he marched over the pleasant country of the valley of Fusagasuga, and returned to the table-land of Bogotá by the mountains of Subya.

The Zipa then prepared to extend his dominions towards the E. and N. He had many encounters with the cacique Ebaque (blood of wood) now Ubaque, to whom all the towns of the valley of Caqueza yielded obedience. He then went towards Chocontá, where Michua, the Zaque of Hunza, awaited him with his army. The battle was fought with such obstinacy that both chiefs fell, and the two armies retired to bury their dead and indulge in prolonged drunkenness, which was the custom when celebrating joy or grief.

Saguanmachica reigned twenty years, and was succeeded by Nemequene (bone of lion), he sent his nephew and heir, Thisquezuza[2], to chastise the Sutagoas, who had rebelled, and for which end he made a wide road by the mountains of Subya, portions of which was seen for many years after the conquest.

To subject the cacique Guatavitá (end of the mountains), Nemequene had recourse not only to force but to cunning, and taking advantage of a mandate of Guatavitas, which ordained that none of his people, who were celebrated for their industry and ability in the working of gold and

---

[1] Chibcha may have been the name given by the Spaniards to the inhabitants, from the divinity Chibchachum, to protect or support. Muisca, means a man. Cundinimarca, from Cundi-rumarca, seems rather an imaginary name for a portion of this country. Velez has but little belief that the people of this part of N. Granada called themselves either Muiscas or Chibchas. Muisca comes from Mu, the body; Isca, five, or body of five extremities.

[2] In the province of Tarapacá, South Peru, is a family named Quispe-Sugso, claiming descent from the Incas.

jewels, that they should not absent themselves to any neighbouring country without two from thence taking their place to work and pay tribute: thus Nemequene filled Guatavitá with his adherents; he also gained over to his side the cacique Guasca,[1] and approaching cautiously one night by the neighbouring heights, and at a pre-concerted signal, by means of fires, the Bogotans surprised the unprepared chief, killing his best soldiers, and in this way was Guatavita added to the dominions of the Zipa.

He then went against Ubaque, who ruled over the temperate valley situated behind the mountains to the E. of Bogota, now known as Caqueza, in which conquest he passed some months.

Proceeding to Zipiquirá he prepared to enter the territory of Ebaté (spilt blood). Although this cacique was the most powerful, he did not rule: neither in Susa (white straw), nor in Simijaca (owl's beak). The chiefs of these places joined the forces of Ubaté, and prepared to defend a narrow pass—the Boqueron of Tausa—a position easily defended, had these three chiefs been of one mind; but it was taken by the Bogotans in consequence of the discord amongst them; and the country was soon conquered to Savoya.[2]

The Zipa now believed that he could revenge old quarrels, resolved to march upon Tunja with more than 40,000 men. The Zaque, assisted by the chief of Suamoz, went out to meet the Zipa near Choconta, and proposed to settle the question by single combat with the Zipa, so as to spare the blood of his people. The Zipas officers would not accede to this offer, telling him that it was beneath his dignity to measure arms with an inferior. A bloody battle then ensued near the stream of the Vueltas. There were 100,000 combatants, and although they had only macanas (a wooden weapon like a sword) darts, tiraderas de carrizo (sort of arrows), and slings, the fight was a terrible one. The Zipa, seriously wounded, was taken from the field, leaving Hunsa victorious. Nemequene was borne on a litter to Muequeta, but five

---

[1] This is a Quichua word for rope; also the name of the last Inca, and spelt Guasca or Huasca.

[2] There was a very ancient Aymará chief in the P. of Tarapaca, S. Peru, named Taita or father Savaya; he was the rival of Taita Jachura for the hand of Mama Husnapa. The rivals fought, and Savaya's head was taken as a trophy to Husnapa. There are three high mountains in Tarapacá named after these worthies; the mountain of Taita Jachura is 17,000 feet above the level of the sea, and was ascended by Mr. Smith and myself when surveying the province. Taita Sayava is 20,000 feet. There is the Indian town of Sibaya to the S. of T. Jachura.—Geographical Soc. Journal, 121, 1851.

days after his arrival he died, leaving as his successor Thisquezuza, whom the Spaniards found ruling the country.[1] Thisquezuza, after having re-organised his army, subjected the Caciques of Cucunubá, Tibirita, and Garagoa, and was on the point of going to war with the Zaque of Hunsa; but, for the intervention of Nompaneme, of Suamoz, who, in consequence of his religious influence, induced them to conclude a truce for twenty moons.

It would appear that at an early period the Chibcha territory was subject to the Zaque of Hunsa, but to prevent civil war he nominated Hunsahua, the pontif of Iraca, to be the great chief, and who was succeeded by his descendants to Thomagata, a great wizard, known under the name of the great tailed chief, because he dragged a tail under his dress, and said he had the power of changing men into animals. Thomagata had no children, and his brother, Tutasua, succeeded him. By degrees his successors lost power in the N. until their lands were threatened under their last Zaque Quemunchatocha, to be incorporated into those of the Zipa of Bogotá. At the time of the conquest, the jurisdiction of Hunsa or Tunja in the E. was to the Cordillera; to the W. to Sachica and Tinjacá; in the S. to Turmequé; but in the N. was the cacique of Tundama, who was independent; and the sacred lands of Iraca or Sugamuxi (the disappeared). This last chief and priest, alternately elected from the people of the towns of Tobaza and Firibitoba, by the four neighbouring chiefs, Gameza, Busbanza, Pesca, and Tocá, so ordained by Nemterequetaba or Idacanza, the instructor of the Chibchas at his death, which he purposely hid from the people, so that his words might have a holy sanction; this law was in force for centuries, when, on a certain occasion, a bold chief of Firibitoba wished to usurp the sacerdotal power, he was abandoned by his people, and perished in a miserable manner.

The Heaven of the Chibchas and Mythological Traditions. —At the beginning of the world the light was enclosed in a very large something the Chibchas know not how to describe, but they called it Chiminigagua or the Creator; the first things that came from it were some black birds, which, flying about the world, threw from their beaks a resplendant air, that illumined the earth. After Chiminigagua, the

---

[1] In 1538 or 9, died near Bogotá, Zaqueszipa, the last Zipa of the Muiscas, "with extraordinary fevers;" these fevers—burnings—are supposed to have referred to the applications of heated horse-shoes to his feet, and other similar torments by Quesada. The object was to make him tell what had become of the treasures of his cousin Tisquesusa, whose kingdom he had usurped, when Quesada murdered him.—Holton, 248.

objects most venerated were the sun and moon, its companion.[1] The world was peopled in the following manner: Shortly after early morn of the first day, there came forth from the lake of Iguaque, four leagues N. of Tunja, a beautiful female, named Bachue or Fuzachogua, (meaning a good woman), with a boy three years of age. They descended to the plain, where they resided until the boy was grown up, when Bachue became his wife; and in them commenced the peopling of the world, which went on with great rapidity. Many years having passed, and seeing that the land was populated, they returned to the same lake, and, turning themselves into serpents, disappeared in its waters. The Chibchas venerated Bachue, and statues of gold and wood are still to be seen representing her and the boy at various ages. The natives believed that the souls left the bodies of the dead, went to the centre of the earth by yellow and black roads and precipices; first passing a great river on floats made of cobwebs, for which reason it was not permitted to kill the spider. In the future state, each nation had its particular location, so that they could cultivate the ground. Bochica was adored as their beneficent Deity, and Chibchacum as the particular Deity of the Chibchas, and especially the one who assisted in the cultivation of the soil, had care of traders and workers in silver. Bochica was the particular Deity of the Ubsaques, Neucatocoa was the Deity of the painters of mantles and weavers, he presided over the customary drunken revels, and the hauling of timber from the woods. He was represented as a bear covered with a mantle and dragging his tail along. To him was not made offerings of gold, beads, &c., as to the others, because they said it was enough that he drank his fill of chicha[2] with them. This Chibcha Bacchus was a slow, dull, and indecorous Deity; he was not held in veneration, and they said he danced and sang with them. They called Fo or Sorro, the Deity who had charge of the boundaries of their fields, and his place in the processions and feasts was called Chaquen; to him was offered the feathers and diadems with which they adorned themselves for battle, or for their feasts.

The goddess Bachue, mother of the human race, had charge also of the fields and their produce, and they burnt moque, and other incense to her honour.

---

[1] In the Chibcha language, Zue, Xue, Sua, Zupa, or Gagua, was the Sun, or the day; Chia, the Moon or Za night; these were adored as the representatives of the Supreme Power, called Ullco, Chibia or Hibia. In the Quichua, Inti was the Sun, Quilla the Moon. Pacha-camac, he who gives life to the Universe, was the Invisible God of the coast nations of Peru, and not that of Incas; and Viracocha is a later idea of God.

[2] Chicha was called in N. Granada, Aba.

They adored the rainbow, under the name of Cuchavira, and was the Deity in particular of those who suffered from agues, and was invoked by women in labour. The offerings made to this Deity were small emeralds, grains of gold, of low standard, and beads, of various colours, procured by barter from the natives of the coast. It is said that Chibchacum, angry at the excesses of the inhabitants of the table-land of Bogotá, resolved to punish them. He caused the waters of the Sapó and Tibitó (principal affluents of the Funza, which formerly ran towards other regions, but were transformed into a lake) to deluge the country. The Chibchas fled to the mountains, and implored Bochica, who appeared at sun-set on a rainbow; he convoked the nation, promised to remedy their ills, by not damming up their rivers, so that their lands might be properly watered. Then, throwing the rod of gold he had in his hands, he opened a breach at Tequendama; the waters fell down the precipice, discovering to them the plain, and more fertile than before[1]. Bochica did not limit his power to this act, and to chastise Chibchacum for having thus afflicted man, he obliged him to bear the burthen of earth, which was previously supported by pillars of guayacan wood.[2] Unfortunately, this measure has brought with it its inconvenience, for since then, at times, there are severe earthquakes, which the Indians say are caused by Chibchacum, tired of being in one position, shifts the weight of earth from one shoulder to the other, and, according to the care with which he does this hoisting, so is the intensity of the earthquake.

Observation leads to the belief that the Andes is one of the last protuberances formed on our planet, and, at the same time, in few traditions is it so plainly seen the geological explanation of a deluge as in this of the Chibchas.

TEMPLES AND PRIESTS.—Their temples were not in general of a sumptuous character, for the reason that they preferred making their offerings in the open air, as to lakes, cascades, and elevated rocks. In these temples, were large buildings, near to which resided the Geques or priests; there were vases of various forms to receive the offerings, or figures of clay, with a hole in the upper part, or plain jars

---

[1] The Indians had a tradition that Chia, Yubecayguaya, or Huitaca, a beautiful but malicious divinity, flooded the country, driving the inhabitants to the mountains. Botschica, her husband, called also Zuhe and Nemquetaba, transformed her into the moon, struck the barrier ridge with his staff, made the falls of Tequendama, drained the plains, and then retired to Sogomoso, where he reigned 2000 years.— Holton, 126.

[2] Huayacan, or holy wood, is a large tree; its wood does not rot under water, but even becomes harder, may be a Guayacum. This same wood was used in Peru, and preferred for their arms and idols, it resisted tools of copper.

buried up to the mouth; these remained open until filled with beads, bars, or tiles of gold, and figures of the same metal, representing animals, and other valuable articles, offered in times of their necessities, preparing themselves previously by severe fasting, the devout, as well as the Geques.[1] These last had a college called Cuca, where those who dedicated themselves to the priesthood, entered when very young; here they submitted for ten or twelve years to a rigorous diet, eating only once a day, and that food a small portion of ground maze with water, and rarely fish, the quapucha. During this period they were taught various ceremonies: the computation of time, the tradition of which, as well as all the others, were preserved by the Geques, who were the depositories of the abstract knowledge of the Chibchas, which was lost immediately after the conquests, because this class of men were the most persecuted by the Spaniards. They had celebrated temples; such a one was that of Sumaoz, burnt by the Spaniards the night they took the town.

WORSHIP OF THE SUN.—This was the only Deity to whom they offered sacrifices of human blood, killing young prisoners, and sprinkling with their blood the stones on which the first rays of the sun shone. These sacrifices, the processions, and solemn dances they performed on the sunas or roads, from the door of the habitation of the Cacique to some particular spot, generally some neighbouring ridge or height; and, lastly, the care with which the Guesa[2] was educated: a victim whose heart was torn from his body, every fifteen years, all had a direct and symbolic relation with the division of time, the calendar, and the ingenious and necessary intercalations, so as to make coincide exactly the course of the heavenly bodies, which directed their times of sowing and harvest.[3] The sanguinary and dramatic character of the sacrifices was calculated upon by the legislator of the Chibcha's to call the attention of the people, in such a way, that they should never forget what so much interested them to know, and was a substitute for the Quipos of the Peruvians.

The principal places of adoration of the Chibchas were lakes, where they could make offerings of the most precious things, without fear of

---

[1] The Muiscas had a great many idols, rudely sculptured, in gold, silver, wood, and wax. A male idol was placed by the side of a female idol. — T. Compans, Cundinamarca, 38.

[2] The sacrifice of a beautiful youth to the god Tezcatlepoca, or soul of the world, is of this character.—Prescott, Con. Mex. I., 62. Here the tragic story of the prisoner was expounded by the priests as the type of human destiny, which brilliant in its commencement, too often closes in sorrow and disaster.

[3] I have made a translation of the memoir by Duquesne on the calendar of the Muiscas, as it stands in J. Acosta's work, which will be found further on.

others profiting by them; for although they had confidence in their priests, and knew that they carefully buried the offerings in the vases destined to receive them, they were naturally more secure when they threw these objects themselves into lakes and rivers.

The lake of Guatavitá was the most celebrated of these sanctuaries; and each town had its path to go down to the lake and offer its sacrifices. Two cords were stretched across the lake so as to form right angles, and to the intersection went the raft with the Geques. Here the miraculous Cacica and her daughter were invoked, whom, they said, lived at the bottom in a delicious retreat, from the period, when in a moment of anger with another chief, her husband threw her into the lake; and here they made her offerings. Each lake had its tradition; and pilgrimages to these sanctuaries were common amongst the Chibchas.

At the period when the chief of Guatavitá[1] was an independent one, he made, annually, a solemn sacrifice, which for its singularity contributed to give celebrity to this lake, even to distant lands, and was the origin of the belief in the El Dorado[2]; in search of which, so many years and so much money was thrown away. On the appointed day, he anointed his body with turpentine (resin), then rolled himself up in gold-dust; thus gilded and resplendent, he embarked on the raft, surrounded by the Xeques, and in the midst of music and singing of the crowds covering the declivities, arrived at the centre. The chief deposited the offerings of gold, emeralds, and other precious objects, and he, at the same time, threw himself into the waters to bathe. At this moment, the neighbouring hills resounded with acclamations. This religious ceremony being over, they commenced dancing, singing, and drinking. In their monotonous songs they repeated the ancient history of their country, and what they knew of its deities, heroes, battles, and other memorable events, which were thus transmitted to posterity. At the door of the chief's dwelling, who presided at the feasts, sat two naked

---

[1] On the edge of the conical summit in which Lake Guatavitá is situated, are two tombs of chiefs, hewn in the sandstone.—Cochrane's Travels, II., 253. La Creation et ses Mystères Dévoilés, par A. Snider, 395. The Lake of Guatavitá is 3000 feet above the sea. At the conquest, the natives were persecuted for their treasures, when they threw their gold and precious stones into the lake. The agents of Capt. Cochrane drained it partially, and found a few small golden figures. Guatavitá is said to mean fire of the mountains, or volcanic fire. I have it elsewhere, end of the mountains. In 1562, gold figures were taken out of the lake, consisting of an alligator, thirteen toads or frogs, and three monkeys. In 1750, another search was made. Also in 1818, by A. M. Joseph, Paris.—T. Compans, 50.

[2] Account of expeditions in search of El Dorado, supposed by some to be near Lake Parima, 3° N. and 36° W. Paris.—Depons III., 275.

Indians, playing upon the chirimia,[1] a wind instrument, sad and shrill, covered only with a fishing net, which was the symbol of death, for, they said, we should never lose sight of death, especially in times of rejoicing. They had, besides, races and betting amongst the young men, the Chief rewarding the more swift.

CIVIL GOVERNMENT.—The government of the Zipa was despotic, as was that of the Zaque of Hunsa. The Zipa made the laws, administered justice, and commanded the troops, and so profound was the veneration in which he was held that no one dared to look him straight in the face.[2] All who approached the Zipa had to bring a present according to his means, but he accepted nothing from those who came to be judged; he had hundreds of concubines called Thiguyes, but one woman only was recognised as his wife. It was considered an honour for the Zipa to ask for the daughter or sister of any one to place amongst the number of his Thiguyes. Illicit affairs with these was severely punished; moreover, the heavy fines imposed upon the culpable one to save him from death, was a considerable item of the revenue of the Zipa.

The Zipa's heir was the eldest son of his sister, who, at ten years of age, was sent to a dwelling at Chia, where he had to undergo a series of fastings, and where he was instructed for some years. This one, as well as all the other chiefs, were inducted into their offices by the Zipa, and the nephew was the chief of Chia until the death of the Zipa.

The cercado, or palace of the Zipa, in Muequetá, had many departments for habitations, and warehouses for clothing and food. He had a country residence and gardens in Tabio, where he went to bathe in tepid waters. He had another dwelling in Tinansuca, a temperate climate, on the descent of the Cordillera, where he passed some months, and finally, in Theusaquillo, a place of pleasure, and where, afterwards, the capital of N. Granada was founded; here he retired after the harvest ceremonies were over, and when the plain was dry and burnt by the summer sun.

CRIMES AND PUNISHMENTS.—Homicide, rape, and incest were punished by death; the incestuous one was put into a subterranean place with venemous creatures, where he died of starvation. Those convicted of unnatural crimes were empaled. He who paid not his contributions or debts, the Usaque sent a messenger with a small tiger (jagua) or similar animals, bred for this purpose, which was tied to the door of the

---

[1] Probably a sort of flute. The Tata was a wooden trumpet.

[2] The Incas of Peru exacted the same observance.

debtor, who had to feed it as well as the messenger, until the debt was paid. He who showed cowardice in war was dressed as a woman and employed for a time in female occupations. Robberies and other offences were punished by flogging in men; women had their hair cut off. When a woman was suspected of inconstancy, they forced her to eat a large quantity of red pepper, if she confessed, she had water given to her, and then she was killed; if she resisted this mode of torment for some hours, she was declared innocent, and an apology made to her.

OTHER LAWS.—Only the Zipa was carried on men's shoulders, on a litter, by his subjects, or by such Usaques whose great services in the field entitled them to this privilege. Permission was necessary to have the nose and ears pierced, so as to wear ornaments, except by the Xeques and Usaques who had this right when they took possession of their office. The Indians generally painted themselves with achote (bixia); also clothed themselves with new and clean mantles, but the mantle with figures and lines made with a brush in black and red, could only be worn by order of the Zipa.

Only by permission of the Zipa could game be eaten, except by the Usaques.

VARIOUS CUSTOMS.—When a man wished to be married he sent a mantle to the parents of his intended bride, and if after eight days it was not returned, he sent another: then, considering himself accepted, he seated himself, at night, at the door of his future bride, and indirectly made it known he was there. The maiden opened the door, holding a totuma[1] or gourd, full of chicha, and having sipped, she gave to her lover to drink. Marriage was celebrated before the Xeque, and the couple being united by their arms, the priest asked the maiden whether she preferred Bochicha to her husband,—her husband to her children—if she loved her children more than herself—and if she would abstain from food whilst her husband was hungry. Then directing himself to the husband, told him to say, with a loud voice, if he wished to have the woman for his wife, and this ended the ceremony.

But a man might have as many women as he could maintain, particularly if he were a Usaque, but only one was the legitimate wife. The matrimonial rites varied in the several Chibcha tribes.

The Zipa being dead, the Xeques abstracted his entrails, filling

---

[1] Tutuma, on the coast of Esmeraldas (Equador).

the cavities with melted resin ;[1] the body was then laid in a coffin of palm-tree wood, lined inside and out with sheets of gold; it was then secretly taken and buried in a cave, made from the day he commenced his reign, in a distant and secret place: these regal and rich tombs have never yet been met with. With the Usaques and other principal Indians were buried their favourite wives and a number of their retainers, who were previously made to take the juice of a narcotic plant; food was put into the tombs, jewels of gold, arms, and chicha made of fermented maize, of which they were very fond. Six days were allotted for mourning, and the anniversary was also solemnized. At this period they repeated, in a singing tone, the life and actions of the departed.

The mass of the people were buried with their jewels, arms and food, in the open country, without any other sign than planting a tree to protect the grave; not naked, but clothed in their best robes. There were also tumuli which served as cemeteries, from whence human bones, objects of gold and deers' horns have been taken, proving that the Indians were buried with trophies of the chase, or, probably, with deer, as provision in the other world. The most considerable cemeteries known, are those of the Hill of the Sanctuary, near the Puente Grande, four leagues W. of Bogotá, and the hills of Caqueza, from whence, on one occasion, 24,000 ducats worth of gold was extracted. In the Province of Tunja, in caverns, are found many mummies, well preserved: some with fine painted mantles, such as were used by the principal Indians, all these bodies are seated, the forefingers tied with cotton strings.

AGRICULTURE, INDUSTRY AND COMMERCE.—It has already been observed that the Chibchas had no cattle; neither did they know the use of iron, and that their instruments for tilling the land were of wood or stone. The potato, sweet potato, maize and quinua, were the principal vegetables cultivated; indeed, they may be called essentially an agricultural people, to whom the frog or toad, as an emblem of humidity, served as a base for their system of numeration, and for their calendar; they had two harvests of potatoes and one of maize, in the colder portions, and it was there the greater number of the people dwelt.

With respect to the cultivation of the quinua, now abandoned, we have no particulars. The seed of the plant is very nutritious, and it is probable it was eaten in the form of a porridge, such as they made with maize, seasoning it with salt, red pepper and savoury herbs. In the hot vallies they had the yuca (jatropha); the arracache (oxalis cremata), in the temperate regions, and some vegetables; but we do not know if they

---

[1] Velez says black bees-wax.

used the fecula of the choco blanco (lupinus) as they did in Quito. We are ignorant if they, as the Mexicans, extracted sugar from the maize-cane, not having the sugar-cane, which was brought from the Old World; or, if they only used honey, found abundantly amongst the declivities of the Cordillera. The plantain, now so abundant in N. Granada, that it may be said to form half the food of the population, was not cultivated in olden times or known, excepting in the province of Chocó. It is calculated that ground, yielding wheat for the sustenance of one man, would grow plantains for twenty-five men.[1]

The most important production, which served these Chibchas to barter with, and for which they obtained gold, was the salt of Zipiquirá and Nemocon; this they prepared from brine springs, by boiling in earthen vessels. At present, rock salt is extracted from these localities.

They had also cotton mantles, woven by the women, when their other domestic affairs were finished.[2] The natives of Guatavitá were celebrated for their ability in working grain gold (extracted from the sands of the Magdalena, or from the province of Guane, Giron, &c.), into figures of animals, the inlaying of shells for cups, used at their feasts, and thin plates of gold which served for belts and bracelets. The painters of mantles, which article was taken to all the markets, were Chibchas. They worked figures in relief,[3] on hard stone, (but we are not informed by what means).

---

[1] The weather affects national character directly, by means of dress, and indirectly through agricultural products, the most important of them in this respect is the plátano, or plantain. The plantain saves man more labour than steam. It gives him the greatest amount of food from a given piece of ground, and with a labour so small that that of raising it to the mouth, after roasting, is a material point of it. "New Granada would be something" says my neighbour Cáldas, " if we could exterminate the plátano and the cane: this is the parent of drunkenness and idleness."—Holton, 23.

[2] The apparatus for spinning is a stick, with a potato or other weight stuck at the other end.—Holton, 289.

The loom for weaving is a square frame; threads of warp, wound as on a reel, (this is for a ruana, or mantle) the colour being changed so as to produce the requisite stripes. The woof simply inserted by their industry, without any apparatus to separate the threads of the warp, and, of course, without a proper shuttle.—Holton, 533.

[3] J. Acosta gives a drawing of one of the symbolic stones or calendar engraved by the Chibchas, of which a copy is given further on. It is of very hard black Lydian stone. I do not find any mention of instruments for cutting or boring hard stones, but for boring a sort of drill must have been used; for cutting some harder stone, such as corundum; the smoothing and polishing would be easy. The Chibchas do not appear to have used copper, tin, lead or iron; their working and war instruments were of hard wood or stone: gold seems to have been the only metal used by them.

The Chibcha was probably the only nation of the New World who used gold coin in their exchanges,[1] this consisted of discs cast in a mould; they had no weights, and for measures they only had that which served for measuring maize, called aba, the name also of the grain. The measures of length were the hand and step.

The most important fair or market of the Chibchas was at Coyaima, in the territory of the Poincas, called by the Spaniards Yaporogos, the name of one of its chiefs. These inhabited both sides of the Magdalena from the entrance of the R. Cuello to Neyva. There was taken salt, emeralds, painted mantles, works in gold, also grain gold. The Chibchas brought from the fairs of the hot countries guacamayas[2] or macaws and parrots, and when they had learnt a few words they were sacrificed to their deities; believing they were a better substitute than human ones. There was another large fair in the country of the cacique Zorocotá, where, subsequently, was founded Puente Real on the river, then called Sarabita, to which came the Northern Chibchas, the Agataes, Chipetaes and the industrious Guanes: here they obtained salt for gold, mantles, and woven cotton cloth of various qualities and colours. In the central point of this fair was a large isolated stone, subsequently broken up, and turned out to be silver ore, from which was extracted some 60 marcs,[3] (8 oz. to the marc), but the spot from whence this mass of silver ore came has never been known.

There was another fair in Turmequé, every three days; and there was seen, independent of other articles, a large quantity of emeralds from Somondoco,[4] although, at the period of the conquest, the mine was almost worked out (qy?).

---

[1] The ancient Mexicans used quills filled with gold dust, pieces of tin in the form of the letter T; also balls of cotton and bags of cacao as medium of exchange. The Peruvians used extensively the pod of the capsicum or aji.—See Numismatics or the New World, by W. Bollaert, Numis. Soc., 1837.

[2] Jameson calls El Guacamayo the sacred river. Huaca means sacred in Quichua. Geographical Trans., 1859. The Poinciana Pulcherrima, the yellow and scarlet variety, is called Malinche (the name of Cortez's Indian mistress) and Guacamayo, in Honduras, the latter being the name given to the large red parrot, called Ara and Lapa, in other parts of South and Central America, a bird the Maya Indians of Yucatan seems to have considered sacred, and dedicated to the sun. At Itzamal, there was a temple to Kinich Kakmé, an idol fashioned like the sun, with the beak of a bird: he is surrounded with rays of fire, and descended to burn the offered sacrifice at mid-day, as the Vacamayu—a bright-feathered parrot—descends in its flight. Froebel's Central America, 181.

[3] This must mean 60 mares, the cajon of 50 cwt.

[4] EMERALDS.—The green varieties are found at Muzo, N. of Bogotá, 5° 28' N. A specimen from Peru (probably Quito) silica, 68·50, alumina 15·75, glucina 12·50, red

Neither the edifices nor the furniture of the Chibchas were in proportion with their other conveniences. The dwellings were of wood and clay, with conical roof, covered with mats of sedge and rushes, some benches and couches, doors of cane entertwined with cords and locks of wood, which form is still used in some places. The strong cercados (enclosures) and vast court-yards flanked by those round buildings, which, in the distance, looked like towers, was the origin of the name of the valley of the Alcazares, given by Quesada to the plain of Bogotá.

The only Chibcha chief who projected the building of a temple, was Garanchaca; he usurped the dominions of the Zaque, pretending to be a child of the sun by the damsel Gacheta. She gave birth to a huaca (something sacred), which was converted into a human being, who was brought up with veneration until he was a man, when he killed Hunsa and put himself in his place. This fabulous Garanchaca pretended, as they say, to build a sumptuous temple to his father, the sun; to which effect he ordered that stones and columns should be brought from the most distant parts of his dominions, but he died ere the building was commenced.

The mysterious personage, who in remote ages was the legislator of the Chibchas, was not venerated as a deity, but as a holy and

oxide iron 1, lime 0·25, oxide chrome 0·30. Tantalic acid and Columbium occur in some varieties. Fine emeralds can be seen at Carthagena, extracted from the mines of Muzo, by a French company. This gem is found in attached and imbedded crystals in alluvium. The finest are from veins, in a blue slate, of the age of our lower chalk, in the Valley of Muzo. One statue of the Virgin, in the Cathedral at Bogota, besides 1358 diamonds and other precious stones, has 1205 emeralds. Not far from the mountain of Itoco, in the country of the Muzos, was found in 1555 two emeralds, weighing 24,000 castellanos, the castellano is 1,415 grs. Three leagues from Itoco is Abipi, where emeralds are found.

The following was a bribe offered to a Chibcha chief: twenty maidens, a hundred loads of cotton, a large quantity of emeralds, idols and figures of animals in gold and silver.

The rainbow was worshipped by pregnant women among the Chibchas, and emeralds offered. In the East Indies medicinal and talismanic virtues are ascribed to this gem.

The heir to Chibcha power, when received as such, was placed on a throne of gold and emeralds. The litter of the Zipa was ornamented with emeralds. In the eyes, ears, nose, mouth and navel of the dead Zipa, emeralds were placed.

The Great Exhibition of 1851 contained the finest known emerald, 2 inches long, weighing 8 oz. 18 dwts. It came from Muzo, supposed to have been brought to England by Don Pedro, who sold it to the Duke of Devonshire.

We are not informed how the Chibchas worked emeralds and other hard stones; but the Mexicans, with tools made of copper and tin, fashioned emeralds into flowers, fish, &c. Cortez sent an emerald to Spain, the base of which was as broad as the palm of the hand.—See Quito Section, for emeralds also.

beneficent man. He is sometimes confounded with Bochica. He is known under the names of Nemterequetaba, Xue, Chuizapagua (or the envoy of God). This ancient individual came, as before-mentioned, from the east; he wore a long beard, and his hair was tied with a fillet; his dress was a tunic without a collar, and a mantle secured by the ends at the shoulders, a dress used by the Chibchas at the time of the discovery of the country, for the poncho and the ruana are of Peruvian origin, introduced after the conquest.

Xue found the people little better than savages, without other clothing than cotton in the rough, tied with cords, and without ideas of society or government. He commenced his exhortations at Bosa, where the Spaniards found a rib, venerated by the Indians, said to have belonged to an animal brought hither by this personage.[1] From Bosa Xue went to Muquetá, Fontibon, and then to the town of Cota, at which place he taught and instructed the people, and such was the concourse that came to hear him, that it became necessary to make a fosse round a hill. Not only did he teach them to spin and weave, but wherever he pleased he left painted, in ochre, in various places, the figure of the weaving machine, so that they should not forget its construction.

Xue then went to the N., descended to the province of Guane, and in the inhabitants there, he found the best disposition for the arts. He not only taught by words, but by works, and passed his long life civilizing the Indians. Ultimately, he disappeared in Sogomoso, leaving a successor to continue the instruction and the guidance of the laws and regulations he had established by general consent, solely by the power of persuasion and example. As a proof of his wisdom, the following regulation was in force at the time of the conquest, that is to say, fourteen centuries after his death: that if the legitimate wife of the Usaque died first she could prohibit the husband from marrying again until five years were passed. In this manner the Usaque was careful in pleasing his wife, dreading her future vengeance; and not being able to do away with polygamy, he invented this method to protect the weaker sex, but it must be stated that the Chibchas behaved well to their wives, and took care of the sick and old.

The Muzos[2] were noted for their continual wars with the Muiscas

---

[1] It is probable this was the rib of a mastodon, bones of this animal are found in the alluvium of Suacha, where, at present, teeth and other fossil remains are met with. Holton, 273, says, this place is famous for the bones of carnivorous elephants once exhumed here.

[2] 1. Mollien's Colombia, 558.

of Bogotá. Their country was very rich in emeralds. They had a singular tradition: that there was, in ancient times, on the other side of the Magdalena, the shadow of a man, called Ari, which amused itself with making wooden faces of men and women, casting them into the stream, from whence they issued in the form of human beings; and these he taught to cultivate the earth: they then dispersed, and from this stock came the Indians who inhabit the surrounding regions.

The Muzos had no gods, nor did they worship the sun and moon, as the Bogotans did: they said these bodies were created after the wooden faces, in order to give them light when they became living beings. During the honey-moon, the wife beat the husband. Their dead were dried before a slow fire, and not buried till a year had passed; the widow was obliged to cultivate the ground for her support until the interment, when her relations took her home.

Some writers say, there is no doubt that Quetzalcoatl the legislator of Mexico,[1] Bochica of Bogotá and Manco Capac of Peru, were Budhist Priests;[2] they also observe, that there is a remarkable analogy between the religion of Budha and Bramah and the Mexican worship; as Bramah, Vishnu and Siva, form the East Indian trimurti; so does Ho, Huitzilopoctl and Tlaloc of Mexico, also Con, Pacha-camac and Huiracocha, of the Peruvians. This appears to me to be a mere idea, and to have no foundation; and as to Con, Pacha-camac and Viracocha, a critical examination shows that such is the confusion as to the history of this said to be Peruvian trimurti, that it is unsafe to follow these wholesale generalisations.

Velasco, the historian of Quito, and other writers of his time, as well as some moderns, have supposed that Peru was peopled from the west, making Easter Island a stepping-stone;[3] this is another fanciful idea,

---

[1] The Mexican deity (sometimes called the God of Air), the Pyxome of Brazil, Viracocha and Bochica, are represented as white men, with flowing beards. Tezcatlipoca, another Mexican god, is described as a black.—Bradford, 301.

[2] Rather say priest of a Budha of the Muiscas or Peruvians.

[3] Easter Island, 27° 05' S. 109° 46' W., 1500 miles from the nearest western island and 2000 from the coast of Peru. The people tatoo and paint. There are three platforms of stonework, in ruins; on each stood four statues, one fifteen feet high, first seen by Davis, in 1686. Population then said to be 6000 to 7000. These people came from the islands of the west. Cook gives a drawing of the ears of the people, pierced, but unlike the Peruvian Orejon. Some of the Mongols have their ears thus pierced and enlarged. Rogweggen, 1722, in Dalrymple's Voyage, mentions the worship of the sun in Easter island; one man there quite white, pendants in his ears, white and round, size of one's fist, appeared to be a priest.—See Delafield's Origin of American Antiquities, 1839. Bradford, 429. Ellis, Pol. Res. iii., 325.; iv., 101.

and the examination of the now delapidated stone (volcanic) idols of that island (not the work of the present race), will help but little this conjecture. Others think that the New World was peopled from the north, at a period before the existence of Behrings Straits!

Huematzin, a Mexican author, towards the close of the seventh century, gives an account of the migrations of the Tezcucans from Asia! Humboldt[1] observes, the predilection for periodical series, and the existence of a cycle of sixty years, which is equal to 740 sunas of the Muiscas, contained in the cycle of twenty years of the priests, appear to reveal the Tartarian origin of the nations of the New World; in another part of his works he modestly says, "I think, I discover in the the Americans, the descendants of a race, who early separated from the rest of mankind, has followed up for a series of years, a peculiar road in the unfolding of its intellectual faculties, and its tendency towards civilization."

"Again,[2] our knowledge of the languages of America is still too limited, considering their great variety, for us as yet entirely to relinquish the hope of some day discovering an idiom which may have been spoken, at once in the interior of South America, and in that of Asia; or which may, at least, indicate an ancient affinity. Such a discovery would certainly be one of the most brilliant which can be expected in reference to the history of mankind."

At the Ethnological Society, in May, 1858, in a communication "On the probable migrations and variations of the earlier families of the human race," Admiral Fitzroy directed attention to the people of South America and Van Diemen's Land, and to the probability of early migrations; for there was a striking resemblance between the Tierra del Fuegians and the Esquimaux; between the inhabitants of Western South America and the aborigines of Van Diemen's Land, and between the people of Eastern South America and the Hottentots of Africa. Sir H. Rawlinson, commenting on the corrections of the assumed chronology, considered the time insufficient to account for changes of language and character, and that physiognomy was a more accurate test of the origin of the people than philology, especially among hill tribes; for instance, in the inhabitants of the mountain districts of Mesopotamia, there was the same character of face as might be seen in the Assyrian marbles.

At Carthagena, 10° 25′ N. 75° 30′ W., the ancient Calamari, I saw numbers of half civilized Indians, some on their way to work on the

[1] Views, ii., 128.
[2] Aspects, i., 177.

Panamá railway; they were active, strong, good-looking, and the hotter and more scorching the sun the merrier they were; they, however, were learning to drink spirits and gamble. Sailing for Colon, in 9° 25' N., the Navy Bay of the English, and Aspinwall of the Americans, we observed the Darien Indians out at sea in their champanes, or canoes, fishing.

At Turbaco, eight miles from Carthagena, in revenging the death of Cosa, at the time of the conquest, Nicuesa and his companions had for their share of Indian booty £62,000 in gold. In the expedition to the river Zenu, in 1534, a Cacica or female chief is spoken of, the cemetery of the surrounding country, where the dead were buried with all their treasure, food and drink, Heredia sacked, finding twenty-four wooden idols covered with sheets of gold; these were in pairs, supporting hamacs, in which were deposited precious objects, brought by the devout. Suspended in the trees, which surrounded the temple, were some gold bells, worth £30,000, and during eight to ten months £1,200,000, in money of the present time, was plundered. J. Acosta[1] gives a description of the tombs of Zenu. Quesada, after the battle of Bonza, returned to Bogotá, when the King's fifth was 46,000 castellanos of gold and 360 of emeralds; a similar sum was set apart for those who had most distinguished themselves. The remainder was divided amongst the army, the foot soldier receiving 512 castellanos of gold (of low standard, guanin) and five emeralds, the horse soldier double.

Macuriz was the name of the chief of Bahaire, near Carthagena. In Ojeda's voyage thither, in 1509, he found the natives to be warlike men, of Carib origin; they wielded great swords of palm-wood, defended themselves with osier targets, and dipped their arrows in a subtle poison. The women as well as the men mingled in battle, being expert with the bow, and throwing a species of lance called Azagay.[2]

The aborigines of the Isthmus have been hitherto known under the names of Dariel,[3] Urabac and Idibae. Their language was said to be similar to the Cunacuna (independent Indians on the S.E. side of the Isthmus). Later researches have shown that four tribes, the Saveneric, Manzanillo, or San Blas Indians, Choló or Chocó, and Bayano,[4] inhabit the Isthmus, and speak different languages.[5]

---

[1] Compendio de N. Granada, 123, 126.

[2] Irving's "Companion of Columbus," 36.

[3] Ludewig, 61. Hervas, i. 27. Darien or Dariel, the people Darieles, also Vocabulary of the Tule language of the Darien Indians. Dr. Cullen on the Darien ship Canal, 1853.

[4] Bayano. Indians of the Isthmus of Panama, about the River Chepo. Ludewig.

[5] Irving's "Companion of Columbus."

Ere the Panamá railway had encroached upon the aboriginal regions of the Isthmus of Darien, the narrow barrier between the Atlantic and the Pacific was traversed from the east by ascending the river Chagrés, in canoes, to Cruces, and then by mule to Panamá, an affair, at times, of many days; at present, the journey is performed by rail in three hours.

In consequence of heavy floods in the river Chagrés having washed away part of the railway-bridge, at Barbacoas,[1] I could only get as far as the bridge by rail, afterwards by canoe to Cruces, then by mule to Panamá, through dense tropical vegetation, and by canclones or roads something like a very narrow railway cutting, caused by continual traffic for the last 300 years in one track.

In vain one searched for the huts of the Indian, they have been replaced by "Yankee hotels!" where, for a glass of refreshment, a dollar is demanded, but one is glad to pay this sum, and even more, for a refreshing drink when travelling in such a sweltering locality.

Captain Liot[2] speaks thus of the San Blas Indians: they resort to Panamá to find a market for the produce of the fertile country they inhabit, and, to a trifling extent, cultivate; they are short in stature, deep-chested and robust, but not remarkable for symmetry; in spite of a listless stolid expression of countenance, they are not without intelligence, and are accounted a jealous and warlike race. I saw some Darien Indians at Panamá, fine looking fellows and not very dark; they went about nearly naked, and the general opinion is, that the white man is not safe in their wilds.

It is said that the word Panamá means a place abounding in fish. Tubanamá was the name of a chief who ruled about here at the time of the conquest.[3] The Indians of Darien called their chiefs Quevi and Saco; this last appears identical with the Saki of Hunsa, in Bogotá.

I had proposed to give an account of the investigations and elaborate surveys for the Panamá railway, from information I obtained of the

---

[1] Barbacoas, or ancient suspension bridges. There are three sorts: one, the bridge of bejucos (ligneous cordage), the true suspension bridge; the second, the tarabita of one rope, for slinging passengers; the third, called tarabita also, of two ropes, for slinging animals. In Chilo, the swinging bridges are made of hide ropes—such as is seen at Santa Rosa de los Andes.—Skinner, "Present State of Peru," 364, Barbacoas, or steps like roads, are cross-poles fixed in the rock, but not fastened at the extremities. Skinner's work is a translation of the more prominent articles of the "Mercurio Peruano."

[2] Panamá, &c., 1849.

[3] Cotu-banamá, was the name of a chief in the Island of Hayti.—Irving, "Life of Columbus," ii., 5.

engineers and others who so bravely carried that operation through under no ordinary difficulties.[1] I must, however, content myself with alluding to its traffic, and making a few observations on a report, by Mr. Hoadley, president of the Panamá railway company, to Mr. Cobden as Chairman to the House of Commons' Contract Packet Committee.

The Panamá railway is forty-seven and a half miles long. Passenger trains run over it in three hours; goods trains in five. During the first four years 121,820 passengers passed; upwards of thirty-four millions sterling of gold, and of silver nearly six millions, was conveyed across it. Almost all the indigo and cochineal is now sent over the Panamá railway, reaching England in less than thirty days; while, if sent round Cape Horn, it would take four months. Coal, timber, guano, munitions of war, ores, heavy machinery, whale oil, cocoa, Peruvian bark, &c., are transported over the line. It has reduced the passage between England and British Colombia from six months to forty days, and its advantages to the trade of the west coast of America is incalculable, in conjunction with the West India Mail and Pacific Steam Navigation Companies, both lines possessing most efficient steamers; indeed, they may be called floating hotels. There is also the United States Mail Steam Ship Company's line, from Panamá to San Blas, Mazatlan and San Francisco; from the latter port there are steamers again to British Colombia.

Although the Australian trade is chiefly in English hands, yet the United States ships, with a million tons of freight, sailed, in 1858, for Australia.

This shows the vast importance of the Panamá route to the Pacific and Australia. The existence of good coal at Vancouver's Island, for the use of steamers, is most important.

Benzoni,[2] who was in the New World, 1541-46, gives the following words as spoken at Suere, near Panamá, which I compare with Quichua:

Suere	Ischia	Chiarucla	Cici
Quichua	Pacha	Ccuri	Ceari and Runa
English	Earth	Gold	Man.[3]

[1] In 1844-5, Captain Liot was commissioned by the Royal Mail Steam Packet Company to examine the Isthmus of Darien, with a view to establish a macadamized road or a railroad across it. The British government discouraged the overtures which were made to them, and suffered the contingent prospect to be abandoned. Years afterwards, citizens of the United States performed the great work of a railway. "Panamá &c., communications between the Atlantic and Pacific Oceans," by Captain Liot, 1849.

[2] Translated by Admiral Smyth, 1857.—Hakluyt Coll.

[3] Garcilasso states that, Panamá, Darien, Santa Marta, &c., were peopled by Mexicans "terribles y crueles," but gives no particulars as to how or when they settled

During my stay in Panamá, the subject of a ship canal was much debated, but the opinion of the majority was against its feasibility. The scheme of a canal appears to be abandoned, although the country between the Chuqunáque and Atrato rivers is said to be level; Mr. Trantwine in describing his surveys of the Atrato river, reports that a ship canal is out of the question.[1]

In the Isthmus of Darien, or Golden Castile, there have been discovered ancient ruins at Cana, 7° 38' N., 77° 31' W.; also at Casas del Principe,[2] 8° 40' N., 78° 04' W.

Repeated aggressions of the buccaneers and others in this auriferous district, where abundance of gold was procured by black slave labour, after the aborigines had been diminished in numbers by oppressive cruelties, induced Spain to close and abandon the mines, for a time, early in the 18th century. Even those famous ones in the mountains of Espiritu Santo, near Cana, from which alone more gold went through Panamá in a year, than from all the other mines of America put together.[3]

Irving[4] tells us that at the conquest, Zemaco was the principal chief of Darien. Careta governed the gold district of Coyba, and gave his daughter to Balboa. Ponca was the name of another chief, at war with Careta. Comagre was a powerful chief, his dwelling was a hundred and fifty paces in length, and eighty in breadth, founded upon great logs, surrounded by a stone wall; the upper part was of wood work, curiously interwoven and wrought with such beauty as to cause surprise and admiration. In a secret part of the building, Comagre preserved the bodies of his ancestors, wrapped in mantles of cotton, richly wrought and interwoven with pearls, gold and certain stones, held precious by the natives. Comagre's son gave the Spaniards much gold, and informed Balboa of the Pacific Ocean. Balboa went in search of the golden

there. Berthold Seemann the aborigines of the Isthmus of Panamá, in Trans. of the American Ethno. Soc., III., 175; 1853. Same author in voyage of the Herald, I. 231, "History of the Isthmus of Panamá," including the more civilized Dorachos of Western Veraguas and their monuments.

[1] Report on Isthmus and Darien, by Capt. Prevost, R.N., "Geographical Soc. Journal," 1854. I was in Panamá when Capt. P. was on his way to explore the Isthmus, and had I not been laid up by the bite in the foot of some venemous animal, I might have been tempted to have accompanied him. In the town library, at Nuremburg, is preserved a globe, made by John Schoner, in 1520. It is remarkable that the passage through the Isthmus of Darien, so much sought after in later times, is, on this old globe, carefully delineated.—King's "Wonders of the World."

[2] Hellert's Voy. à l'isthme de Darien.

[3] Fitzroy on the Great Isthmus.—"Geogr. Soc. Journal," 180, 1853.

[4] Companions of Columbus.

temple of Dobayba, mother of God, who created the sun and moon. The temple was not found, but from an abandoned village he gathered jewels and pieces of gold. The chief Abibeyba reigned over a region of marshes and shallow lakes. Balboa, on his journey across Darien, was told by Ponca that the Pacific Ocean was called the great Pechry. The chief, Quaraquá, and his people were sacrificed by the Spaniards, and their village plundered of gold and jewels. On the 26th September, 1513, Balboa first beheld the Pacific Ocean; he then passed through the country of the chief, Chiapes, who gave him five hundred pounds weight of gold. On the 29th, St. Michael's day, Balboa took a banner, upon which was painted the Virgin and Child and the arms of Castile and Leon, then drawing his sword, he marched into the sea, and waving his banner took possession of the seas and lands from the Arctic to the Antartic poles. Balboa then fell in with the chief, Túmaco, who gave him pearls and gold, and here he was again informed of Peru. Teaochan conciliated the Spaniards by gifts of pearls and gold. Poncra, supposed to be rich, and not yielding, was torn to pieces by bloodhounds. Balboa took Tubanamá prisoner, who gave as his ransom armlets and jewels of gold to the value of 6000 crowns.

On Pizarro's first journey across the Isthmus, the names of the Caciques, Tutibrá, Chucuma, Chirucá and Biru are mentioned, and the chief of Isla Rica gave him a basket filled with pearls; one weighed twenty-five carats, another three drachms, and the size of a muscadine pear.

COAL[1] exists at Cienaga de Oro on the R. Sinu; on the banks of the Carare, a branch of the Magdalena; at Conejo, below Honda; also near Bogotá, and is used at Mr. Wilson's iron works. Coal occurs in Veraguas, Chiriqui and Costa Rica, also on the I. of Muerto, near David Chiriqui; this coal "was found to burn equally as free as English coal." Coal was recently discovered at Tarraba, Costa Rica. I find no geological description of the country these coals are found in, but in all probability they may be classed with those of Chile which are of tertiary formation,[2] excepting, perhaps, the coal found near Bogotá, which may be of the carboniferous period.

GOLD.—The king's fifth from a mine near Bogotá, was 300,000 dollars. Captain Fitzroy ascertained the position of the concealed mines of Cana. Between Panamá and Pacora, the gold dust collected was twenty-two carats fine. Near S. Bartolomeo, in the Ceno, del Pilon de Oro, is the mountain of the Block of Gold, whence, it is said, a

---

[1] See my paper on Chile coal, "Geographical Soc. Journal," 185
[2] S. American Comp. Report, London, 1859.

Spaniard from Lima once extracted a large block of gold. Major Doss, in 1849, found gold in all the streams of the Chepo, each pan full of earth yielding from twenty-five to thirty cents. One person, in a day, worked out five ounces.

The following is from Berthold Seemann.[1] The aboriginal Isthmians were rude and barbarous savages, who, divided into many hostile tribes, waged continual warfare with each other. It is only in Western Veraguas that traces of a more civilized people are found. These parts were inhabited by a numerous tribe, the Dorachos, where still are found their remains, tombs, monuments and columns of different sizes, covered with fantastic figures, or representations of natural objects, differing entirely from either the hieroglyphics of Mexico or those of Central America. At Caldera, a few leagues from the town of David, lies a granite block, known to the country-people as the "Piedra pintal," or painted stone. It is fifteen feet high, nearly fifty feet in circumference, and flat at the top. Every part, especially the eastern side, is covered with figures. One represents a radiant sun; it is followed by a series of heads, all with some variation, scorpions and fantastic figures. The top and the other sides have signs of a circular and oval form, crossed by lines. The sculpture is ascribed to the Dorachos, intended, probably, to commemorate their annals. The characters are an inch deep; on the weather side, however, they are nearly effaced. As they, no doubt, were all originally of the same depth, an enormous time must have elapsed before the granite could thus be worn away, and a much higher antiquity must be assigned to these hieroglyphics[2] than to many other monuments of America.[3] Several columns are seen in the town of David, where they are used for building purposes; the characters in them differ from those of the "Piedra pintal," by being raised and considerably smaller. The tombs of the Dorachos are numerous; they are of two descriptions. The better sort consist of flat stones put together, resembling the coffins used in northern Europe; they are slightly covered with mould, and earthen vases are found within; the vessels are of good workmanship, and in the shape of basins or of tripods, the legs being hollow, and containing several loose

---

[1] Voy. of '*Herald*,' 1848, and Trans. Amer. Ethno. Soc., 175, 1853. Mr. Seemann has kindly allowed me to introduce into my work, the two drawings he made of this interesting monument.

[2] Messrs. Whiting and Shuman, in their report, 1851, on the coal formation of the Island of Muerto, near David, in Chiriqui, say they found monuments and columns covered with hieroglyphics, similar to those discovered in Yucatan, by Stephens.

[3] Something of this sort, is the old sculptured stone in the Pampa del Leon, in Tarapacá, Peru.

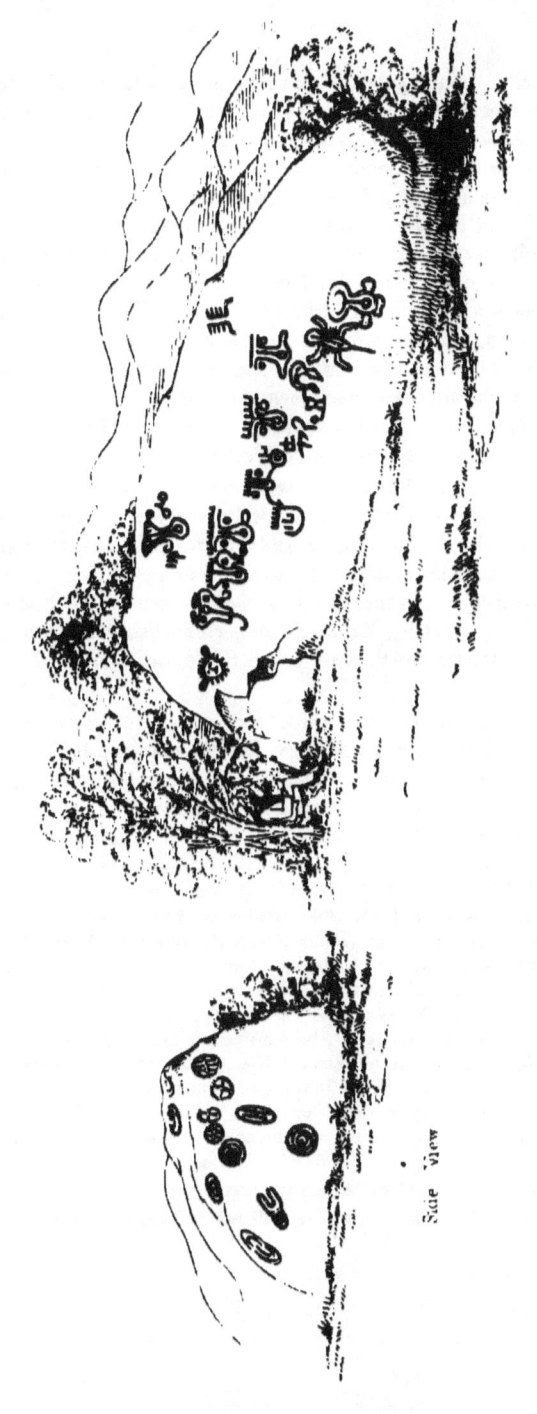

PIEDRA PINTA OR ENGRAVED STONE
Caldera, Nature, Veraguas

Side View

balls. Occasionally, round agates, with a hole in the centre, and small eagles have been met with. It seems to have been customary among the Doracho tribe to wear these eagles around the neck by way of ornament. Ferdinand Columbus frequently mentions them when speaking of Veraguas and the adjacent Mosquito shore. Several have been found in the last few years; most of them measure from wing to wing, about four inches. Tombs of the second class are more frequent, they consist of a heap of large pebbles, from three to four feet in height, and descending as much below the surface; no vases or ornaments are found in these graves, but always one or more stones for grinding Indian corn, made like most of the vessels, with three legs. Bodies have been met with, which, at the slightest touch, crumbled into dust. The inhabitants of Alenje speak of other remarkable remains in the northern Cordillera, one of which is said to be a rocking-stone.

RECENT DISCOVERY OF HUACAS, CONTAINING VARIOUS OBJECTS IN GOLD, IN CHIRIQUI[1].—Much excitement was lately occasioned at Panama[2] by the accidental opening of Indian graves in the Chiriqui district, 150 miles distant, and the discovery therein of large quantities of golden images. As there are supposed to be many thousands of these graves equally wealthy, hundreds of persons had gone thither, and thousands of dollars worth had been taken out and sent to Panamá.

DESCRIPTION OF GOLD IMAGES FROM THE CHIRIQUI HUACAS.—
1. A bat, with outspread wings and legs, having a dragon-like head, surmounted by four horns, curling inwards, of the purest gold, and weighed six ounces. 2. A frog[3] with large protruding eyes, the eye-balls being enclosed in the sockets like the balls in sleigh bells;

---

[1] See "Obs. on Chiriqui," by J. H. Smith, "Geogr. Soc. Journal," p. 257, 1855. The aborigines never failed to leave valuable remains in their burial places or guacalis. This region contains a great number of such old graves, the burial-places of a once powerful tribe, not migratory. Many of these guacalis have been opened and found to contain images of birds, beasts and trinkets of gold. I had the pleasure to assist Mr. Smith and Dr. McDowall to draw up this paper, and we laid down the district in which these recent discoveries have been made, in a line running east from the Bay of Guanabano to the Cordillera, and call it a region abounding in Indian antiquities. We also place Las Breñas, old Indian gold mines, in a quartz formation, 16 geo. miles W. of the ancient graves. At Charco Azul, on the coast, are indications of gold and copper at Punta Banco. David, the capital of Chiriqui, is in about 8° 17' N., 82° 30' W.

[2] *Times*, August 11, 1859, Panamá and American papers.

[3] The existence of the frog here shows an alliance to the Chibcha race of N. Granada.

this is alloyed with copper,[1] and weighed about two-and-a-half ounces. 3. Has the body and legs of an alligator, with the head and ears of a lamb,[2] only with an enormous mouth and dragon-like teeth, and weighed about two ounces. 4. An idol of hideous and obscene conception, with legs and arms extended; the head flat, having a fan-like crown at the back, a wide open mouth, and a hooked nose, under which curls something like the latest form of moustache. This weighed about two ounces, and was of pure gold.

Besides these, there were a frog, an eagle,[3] very small twin frogs, an armadillo, and a small bell.

The accounts we continue to receive of the wealth of the huacas, in golden images, are every day growing more wonderful. A bat has been found of very fine gold and great weight; also a "gold woman." It is the poorer class of people who are turning up the graves and selling the gold images at from 3 to 4 dollars the ounce. These tombs are of great extent, some of them having contained many hundreds of bodies. The gold is contained in earthen vessels, by the side of the body. The ground where the huacas are is covered with trees, and it was by the falling of a large tree, growing out of the top of a mound, that the deposits were discovered. The roots of the tree took with them the earth and mason-work of one of the mounds, leaving the gold exposed, which was accidentally seen by a man when passing close to it. Many of these golden objects reached London, but soon found their way into the melting pot.

In November, this year, Messrs. Pixley & Co. allowed me to examine five thin circular gold plates, from Chiriqui, weighing 7 ozs. $\frac{7}{10}$. The largest had seven circular embossments (these had been battered, and any figures that may have been there were obliterated), and was $7\frac{1}{4}$ inches in diameter; two were $6\frac{1}{4}$ inches in diameter; the other two $4\frac{1}{4}$; these were plain. The plates appeared to be alloyed with silver, and probably used as breast plates.

Irving[4]—"Voyage along Costa Rica and Veragua," says:—"Here for the first time on the coast, the Spaniards met with specimens of pure gold; the natives wearing large plates of it suspended round their necks by cotton cords: they had, likewise, ornaments of guanin,

---

[1] This may be alloy, or a natural mixture, and was known under the name of guanin, its specific gravity 11.55.

[2] Rather say: resembling a lamb, more probably a deer, as the sheep was introduced by the Spaniards.

[3] The existence of the eagle leads me to think these may be remains of the Doracho nation. (See Seemann Voy., *Herald*, 1848).

[4] Life of Columbus, II., 178.

Bollaert's Antiq: S America.

Huaca Mayo, or Sacred Parrot.

Idol

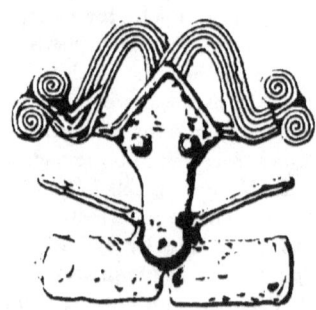

Idol

The figures half the size of the originals.

gold of low standard, an alloy with copper, or a natural metal, rudely shaped like eagles.

"They met with canoes of Indians, their heads decorated with garlands of flowers, and coronets formed of the claws of beasts and the quills of birds; most of them had plates of gold about their necks. An Indian had an eagle (in gold) worth twenty-two ducats. Seeing the great value which the strangers set upon the metal, they assured them it was to be had in abundance within two days journey."

The eagle here spoken of may be a representation of the Guacamayo, sacred macaw or parrot, so known to the Chibchas.

Thirteen leagues from the Gulf of Nicoya is Carabizi, where the same language was spoken as at Chiriqui. The country on the Pacific, in the same latitude with Chiriqui, was called Cabiores, and next to it was the province of Durucaca.[1]

Mr. Squire,[2] in his elaborate paper on Nicaragua, says, upon the low alluviums, and amongst the dense dark forests of the Atlantic coast, there existed a few scanty and wandering tribes, generally corresponding with the Caribs of the islands. A portion of their descendants may yet be found in the wretched Moscos or Mosquitos, (little Moscos), "who, by a brazen fraud, are attempted to be passed off upon the world as a sovereign nation." The few Melchoras, in the river San Juan, are of the Carib stock, and it is more than probable that the same is true of the Woolwas, Ramas and Poyas, and also all the other tribes on the Atlantic coast, further south, towards Chiriqui, Lagoon, and collectively denominated Bravos.

As there are Carib affinities with the Moscas or Muiscas of Bogotá, these, I think, may have, in early times, come to the coast of N. Granada, and have been the conquerors of the nations, who built at Tunja, or the more ancient Timaná.[3]

Some of the names of places and natural objects within the Nagradan (Nicaragua) area, seem to have a relationship to certain Peruvian names. Thus Momobacho Momotombo and others, sound wonderfully like Moyobamba (mud plain) in Chachapoyas, Tambobamba, Guambacho, &c. It would be interesting to take up the sug-

---

[1] Oviedo and Trans. Amer. Ethno. Soc. 106. 1853.

[2] Trans. Amer. Ethno. Soc. 94, 1853.

[3] The present Moscos of Central America are said by Ludewig to be a mixed tribe, the issue of aboriginal Indians with Negroes, shipwrecked on the coast, or escaped from the Spanish settlements of the interior.

gestion, and inquire whether there is really any relationship between the languages of Peru and Central America.[1]

Herrera says, among the people of Nicaragua, those speaking Cholutecan were the original and most ancient, they held the estates, and had cocoa-nuts which were the money and wealth of the country.

The Eagle, in Chorotegan, is called Mooncayo.

ANTIQUITIES OF NEW GRANADA.

I am rather surprised that larger numbers of monuments, some of more ancient nations than those first seen by the Spaniards, have not been met with. Perhaps dense tropical forests cover many such remains, and are awaiting the footsteps of the emigrant or the enthusiastic antiquarian explorer.[2]

We have to thank Humboldt for much that we know about this region of the New World, for his examination of the Muisca or Chibcha calendar, to T. Compans, for his "Essai sur l'ancien Cundinimarca," also to Colonel J. Acosta.

Rivero and Tchudi, "Antiguedades Peruanas," (plate xli.) gives representation of two animals, carved on a slab of stone, from Timaná (about 2° N. 75° 15' W.) which, they think, may have some connexion with the Muisca calendar. Plate xxxiii. is a club from Tunja (5° 30' N., 73° 50' W.), in it are some marks which, I think, may be hieroglyphics of the name of the owner; the second figure from the top has a slight resemblance to Cuphupqua: seven, or the ears of the Muisca calendar, always listening.[3] In Brantz Mayer[4] the sculptured stone at Mapilca, in Mexico, has something of this character.

Humboldt gives a head engraved on green quartz (coloured by oxide of nickel) of the Muiscas. It is perforated, and probably done

---

[1] Squire in Trans. Amer. Ethno. Soc. 99, 1853.

[2] See "Les Antiquités Américaines au point de vue des progrès de la Geographie," par M. Jomard, in Bulletin de la Societé de Geographie, Paris, 1847.

[3] Rivero and Tschudi, Antiq. Amer., Plate xli, is an engraved stone, from Junin, in Peru, seems to have analogy with the figure 7, or Cuphupqua, the ear. If such be the case, it would be interesting. From what I can learn, the department of Junin, in Peru, deserves careful investigation.

[4] II., 198.

by a tool of copper and tin, as iron was unknown to them; this must be looked upon as a fine specimen of work in stone.[1]

In the country of Antioquia lived the Catios: they were a superior people, well clothed, lively and intelligent, wrote their history in hieroglyphics, and painted on mantles. I have noticed something of this sort on the skin mantles of the Comanches in Texas.

The following, on the antiquities of New Granada, is from the "Bulletin de la Societé de Geographie," Paris, 1847. The researches were made by Señor Velez de Barrientos. Velez was informed that there existed in the Canton of Leiva,[2] in Tunja, ruins of a temple and palace of the ancient Indians. He went in search of them in June, 1846. He got to Moniquirá (about 6° N, 73° 45' W)., and first fell in with stone columns; one, 4 to 5 yards in length, by 3½ in diameter. He then found 13 large columns, arranged in a circle of 50 yards in circumference, appearing to him as if designed for a temple[3] or palace. Some of these columns were oval, like those of Ramiriqui (see further on), and had notches at the ends, showing they had been dragged from a quarry. Four hundred yards from the 13 columns he found the main ruins, composed of cylindrical columns, some 29 in number, well finished, fixed in the earth, and occupying 45 yards in length E. and W., by 22 broad.

The columns were 1½ yards in circumference; their original length cannot be determined, as they are so worn, the highest not being more than one yard above the ground, others are hardly visible. These are, by their lightness and elegance, a great contrast with the 13 columns before mentioned; some of these looked as if they had been worked on their sides.

One hundred yards distant he found amongst dense underwood a considerable number of stones, which appeared as if they had been wrought; no mortar or cement was observed. The ground on which these ruins stand may be about two miles in extent, and had been the site of a city, and, in all probability, of a nation much more ancient than the Muiscas.[4]

---

[1] Vues, plate 66.

[2] Probably named after Andres Venero de Leiva, who entered Bogotá, 1564.

[3] See J. Acosta: The Muiscas had temples to the sun with stone columns, remains of which have been discovered in the valley of Leiva. Humboldt, Aspects, II., 309.

[4] Velez says he believes it to be an error to call the ancient inhabitants of the country by the name of Muiscas. Muisca is said to mean man, and it is a compound word. Mu signifies the body, isca five, or body of five points or extremities (as legs, arms, head). It is probable the Spaniards understood by the word Muisca, that

The natives now call these ruins of Moniquirá, whether temple, palace, &c., "Little Hell," and it is Velez's opinion that these have afforded materials in the building of the towns of Mouiquirá, Leiva, and of a convent; in the Church of Moniquirá he thought he observed columns and other stones similar to those of the ruins.

The beginning of 1846, Velez saw, at Tunja (5° 30' S., 73° 50' W.), the two stones known as the "Devil's Cushions;" they are on a hill six cuadras (the cuadra is 600 yards) from the town to the W.; the rock is wrought, surmounted by two stones in the form of mill-stones, but a little larger and something like cushions. At this spot the ancient inhabitants may have adored the rising sun.

Our explorer then went by Boyacá to Ramiriqui to examine the large columns (Boyacá is a few miles S. of Tunja) known as the "Devil's Stone-beams" (Vigas del Diablo). At a short distance from the river of Ramiriqui, he found three large eliptical columns laying on the ground, one 7¼ yards in length; at their extremities were notches to aid in hauling them from the quarry. Another column was 4½ yards long, not cylindrical, but with several sides. The curate of Ramiriqui took Velez to another part of the parish were there are five or six similar columns. J. Acosta wrote to Velez that it was said the great stones, four leagues from Raquira (between Moniquirá and Gachantiva) had been taken at the time of the conquest to the plain of Tunja, where the Indians were constructing a temple. This Velez does not believe.

The stones seen at Leiva and Ramiriqui are of Asperon, a sort of whet-stone.

Velez's opinion is, that this country was anciently inhabited by a more civilized people than those found by the Spaniards. As a proof, in the district of San Augustin, in the elevated parts of Nieva, 3° 15' N., are found monuments, such as the great stone table, said to be of sacrifice, supported by cariatides, statues of large dimensions, and numberless other objects, artistically wrought. At the conquest the Spaniards only found hereabouts the Pijados, Pantagosos and other tribes, who, although brave, were barbarous. We cannot attribute to these the construc-

which may have been the name of a particular family or tribe, or the expression for a body of five parts, and they concluded that all the people of the country bore the name of Muisca. He observes that he does not find the country in question was called by a generic name. Tunja only was known as the country of Yravacá, but in the plain now called Bogotá there did not exist a common name, because the Zipas who had been subjected to the chief of Tunja, had thrown off the yoke about sixty years before the conquest, during which time the Zipas had extended their dominions by force of arms.

tion of the works now in ruins, such are of more ancient and civilized times.

Another proof of ancient origin, and that this part of the country was well populated, in Antioquia, in the Canton of Santa Rosa, Velez's parents had occasion to dig; it was through granitic debris, and, at eight yards depth, a thick bed of well preserved trees was met with, particularly the oaks, and like the forest above. Under this bed of trees, buried by inundations, was discovered an ancient weapon, the macana, of palm wood, two yards long, one end like a lance, the other a narrow blade like a sword, with curious carvings: this was given to a Dr. Jervis, who sent it to England.

Velez describes a cavern used as a burial place. It is situated in the direction of Gachantiva, Canton of Leiva, near the copper mines of Moniquirá. Not long since a man belonging to the smelting works, while chasing a fox with a little dog, the fox and the dog disappeared through a hole. The man began to enlarge the opening to rescue his dog; some stones being cleared away, a cavern was discovered full of mummies, clothing and other objects. At the entrance of the cavern one of these mummies was sitting on a low wooden seat, with a bow and arrow, in the attitude of defending the place; it was said that this mummy, when first seen, had a crown of gold on its head. The cavern was explored; many objects in gold were taken from the mummies, also cloths of fine cotton, in a good state of preservation; some of these were worn by the present inhabitants, and used for their mules. Velez arrived there in June, 1846; at the mouth of the cavern he saw bones of the mummies that had been thrown outside. The cavern had been dug in a calcareous rock He saw, taken from this tomb, in the possession of Dr. Garcia, curate of Guateque, emeralds; one large, and in the rough, the others somewhat worked. He succeeded in getting the low wooden seat, a bust in terra cotta, pieces of mantles, a bone collar artistically worked, two little figures of animals in gold, ear-rings of tombag,[1] in good taste, the skull of a deer, its horns covered with black beeswax, which led him to suppose that this wax was used as a preservative, and it was possible that this wax was also used to embalm the bodies.[2]

The museum of Bogotá has lost the rare pentagonal calendar stone investigated by Humboldt. Since then was found in the ravine of San Diego, near Bogotá, another calendar, now in the possession of Velez; it is small, long, squared, and of basalt, with similar signs to

---
[1] A mixture of gold with copper, probably guanin.
[2] Melted resin was used as an embalming material by the Muiscas.

those described by Humboldt. Velez mentions, that his collection contains five such pentagonal stones, idols, collars and other ornaments, in hard stone and gold, mummy cloth, printed in colours and rich in design, probably from Lieva.[1]

My esteemed friend, General José Hilario Lopez, late President of New Granada, when I had the pleasure of meeting him in Paris, in 1857, informed me that on one of his estates near Nieba, S. of Bogotá, are some very ancient monuments and promised to procure details of them. General Lopez, during his presidency (1852), was most instrumental in giving freedom to the negro, also causing all religious sects the public use of their rites and ceremonies.

My old fellow traveller in Texas, A. Snider, also knew General Lopez in Paris. He gives the following from conversations with him.[2] In New Granada, near Neyba, is a cavern, at the entrance of which stood, as a guardian, a colossal tiger (jagua). A short distance from this cavern General Lopez has made excavations, and from the depth of two to five metres has extracted colossal statues, of great beauty, representing horses! (rather say of the Llama, or deer tribe),[3] monkeys, toads, and of men and women. Near to this spot was discovered a large stone table, which fifty men could scarcely lift: this table was well polished, on four feet in the form of paws, coming from a central pillar. Upon some of these monuments are still to be seen remains of inscriptions (hieroglyphics).

T. Compans[4] states, that the Sutagnos, which comprehended the Neybas and others, lived between the rivers Pazca and Suma Paz. The Indians had idols of gold and silver.

Velasco[5] says, the province of Nieva, in 3° 10' N., was only in part conquered by Hospina, one of Belalcaza's officers, in 1543. It was a hot and unhealthy place. He speaks of the Nieva nation, the Anatagoimas and Coyamas, as principal tribes, numerous, alert, and brave; they, however, became violent enemies of the Spaniards, and even dictated terms to them.

---

[1] In the British Museum is the body of a female mummy, from the cavern near Gachantiva, or Gachansipa; also a head. There are specimens of pottery, from N. Granada, in the Museum of Practical Geology.

[2] La Creation et ses Mystères Dévoilés, &c., 299. Paris, 1858.

[3] The Cervus Peronei, similar to the C. Virginian, but smaller, is common in N. Granada.

[4] Essai sur l'ancien Cundinamarca, 4.

[5] III. Vol., His. de Quito.

I have lately examined, through the kindness of Mrs. Harrison Smith, late of Panamá, four figures in gold from Tumuli, in the valley of Antioquia, 6° 45′ N. 75° W., near the river Cauca, found by General Herrera;[1] a shark three inches long, a toad one inch, a head of an animal, and a deity. The gold of these figures is of low standard, containing copper, and probably some silver. Is this a natural form of the gold, or has it been alloyed by the natives? Columbus procured, at Paria, plates of gold, of low standard, called guanin, or gianin, which class of metal was known as far as Honduras. It was assayed in Spain, and found to consist of sixty-three gold, fourteen silver, nine copper.[2]

A recent analysis of gold from Titiribi, in Colombia, gave gold 76·41, silver 23·12, copper 0·3.

My friend, Don Liborio Duran, of N. Granada, tells me that near Nieva, 3° 10′ N., (Old Nieva is in 4° 43′), there is a locality called "La Cindad de la Plata," where very rich silver mines were worked by the first settlers, who enjoyed but for a short period their prize. The settlement was destroyed[3] by the Paes, Pijaos, Andaquis,[4] &c.,

---

[1] Cauca, sometimes called Guaca (sacred in Quichua), this last name probably given to it by the Spaniards, some of whom had been in Peru. This country was well peopled at the period of the conquest. The natives clothed in cotton mantles, were rich and industrious, and the Chief was borne on a litter covered with gold.— J. Acosta, 144.

On the Cauca, about Cali and Vijges, Holton, 569, describes huacas or graves. Some are square pits, excavated in the ground, covered over first with logs and then with earth. Others have side excavations, and very often small passages running from one to another. Bones and relics are found in them; but I find very few of these in the hands of people here. They are diligently hunted for gold. A man who has a passion for this (and it very naturally becomes a mental infirmity), is called a guaquero, or Indian grave hunter.

[2] Velasco, i. 31. Tumbaga, or pucacuri (bad gold), is an alloy of gold and copper. It is found in a natural state in the mines of Patia de Popayan and Villonaco de Loja. This Guanin is first mentioned by Columbus as forming the ornament of a chief, when coasting along the south side of Jamaica, in 1494.

"Life of Columbus," by Irving, ii., 177. In 1503, Columbus, when on the Mosquito coast: "there was no pure gold to be met with here, all their ornaments were of guanin; but the natives assured the Adelantado that in proceeding along the coast, the ships would soon arrive at a country where gold was in abundance," p. 178. On the coast of Veragua pure gold was met with for the first time.

[3] See J. Acosta, 349. Velasco, iii. 22. When the destruction of the Spaniards is detailed.

[4] I mention as one of the confederated tribes with the Cherokees, the Unataquas, or Andarcos, as existing in Texas. See my Obs. on Indians of Texas, "Ethno. Soc. Journal," 1850.

and, in lapse of time, the position of the mines were forgotten, except by a few Indians, who taught their children that it would be criminal ever again to impart to their sanguinary conquerors the knowledge of the site, and if they did so, they would die. Duran's father became compadre, or godfather to the daughter of a chief, in whose family it was believed the secret was known. The child was induced to become an inmate of the Duran family, and on being questioned, promised, but unwillingly, to lead her friends to the spot. The journey was commenced, and on arriving, as it is supposed, near to the place, the child became sad and deaf to further entreaties to proceed; she refused food for several days, and the party, fearing the child would be starved, returned, but the little girl died not long afterwards.

I find a "La Plata," in 2° 20' N. 75° 45' W., and to the N.E. some 15', a spot called "Carniceria," or the butchery. Velasco[1] gives the latitude of San Sebastian de la Plata, 2° 20', and the "Asiento," probably the mines, in same lat. and long. 3° E. of Quito. He also says, that the ancient Indians, of Nieva,[2] used hieroglyphics and characters, cut in relief on stone, many of which monuments are still to be seen, especially at Piedra Pintada (the engraved stone), and that he himself saw there large stones, full of hieroglyphics, figures of animals, branches of flowers, and other strange characters of various angles, figures that appeared to be numerals; these, as well as those at Timaná, are in the old country of Popayan, but Velasco says nothing about the ruins of Timaná.

On the route from Puerto Cabello to Valencia, about 10° 15' N. 68° 30' W. (in Venezuela), is a large rock, covered with hieroglyphics.[3]

In the plains of Variñas, 7° N., are tumuli, found between Mijagual and the Cano de la Hacha.

Humboldt[4], informs us, that near the southern entrance of the Raudal of Atures, about 1° 30' N. 68° W., is the celebrated cave cemetery of Ataruipe, the burial place of an extinct nation, the Atures, pressed hard and destroyed by Cannibal Caribs. Here skeletons were preserved in mapires, or baskets of palm leaves. Besides the mapires were found urns of half-burnt clay, which appeared to contain the bones of entire families. The larger of these urns were about three feet high and nearly six feet long, of a pleasing oval form

---

[1] His. de Quito.
[2] This Neiva, Nieba, or Neyva, south of Bogotá, must not be confounded with Leiva, which is near Tunja, and N. of Bogotá.
[3] Bulletin de la Société de Geographie. Paris, 1817.
[4] Aspects, I., 227.

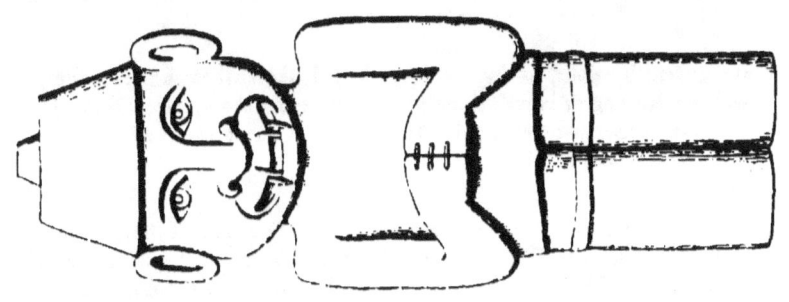

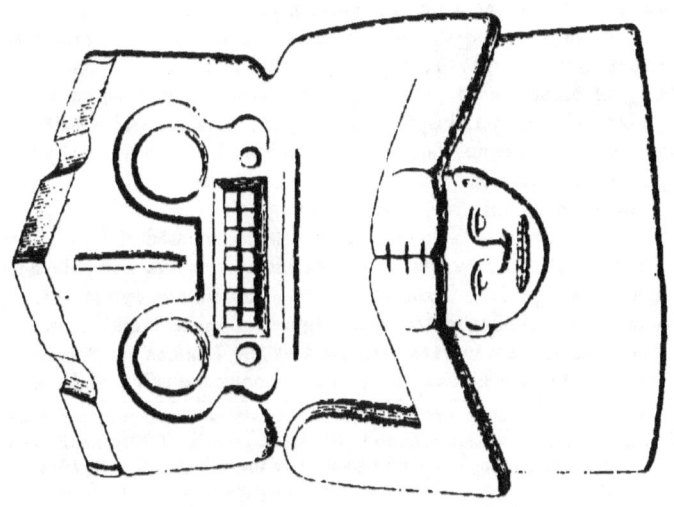

and greenish colour, having handles shaped like snakes and crocodiles, and meandering or labyrinthine ornaments round the upper margin.

These ornaments are similar to those that cover the walls of the Mexican Palaces at Mitla.

The following on the antiquities of N. Granada, I have translated from the beautiful work of Rivero and Tschudi, "Antiguedades Peruanas," published at Vienna, 1851. In Dr. Hawk's English translation of this work, 1854, he has omitted what appertains to N. Granada. In the frontispiece of the Spanish edition are figures in gold, said to be of the Muiscas, found at Timaná, one represents an owl with a serpent in its mouth, another a face with large canine teeth, like the canine teeth in the statues of Timaná, of much better workmanship (though apparently of an earlier date) than those I have described from Antioquia.

In reference to plate xxxix, they observe, as but few examples of the antiquities of the Muiscas have been published, these are offered, say of the times of Bochica. They have a distinct type compared with the Incarial.[1] The stone idols are found near Timaná: these monuments, of which there is a large collection, are in the interior of a dense forest. There is no tradition as to the history of these statues. Fig. 1 is a statue, one yard eight inches in height; the characters marked on the cap have been placed by the Spaniards. Fig. 2 (A) is one and a half yards high, and has a pleasing face (both these have long canine teeth).[2]

Plate xlii., two stone statues, (B) is one of them.

Plate xl., a stone statue, also form of an animal.

Plate iiil., a square table of stone, the feet composed of four columns and one in the centre, which is not cylindrical as the rest; its height is nearly two yards. Upon the central column are two stones. On the two front columns are engraved figures of the sun and moon.

The table appears to have been used by the Muiscas for the sacrifice of offerings to their deities, and is found among the ruins of Timaná.

---

[1] M. E. Rivero wrote a small work, "Antiguedades Peruanas," published in Lima, 1841, at p. 51 of this work, and plate xxxiii. of Atlas of Rivero and Tschudi, Antig. Peruv., in alluding to the hieroglyphics on the club, it is said that Dn. M. E. Rivero obtained it at Tunja. Thus I cannot but suppose that he was also at Timaná, and made sketches of the stone statues, as well as the sacrificial table.

At San Augustin, and in the forest of Laboyas and Timaná, there are columns, idols, altars, images of the sun, and other evidences of the former existence there of a great nation now extinct.—S. American Co's pamphlet, London, 1859.

[2] The gold ornament I describe further on, as coming from Cuenca, in Quito, has those canine teeth, of large proportion.

I find that Timaná, founded by the Spaniards, in 1540, was in the jurisdiction of Popayan, and in the country of the Timanáes, and according to Velasco, in 2° 15' N. 3° 30' E, of Quito, but in J. Acosta's map, 1° 45' N. 78° 45' W., of Paris, a woody, mountainous and hot country. Velasco does not advert to these important remains, but he does to those of Nieva. The ruins at Timaná are more than 2° S. of the territory of the Chibchas, and are in all probability of an earlier date than Chibcha or Muisca[1] remains, and of another nation. Besides the Timanáes there were many other nations, who cultivated the land, as the Yalcones, 5000 warriors strong, the Apima, Pinaos, Guanacas, Paeces, &c.

MUISCA CALENDAR.

Account of the Muisca Calendar[2] of the Indians of New Granada, Dedicated, in 1795, to Don Jose Celestino de Mutis, by Don José Domingo Duquesne, Curate of Gachancipá.

I now communicate some observations in regard to the history of the Muiscas, to explain what concern their computation of time, by interpreting certain signs which I have investigated. This interpretation is founded on a knowledge of the customs, history, idolatry and language of the Muiscas. The language, although it has been of use to me, has given me much trouble; for, at the present time, it is not spoken, and I have been obliged to work it out from the cartapacios (small books, probably MSS.), where it was reduced to the Latin form, but with which it has no analogy.

The Muiscas counted with their fingers.[3] They only had names for numbers up to 10, and the number 20, viz., 1, ata; 2, bosa; 3, mica; 4, muyhica; 5, hisca; 6, ta; 7, cubupcua; 8, sahuza; 9, aca; 10, ubchihica; 20, gueta, concluding these, they turned their hands, went to their feet, repeating the same words, putting before them the

---

[1] These ruins appear to have some analogy with the earlier ones of Tia-Huanacu as compared with Incarial. The monuments of N. Granada require detailed examination.

[2] Translated from J. Acosta's "Compendio, &c., de la N. Granada," Paris, 1848.

[3] The word expressing the number 5, in the Carib of Essiquibo, the Moscan of Nicaragua, and some others, means one hand; that expressing 10, two hands; that expressing 20, a man; *i.e.*, both hands and feet. The Peruvians and Cunacunas had a purely decimal system. Trans. Amer. Ethno. Soc. iii., 1853.

word quihicha, as, thus says the foot; quihicha ata, 11; quihicha bosa, 12, &c.

The number 20, expressed by the word gueta (house, or the time of sowing), included all the property and happiness of this nation, and here ended their numbers. Thus having finished with one 20, they commenced counting another 20, uniting it to the first until 20 twenties were obtained.

Thus as mathematicians have given to the circle 360° to facilitate its subdivision, the Muiscas divided their accounts into four parts, and again subdivided each part into fives: thus their prime numbers were 5, 10, 15, 20, which served them in the arrangements of their affairs.

The moon was the object of their observations and religion. This planet, on which they gazed with adoration, gave to them the idea or model for their habitations, enclosures, temples, fields, in a word, was connected with all their doings. They fixed a pole in the earth for a centre, and with a cord from it described a circle;[1] this pole and the cord, if we carefully examine the characters and symbols described, will be seen to be the principal elements for instructing.

The various meanings of the numbers in their language, alludes to the phases of the moon, agricultural operations, and the superstitions of idolatry; and in this way we are conducted to the formation of a calendar.[2]

The Indians had mentally in their hands these symbols, as we have the notes of music; and thus, by merely giving a turn to the fingers, they knew the state of the moon, and the position of their agricultural and other affairs.

The year consisted of twenty moons, and a century of twenty years;[3]

---

[1] The Bakwains have a curious inability to make or put things square; like all Bechuanas, their dwellings are made round. "Livingstone's Africa," 40.

[2] M. Duquesne has made various etymological researches on the words which denote numbers in the Chibcha language. He asserts, "that all these words are significant; that all depend on roots which relate either to phases of the moon, in its increase or wane, or to objects of agricultural worship." As no dictionary of the Chibcha language exists, we cannot verify the justness of the assertion; we cannot be too mistrustful of etymological researches, and shall satisfy ourselves with here presenting the significations of the numbers from one to twenty, as given in the MSS. which I brought from Santa Fé. Humboldt, Views, II., 118. The late Colonel Joaquin Acosta, author of the "Compendio," &c., had a "Diccionario y Grammatica de la Langua Mosca Chibchá," MSS., in 12mo., which, I think, he gave to the Geographical Soc. of Paris. See Ludewig, p. 128.

[3] Among the Muiscas, the day was divided into four parts; three days made a week, and ten weeks a lunation or month. The rural year was composed of twelve Sunas, and, at the end of the third year, another month was added, a method similar to one

they commenced a month from the full-moon in the sign of Ubchihica. which signified brilliant moon: counting seven days on the fingers, beginning at Ata, which follows Ubchihica, they found the quadrature in Cuhupcua; counting from this, seven, they found the next immersion of the moon in Muyhica, which meant anything black; and the following day, the conjunction symbolized in Hisca, which, in their idea, was the union of the moon with the sun, represented the nuptials of these planets, which was the capital dogma of their belief, and the object of their execrable rites; then counting eight days, they found the other quadrature in Mica, which meant a changing object, thus denoting the continual variation of its phases. The first aspect of the first phase was signified in Cuhupcua, and as in this symbol fell the quadrature, they gave it two ears, calling it deaf.

These same symbols served to count the years, and contained a general doctrine, in regard to the sowing season. Ata,[1] and Aca represented the waters in the sign of the toad,[2] for when this animal most loudly croaked it was a signal showing that the time for sowing was near.

---

used in China. The civil year, or zocam, consisted of twenty sunas and the ritual. or sacred year of thirty-seven sunas. Five ritual years made a small cycle, and four of these a great age, equal to a real solar cycle of sixty years, an astronomical period of the same duration as one used in Oriental Asia. His. of China, by Davis, I., 282. The Mexican week was of four days, as was also that of Java. See Calendar of Nicaragua and Mexico, which was of this character. Trans. Amer. Ethno. Soc., 153, 1853.

[1] Atl, water, in Mexican.

[2] Frogs are very common in N. Granada, and very large ones are to be seen particularly at Baranquilla, near the mouth of the R. Magdalena.

The frogs or matlamétlo of Africa are of enormous size, when cooked look like chickens, and are supposed by the natives to fall from thunder clouds, because after a heavy thunder storm the pools, which are filled and retain water a few days, become instantly alive with this loud-croaking pugnacious game. It would no doubt tend to perpetuate the present alliance, if we made a gift of it to France. "Livingstone's Africa," 42.

The Maopityans or Frog Indians are a small tribe in Guiana, from mao, a frog, and pityan, people or tribe. Schomburgh on Natives of Guiana in Ethno. Journal, I. p. 265.

On the Oronoko were Indians, who rendered honours of divinity to toads in order to obtain rain or fair weather; but the animals were beaten if the prayers were not promptly complied with. Depons, I. 198.

The Creeks and Cherokees, indeed, amongst all the Floridian nations, had a great annual festival in July or August, called Boos-ke-tau, at which they danced the Toc-co-yule-gan, or Tadpole dance, by four men and four women. Trans. Amer. Ethno. Soc., 1853.

The rana arunco, or land toad is called by the Araucanos of Chilé, Genoo, or lord of the waters. Molina, I., 179.

Bosa, an enclosure for sowing, made round their grounds to preserve them from injury.

Mica, to look for, find, choose small things, means the care they should have in choosing seeds for sowing.

Muyhica, black object, represented dark and tempestuous weather. Its root signified that plants grew, for with the benefit of rains, the seeds gave out plants.

Hisca, green things, as the rains made the fields look beautiful and gay. It likewise meant to rejoice, make merry. The most forward plants in their fields, they praised in hope of their fruitfulness.

Ta, enclosure for sowing. The sixth month of the season; this corresponded to the harvest.

Cuhupcua, their granaries, have a snail shape or winding like the ear.

Cuhutana, has the same root, signifies the corners of the house where the grain is deposited, the harvest.

Sahuza, tail, the month, or the end of the sowings; has allusion to the pole fixed in their (calzadas) the ground for describing the circle where they had their solemnities at harvest time.

Aca, two frogs, coupled.

Ubchihica may allude to their feasts.

Gueta, house and field, marked with a toad at full length, the emblem of felicity.

The Muiscas looked upon these things, as so many oracles; they taught their children with great care the doctrine of their forefathers, and not content with these precautions, not to lose the plan for the government of the year, they marked the period by the sacrifice of many victims.

They did not repeat the word Zocam (the year) without its corresponding number, as zocam ata, zocam bosa, &c. In the same way with the word suna (calzada or platform), where, at sowing and harvest time, their feasts and sacrifices were held, as suna ata, suna bosa, one platform, two platforms, and thus it was that these places were like books in which were registered their doings.

Twenty moons, then, made a year; these ended, they counted another twenty, and then successively going round a circle, continuously, until concluding a twenty of twenties. To intercalate a moon, which is requisite after the thirty-sixth moon, so that the lunar year shall correspond with the solar, and to guard the regularity of the seasons, was easily done. As they had in their hands the whole of the calendar; they sowed two enclosures successively, with a sign between them, and the third with two. Upon this principle was conducted their astronomy, idolatry, politics, economy and what is not less interesting, their surveying.

We will now distribute these Muisca signs with the fingers, and this digitated table will give us all the combinations. Let us suppose that ata, which is made with the first finger, corresponds with January, the proper month for sowing. Continuing with the fingers we come to the second enclosure in Mica, intercepting Bosa, which is between Ata and Mica. So that this enclosure is made in the thirteenth moon in respect to Ata.

Proceeding with the fingers from Mica, the enclosure corresponds in Hisca, intercepting Muybica, which is between Mica and Hisca, so that the enclosure is in the thirteenth moon.

Lastly, let us run the fingers from Hisca, then the enclosure will be in Suhuza, intercepting two signs, Ta and Cuhupuca, which are between Hisca and Suhuza; this is in the fourteenth moon in respect to Hisca.

This moon Cuhupcua (deaf) is that which is intercalated, because it is the seventeenth of the second Muisca year, which number, added to the twenty moons of the first year, produces 37, making the lunar and solar years equal, and Suhuza, becomes a true year.

This intercalation, which is perpetually verified, leaving aside 37, or deaf moon, leads to a belief that between the two ordinary years, of twenty moons each, there is another hidden astronomical one of 37 moons, so that moon 38 is the true year. The Muiscas, without understanding the theory of this proposition, which has embarrassed many learned nations, found it necessary to add this moon at the end of each three lunar years, in consequence of the twelve anterior ones being of twelve moons, and the third of thirteen. They had thus a great facility in the intercalation, following this method, and preserving the astronomical year, so that the people noted no difference in the ordinary years of twenty moons.

The ordinary year of twenty moons served for the period of truces in their wars, for purchases, sales, &c. But the astronomical year and the intercalated of 37 moons, which counted for three sowings, served principally for agriculture and religion. The account was kept by their Xeques noting the epochs by particular sacrifices and engraving them on stones, by means of symbols and figures, as is seen in a pentagon in my possession, which I will presently explain.

The Muisca century consisted of twenty intercalated years of 37 moons each year, which correspond to 60 of our years, composed of four revolutions, counting five in five, each one of which was of ten

Muisca years, and fifteen of ours, until twenty were completed, in which the sign Ata returned to where it had first commenced. .The first revolution was closed in Hisca, the second in Ubchihica, the third in Quihicha Hisca, and the fourth in Gueta.

The week was of three days, and was signalised by a market on the first day at Turmequé, a most important one, as may be seen by reference to Father Zamora.

They divided the day Sua and the night Za thus: Sua-mena, the morning, from sun-rise to noon; Sua-meca, noon till sunset; Zasca, time for food, sunset to midnight; Cagui, midnight to sunrise, morning meal.

The founder of the Muiscas did not make the working of the calendar easy for the nation. He ordered that they should consult their chiefs; thus the people believed the chiefs had command over the stars, and were absolute masters over good and evil. Nothing was done without the advice of the Xeques, for which they received large presents, and thus it was that these calendars were highly paid for.

Care was taken to signalise the annual revolutions by notable acts. Sowing time and harvest had their sacrifices. Each town had a causeway (calzada), level and broad, commencing at the cercado, or house of the Tithua or chief, of half a mile in length, at the end of which there was a pole like a mast, to which was tied the unfortunate creature to be offered to the sun or the moon, so as to obtain an abundant harvest.

The Indians came in troops, adorned with jewels, figures of moons and halfmoons of gold, some disguised in the skins of bears, jaguars, and pumas: some with masks of gold, having tears imitated on them; others followed whooping and laughing, dancing and jumping wildly; others wore long tails, and arriving at the end of the causeway, sent a shower of arrows at the victim, causing a lingering death, the blood was received in various vessels, and the barbarous proceeding terminated with the accustomed scenes of drunkenness.

It appears that this procession was symbolic of the calendar, and had it been depicted, it would have aided inquiry or a better knowledge of the signs and the characters attributed to them.

But the victim destined to solemnize the four intercalated moons at the commencement of the century, underwent a peculiar induction. He was a youth taken from a particular town, situated in the plains, now known as those of San Juan.

His ears were pierced, and he was brought up in the Temple of the Sun; at the age of ten years (our) he was led out to walk, in memory of the perigrinations of Bochica, the founder, who, they believed, resided in the sun, living there, in an eternal happy state of marriage with the moon, and having a brilliant family.

The youth was bought at a high price, and deposited in the Temple of the Sun until he was fifteen, at which age he was sacrificed, when his heart and entrails were torn out, and offered to that deity.

The youth was called Guesa,[1] this means without home. Again, he was named Quihica, or door, as was Janus, or the beginning of the year, among the Romans. Guesa signifies also month, because he interceded for the nation with the intercalated and deaf moon, which heard his lamentations from the earth. The people believed that the victims implored for them from within their habitations, so they sacrificed many parrots and macaws, sometimes as many as two hundred of these birds were offered up at a time on the altars, but not before they could repeat their Muisca language. Notwithstanding all the sacrifices, the intercalated and deaf moon went on its way without any alteration in the calendar.

The many precautions taken by the Muisca legislator for the government of the year, made the people very attentive in its observance. It was looked upon as a divine invention, and its author as a god, who dwelt amongst the stars. Thus Bochica was placed in the sun, and his wife, Chia, in the moon, that they might protect their descendants.

To Bochica was given two companions or brothers, symbolised by one body and three heads, and one heart and one soul. Bochica, from the sun, directed their agricultural operations.

The toad or frog had its place in the heavens, as a companion to the scorpion and the rest of the Egyptian animals.

Not content with having deified their first legislator, they worshipped another of their heroes in the same calendar. This was the powerful Tomagata, one of the oldest Zaques. He had only one eye, but four ears, and a long tail, like a lion. The sun had taken from him all procreative power the night before his marriage, so that his brother, Tutasua should succeed him. He was, however, so light of foot that every night he made ten journeys to Sogomosa from Tunja, visiting his hermits. He lived a hundred years, but the Muiscas say he lived much longer. The sun gave him the power to turn those who offended him into snakes, tigers, lizards, &c. The Indians called him the cacique rabon (great tailed). His name, Tomagata, means fire that boils. They passed this strange creature into their astrological heaven,

---

[1] See Prescott Conq. Mex. I. 62. On the Sacrifice of a beautiful youth to Tezcatlepoca, the soul of the world.

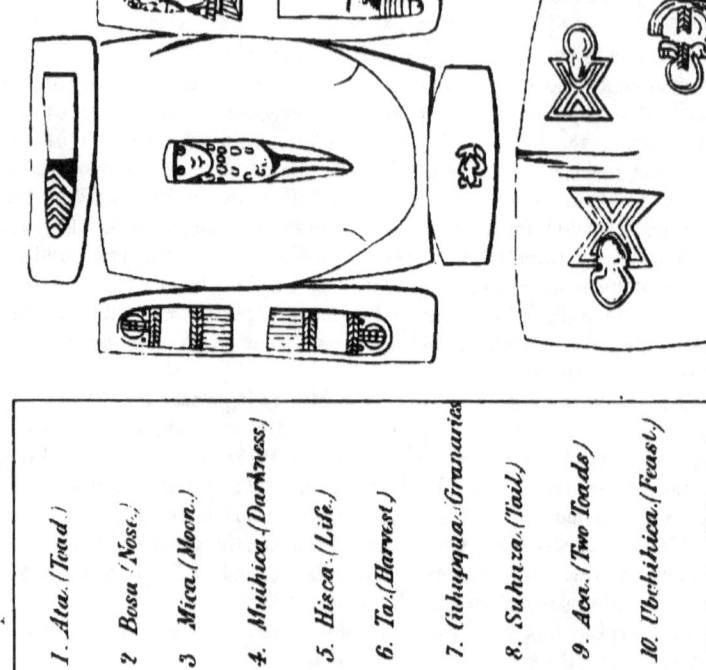

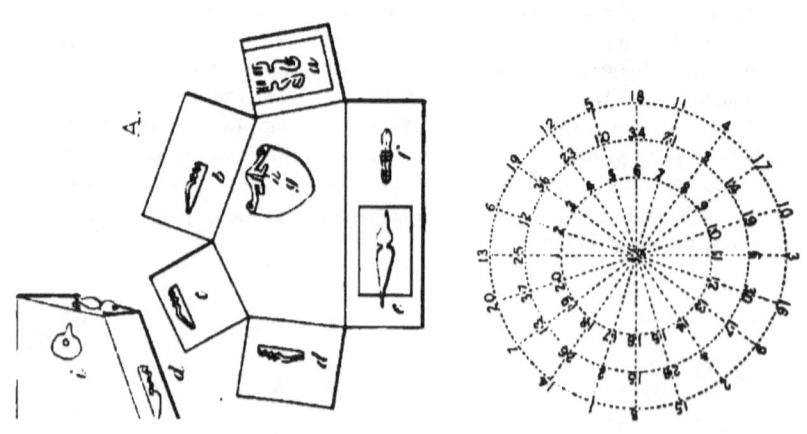

1. *Ata. (Toad.)*
2. *Bosa (Nose.)*
3. *Mica. (Moon.)*
4. *Muihica. (Darkness.)*
5. *Hisca. (Life.)*
6. *Ta. (Harvest.)*
7. *Cuhupqua. (Granaries)*
8. *Suhuza. (Tail.)*
9. *Aca. (Two Toads)*
10. *Ubchihica. (Feast.)*
20. *Gueta. (Felicity.)*

and, I think, he may be considered rather as the eunuch to the virgin gleaner, than as the companion to Sagittarius.

Such was the heaven of the Muiscas, full of animals, like that of the Egyptians. We see introduced into it Bochica and Chia, like Osiris and Isis, the transformation of these into the ram, the bull and other animals, and imitated in the transformation of Tomaguta, &c.

Ata is a toad in the position of springing, which well characterises the beginning of the year. Aca is a toad from whose tail another is forming, symbol of that moon in which these animals begun existence, and their croaking announced the rainy season, and was the sign that sowing must commence. Here is an allusion to the sign Pisces. Gueta is the toad, laying at full length, meaning abundance and felicity. To other signs they gave human characters, as we ourselves sometimes picture the sun and moon with eyes and nose. Bosa represented a nose; mica, two open eyes; muyhica, two closed eyes; cuhupcua, two ears; ubchihica, one ear. They probably wished here to give an idea of the moon's phases. Cuhupcua looks like a basket, to signify the harvest. Ta and Suhuza are figured by the pole and cord, by which they made the circle for the plan and foundation of their houses and fields. Hisca, the union of two figures, was the symbol of fecundity, as Gemini. They had various other significations.

We have seen the Muisca calendar by means of the fingers, also engraved on stones, by means of symbolic figures. In this country (New Granada), up to the present time no one has occupied himself in working on the iconography of the Muiscas, and these few observations are the first elements of this study.

The toad is, without doubt, the symbol of the first moon of the year and century. The Indians put it amongst their divinities, and represented it in various ways. When springing it corresponded to the first sign, Ata, and is thus engraved on many stones. I have observed it on the other stones engraved with a tail, which, I suppose, represents quihicha ata, or the number 12; for, continuing the springs or jumps, so as to denote future months, he designates, with his tail, those he leaves behind. On some stones, the toad is seen without feet, which appears to me to represent Gueta, a sign of quietude or rest, not influencing agricultural operations. Sometimes the head of the toad is united to the head of a man; at others the body without feet, turned into an idol, with a tunic, also the tailed toad without feet.

The figure I am now about to describe is a pentagon (a).[1]

(a) is a toad on a plain surface, in the act of jumping.

---

[1] Of Petro-Silex, of a green colour.

(b) is a sort of finger, having three lines.

(c) is the same, but is outside the centre of the line, followed by the others.

(d) is the same, preserving its central position.

(e) is the body of the toad, without feet.

(f) is a snake.

(g) is a circle on the plain part of the stone, in the segment of which is the figure (h).

(B) is the reverse of the same stone.

(i) is a circle with two segments formed by a cord and a radius.

(h) is a snake, &c.

INTERPRETATION.—On this stone[1] (at A) is symbolised the revolution of the first Muisca year, commencing in ata and ending in hisca; this includes nine years and five Muisca moons.

The Indians, who for all things used the circle, here preferred the pentagon to signify that they spoke of five intercalated years.

(a) The toad in the act of springing begins the year and century.

(b) This species of finger[2] signalises by the three thick lines, three years. Omitting, then, the finger (c) which is on one side, they count on the finger (d) another three years, which, together with those of finger (b) produce six. This denotes the intercalation of quihicha ata, which succeeds the six Muisca years, as is seen in the table; and is of much moment among the Indians, as belonging to the toad, which regulates the whole of the calendar.

(e) is the body of a toad without tail and feet: symbol of quihicha ata, and wanting the feet, properly expresses its intercalation. The intercalary month is not computed for the sowing, and thus they imagined it without action or movements. There is seen, on the plain part, the toad ata, which appears to signify that in both places the toad is meant.

(f) this serpent represents the sign suhuza, which is intercalated after

---

[1] REFER ALSO TO THIS FOR FURTHER EXPLANATION.—(a) Toad or frog without head, sign of ata, emblem of water.

(b c d).—Three small pieces of wood, each marked by three transverse lines.

(e).—Tadpole, with long tail, and without feet; frog in repose; useless.

(f) indicates by eight transverse lines, divided into five and three, that at the 8th Muisca year, the moon governed by Suhuza is intercalated; this is represented at (i) by a circle, traced by means of a cord round a column.

(f h) represent serpents—emblems of time.

(g).—The sign hisca, alludes to the nuptials of Bochica and Chia.

(b c d).—The nine strokes are the nine Muisca years.

(h) the lock which closes the temple.

[2] Humboldt calls these figures pieces of wood, marked by transverse lines.

quihicha ata, at the two Muisca years, represented by the two thick lines on the back, corresponding to the eighth year, as is seen on the table.

We now go to the plain or flat part (B). The serpent (h) is a reproduction of suhuza, and as it is laying on a sort of triangle, is the symbol of hisca, signifying that it is intercalated immediately after suhuza, in the second year, which is also figured by the two thick lines it has on the back.

As the principal end of this chronological stone is to signalise the intercalation of the sign hisca, as being the end of the first revolution of the Muisca century. For greater clearness, these years are counted in the three fingers (b c d), together producing nine years, which give, punctually, this notable intercalation, happening at nine years and five months, as is seen in the table.

(g) at (A) is a closed temple. (h) is a wooden lock of the same form as used by the Indians of the present day. The holes of the two ears serve for the stakes they use, and the two interior hooks to fasten the door, signifies the first revolution of the century, closed in hisca. To continue the time it was necessary to imagine that Guesa opened the door with the sacrifice already alluded to, the circumstances of which were symbolical, and related to these revolutions of the century.

The serpent has been the symbol of time with all nations. This first revolution of the century was consecrated principally to the nuptials of the sun and moon, symbolised in the triangle, not only by the Indians but by other nations.

Explanation of the diagram of circles of the Muisca year (c) : The first or interior circle represents the twenty moons of the vulgar Muisca year, all of which signs are intercalated in the space of a century. The second circle expresses the Muisca years corresponding to the intercalation of each sign. The third circle expresses the order of this intercalation. Example: I wish to know in which Muisca year the sign mica (the third year of twenty moons) is intercalated. I see in the diagram the number 3 (which represents mica) in the inner circle; I find that in the second circle it corresponds to number 36[1], this is the year sought for; I see in the third circle that it corresponds to

---

[1] Duquesne gave the arrangement of the numbers in tables as at p. 55, and in three circles, one inside the other. See J. Acosta and Humboldt.

In the diagram of circles, given by Humboldt and by J. Acosta, by some error the number 30 is given instead of 36. The numbers in the diagram stand thus: 3, 36, 19.

number 19; and thus the intercalation of mica is in order or the 19th of the century.

The intercalation of Gueta 20, is the last of the Muisca year 37. This is after the vulgar Muisca century of twenty moons, and seventeen years more, so that, the century ending with the astronomical revolutions of twenty intercalated years of thirty-seven moons each, three vulgar years are required to complete two vulgar centuries.

Arriving at this point, they took no account of those three vulgar years; they did not require, for agriculture, religion, or history, beginning again in ata (which had been arrived at in its turn), a vulgar year, the beginning of a fresh century, like the last already described.[1]

Note by J. Acosta: I have wished to preserve this document without addition or correction

Note by W. B. I have omitted such observations as have but little to do with the document.

In a note, J. Acosta[2] says: That this calendar of Duquesne is lost.

(D). Is the representation of another stone calendar, showing all its sides, of the original size, procured by Dr. Roulin, in N. Granada. It is larger and more perfect than that of Duquesne, not of petro-silex, but of Lydian Stone.

J. Acosta gives no explanation of this engraved stone calendar. What I call the upper surface has a pointed figure with male human head: it may represent gueta, 20, quietude or rest, or zue, the sun. The upper side has an oblong figure with seven angular marks: may be the tail of a serpent, emblem of time. The lower side is a toad or frog, probably the symbol of the first moon of the year and century. The right hand side has a half female figure, may be za, the moon: under the figure an oblong with six straight lines, may be tail of serpent. The left hand side has two complex oblong figures, both alike, each having six straight lines, two sets (six each) of angular marks, a circle with three lines drawn from top to bottom, and two very small circles, I cannot offer any explanation to this last, but it has to do with computation of time.

The underneath part (E) has three figures of toads or frogs, one has two sets of six angular lines, may be the first sign, ata. In another is traced nine large angular lines and two smaller, may mean gueta or 20.

---

[1] J. Acosta says of this green stone calendar, "supposed to be of the Chibchas."
[2] 418.

NOTE.[1]—On some Muisca stones by M. Jomard. The collection I purchased in 1840, which came from the table-land anciently known as Cundinamarca, contains six stones analogous to that published by Humboldt as the Muisca calendar, in his "Views of the Cordilleras," &c. There appear always the same figures, viz.—the human head, the frog, instruments, a fish or a part of one, insects, crustaceæ, the carcaj or arrows, the rencunjo (spawn of frogs or young frogs), not the perfect animal, a sort of rectangular tambor, with a Grecian border (Græca), which has always one of these figures, alone or repeated, seen sculptured in relief on the upper and lower portions, and on the facets of the ancient stones alluded to.

Humboldt, founding his opinion on the numeration of the Muiscas, subject to the number five and its multiples, as well as the Muisca calendar, and observing that the pentagonal stones had 10 sculptured figures on its facets, considers that it is a calendar, thereby adopting the opinion of Duquesne.

The particulars of the six stones in my cabinet are as follows:

1. Stone irregular pentagon, with nineteen figures. It is possible that the twentieth has been rubbed out.
2. Another pentagon rather regular, ten figures, two facets empty, or only marked, with two cross lines.
3. Another trapezoidal, regular, has five figures.
4. Another stone (esquisito verde) is broken; appears to have been a pentagon; seven figures remain, but adding the three facets there would be ten.
5—6. Two stones much worn; their original form cannot be made out; in these are seen some figures like those on the first described.

This examination confirms the conjecture of Humboldt, but only in relation to the No. 5 and its multiples; but if these stones are calendars, how is it that similar figures represent different days of the week? Then the Muisca week of three days does not agree with the numbers 5 or 10, and it would only be from the number 15 and its multiples, where the divisions in 3 or in 5 could be considered. In regard to 20, we should have to go to 60 to have at one time a multiple

---

[1] M. Jomard has prepared this note: it contains the description of the objects in his cabinet connected with the Chibchas. This collection is the most complete I have seen in Europe or America; for, independent of the stone calendar I possess, which is the most perfect known (the drawing D in plate) I only know of one other in N. Granada, very much used, belonging to Dr. M. M. Quijano, of Bogotá.

of 20 and 3, then 60 days do not correspond to any of the divisions of the solar or lunar year, although on the other side, according to Duquesne, the Muiscas had a division or period of 60 rural years, or 20 great years of the xeques or priests, each of which embraced 37 moons but the civil year had only 20 (signed)—Jomard.

Besides these stones, the cabinet of M. Jomard contains various drawings of idols and ornaments, vases and other utensils of the nations of N. Granada, especially from Antioquia (some 200), which being of gold and heavy were drawn before they were melted down. (Signed) J. Acosta.

(F) from 1 to 20 are the only hieroglyphics I have found of the Muiscas.

LUNAR DAYS OF THE SUNA OF THE MUISCA INDIANS, DIVIDED INTO TEN SMALL PERIODS OF THREE DAYS.[1]

FIRST SERIES.

Ata	Muyhica	Cuhupqua* last quarter	Aca
Bosa	Hisca		Ubchihica
Mica	Ta	Suhuza	

SECOND SERIES.

Ata	Muyhica	Ta	Aca
Bosa	Hisca* conjunction	Cuhupqua	Ubchihica
Mica		Sahuza	

THIRD SERIES.

Ata	Muyhica	Cuhupqua	Ubchihica* full moon
Bosa	Hisca	Sahuza	
Mica* 1st quarter.	Ta	Aca	

THREE FORMS OF ZOCAMS OF THE CALENDAR OF THE CHIBCHAS OF MUISCAS.

RURAL YEAR OF TWELVE AND THIRTEEN MONTHS.		YEARS OF THE PRIESTS OF THIRTY-SEVEN MOONS.		VULGAR YEARS OF TWENTY MOONS.	
I. Ata		1. *Ata*	1	I. *Ata*	1
		2. Bosca	2		2
		3. Mica	3		3
		4. Muyhica	4		4
		5. Hisca	5		5
Common year		6. Ta	6	Harvest	6
		7. Cuhupqua	7		7
		8. Suhuza	8		8
		9. Aca	9		9
		10. Ubchihica	10		10
		11. *Ata*	11		11
		12. Bosa	12		12
II. Mica	1	Mica	13		13
	2	Muyhica	14		14
	3	Hisca	15		15
	4	Ta	16		16
	5	Cuhupqua	17		17
Common year	6	Suhuza	18	Harvest	18
	7	Aca	19		19
	8	Ubchica	20		20
	9	*Ata*	21		21
	10	Bosa	22	II. *Ata*	1
	11	Misca	23		2
	12	Muyhica	24		3
III. Hisca	1	Hisca	25		4
	2	Ta	26		5
	3	Cuhupqua	27		6
	4	Suhuza	28		7
	5	Aca	29		8
	6	Ubchihica	30		9
Embolismic year	7	*Ata*	31	Harvest	10
	8	Bosa	32		11
	9	Mica	33		12
	10	Muyhica	34		13
	11	Hisca	35		14
	12	Ta	36		15
Deaf month.	13	Cuhupqua	37		16
					18
IV. Suhuza	1	II. Suhuza	1		19
	2	Aca	2		20
	3	Ubchi	3		
	4	*Ata*	4	III. *Ata*	1

[1] Humbolt's "Views," 126, 130.

PANAMA.—The approach to this city from the Atlantic is by tracks through the most dense tropical forests; here and there the scorching sun's rays dart through openings, and teach one how to appreciate the shade. As Panamá is neared and the low mountains of the Isthmus left behind, a pleasant grassy savanna is entered.

Who can help musing in such a locality on the discovery of the New World by Columbus, his sorrows and sufferings; the proud feelings of Balboa, his melancholy fate; and the history of the bold but cruel Pizarro, the conqueror of Peru?

I was still north of the equator in 8° 56', it was the winter month of this region, the sultry atmosphere of the woods was somewhat tempered by the sea breeze, and a good bit of road presented itself; on either side were the huts of the half-Indian people, some swinging in their hammocks and very lightly clad. Their cabins were shaded by bananas and palms, orange and pomegranate groves, and the beautiful maize waved gracefully in the plantations.

On entering Panamá, black clouds rose from the horizon spreading themselves rapidly. A thunder-storm succeeded with torrents of rain, when the weary traveller drenched to the skin found shelter in the "Louisiana Hotel." After such a soaking, it is customary to rub the body with brandy, comforting also the inner man with a portion: this is said oftimes to prevent an attack of fever.

I had a letter of introduction from Mrs. Harrison Smith (then in England) to her brother-in-law, who located me in, perhaps, the best house in the city, for which I was most thankful.

I did not find any ancient ruins here; there are, however, some interesting modern ones; the Jesuits' college, destroyed by fire, monasteries, convents, and churches, the walls of which are covered with trees and shrubs, their descending roots breaking out the masonry. Worthy of note also is the cathedral and some of the churches, the upper portions are studded with pearl shells, giving them a quaint and sparkling appearance.

Since the discovery of the gold regions of California, from a lifeless place, Panamá has sprung into activity and opulence, added to which is the circumstance of its being the point of transit to the west coast of South America.

There are here many interesting views, amongst which may be mentioned, that of a portion of the city from the ramparts, on which there were some brass guns off their carriages, and it was said that a couple of stout lads with sticks would have no difficulty in taking the arsenal; another good view is that of Playa Prieta, with its luxuriant vegetation rising from the shores of the Pacific; a third is from opposite the cathedral, with the Cabildo and busy Calle de la Merced to the left, and a group of buildings to the right.

Although Panamá is a New Granadian city, Brother Jonathan really rules here; it is a lively commercial place, and its residents most obliging and hospitable, with a population of 20,000 souls.

I saw the arrival of a large party of diggers from California and their departure for the Atlantic side; they enjoyed themselves much after a sojourn in the gold regions.

The "difficulties" that occasionally arise are amongst gamblers, rowdies, and loafers, when the revolver and bowie knife comes into play oftimes with fatal consequences. Panamá ought to be kept cleaner, for there is abundance of rain to wash it.

After the white population, principally foreigners, the negro element preponderates amongst the work-people and servants, who are a gay and saucy set; they are very fond of dancing, and on moonlight nights they assemble and dance till morning, accompanied by singing, their music being on a drum made of the hollow trunk of a tree, and an instrument of bamboo filled with pebbles.

This is an expensive place, washing is charged from twelve to sixteen shillings a dozen.

Formerly, when in the tropics, I wore linen clothing, but I found it more pleasant to dress in a very thin woollen shirt, trousers, and blouse of same material. If a Panamá straw hat and white leather boots be added to the above, these form a most enjoyable costume, being more conducive to health than either linen or cotton, particularly if there be much rain.

As I was lame in the foot from the bite of some venemous reptile,[1] the night I slept at Cruces, I could not conveniently go abroad. My kind host, Mr. G. Smith, invited an evening party to meet me, consisting of the principal merchants, consuls, gentlemen connected with the railway, editors of eight newspapers, and other notables, including Mr. Joy, well known for his energy and activity in affairs connected with the Isthmus; he has now steamers on the river Magdalena, and a great boon they must be to the country.

I visited El Señor Plece, the Panamá pearl merchant. His pretty treasures were kept in little bags; one beautiful pearl he showed me, pear-shaped, nearly an inch and a half long, by an inch broad in the thickest part; he hoped, in time, to fall in with another to match, when his price would be £4000; he intended to offer the pair for purchase or refusal to the Queen of England.

---

[1] The blood-sucking vampire bat is common in the Isthmus.

Mother-of-pearl shell was selling at £7 per ton.

One of the interesting sights of Panamá is the patio or court-yard of the British consulate, piled up with bars of silver from Peru and Chile, on their way across the Isthmus.

From January 1st, to September 30th, 1853, specie, gold-dust, and silver in bars from California, Mexico, Peru, and Chile, amounting to nearly 43,000,000 of dollars crossed the Isthmus. Of passengers there arrived 7,041, and sailed 7,447.

My friends made a party on horseback to show me something of the surrounding country. Having trotted over the grassy plain, we reached the hills, from the tops of which we enjoyed exquisite views of mountain scenery, particularly at the Losaria, where there are many country seats; forming, with the Pacific on the west, an interesting panorama.

One mile from Panamá is the Cerro de Ancon, 500 feet high: from its summit is seen the city, the islands in the bay, the neighbouring plantations, the range between Panamá and Porto-Bello, the Rio Grande, the low lands towards Old Panamá, and the Chepo and Pecora rivers.

20th of December. As I was to be at sea on the 25th, my good friends Mr. and Mrs. Jones kept this as Christmas-day. I had passed a very happy time of it, and when retiring to bed, I heard bitter lamentations in an adjoining room. I enquired the cause, and found that a young lady had just died of fever, after a very short illness. I could not rest, so sallied forth, lit my cigar, found a billiard-room open, sipped some iced drinks, and, at 3, a.m., the temperature being 86°, I went home.

Col. Lloyd, in his observations on the Isthmus of Darien,[1] says, Porto-Bello is one of the hottest and most unhealthy places in the world. It is a beautiful locality, but so fatal to human life as to be called the white man's grave; at Panamá, on the contrary, it is healthy, the thermometer in the rainy season does not rise higher at night than 82° to 87°, in summer 90° to 93°.

WATER.—The supply is limited for the city, and it is slightly saline, 2d. to 3d. per gallon is paid for drinking water. It was proposed in 1850, by a company that required a capital of a million dollars, to bring good water, by pipes, from the river Pecora, but as yet this has not been effected; 15 to 20 per cent. dividend was promised.

Panamá, its environs, and Taboga expend for water of indifferent quality nearly £56,000 annually.

OLD PANAMA is distant five miles by water from the present city; it

---

[1] Geogr. Soc. Journal, 1., 69.

was destroyed by Morgan, the Buccaneer, in 1673. It had once 20,000 inhabitants. The Spaniards say they had been weary of the place, and determined to leave it on account of its having no harbour. The spot is now deserted, and it requires a practico or guide to find it.

Some watch-towers, solidly built, an arch, two or three piers of a bridge, fragments of church and convent walls are now the only remains to be found. On the top of the convent walls trees and shrubs grow from thirty to forty feet high, their roots running like wedges into the walls, and starting the masonry. A few negroes live in the vicinity. Seemann, the naturalist, describes Old Panamá as surrounded by flat hills, copses of wood, savannas; grassy slopes lose themselves in wild thickets or wooded glens, and the trees stand as in a park. Roads are wanting, and in the wet season, which comprises nearly three-fourths of the year, the country is almost impassable.

December the 22nd, got on board the "Bogota" steamer, commanded by that excellent skipper, Captain Bloomfield, on my way south. We ran over to the island of Taboga, twelve miles distant, in search of a ship's cook, we got a black boy, for whose services we paid six pounds a month. This densely wooded island is two miles long, its highest parts 935 feet. It is an interesting bustling place, with its habitations, hotels, cafés and huts picturesquely scattered about. Supplies of beef, pigs, fowls, eggs, yams, bananas, pine-apples, sweet potatoes, &c. are daily taken from hence to Panamá. Here the Pacific Steam Navigation Company have a gridiron and depôt.

At Taboga has resided, for forty years, a most benevolent individual well known as Doña Ana, and called the Queen of the Island; she is a Jamaica creole of tall and commanding appearance, and reputed to be the daughter of an English nobleman. Her attendance on sick sailors and others is above all praise, and from her knowledge of the medicinal herbs of the country she effects many a cure. She resides with her black husband in a small hut like any other on the island.

By dint of industry she had saved rather a considerable sum of money, which she entrusted to an Englishman at Panamá to invest for her, but he like a scoundrel ran off with her hard earnings; she has, however, the blessings of many a sailor who, having been prostrated with fever, but for her care would perhaps have found a grave in Taboga.

A story is told of the land crabs of Taboga, who, about the latter part of Lent, are observed descending the hills in great numbers, they even climb over any huts that may be in their way " and join the religious procession on Good-Friday."

BAROMETRICAL AND THERMOMETRICAL OBSERVATIONS FROM THE AMERICAN HOSPITAL'S REGISTER FOR 1853. THE BAROMETER WAS FIFTY FEET ABOVE LOW WATER.

MONTHS.	DATE	6, A.M.	NOON.	6, P.M.	6 A.M.	NOON	6 P.M.	WINDS.
January..	1	30.00	30.00	30.00	78	78	77	N. and N.W.
"	15	29.91	29.93	29.86	75	84	86	W.
February.	1	30.02	30.03	30.00	75	85	80	N.W.
"	15	29.92	29.93	29.92	76	86	79	N.W.
March..	1	29.87	29.90	29.86	77	87	83	Calm, and N.W.
"	15	29.90	29.77	29.90	75	87	80	Do.
April...	1	29.90	29.99	29.90	75	87	83	N.W.
"	15	29.92	29.98	29.92	77	87	83	N.W.
July...	1	29.90	29.99	29.90	77	82	81	W. and N.W.
"	15	29.91	29.92	29.90	79	87	84	N.E. and S.W.
August..	1	30.02	30.01	30.00	74	85	75	W. and N.W.
"	15	29.96	29.97	29.91	75	84	76	N.W. and S.S.W.
September.	1	29.96	29.96	29.95	80	87	76	N.W. and S.E.
"	15	30.00	29.98	29.98	76	83	74	N.E. and S.W.
October.	1	29.94	29.93	29.92	77	80	77	N.W. and N.E.
"	15	29.98	29.93	29.96	78	87	82	S.W. and W.
November.	1	29.94	29.93	29.91	74	79	74	W. and N.W.
"	15	29.92	29.98	29.90	79	86	79	S.

Rainy weather predominates, with sultry periods and much lightning and thunder, also heavy thunder storms. I found no record of earthquakes.[1]

On the 16th of June. 1854, in Panamá from 4.30, p.m. until dark, the atmosphere was darkened by a flight of large black-striped yellow butterflies; such an occurrence had not been seen before by my informant during a four years' residence.

ON THE CHIBCHA, MUISCA OR MOSCA LANGUAGE.

In Ludewig's useful work on the literature of the American aboriginal languages, he refers to collections of words, vocabularies and grammars; some of these, however, are still in M.S.S. I give first a list of words, the result of my own reading on the subject; other lists are from T. Compans, Duquesne, Holton, Seemann, &c.

Humboldt says, the Chibchas were unacquainted with the b and d, and characterised by the frequent repetition of the syllables cha, che, chu; as, for instance, chu, chi, we; hycha chamiqui, myself; chigua chiguitynynga, we ought to fight; muisca cha chro guy, a worthy man; the particle cha added, Muisca, denoting the male sex. It would appear that the Spaniards gave the name of Chibchas to the natives of the Plateau of Bogotá, in consequence of the very frequent repetition of the word chi; and as muisca means man, we are left rather in

[1] A long-continued earthquake was felt at 10, p.m., on the 27th June, 1859.

ignorance as to the real name of the nation, or of their country; for Bacatá or Bogotá, means limit of the cultivated land; Cundi-rumarca or Cundinimarca, apparently an imaginary term for the country.[1]

Colonel J. Acosta gave his M.S. dictionary and grammar of the Lengua Mosco Chibcha to the Paris Geographical Society, 12mo, of 296 p.p. His dictionary is the only one existing; the grammar is different from that of Fray B. de Lugo: this last is very rare, printed in Madrid, 1613.[2]

Hervas[3] says, the Muisca language was spoken in the country of the Zippa (Bogotá). The language is lost, but there are some M.S. vocabularies.

The Tunja language was different from that of Bogotá.

Bacatá, Bogotá	limit of cultivated land, probably from proximity to the mountain wall. Also from a chief of that name.	Sugamuai, Sogomoso	mysterious one, or disappeared country.
		Chiminigagua	the Creator.
		Bochica, Botschica	beneficent deity.
Zomi, Turma	potato, yam.	Bachue, Fuzachogua	good woman.
Batatá	sweet potato.		
Zipa	principal chief, residing at Bogotá.	Zue, Sua, Zupa, Gagua	sun or day.
Zaque	another great chief.	Chia, Za	moon or night.
Usaques	lesser chiefs.	Ulleo, Chibia, or Hibia	supreme power.
Guechas	military chiefs.		
Ebaque	blood of wood, name of a chief.	Aba	strong drink, made from maize.
Nemequene	bone of lion, a chief of Bogotá.	Neucatocoa	Chibcha Bacchus.
		Fo, Sorra	deity of boundaries of fields.
Guatavitá	end of mountains, lake of.	Chaquen	feast of Fo.
Ebate	spilt blood, a chief.	Cuchavira	rainbow.
Susa	white straw country.	Huayacan	holy wood, very hard.
Simijaca	owl's beak country.	Gueques[6], Chuque	} priests.
Macana[4]	a wooden sword.		
Tomagata[5]	great tailed wizard, and fire that boils.	Sunas	sacred paths.

[1] I suppose it was called Thousaquillo.

[2] Ludewig, 128.

[3] Catalogo, &c., I. 229.

[4] Maquahintle, in aztec.

[5] Famagostad of the Nicaraguas, was their uncreated first man—appears to have affinity to Tomagata.

[6] Squire says the councils of old men, called guegues, in Nicaragua, appointed the war-chief. Guegue he takes to be a Mexican word, formed by the reduplication of hue or gue, old; huehue or guegue, literally old-old. Trans. Amer. Ethno. Soc. 125, 1853.

[7] On the Amazons this plant is called uruca; Valley of Amazons, Hakluyt. Soc. 1859. Called achiote and tile in Nicaragua.

Guesa	the name given to the beautiful youth, sacrificed every 15 years. He is sometimes called Quihica, or the door.	Yuca	jatropha manhiot.
		Arracache[1]	a valuable esculent tuber.
		Aba	maize,[2] and a measure for.
Chirimia	wind instrument.	Guacamayo	the macaw, sacred bird.
Tata	wooden trumpet.	Barbacoa	suspension bridge.
Thiguyes	the Zipa's concubines.	Guanin, Gianin	gold of low standard, by this name it was known on the coast.
Bija or Achote	vegetable colours (bija orellana).		
Totuma	a calabash vase (crecentia cujete).	Capisuyo	Indian tunic.

FROM T. COMPANS, WHO QUOTES FROM PIEDRAHITA, SIMON, &c.

Chibchacum	special protector of the natives, who either called themselves Chibchas, or were so named by the Spaniards. Cum means a stick or support.	Chircate	mantles for females.
		Chumbi, Mauri	girdle.
		Liquira	female mantle, for upper part of body, fastened by a large pin.
		Thyhuas	palaces, houses.
		Nigua	insect, the chigoe.
Nompanim	the lion's vase, a chief.	Sua-mena	from sun-rise to mid-day.
Huacata	the emerald.		
Muequetá	a country in the plain, or Bogotá.	Sua-moca	from mid-day to sunset.
Gueta	house.	Zasca	from sunset to midnight.
Fo	a fox, deity of the goldsmiths and weavers.	Cagui	from midnight to sunrise.
Chunsna	grand sanctuary.	Zocam	the civil year of 20 moons; the week of 3 days and 10 weeks made a lunar month. The sacred year was of 37 moons, and 20 of these formed the Muisca cycle.
Moque, Mocoba	a resin, incense.		
Huan	feast of the sun, in December.		
Zaga	fasting.		
Chuncho, Tunjo	sacred place.		
Jana	a measure, palm.		
Ypguagua	a fathom.		
Jugua	the Jaguar, also a fruit.	Suna	new moon.

FROM HERVAS.

Tighi	woman.	Zagá	fasting.
Ramza	tribute.	Quimi-Zaque	country of the Zaque.
Zuha	son of the sun.		

---

[1] Seemann's Voy. of Herald, i. 200. Arracachia esculenta of Holton.
[2] Called "Mamaix in Mexico and West Indies." Hakluyt Coll., 1859.

FROM HERRERA.

Chiquachi	a district in N. Granada, means caracoles or shells, many found there.	Tunja	name of a chief.
		Tyrona	a forge or furnace.
		Tamalameque	town of the palms.

FROM HOLTON.

Achira	species of cane.[1]	Jipetera	disease from eating earth.
Bejuco	climber, affords ligneous cordage.	Moro	fustic, morus tinctoria.
Cacào	chocolate tree.		
Caiman	alligator.	Mòya	cake of salt.
Cocò	cocoanut.	Múcura	an earthen vessel.
Còto	goitre.	Neme	bitumen.
Galapagó	terrapin.	Name	yam, dioscorea.
Guacamayo	macaw, ara glauca, a sacred bird.	Ora	oxalis tuberosa.
		Paica	worm-seed, chenopodium.
Guácharo	the mysterious bird (steatornis caripensis).	Paramo	frozen regions of the Andes.
Guadua	large bamboo.	Poyo	a bench
Guambia	a bag.	Quina-Quina	Peruvian bark tree.[2]
Guaricha	a low girl, from this class wet nurses are at present procured.	Quingo	zig-zag.
		Sagu	arrow-root.
		Tutuma	a fruit, vessel of calabash.
Iraca	carloduvica palmata, also called jipijapé, from which the so-called Panamá hats are made.	Tulpas	three stones, forming a fine place.
		Yuca	manihot utilissima.

FROM ULLOA.

Caobo or acajou	mahogany	Chacara	farm, from which chacra.
Tulcan	toucan or preacher.		

---

[1] Achira (canna discolor) has tuberose roots, and looks like the sweet potatoe. Seemann's voy. of Herald, I., 180.

[2] CINCHONA.—Near to Bogotá Holton passed a cinchona bush in flower; he says it was a useless species. N. Granada, 125.

Near Pandi the ground rises steadily to the E. covered with huge trees, that must include an unknown quantity of cinchona, 308.

QUININE.—At the Hacienda of Tequendama, M. Louis Godin has a quinine factory. The quinine made here is not esteemed at Bogotá, but I am satisfied that it is skilfully made and of pure white: there may be worse—there can be none better. The bark is pulverised entirely by hand, and comes from places on the mountains south of here, as nearly as I could ascertain. Every man keeps his own quina secrets. 286. From Markham's notes on the culture of cinchona; the varieties are C. Con. (var. Pitayensis and Lancifolia), C. Cordifolia. Found in the warm regions of the Andes of Bogotá, at the margins of the forests, altitude 5000 to 9000 feet above the level of the sea; grows in thickets, in sunny exposed places.

FROM SEEMANN.

Aracacha	oxalis crenata	Chupa	gustavia speciosa.
Baco	Gustavia Augusta.	Corinso	godoya antioquiensis.
Bejuco de Guaco	mikania guaco.	Cucua	brosimum namagua.
Bleo	peirescia bleo.	Guayavo de Anselino	campomanescia cornifolia.
Candia	abelmoschus esculentus.	Quereme de Cali	Thibaudia quereme.
Caspi de pasto	rhus glandulifolia.	Ruda	dysodia chrys.
Cauchuc (Popayan)	siphocamphylus caouts-chouc.	Sarzileja	chaetogastra canescens.
Cedron	simaba cedron.	Tagua	phytelephas, macrocarpa.
Chigua	zamia chigua.		
Choco	erythrina rubinervia		

FROM DUQUESNE'S ACCOUNT IN THE CALENDAR.

1. Ata, also a toad or frog; waters; and that the time of sowing was near; corresponds with January.
2. Bosa, nose with extended nostrils; part of moon, figured with face; round enclosure for sowing.
3. Mica, two eyes open of moon; care in choosing seeds for sowing, etc.
4. Muyhica[1] two eyes closed; black object; darkness; tempestuous weather.
5. Hisca,[2] two figures united; hope of fruitfulness; nuptials of sun and moon; conjunction; green things; plants.
6. Ta,[3] a stake with a cord; enclosure; harvest.
7. Cuhupqua,[4] two ears, a snail shape or winding of the ear; granaries.
8. Sahuza, tail; the end of sowing (this reading doubtful).
9. Aca, two frogs coupled; toad on waters.
10. Ubchihica, an ear; may allude to feasts; full moon; harvest.
20. Gueta, probably a sign of quietude or rest; frog extended; house and field; felicity.

FROM JOMARD'S OBSERVATIONS.—"Bulletin de Geographie," 1847, p. 88, part II.

11. Quicha.ata.
12. Quicha-bosa, &c.
20. Quihcha-ubchihica or gueta.
21. Gueta-sasaqui, ata, &c.
30. Guetas-asaqui, Ubchihica.
40. Gue-bosa.
60. Gue-mica.
80. Gue-muyhica.
100. Gue-hisca.
Quihicha, or qhicha foot.

COCONUCO AND PUBENANO WORDS.

Manche	supreme power, spirit	Indé	a word of affirmation, indeed.
Palash	heaven.		
Cuai, pansig	devil.	Puil	evil, the moon.
Cashu	chief.	Puitcher	author of good, the sun.
Carabics	inferior chiefs.		
Bura	maize.	Sil	stars.
Hayo	the coca of the Peruvians.	site-silg	pleiades.
		silg or sull	planets.
Pic or Mambi	alkaline ash, chewed with hayo.	Canapuil	a month or moon.

Other ways of spelling—[1] Mhuyzca. [2] Hiesca or hysca. [3] Taa [4] Qhupca.

WORDS IN THE LANGUAGE OF THE INDIANS OF CHOCO
Mollieu's Columbia, 450.

Copdour	chief.	Carpemara	how much.
Ouenmehor	man-eater.	Ambs	one.
Decoupera	woman.	Noumi	two.
Hemeora	man.	Conoupa	three.
Babkoukena	white.	Aiapa	four.
Gaeuna	Indian.	Conambo	five.
Niagour	black.	Audkinanamba	six.
Ourima capua	come here.		

CHIRIQUI WORDS, from J. Harrison Smith. Geogr. Soc. Journal, 1854.

Caraña	Chiriqui incense.	Arnotto	bixia, dye wood.
Tacamahaca	dye wood.	Paraguatan	dye wood.
Aguacate	laurus persica, dye wood.	Angoli	sesamum orientale, dye wood.
Capana	dye wood.	Guacalis	ancient Indian graves

CHIRIQUI WORDS from Panamá, "Star and Herald," edited by John Power, Esq., F.R.G.S., who went to the Chiriqui Guacalis, and reported on them in his journal, August to October, 1859.

Tuyra or Tavira	devil.	Dorache	extinct nation of Chiriqui, or "martial tribes" of Veraguas.
Tequina	priest, master.		
Cauques	chiefs.		
Sacos	inferior chiefs.		
Cabras	dependent on chiefs, and who had slaves.	Bugaba	Chiriqui tombs.
		Mamude	ditto.
Espaves	wives of chiefs.	Boquete	ditto.
Ira	women.	Guacalis	objects found in the tombs, those of gold s. g., 17-44; those alloyed with copper known as guanin and tumbaga, e. g., 11-55.
Chui	men.		
Xangui	black dye.		
Boxa (bixia)	red ditto.		
Baio	house of canes.		
Areytos	songs.		

See my paper to Antiq. Soc., read December 8, 1859, "On Discovery of Gold Objects, &c., in the Tombs of Chiriqui."

WORDS from Suere, near Panamá. See Benzoni, in Hakluyt Coll., 1859, which I compare with Quichua.

Suere	ischia.		Chiarucla	cici.
Quichua	pacha.		Ccuri	ccari and runa.
English	earth.		Gold	man.

J. Acosta, p. 31, gives the following as the numerals of Careta (Coyba), on the Isthmus of Darien : 1, quenchecoo ; 2, pogua ; 3, pagua ; 4, paquogua ; 5, atale ; 6 nergua ; 7, anvege ; 8, cugule.

Paravey, Paris, 1853, published a memoir on the origin of the Japanese, Arab, and Biscayan, with the people of Bogotá !

FROM TRANS. AMER. ETHNO. SOC. 134, 1853.

I here compare the Muisca of Bogotá, with the Waikna or Mosca, Woolwa, and Nagradan.

English.	Waikna or Mosca.	Woolwa.	Muisca.	Nagradan.
Man	waikna	all	muisca, body of 5 parts	
Woman	mairen	yall	tighi	
Foot	meña	calni	quihicha	
Water	lia	wass[1]	ata[2]	
House	watla	u	thyhuas	
Maize	aya	.	aba	
One	kuuni	alaslaj	ata	imba
Two	wal	muyebu	bosa	apu
Three	niupa	muyebas	mica	asu
Four	wal-wal	muyerunca	muyhica	acu
	matasip	muyesinca?	hisca	huisu
Six	.	dija or muy-dijca	ta	mahu
Seven	.	bajca or muy-bajca	cuhupqua	niquinu
Eight	.	muyacca	sahusa	nuha
Nine	.	yaccabavo	aca	melnu
Ten	.	muyhasluy	ubchihica	guha
Chief	wati	.	saki	
Moon	kati	.	chia, za	
Sun	lapta	.	sua	
Old man, chief	.	.	gueque	gueque
Male, un-created, who created the world	.	.	tomagata	famagostad
Female, ditto	.	.	.	zipa-ltonal
Priest of the temple, chief	.	.	sogomoso	tamagoz
Rainbow	.	.	cuchavira[3]	

[1] Probably from water.
[2] Atl (Mexican) ; oka (Choctaw).
[3] Ccuichi, in Quichua.

FROM ULLOA.

Serpo	toad, Portobello	Yabira	a virgin, Darien
Chacara[1]	farm-house, do.	Capeti	the sleepy, do.
Hato	do. do. Lloyd	Pucro	light wood, at Guayaquil, called balsawod, do.
Guana	lizard like animal, eaten, Portobello.		
Guazan	name of chief near Panamá	Zeti-gaati	species of willow do.
Chepo, chepauri	chief, do.	Paparos	peasants, do.
Pononomi	chief, do.	Bejucos	bridge of six ropes ligneous cordage, do
Escolia	chief, do.		
Parita	chief, do.	Tarabita	of one and two ropes, do.
Urraca	chief of Veraguas		

DARIEN—FROM SEEMANN.

Anta	phytolephus sp.	Cucua	brosimum namagua
Chigua	zamia chigua		

From aborigines of the Isthmus of Panamá by Berthold Seemann. Trans. Amer. Ethno. Soc. 175, 1853.

VOCABULARIES OF SAVANERIC, CHOLO AND BAYANO.

English.	Savaneric.	Cholo.	Bayano.
Man		chumaquira	
Boy		guarra	
Woman	su-ich	huena, huera	purra
Girl		huenajauna	
Child		quarchaque	
Friend			nugliete
Thief			trusaso, transolico, campanucho
Hair	chugaga	puda	saglaga
Face		quirù	
Nose	vas'e	quejunbue, jun	asagua
Mouth	ca	itai, ji	cagüig
Teeth	dajù	tida	nugula
Tongue	cavira	quirame	
Ears	oló	quevatl, jurù	ou a
Breast	jusolé	jù, bi	
Arm		jupatù	
Hand	covarè	jiqua, jua	arcana
Finger		jevachaque	
Body, perhaps belly		cacuà	
Leg	suaguet	jeremumuli	
Thigh		macarà	

[1] Chacra, in Quichua, means estates, farms, plantations.

English.	Sarnueric.	Cholo.	Bayano.
Foot	sera	jerà	naca
Fire	jivita	quebuejiue	
Water	chi		
Earth	lavi	quebue, itro	
Silver	. . .	paito	manila
Sugar-cane	en-que	chaso	
Plaintain	bla	pata	
Tree	. .	panijo	
Pine-apple	. .	chijo	
Calabash-tree	. .	giatahu	noca
Maize	chugapa	nepe, nearà	
Guayavo	. . .	painiso	
Another plant	. . .	bija (bixia?)	
Vegetable ivory	. . .	anta	
Wood	. . .	pajura tupa	
Cock	antana		
Hen	cog		
Egg	coyquigua	necomù	
Turkey	. . .	chamù	
Parrot	. . .	jari	
Dog	tò	uaà	
Pig	chunchi[1]	china	
Hour	ju	tee	
Ladder	. .	dumè	
Pot	uu	ecohurì	
Knife	. . .	neco	
Canoe	. . .	jampa	
Flask	. . .	mamasand[2]	
Shut	singom		
Sun	chuhi	becia, bichia	
Moon	datu	jedecò	
Stars	behugupa	chintahu, cocohi	
I have	chacri	iru vuma	
I had	. . .	vuru ira basima	
You (instead)	. . .	confero	
Good-day	baguiche		
Yes	. . .	nano	
No	. . .	seva	
1	. . .	abà	quenchique
2	. . .	umè	povuar
3	. . .	umpea	pavuar
4	. . .	quiramani	paquevuar
5	. . .	guasoma	atate
6	. . .	guaquiranamba	nercua
7	. . . .		cugle
8	. . . .		pavaque
9	. . . .		paquevae
10	. . . .		ambuc
100	. . . .		ambuc-ambuc

See Dr. Cullen's vocabulary of the Bayano language, in the Geographical Society's Journal. The Bayano or the Yule or Tule is spread along the northern shore of Darien, from the Atrato to the coast of San Blas.

---

[1] Chancho, Spanish.
[2] Mama-Juana, Spanish.

PANAMA. From Berthold Seemann's Popular Nomenclature of the American Flora.

Acabú	zanthoxylum spinosum.	Guanabano blanca	annona muricata.
Achote	bixia orellana.	Guanabano de torete	" obstrusifolia.
Agalla[1]	caesilpina coriacea		
Aji	capsicum, Chile pepper.	Guandú	cajanus bicolor.
		Guaruma	cecropia peltata.
Amaosig	bursera gummifera.	Guatatuca	gesnerin.
Amistay	impatiens balsamina.	Guateguate	passiflora fetida.
Anamu	petiveria alliacea.	Guava real	inga spectabilis.
Anona	anona laurifolia.	Guayacan	Tecoma flavescens.
Añil	indigofera añil.	" (Mex.)	guajacum off.
Aqui	cupaniasapida.	Guzuma	guazuma.
Bala	gliricidia maculata.	Guepero	brosimum namagua.
Balsa	achroma lagopus.	Guineo	musa sapientum.
Bejuco de estrella	arstolochia.	Icaco	chrysobalnus icaco.
Bejuco de sajino	dioscorea.	Ichu (Peru.)	stipa ichu.
Cabuga	agave tuberosa.	Iguana	machaeruim triste.
Cacique	diphysa carthag.	Jagua	genipa caruto.
Cadilla	amaranthacea.	Jercaco	ocimum basilicum.
Caffé	coffea arabica	Jipejapa	carloduvica palmata.
" "	" racemosa.	Jobito	spondias.
Caimitillo	miconia myriantha.	Jobo	"
Caimito	chrysophyllum carinito.	Macano	diphysa Carthag.
		Maguey	agave.
Cainillo	cremanium compressum.	Mammey	mammea, mangrove.
		Mangle	rhizophora M.
Calabazu	crecentia cunefolia.	Mango	mangifera indica.
Calahuala	goniophlebium attenautum.	Mani	arachis hypogaea.
		Maquenque	palma.
Camaron	hirtella racemosa.	Maroñon	anacardium off.
Caoba	swietenia mah.	Marfil Veg.(Veg. ivory.)	phytolephus.
Caracucha	pluiveria.		
Cauchuc	india rubber.	Matapalo	ficus sp.
Ceiba	eriodendron saumauma.	Matamba	desmoncus.
		Monca	cyphomandra betacea
Chamico	chamico D. stram.	Nance	brisonima continufolia
Chiriqui	compósita.		
Chonta	palma.	Naju de culebra	peirescia bleo.
Chumico	curatella amer.	Orusul	lippia dulcis.
Chunga	palma	Otó	arum esculentum.
Ciqua	canela, laurines.	Pacay	palma.
Cocla	bauhinia multinervia.	Puica	
Coco	cocus nucifera.	Panamá	sterculia Carthag.
Cocobolo		Papayo	carica papaya.
Cope	clusia.	Pava	panax.
Corozo	bactris.	Pijibaya	palma
Corotú	enterolobium tinbova.	Pitajaya	cereus pitaya.
		Platano	musa paradisica.
Corpache	croton pseudo-china.	Poropopo	cochlospermum hibiscoides.
Cubita	carloduvica palmata.		
Cuipo	sterculiacea.	Quira	machaerium schomb.
Culantra	eryngium faetidum.	Sajino	rhopala diver

[1] Looks as if of African origin.

Culen	psoraralea glandulosa	Sandilla	citrullus vulg.
Cutarro	suartzia pinnata.	Sapallo	curcubita melopepo.
Dividivi	caesalpina coriacea.	Sumbo[1]	cucurbitacea.
Espavé	anacardium rhin.	Té[2]	corchorus mompoxensis.
Guachapali	schizolobium excelsum.	Tula grande	cucurbitacea.
Guaco tree	cratevia tapioides.	Yerba de Chiva	hydrolea spinosa.
Guagra de Puerco	aroslichum aureum.	Zanora	Iriartea exhoriza.
		Zanco	sambucis Mex.

FROM LLOYD'S NOTES ON THE ISTHMUS OF DARIEN
Trans. Geogr. Soc. I., 69, and Dr. Cullen.

Bongo[3]	cork-wood tree, "noble Bongo tree," canoes made from	Guallavo	infested by ants.
		Juasimo	hard wood.
		Majagu	for making ropes.
Carrasca	species of bamboo.	Siti	hard wood.
Corutu	like elm.	Tangare	like mahogany.
Carati	hard wood.	Totumo	calabash tree.
Ciquarri	bastard mahogany.	Yalla	like box.
Cucuma	for making mats, &c.	Cauchuc (Palo de Vaca)	milk or Indian rubber tree.
Guachapali	like walnut.		
Guayavite aseyjan	white wood.		

Lloyd gives the following Indian names of places in the district of Panamá, Pecora, Chepo, Cheman, Gorgona, Taboga, Areyjan, Capira, Chame, Perí, Pocri, Macoiscas, Ocu, Penonome, Ola, Chagres, Palenque, Fichichi, Pinogana, Fucuti, Cana, Chipigana, Punaga, Colubre, Sorá. Alange, Gualaca, Biyaba, Dolega.

[1] Looks as if of African origin.
[2] Spanish for tea.
[3] Looks as if of African origin.

EQUADOR OR QUITO.

Pizarro.—Guayaquil.—Puná.—Coal.—The Historian Velasco.—Villavicencio.—The Patriotic Bishop Calama.—Description of Equador.—Canelo-Cinchona.—Cedron.—Roads to Quito.—Quito.—Chimborazo.—Quitus.—Invading Caras.—Manta.—Fossil Bones.—Malabas.—Tortolas.—Negroes.—Conquest of Quito by the Caras.—Emeralds.—Conquest of Quito by the Incas.—Antiquities.—Gold Mask from Cuenca.—Chronological Table.—Population.—Ethnology.—Popayan.—Equador Land Company.—Vocabularies.

After leaving Panamá, many classic spots were passed, one in particular, the island of Gallo, in 2° N., where Pizarro, when about to be forced back to Panamá, drew his sword, and traced a line with it on the sand from east to west. Then turning towards the south, "Friends and comrades," he said, "on that side are toil, hunger, nakedness, the drenching storm, desertion, and death; on this side, ease and pleasure. There lies Peru, with riches: here Panamá and its poverty. Choose each man, what best becomes a brave Castillian. For my part, I go south." So saying, he stepped across the line.[1]

Running along the steep coast, with high mountains in the rear, we steamed between the island of La Plata and the main. This island was so called by Pizarro, on seeing silver in the hands of its inhabitants. The bucaniers of old used this spot as a rendezvous to share their booty. We now entered the bay of Guayaquil. The island of Puná, twenty-four miles in length by twelve broad, is of recent sandstone, and thickly wooded. The sky was cloudy, so we could not see the colossal mountains to the east, including Chimborazo which shows itself from February to June.

The river Guayaquil is thickly lined with mangroves, other trees, and canes. The anchorage is before the city, which is built at the base of some hills, and has a population of 20,000 souls.

The great business part of the city is the Malecon in front of the river, and, as evening draws on, the population makes for that spot to

---

[1] Prescott, Conq. Peru, I., 172.

walk or trade, where, among other objects offered for sale, is the famed Panamá hat. When the lamps are lighted on the Malecon, in the streets and houses the effect is very good. Some of the streets and buildings would delight the artist.

There are many fine looking men and women, but the majority of the population is a mixed race of White, Negro, and Indian.

Guayaquil, formerly known as Culantá, is in 2° 12′ S., on the river Guayas, fifty miles from its mouth, and the principal port of Equador. It takes its name from Guayas, a chief, who was feudatory to Atahualpa (Oviedo spells it Atabaliva); he was accidentally killed by one of the Spanish conquerors. The natives of this district were called Guancavilcas or Guayaquiles.

The island of Puná, when first visited by the Spaniards, had a temple, dedicated to the god of war, Tumbal, a frightful figure; at its feet were military arms bathed in the blood of prisoners who had been sacrificed on an altar in the centre of the temple, which was dark, and its walls covered with horrible looking paintings and sculptures. The islanders were nearly all destroyed in the defence they made against the Incas and the Spaniards. When first visited by Pizarro, in 1530, it is said there were 20,000 inhabitants; in 1734, only 96 remained. Valverde, the priest and co-murderer with Pizarro of Atahualpa, was killed with forty-two Spaniards, by the Indians of Puná, flying from the partizans of Almagro, after the latter had assassinated Pizarro.[1]

The first account we have of the nations south of Panamá, is by Pizarro. The Indians abandoned their dwellings, leaving food and ornaments of gold; and human flesh was found roasting. At Point Quemada, 7° N., the natives are described as warlike, armed with bows and arrows and other weapons. Near the equator, in the open sea, was discovered a balsa or raft (huampu), with two masts and square cotton sails,[2] with men and women; two of the persons were from Tumbez. At Tacames or Tacumez, 1° N., a town was visited containing 2000 habitations; the people were warlike and had canoes; one of which had a gold mask as a flag. The island of Santa Clara[3] was uninhabited, but

---

[1] Benzoni, 246, translated by Admiral Smyth, Hakluyt, Soc.

[2] Cotton grew in abundance on the coast of Quito, white, brown and dark violet. I do not find that the seal-skin balsa was known to the natives before the conquest, only those of light-wood, reeds and calabashes.

[3] COAL.—On the island of Amortajado, Mr. Peacock noticed, in 1841, the existence of coal, but no geological description is given, and it is supposed that a similar coal is to be found on the islands of Puná and Santa Clara, at S. Elena and the coast of Chocó. Mr. P. also found orchilla weed and guano on these coasts. Official correspondence, testimonials, &c., of Mr. Geo. Peacock, 1859.

occasionally visited by the people of Puná for purposes of sacrifice and worship. The Spaniards found in this spot some pieces of gold, rudely wrought into various shapes, and probably designed as offerings to the Indian deity.[1] At Carapoto, in 0° 44′ S., Benzoni saw one of their temples containing an idol made of clay shaped like a tiger (jagua), also two peacocks with other birds intended for sacrifice. I may remark that the peacock is an eastern bird, and was not then known in the New World, those seen were turkeys.

The turkey was introduced into Europe from Mexico, called by the Spaniards gallopavo, from its resemblance to the peacock.

Tumbez, 3° 30′ S., was first visited by the Spaniards in 1526. Ulloa mentions that this town was built of stone. It is likely that adobe or sun-dried brick was also used, for he adds, when he passed through the place, about 1736, no vestiges were remaining. Prescott[2] says, the town was built of stone and plaster, and a Curaca ruled the district. Here Pizarro met with an Inca noble or orejon. The fortress was built of rough stone, surrounded by a triple wall. The Temple of the Sun was blazing with gold and silver. The convent appropriated to the Inca's destined brides, the garden of which glowed with imitations of fruit and vegetables in gold and silver.

Tupac-Yupanqui had built the fortress, and peopled the place with mitimaes, colonists forced by the Inca to settle there. The Temple[3] and the House of the Virgins of the Sun had been erected by Huayna-Capac. In less than half a century Tumbez was to be traced only by the mass of ruins that encumbered the ground.

Much that I have to say about ancient Quito, I am indebted to the interesting work of the Jesuit, Juan de Velasco, a native of Quito. He retired to Italy after the expulsion of his order from the Spanish colonies, and composed his "Historia del Reino de Quito." A MS. copy, written in 1789, was taken from Europe by Don M. Larrea, and printed in Quito 1841-4. The first volume contains the Natural History; second, Ancient History; third, Modern History. A portion of this work has been translated by Ternaux-Compans, vol. 19, Paris, 1840.

I have also freely used the "Geografia de la Republica del Ecuador," por Manuel Villavicencio, New York, 1858; who says that Velasco's

---

[1] Conq. of Peru, I., 178.
[2] Prescott Conq. Peru, I., 178.
[3] According to Benzoni, at the gate of the temple of the Sun were tame animals like lions (pumas), and two tigers (jaguars).

work is the richest fountain from which can be drawn materials for the history of Quito. Villavicencio's volume is a standard authority for the geography of Equador, and deserves to be translated.

Quito,[1] in consequence of the productiveness of its commerce, was formerly one of the most opulent provinces of S. America. At the commencement of the 18th century, it fell into so sensible a decay, that its plantations, manufactories, &c., were reduced to a fifth part of what it had heretofore been.

To give it new vigour, Count Casa-Giron, after having, at great expense, procured from Europe skilful artists to re-establish manufactures, set on foot a patriotic society in 1789—" the School of Concord," consisting of twenty-six associates and twenty-two corresponding members. In 1791, the patriotic Bishop of Quito, Calama, undertook the direction of this society. In 1792, its secretary, Xavier, commenced the publication of a periodical, "The First Fruits of the Culture of Quito."

Bishop Calama, in his pastoral edicts, which are utterly divested of bigotry, displays the most benevolent views. Being at Ambato, in his edict he says, "Seeing that in this department there is abundance of flour, we offer a premium of fifty dollars to the baker who shall make and present to us a specimen of wheaten bread well fermented, well kneaded, and well baked."

An interesting project of this prelate, was to establish a communication between Ibarra and Otabalo, also with the provinces of Asquande, Chocó, and Barbacoas, the want of which prevented the exportation of the productions and manufactures, reducing the inhabitants to a state of extreme misery. One of the beneficent results was the discovery of several gold mines.

Bishop Calama's discourse at the opening of the Economical Society, displayed sound policy and masterly eloquence. It finishes with this sentence:—" We are all poor, but we shall all be rich, if we propose to ourselves, as our guide, to be loving friends of our country. I am aware of the superior obligation which the character of bishop imposes on me; and it is full in my remembrance, that one of the five vows I made was, that all my income, all my books, and all my voice and pen, although weak, should be employed for the benefit and succour of my beloved diocess."

The Republic of Equador[2] is divided into three natural parts by two

---

[1] "Mercurio Peruano," and Skinner's " Present State of Peru," 1805.
[2] Explorations in Equador, by G. J. Pritchett, Geogr. Soc. Proc., 1859.

parallel chains of the Andes. The centre division being on an average level, much more elevated than the others, from 5000 to 11,000 feet, possesses an equal and agreeable climate, a clear bright atmosphere, and is the seat of the chief cities.

The eastern and western slopes of the Cordilleras are densely covered with every species of timber, including a large mahogany, out of which the Indian scoops his canoe. The cotton and india-rubber plants grow wild, as also cocoa, canelo[1] (called by some cinnamon), coffee, the gunyusa or tea plant, vanilla, tobacco, indigo, orchilla, wax palms, copal, storax, spices, dyes, sugar-cane, rice, maize, quina or cinchona bark,[2] cedron,[3] &c.—indeed, a paradise for the botanist. In the more temperate parts, there are large grazing and arable farms.

As to mineral productions, they are in abundance; the entire range

---

[1] CANELO, translated, is the cinnamon tree, but is a very different plant to the oriental. The native name was annawon. Fine cinnamon is C. verum, class ix., order 1 flourishing in Ceylon. Canelo or canella. is canela alba, laurifolia, and other varieties growing in Equador in particular; class ii., order 1. Pritchett says, " Cinnamon (canelo), the bark of a species of laurel; and ishpingo is the calyx of the flower: three to four thousand pounds are annually gathered of it." The canelo of N. Granada is called by Holton drymis winteri or winters bark. Seemann mentions canela de Chile, drymis Chilensis—(this is the boighe of the araucanos, a sacred tree) C. de Chisro Brazil), Oredaphne opifera; C. de Ermi (Brazil). See expedition of Gonzalo. Pizarro, A.D., 1539-42, to the land of Cinnamon, by Markham, Hakluyt Coll., 1859. Prescott Conq., Peru II., 97.

[2] CINCHONA.—See Ulloa's " Noticias Secretas," and " Narrative" on the destruction of this tree. The bark known as quina-quina was used in the time of the Incas; it takes its present name from Chinchon, a viceroy of Peru.

The following is from Markham's Notes on the Culture of Cinchonas. The mean temperature of the Cinchona region is about 62° F; from 4000 to 10,000 feet above the level of the sea; and the region extends from 10° N. to 19° S. lat.

CINCHONAS OF EQUADOR.—C. Condamines, is found in the forests near Loxa and Cuenca, growing to the height of thirty to forty feet, in a formation composed of gneiss or micaceous shists, on the declivities of mountains, between 3° 42' and 4° 40' S. lat.; 5000 to 9000 feet above the level of the sea. Mean temperature 64° to 68° F. it flowers in May, June, and July.

C. Cond. (var. lancifolia) a variety, growing as high as 10,000 feet, on the declivities of the Andes, and is sometimes exposed to frost at night. C. Succirubra, " the red bark," growing near Huaranda, between Quito and Guayaquil, in a formation of micaceous shists, 2° 16' S. lat.—a very valuable species, as yet little known.

B. Seemann calls the C, cond : Cascarilla, fina; C, humb: Cascarilla, peluda.

[3] CEDRON.—Seemann, Voy. of " Herald," II. 74, mentions that the kernel of the Simaba Cedron is intensely bitter. It is used in fevers and snake bites. May not its active principle be as important as the alcaloides of the Cinchonas ?

of the Cordilleras abound with gold, silver, and copper. Gold is also found on the banks and in the channel of every river which has its source in the high lands.

The mountain range of Llanganate (beautiful mountain), S. S. E. of Quito, in Canelos, is known as the mother of the gold found in the streams that run from it. Quicksilver is seen to ooze out of the ground in Cuenca; and the district of Esmeraldas only requires searching in its streams and rocks for the beautiful gem that gives name to that part of the country.

The Caras, on their way from the coast of the Pacific to the conquest of the capital of the Quitu (Quito), ascended the river Esmeraldas. The port of Tacamez is at its mouth, and to the river Silanche, thirty-five leagues, is navigable for small vessels, then by land to Niguas, Mindo, and Cotocallo. There is another and a much shorter route to Quito from the port of Pailon, 1° 21′ N., crossing numberless ravines and streams that flow into the Mira, then along its banks to Ibarra,[1] a distance of only forty-five leagues to Quito, whereas, from Guayaquil it is nearly ninety.

The route to Quito from Guayaquil is, first, twenty leagues by the river to Bodegas, but in the rainy season seven leagues further to Sabanetta.

To arrive at the vicinity of Chimborazo, a series of lower mountains are traversed, presenting the most beautiful variety of undulation and colour, and of an extent that gives boundless room for every kind of atmospheric effect. At Huaranda,[2] the mules of the traveller are changed for others of harder hoofs and surer tread, to climb the rough incline of the mountain. From Huaranda, after a steep ascent of four hours, the highest point of the road is reached, which traverses round Chimborazo. Passing the tambo of Chuquipoyo, a few leagues further is Mocha. Five leagues more is the large town of Hambato. Here

---

[1] Near this is Salinas, where there is much salt and some nitrate of potash. A few miles N. E. of Ibarra is Yaguarcocha or Lake of Blood. The Cañares having been traitorous or rebellious, the Inca, Huayna-Capac, ordered the execution of 30,000 of them. Their bodies were thrown into the lake, the water of which became reddened with blood.

[2] A beautiful oil-painting, by F. E. Church, was exhibited in London, in July, 1859, called "The Heart of the Andes." The view is taken from near Huaranda, when the sun is descending in the west, and under the shadow of Chimborazo. "Here is a picture of the grandest design, singularly original, simple and perspicuous, of quiet purpose and intention, fully carried out. One beholds Italian landscape in more than Italian perfection, and in grandeur cannot be surpassed."

Bolkerts Antiq S America

Atahualpa gained his first victory over the Incarial forces, after which he punished severely the Cañaris for taking side with Huasca. And seven more the city of Latacunga, at 10,285 feet above the sea, in the valley out of which rises the active volcano of Cotopaxi. Five leagues more is Tiopuyo, and then thirteen to the city of Quito, which is on the east side of the volcano of Pichincha.[1]

The city of Quito was taken by Belalcazar from the Indians in 1533. It is in 0° 15' S., 81° 5' W. of Paris; 10,234½ Spanish feet above the sea. Its mean temperature is 60° F. The winds in summer are N.E., in winter S.W., and its population 80,000.

On the south of the city of Quito is the hill Panecillo, called by the Incas Yavira, which word, in one of the dialects of Darien, means virgin; but ere the Peruvians worshipped the sun from its summit, the Quitus and Caras had their temple there. The ground on which Quito is built is very uneven; most of the houses are of two stories, many are built of brick; the principal edifices are of stone, the rest of adobe, covered with tiles; these last resist the frequent earthquakes pretty well. In the university is placed a marble slab to commemorate the labours of the academicians in 1736. There are many churches, convents, monasteries, two hospitals, two colleges, and several plazas or squares. The city is situated in the centre of many hills. From their summits there is a beautiful panorama of the Andes, with the icy cones of Cayambi, Antisana, Cotopaxi, Sinchiolagua, Corazon, Iliniss,[2] Pichincha, and Cotocachi; to the south of Quito, is the lovely valley of Chillo, full of gardens.

I am indebted to my old friend, Mr. George Pritchett, for the drawing of the city of Quito, taken not long before the late severe earthquake of the 22nd of March, 1859. It occurred at half-past eight, a.m., and almost destroyed Quito. The churches, convents, and government buildings, were most of them thrown down, besides many of the private residences. The damage was estimated at three millions of dollars. Many deaths were reported. A number of towns north of the capital have been destroyed, and in Guayaquil the shock was severely felt, doing some damage.

This is the land of the mighty Chimborazo (Chimpu-razu—snow of

---

[1] At certain periods of the year the journey from Guayaquil to Quito, some 270 miles, most of it very bad road, takes many days; under favourable circumstances it can be done in a few days, Lord Stanley performed the journey in three-and-half days.

[2] Balbi, Geo. says: There are ancient remains about this mountain.

Chimpu), rearing itself above the chain of the Andes, like that majestic dome, the work of the genius of Michael Angelo, upon the ancient monuments which surround the capitol; and as having been the seat of a very old civilization, long before it was conquered by the Caras, or by the Incas of Peru.

Quito, or the country of the old Quito nation was composed of forty districts, governed by chiefs called Quitus, having nations allied with them, as the Yambaya, Latacunga, Puruhá Cañar, &c., under their Curacas or despotic Chiefs. In Cañar was a temple dedicated to Supay Urcu, or the devil, on the hill of Guagual-Suma,[1] here children were sacrificed to ensure a good harvest; neither the Scyris or the Incas could prevent this barbarous custom.

Quito was conquered by the Cara nation who came from the coast of the Pacific about 1000 A.D. Garcilasso says the Indians of the coast of Peru, came from Mexico by the way of Panamá, and that they were cruel and terrible Caribs. The Caribs often are alluded to in this direction, as connected with the Muiscas, Indians of Darien, Popayan, &c. Again, they are mentioned by Prescott[2]—" an immense army, it was reported, was mustering at Quito, and 30,000 Caribs were on their way to support it." This army was coming to Cajamarca to rescue Atahualpa from the hands of Pizarro. Morton and others suppose there was a Toltec emigration to the coast of Peru about 1050 A.D. retreating from before the Aztecs. Prescott, when speaking of the dispersion of the Toltecs, says they spread over Central America and the surrounding isles in the eleventh century.

This invading nation, the Caras, had taken possession of the coast now known as that of Cara some two hundred years before, say 800 A.D., and had had eight or ten chiefs called Scyris, Shyris, Sciras, Schyris, or lords of Caran. After these first Caras left the coast for Quito, other Indians took possession of their country, calling themselves Caras; these last had the custom of compressing the heads of their children.

Bravo Saraiva,[3] after having examined traditions and proofs, assures us that the Peruvians and Caras came from beyond sea, or from the west; however, we have only his word for this.[4]

---

[1] Suna, is sacred path in the Muisca.
[2] Conq. Peru, I., 310.
[3] Chron. Peru. c. 52.
[4] The present Bay of Cara-ques takes its name from the ancient city of Cara, in 0° 43′ S.

The Cara nation came, most probably, from the north coast of Peru,[1] for it seems they knew that coast, and navigated on rafts with sails. As to their abandonment of the coast of Cara, two reasons are given, one to escape from the said to be giants of Manta, who, we are told, came to the coast on floats of rushes; the other that Cara was unhealthy.

Tradition adverts to the giants who lived near Manta, 0° 57′ S., and Punta Santa Elena, 2° 11′ S.; these killed the men of Cara to obtain possession of their women. Pizarro saw ruins attributed to the giants, also deep wells sunk through rock, and stone statues, eight feet high, some naked, others with mitres and priestly insignia. Montesinos[2] (not the best of authorities), says that, under the twelfth Inca, according to his list, giants entered Peru, settling at Punta Santa Elena and other places; they became very wicked, when the divine wrath annihilated nearly the whole of them. Some fled towards Cuzco, but were met by the Inca and dispersed at Lima-tambo.

When Manta was subdued by Huayna-Capac, there was a temple dedicated to Umiña,[3] the goddess of health, which contained an idol:

Near Ibarra was the city of the Caran-qui. These were probably the descendants of the Caras; and in the vacinity of Angel, at the mouth of the R. Mira, are ruins of a fortress.

On the road to the coast from Ibarra, is the valley of Pala-cara; also the mountain of Cara; the River Caran, near to the Pailon.

Can Cara-ibes, or Caribs, have any relation to these Caras?

Pu-cara means a fortress in Quichua.

Cara-pongo is the name of a ravine, near Lima.

Cara-manta, is on the R. Cauca, in N. Granada.

Caras, the name of a village in Huaraz, Peru.

Cara-pucho and cara-macho, are points on the coast of S. Peru.

Cara, in Auracano, is city; Pu-cara, cities; Cara is a Japano-Chinese word, for the north of China or Tartary. According to P. Martyr, the word carib means "stronger than the rest." The other Indians call them caribs or cannibals.

I gave this list seeing that we do not know from whence the Caras came.

Cari-bana, east of the Bay of Uraba, on the main, supposed country of the Caribs. Karabà and Carabalis, a nation of Africa.

[1] Velasco I. 92. The language of the Caras, or Scyris, was a dialect of the Incas language, or of the Quichua; and more than one author has said that the Incas were surprised when, on their conquest of Quito, to be able to understand the nation they were invading. Hervas "Catalogo de las Languas Conocidas," I., 276, he follows Velasco in this subject. We know little or nothing of the ancient Quito language; the Scyri, which introduced the letter o, is often called a dialect of the Quichua: I would rather say that it had affinities only. See Hervas's Catalogo, Vol, I.

[2] Montesinos, memorias antiguas del Peru, in T. Compans, also in Rivero and Tschudi.

[3] U'miña, in Quichua, means emerald.

the face was half human and made of an emerald;[1] and Garcilasso describes the heads of the natives here as deformed by artificial pressure; other Peruvian nations did the same, and four varieties of deformed crania have been observed.

Villavicencio[2] says, two leagues N. of Monte Christo, in the district of Manta, on the flat summit of a low mountain, is a circle of thirty stone seats, with arms, and that they, in all probability, were used on solemn occasions by the chiefs of Cara ere they conquered Quito. Two of these chairs are to be seen in the museum at Guayaquil. Benzoni states, that the chiefs of Manta had an emerald the size of a hen's egg, which they worshipped. At Puerto Viejo, 1° 5′ S., the natives painted their faces, made holes in their nostrils, lips, ears and cheeks; and they put jewels into them on feast days. Their usual dress was a shirt without sleeves: some went naked, and occasionally dyed the body black: they used balsas or rafts. At Colonchi they sometimes drew five or six of their upper teeth for beauty's sake.

At Punta Santa Elena, as well as at Manta, large bones have been met with. In a paper of mine read at the Geological Society, on the fossil bones of Mastodon in Chile, I have adverted to the bones found at the above places.[3] Humboldt states, from the information of others, that these bones "are enormous remains of unknown cetaceous animals." A friend of mine was offered a specimen when there, but, unfortunately, did not become its purchaser. Stevenson saw a grinder from this spot, which weighed 5 lbs. 3 ozs.; the enamel spotted like the female tortoise shell.

The pearl fishers at Panamá are said sometimes to be squeezed to death by a fish called manta; it is broad like a mantle. Was the country of Manta so called from finding this fish about here? The Turbines or Caracolillo,[4] a shell fish, is found in this district, growing on rocks, larger than a nut, and full of juice, which becomes purple, dyeing silk, cotton, &c., by merely drawing the things to be dyed

---

[1] Manta has an emerald mine. The emeralds are found in crystals in the rock, and something of a vein-like character. Some are half white, others half green, but they get ripe and come to perfection. Herrera II., 37 Des.
At Tezcuco, in the "Tribunal of God," there was a skull crowned with an emerald.
[2] Geografia del Equador, 448. Manta is the seaport to Monte Christo.
[3] See my obs. on Texas, Geographical Soc. Journal. xx., 1850. The elephants bones found here are fossil, and well silicified. I have deposited a grinder in the British Museum, which appears to be of a new species, see my paper on Mastodon bones in Chile. Geological Soc. Journal, 1857.
[4] A murex.

through the liquor, which is at first milky, then green, and then purple.

Before proceeding with the history of the Caras, I will advert to some Indians of the coast.

Stevenson[1] gives an account of the still wild Malabas. They live on the river San Miguel (in Esmeraldas), which joins the Cayapas. They understand Quichua. He visited them about 1815: the name of the chief was Cushi-cagua, and his tribe consisted of 200 Ischcay-huarango families. According to the tradition of the Malabas, they and other tribes, are descendants of the Puncays, or chiefs of Riobamba; and, although the Conchocando of Lican, the chief of Riobamba became the vassal of the Inca Tupac-Yupanqui, the Malabas were never conquered. The men wear an ornamented piece of leather round their heads—the wincha. On seeing a watch, they exclaimed, "manan, manan! chy trapichote,' which in quichua means, no, no: it is a sugar mill.

Velasco[2] speaks of San Miguel as having once been a considerable Spanish settlement, where mines of very fine gold were worked. The wild Tortola Indians, fearing they would be enslaved by the Spaniards, attacked and destroyed San Miguel.

The Cayapas Indians are faithful, brave, and rich; they have mines of fine gold.

The mouth of the river Esmeraldas is in about 1° N., 79° 45' W. The "city," San Mateo, not containing one hundred houses, is two leagues from the mouth of the river. Here there is much of the negro element. Stevenson[3] says the natives of Esmeraldas, Rio Verde, and Atacamez (Tucamez) are Zambos, or a mixture of negro and Indian. The tradition is, that a ship having negroes on board arrived on the coast (for soon after the conquest, great numbers of negroes[4] were taken from Africa to the West Indies and shores of the Isthmus of Darien, across it to Panamá, and from thence to the various Spanish

---

[1] II. 411. [2] III. 108. [3] II. 388.

[4] Ferdinand, the Catholic, sent negro slaves on his own account to America in 1510. In 1516 the privilege was granted to Señor Chevres, who ceded it to some Genoese merchants for 23,000 ducats, and who sent their first shipment of 500 African negroes (men) and 500 (women) in 1517. "Mercurio de Lima," I. 216.; Lima, 1791.

About 1555, Ursua fought against the cimmarones (wild) or rebellious negroes, on the Isthmus of Panamá. "Valley of the Amazons," Hakluyt Soc., 1859. In later times there were so many negroes in Lima, that they constituted ten different classes; they had two head-men or captains, and appear to have been pleased with church

settlements on the Pacific), and having landed, killed the male Indians, kept their widows and daughters, and thus laid the foundation of the present race. Their language is different from the Quichua, which, mixed with Quitu, is the general one of the Indians, being rather nasal, and appears scanty of words.

A woman is teona; a man, qual teona; a bitch, shang-teona; these words are of African origin. It is harmonious, and some of their songs are not devoid of melody. They have the chambo and marimba[1] as musical instruments.

Herrera[2] mentions about Quatro Rios (Esmeraldas), some negroes saved themselves from a wreck, they mixed with the Indians, and live here.

I am indebted to M. Bourcier, late Consul-General from France to the Republic of Equador, for the following observations on the Indians of Esmeraldas. They live retired from the Spaniards; grow tobacco, coffee, cacao, rice, &c; collect caucho or indian rubber, gums and resins; they make straw hats, nets, hammocks, and weave cloth; they cut timber, fish and hunt.

They speak Spanish, but their own idiom is a mixture of the old languages of Quito and Quichua; they are slow and inoffensive, honourable and truthful, but fond of drink.

In the district of La Tola are the Cayapas, who speak a different language; they profess Romanism, and, although subject to the government, have preserved their old customs, and do not marry with other tribes. All they require of the whites is salt and iron. They are robust, well made, face oval, roman nose, eyes and hair black and copper coloured. Their dress is a white tunic, without sleeves, and short trousers. The hair is combed back and tied. Male and female wear round the neck large collars of shells, small fruit, eggs, jaguar, caiman and snake's teeth; also talismans, composed of a mass of huaco (probably the mikania guaco), to preserve and cure them from the bite of poisonous reptiles.[3]

They despise gold, but like silver, and on their collars have five or six

ceremonies. They did much of the laborious work, but when dancing and singing to the sound of their marimba (thin tablets suspended over the mouths of calabashes), they had at least that short period of joy allowed to them by their masters. Skinner "Present State of Peru," 291.

[1] This is an African musical instrument.
[2] II., 38, Descripcion.
[3] Stevenson, II., 243, says, the leaves of the huaco are bruised and pressed together in the form of a cake, which they eat for snake bites

dollars, preferring those with the head of the King of Spain to the Republican coin.

The inhabitants of the settlements, and who consider themselves descendants of the Spaniards, are in part Zamboes (from negro and Indian), mulattos (from white and black), or Guasos (from white and Indian). These are without education or manners; their only occupation is to make money and cheat the Indians.

This district derives its name from the famed emerald mine said to exist not many leagues from the city of Esmeraldas. Since the period of the conquest its position has not been known. If the present Indians know the spot (of which there is a doubt), they carefully conceal it from the whites. That it exists is a fact, for the ancient rulers of Quito drew from it those large emeralds, emblematic of their sovereignty, and so much valued by the Conquistadores, some of which are among the crown jewels of Spain.

M. Bourcier purchased a drilled emerald, such as the Incas wore, suspended from the neck, from a Cacique, who had a small plantation on the banks of the river Esmeraldas; it weighed sixty-four quilates (the quilate or carat is four grains), equal to 256 grains. The Cacique told him he had inherited it from his ancestors; and M. Bourcier believes it came out of the mine in question.

Nine leagues from the village of La Tola, in a distance of five leagues, are annually found, after the heavy rains, gold ornaments of crowns, stars, spoons, birds and animals. About six pounds weight of these gold figures are found per year. Rough pottery is also met with.

The ancient Indians had stone and bronze hatchets. Large earthen vessels, containing chicha, have been disinterred, also a male skeleton, which had false teeth, secured to the cheek-bone by a wire of gold.

To return to the Caras, they, bent on conquest, moved north of Tucamez, 50′ S., and by the river Esmeraldas, which has a course of more than 500 miles, rising near the volcano of Cotopaxi, they found their way to Quito about 1000 A. D. The Caras were more civilised than the Quitus. They adored the sun and moon: the temple to the sun, on the hill of Panecillo, was of stone and square, and had a pyramidal roof, with its door to the east, so that the first rays of the sun fell upon a gold image of the same; the temple to the moon and stars was on an opposite hill—it was round, and had openings, so as to admit the moon's rays to fall upon a silver image of one imitated thereon, the ceiling was blue, with stars of silver. Their idiom, which introduced into the Quitu the letter o, is generally stated to have had affinities with Quichua.[1] Their clothing was of skins and woven cloth of cotton and wool. Their year was regulated by the solstices; they had on each side of the door of their great temple to the sun, two "most ancient" columns to observe the solstices; they had also twelve pillars round the temple which served as gnomons to show the first day of the month. Quito, which lay under the equator where the rays of the sun threw no shadow at noon, was held in especial veneration as the favoured abode of the great deity. They adored Pacha[2] and Eacha, who were gods or Cara heroes, and they preserved the idols of conquered nations.

Although the Scyris adored the sun, they did not, as the Incas, call themselves children of the sun. The government was monarchic and aristocratic, the regal emerald descending to sons, not to brothers, but to nephews.[3] The Quitus buried their dead in graves, but the Caras placed theirs on the earth with arms and objects of value, building a tomb (tola) of rough stone over the body.

The Scyri had one legitimate wife, but many concubines. Their principal arms were the lance and club. A plain wreath of feathers was worn by all who bore arms; two by chiefs, and the Scyri added to his wreath or crown of feathers, a large emerald.[4] Their architecture

---

[1] Ulloa II., B. At Piura, 5° 12' S., the natives use a different language to those of Quito and Peru; and this is the case in many of the vallies. Their accent is also different, having a melancholy singing tone, contracting half of their last words as if they wanted breath. The original Quito u is retained in many words, although the o was introduced by the Caras. The Poechos are placed about here.

[2] Pacha is earth, in Quichua. Pacha-camac, creator of earth, or God.

[3] A similar custom was observed among the Zipas of N. Granada.

[4] EMERALDS. I was surprised not to see emeralds at Guayaquil, when, at the conquest, they were so abundantly found in Equador. This gem cannot have disappeared, but awaits intelligent searchers, particularly as we now know their geological position. Emeralds were obtained in considerable quantities from the district of Tucamez, and the River Esmeraldas is said to be so called from the ancient quarries of this stone. It is also mentioned that the name of Esmeraldas was given to this part of the country, seeing that it was so green with vegetation, by some of the conquistadores who had been on the desert coasts of Peru. Stevenson (II., 406), says: he did not visit the mines owing to dread of the natives, who assured him it was enchanted, and guarded by a dragon, which poured forth thunder and lightning. The locality of the emeralds may be arrived at by the river Bichele, the alcalde of which place gave Stevenson three emeralds found in the sands at the mouth of that river. These mines were worked by the Jesuits. An emerald, as large as a pigeon's egg, fell into the hands of Pizarro's followers, at

was not so far advanced as that of the Incas, but Velasco says they knew how to construct arches and vaulted roofs: their fortresses were square earthworks. The cutting and polishing emeralds appears to have been known to them ere they conquered the Quitus.

Instead of the Peruvian quipu, they had small pieces of wood, clay and stones of various sizes, colours and forms, by which they expressed principal occurrences; these were kept in compartments in their temples, tombs and dwellings.

Coaque; but not knowing their value, broke many into pieces. Velasco I. 29, says: the Beryl, sky blue and green emeralds, is found in the cordillera of Cubillan; also when Alvarado landed on the coast of Esmeraldas with five hundred men, they collected many loads of gold and emeralds, but found their booty so burdensome on their march to Quito, that they threw it away.

It is often stated that Peru is rich in emeralds, it should rather be said the coast of Equador. I have never heard of this gem having been found in Peru. The XI. Inca, who died about 1475, A.D., commenced inroads on Quito, his son Huayna Capac, conquering the country. About this period, I conceive the Peruvians became acquainted with the emerald. Rivero and Tschudi say: the image of the sun, at Cuzco, was made of a plate of gold, with a human face and many rays, with emeralds and other precious stones, the robes of the Incas were garnished with emeralds; may not these emeralds have come from Quito? However, I cannot but think that the emerald-bearing rocks are to be met with in Peru. Molina His. Chile, I. 63, mentions that a beautiful emerald was found in Coquimbo. The pyx, in a church at one of the missions in Paraguay, was set round with *emeralds* and other precious stones.

At the Museum of Practical Geology, in London, there is an instructive collection of emeralds, and the rocks in which they are found. They are arranged as follows: Beryl, a silicate of alumina and glucina. 1. Gneiss, containing crystals of green beryl from the United States. 2. Coarse grained granite, ditto ditto. 3. Beryl in quartz. 4. Precious beryl from Siberia. 5. Ditto from granite, near Dublin. 6 Emeralds associated with calcareous spar and iron pyrites, in a vein of black carbonaceous limestone from Muzo, New Granada.

Parisite, a brownish-yellow crystal, composed of carbonate of lanthanium and didymium with flouride of calcium, is also found in the emerald mines of Muzo.

We know nothing as to the process the natives of Quito, or Peru, had for cutting, boring or polishing precious stones; they may have had hardened copper or brass instruments, and something approaching the drill, for the regal emerald had holes drilled through it to keep it fast on the head.

When Gonzalo Pizarro built his brigantine, and started from the junction of the Coca and Napo, he put on board more than 100,000 dollars in gold, and many fine emeralds.

Wallace, Travels on the Amazon, 1853, 278, Ornaments of the Uaupés Indians. "I now saw several men with their most peculiar and valued ornament—a cylindrical, opaque, white stone, which is quartz imperfectly crystallized. These

According to the reading of the coloured stones by some, 700 years is given for the reigns of eighteen or nineteen Scyris; other readers give fifteen Scyris and 500 years up to the death of Cacha Duchicela in 1487, A. D.

The eighth Scyri conquered towards the south, making inroads upon the Puruhás, whose capital was at Riobamba, 1° 38′ S., 5′, W. of Quito. The temple of the Puruhás was oblong. Neither the sun or moon was adored, but an idol of clay, their deity of war and vengeance; it had a human head, and was in the form of a vase; the mouth was at the top of the head, and it was by this orifice that the blood of the sacrificed was poured: the Scyris abolished these sanguinary rites.

By the death of the eleventh Scyri, about 1300, A.D., the male line of the Scyris became extinct, when Toa, his daughter, was declared his

---

stones are from four to eight inches long, and about an inch in diameter. They are ground round, and flat at the ends—a work of great labour,—and are each pierced with a hole at one end, through which a string is placed to suspend it round the neck. It appears almost incredible that they should make this hole in so hard a substance without any iron instrument for the purpose. What they are said to use is the pointed flexible leaf-shoot of the large wild plantain, triturating (twirl with the hands) with fine sand and a little water; and thus no doubt it is, as it is said to be, a labour of years. Yet it must take a much longer time to pierce that which the Tushua (chief) wears as the symbol of his authority, for it is generally of the largest size, and is worn transversely across the breast, for which purpose the hole is bored length ways from one end to the other, an operation which, I am informed, sometimes occupies two lives. The stones themselves are procured from a great distance up the river, probably from near its source at the base of the Andes; they are therefore highly valued, and it is seldom the owners can be induced to part with them, the chiefs scarcely ever."

Orellana, in his descent of the River Amazon mentions, that in an Indian village below the junction of the Putumayo, in a country house, they found "good jars of earthenware. *vases, goblets of glass enameled with many bright colours, resembling drawings and paintings.* The Indians of this place said these things came from the interior together with much gold and silver." This requires investigation. I do not find that glass was known to the people of the New World.

See "Valley of the Amazon," Hakluyt Collection, 1859. One hundred leagues farther down the river, in the territory of Paguana, they saw the sheep of Peru (llamas).

See Wilke's American Exploring Expedition, v. 17. On Bowditch Island, in the Pacific, the hand drill used, pointed with hard stone, for drilling shell. Could such an adaptation have been employed by the Emerald drillers of Mexico, Bogotá and Quito?

successor; she became wife of Duchicela, the eldest son of Condorazo[1] chief of the Puruhá.[2]

Duchicela reigned seventy years; he was succeeded by his son Autachi Duchicela; he reigned sixty years. Guallca, his eldest son, would have succeeded him, but being of a bad disposition, his brother Hualcopo was put in his place, who died in 1463. In this reign Tupac Yupanqui, Inca of Peru, commenced his inroad upon Quito, and having taken the fortress of Tiocajas, 1° 58′ S., 14′ W. of Quito, the Quitenos, after a loss of 16,000 men, were routed, and the Inca returned in triumph to Cuzco in 1460, A.D.[3] The following was a favourite maxim of this Inca:—" Science was not intended for the people. Persons of low degree are only puffed up by it, and rendered vain and arrogant: neither should such meddle with the affairs of government, for this would bring high offices into disrepute and cause detriment to the state."

Hualcopo, who died mainly of grief, was succeeded by his son Cacha, the fifteenth Scyri; he reigned twenty-four years. He annihilated an Incarial army and demolished the fortress at Mocha, 1° 26′ S., 14′ W. of Quito: his only daughter, Paccha,[4] succeeded him.

---

[1] Villavicencio, 207. A son of the Scyri married a daughter of the Puruáh chief.

[2] The Inca or Quichua language had not been introduced into Quito long prior to the Spanish invasion, where the now wholly extinct Puray (Puruhá) had been previously used. Humboldt, Views, 235

The Quiteño, at the period of the Spanish conquest, appears to me to have been a mixture of Quitu, Cara, Puruhá, some others, and Quichua. There is a grammar of it, published in Lima, 1753.

[3] Humboldt says, at this period Quito was governed by the Conchocando of Lican (about 1° 24′ S.) and Guastays, or tributary princes; but, in another part of his writings, states that Lican was the residence of the Conchocando, chief of the Puruáys. Subsequently there was an Apu, lord or chief of Lican, who was descended from the Conchocandos ; speaks also of a river Lican.

Villavicencio states that Lican is a short distance N.W. of Riobamba ; that the latter had Incarial buildings. Velasco, II., Liribamba was the ancient name of the capital of the Puruhá, in a plain now called Gatazo. On another, the centro plains was Cajabamba, and the southern one, which was the coldest, Ricbamba (Riobamba)

It would appear that under the Scyris, these three narrow plains in the mountain were joined and had a population of 60,000.

Stevenson. II., 269, passed an evening with the Cacique of Riobamba, the only person he ever saw who could knot and interpret the Quipus. He boasted of the Huasta-Puncay, the ancient lord of the surrounding country.

[4] She is sometimes called Paccha-chire. Paccha is waterfall in Quiteño ; in Quichua fountain ; and in the same language pacha the earth.

Huayna-Capac went against Quito in 1475, to revenge the Incarial loss at Mocha, and in the last fight at Hatun-taqui, 20' N., Cacha[1] was pierced by a lance, which proved mortal; and the victory was for the Inca. About this period, the kingdom of Quito extended north and south some six degrees, or from Pasto to Paita.

The Inca gave orders that Cacha should be buried with all pomp at Quito.

The Scyris were buried in a large sepulchre of stone, of a pyramidal form, so covered with pebbles and sand as to look like a hill. The door was to the east. The embalmed bodies, arranged in order, with their insignia and the treasures the Scyri had commanded, should be interred with him. Over each was a niche, in which was found a hollow figure of clay, stone or metal; within were small stones of divers colours and shapes, which denoted his age, years, months of his reign, &c.

Huayna-Capac deemed it politic to make overtures of marriage to Paccha: she was then twenty years of age, and by the law of Quito, whosoever she married could reign with her. Paccha consented, and on the day of marriage Huayna-Capac added to his Incarial llautu (fillet) or crown, that of Quito with its large emerald.

Before the conquest of Quito by the Peruvians, the Cara-Quitus built their temples and habitations of stone and adobes; aqueducts, fountains and baths were known to them. Hualcopo, about 1430, A.D., erected palaces, particularly that in the plain of Collo in Llactacunga, now used as a farm-house. It is entered through a passage leading to a court, round which are three spacious halls, each having several compartments; there are other smaller rooms, and one supposed to have been a menagerie. The whole is built of black stone and cyclopean. These ruins are sometimes called the Aposentos de Mulalo, 50' S., and are 9,480 Spanish feet above the sea.

The fortresses in Quito were of earth; that of Hatun-Taqui would hold 6000 men: these must not be confounded with subsequent Incarial works.

Humboldt speaks of walls of unburnt brick which owed their origin to the more ancient inhabitants.

The Peruvians at least knew how to make a mortar for cementing, calling it sanguaga. Lime or iscu they burnt, mixing it with bitumen,

---

[1] Hatun-taqui or tontaqui, said to be a Quichua word, means the large war-drum or gong of hard wood. Here the Scyris had a fortress. Many tolas or conical tombs are met with at this spot.

which made a most adhesive cement. Burnt sulphate of lime, pachachi also was employed. For bricks the clay was called tica; for pottery a finer sort was used, known as llanca. The adobe or sun-dried brick[1] was one of the ordinary building materials for the dryer parts, and the walls or tapias were of much larger size.

In Quito there are many sorts of clay, especially for the manufacture of pottery. In Latacunga there are two localities, Pugilli and Saquisili, the red pottery from whence, as jars, pans, pitchers, &c. has a most delicate fragrance. There is another place in Collas where fine pottery is made, such as is called majolica in Europe.

Majolica, Raffaelle or rather Moorish ware, was first introduced into Mayorca, and from thence spread over Italy.

Huayna-Capac reigned thirty-eight years over Quito; at his death the kingdom of Quito was given to Atahualpa[2] his son by Quito's queen, the empire of Peru to his half-brother Huasca. Atahualpa is said to have married his sister, Cori (Coya or queen) Duchicela.

In 1529,[3] three years after the death of Huayna-Capac, the chief of Cañar, (Cuenca) raised the standard of revolt against Atahualpa, sought and obtained the protection of Huascar. Then the fratracidal war ensued, and many severe battles were fought, when, in 1532, Huascar was made prisoner.

The Incas having conquered to the south, east and west, turned their arms towards the north, having Quito for the prize, and, to facilitate their movements, constructed roads of great length, many of them lined with stone, which have been compared to the best Roman roads. The Incas erected on their route palaces, temples, houses for the virgin of the sun, tambos or resting places, fortresses and other buildings. The city of Quito having become the residence of Huayna-Capac, it partook of the Incarial architecture, religion, customs and language. This Inca added to and beautified Hualcapo's palace at Llactagunga or Tacunga, calling it after his bride Pachasula.

---

[1] Adoub was the Egyptian word for this kind of brick, and it is still used by the Copts, &c. Doubtless the Saracens derived it from the Egyptians, and carried it to Spain; thence it went to America, and from America to the Hawayan Islands; continuing westward, it may arrive at the land of its birth.

It will be observed, that adobe or unburnt bricks was known to the more ancient races in Quito and Peru.

[2] The hen, hatuallpa; the cock, arca-huallpa. Osculati spells the above, atuhualpa and orco-hualpa.

[3] General Miller's Peru, Frazer's Mag., 1844.

Many Incarial ruins are met with in Quito; Tupac-Yupanqui built the palace, fortress and a sort of labyrinth at Cañar, known as the Paradones del Inca in 2° 30′ S., 13,258 feet above the sea. To the S.W. is the Inga-pirca or fortress of Gran Cañar, 10,640 feet above the sea, near which is the Inti-huaicu or ravine of the sun. In this solitary spot, shaded by luxuriant vegetation, rises an insulated mass of sandstone. On the surface of the rock are concentric circles representing the image of the sun. The foot of the rock is cut into steps which lead to a seat hollowed out, and so placed that from the bottom of a hollow the image of the sun may be seen.

To the N. of Cañar is the Inga-Chungana, the play or sport of the Inca; at a distance it resembles a sofa, the back of which is decorated with a sort of arabesque; here the Inca could repose and enjoy a delightful prospect over the valley of Gulan.

La Condamine saw in an old building in this district, ornaments of porphyry (Velasco says granite) representing the muzzles of animals, in the perforated nostrils of which were moveable rings of stone.[1]

Huayna-Capac built the bridge of Rumichaca (stone bridge) over the Augasmayu in Pasto.

Mocha, once the seat of the Mucha, a warlike tribe, was celebrated for its Incarial palace, temple and fortress; here the Indians defended themselves successfully against Alvarado.

---

[1] We know that the Peruvians used tools of brass. Velasco II., p. 70, states that when Huasca was taken prisoner by his brother, as he was being incarcerated, a woman gave him secretly a bar of metal—silver with bronze, brass, or an alloy of silver, copper and tin—that during the night the Inca, by help of the bar, broke through the wall of his prison and escaped. I allude to this as showing that silver was also alloyed with copper so as to give hardness to metal bars or tools for quarrying, there is no account of iron being employed. There was some quillay, or iron ore, particularly at Cuenca; but it was not smelted by the Indians, being too serious an operation for them. Gold and silver was merely melted, but the chloride and sulphuret of silver by aid of fire and air could be reduced by them.

In Vol. I., Mercurio Peruano, p. 201, 1791, the following mines are mentioned as having been worked by the Incas:—Escamóra, Chilleo and Abatanis, of gold; Choquipiña and Porco, of silver; Curahuato, of copper; Carabuco, of lead (probably the vicinity of Oruro yielded tin); and the magnificent iron works! of Ancoriames 16° 25′. S., on the east margin of Lake Titicaca, are particularised. Tools of copper, brass, and brass and silver have been met with; but I find no account of iron tools, or manufacture of iron. Don M. E. de Rivero on the analysis of ancient copper chisels, hatchets, &c., found from five to ten per cent of silex; it is difficult to say if this silex was introduced, or was an impurity. (R. and T., p. 215, English Edition.)

Cayambé, about 6' N., is celebrated for its ruins and tombs, some as old probably as the time of the Quitus or Scyris. Huayna-Capac built here a palace and fortress, also a tambo or resting place. Near the tambo was a small temple to the sun (now a church), behind which are warm baths (of marble). One of these baths had the figure of a puma, the other that of a lizard, with water issuing from their tongues. The snowy mountain of Cayambé, through which the Equator passes, is reputed to be rich in silver. Ulloa[1] mentions that near the town of Cayambé is a circular temple of adobes or unbaked bricks. Tiquizambi, now Tijan, 2° 10' S., 6' W. of Quito, had its tambo and fortress: Velasco[2] says ruins of these were seen in his time, but Villavicencio states that they were buried and lost in the earthquake of 1699. In a S.W. direction from Tijan are portions of the Incarial road, also ruins, and a rivulet, the Culebrillas, which has three hundred bends, and then runs into a lake.

At Palta-pamba (plain of the palta, a fruit), in the district of Nanegal, N.W. of Quito, are the remains of a causeway, stone buttresses and cope, a mineral pitch used as cement[3] for the building a bridge. In the vicinity are ruins of a temple, a conical tower, and many tombs containing mummies with objects in silver. Villavicencio[4] supposes these remains to have been the work of the Caras, when on their way to the conquest of Quito.

In the canton of Molletura, 2° 38' S., 54' W. of Quito, the mountain of Caushin has a spiral road up it of six to eight yards broad: here there seems to have been a fortress, and part of the Inca's road passed this spot: many tombs have been met with. At the foot of the mountain of Curitaqui is a cavern, and from the number of bones of children and animals met with, was probably a place of sacrifice. Gold ornaments are often found in this locality, having been washed out of the old tombs by rains.

At Tambo-blanco, 3° 46' S., 45' W. of Quito, in Loja, are Incarial remains of a palace, other buildings and tombs; and at the quarries of Cariamanga, 4° 17' S. 1° 22' W. of Quito, are hewn stones seven yards long, probably intended for Incarial buildings.

Walls, ruins and roads are seen in many parts of Equador; in the plains, sides of mountains and on their summits; the more irregular

---

[1] 267.

[2] I., 467.

[3] Cope, a mineral pitch, is found near Point St. Elena, and Amotape, near Piura. It abounds in Realejo, and at Chumpi, near Guamanga in Peru.

[4] Geo. Ecuador, 294.

are thought to be the work of people long before the conquest of the country by the Incas.

One league from Gonzonamá 4° 15′ S. near the deserted Spanish city of Zamora,[1] are the ruins of a village built by the Incas. There is one large house, two hundred and fifty feet long and fifty feet in breadth, standing east and west. The walls are three feet thick, and built of stone; the doorways six feet broad. Nothing is standing save the walls, and these are very low and decayed. The art of building arches was unknown to the ancient Peruvians; the roofs of the houses and those of the temples were thatched with straw.

I have already alluded to the mode of burial of the Quitus and Caras in their tolas, which is different from that practiced by the Peruvians in Quito: the graves of the latter were called huacas.[2] The embalmed (?) or dessicated body, wrapped in cotton or woollen cloths, was laid in a grave of stone or bricks; curiously fashioned earthen vessels, some containing chicha and food, were deposited with the body. From these huacas many interesting objects have been taken, including small copper and brass axes, mirrors of polished stone and metal, known as the Inca-stone or Ingarirpo. Velasco says it was composed of silver, gold and other metals. Molina calls it auriferous pyrites; and Ulloa adds, it was not transparent, but of a lead colour, and smooth as glass. The mirrors of the Gallinazo-stone were hard, brittle and black, probably obsidian. Stone spear-heads, gold nose jewels, collars, bracelets, ear pendants, hollow idols of gold and silver, copper nippers for pulling hair out, from the face in particular, large metal pins, &c.

GOLD MASK FROM INDIAN TOMB AT CUENCA.—In January, 1859, Mr. Gerstenberg, chairman of the Equador Land Company, at my request, exhibited to the Royal Society of Antiquaries, a gold mask, with tusks and rings, found in the Indian tombs of Cuenca.

DESCRIPTION.—The centre or face is embossed, more than half an inch high; the rim is flat; a small circular raised plate and wire attaches the mask to three hollow rings. There are twelve small globular bodies, joined six and six, moveable on a wire. There is the appearance of soldering about the large hollow rings. The embossing over the face looks like an hieroglyph. This ornament was worn by a chief or priest, and may be the head of a war-deity. There is attached a flat pear-shaped piece of gold.

---
[1] Seemann's Voy. of Herald I., 170.
[2] An old Indian grave is generally called a huaca, but machay is a tomb. The dead body mallqui or manoa. Anything found in a tomb is huaca or sacred.

Bollaert's Antiq. S. America.

Probably an Hieroglyph.

It weighs four ounces, nineteen pennyweights; its specific gravity is 14.07 (pure gold is 19 3). It is of a light colour, owing to alloy with silver; but whether alloyed by the natives or found in this state is a question: if the latter, then we may look upon it as an aururet or electrum, and would contain about 39.50 per cent. of silver. (Gold from Titiribi, in Columbia, gave—gold. 76.41; silver, 23.12; copper, 0.3.)

Between Cuenca and Guayaquil, the Equador Land Company have acquired a district of land, the Molletura, where similar remains are found.

At the Pailon, another district obtained by the Company, in one of the valleys there are often found such ornaments after the rainy season; they are washed from the ridges of the mountains, where the chiefs and others were buried. The gold articles are mostly broken up and melted by the finders or purchasers.

Cuenca is in 2° 57′ S., 29′ W. of Quito, the beautiful country of the Cañaris, a nation contemporary with the Cara dynasty of Quito.[1]

The face of this gold object from Cuenca may be compared with that of the stone statues of Timaná in 2° N.

TABLE OF THE CHIEFS OF QUITO, OF CARA OR OF THE SCYRIS, AND THEIR ALLIANCE WITH THE PURUHAS AND PERUVIANS.

FIRST EPOCH.

The rulers of Quito or the Quitus, how long they were masters of the country, or the number of them, is unknown; the last was called the Quitu, who was conquered by the Caras, about 900 or 1000, A.D.

SECOND EPOCH.

The Scyris settled at Cara came on the coast of the Pacific, about 600 or 800, A.D.; conquered Quito, about 1000, A.D.

THIRD EPOCH.

YEARS

Eleven Scyris reign in Quito . . .   320 from 980 to 1,300

---

[1] Indians of Cuenca.—Seemann Voy. of Herald, says, they are, perhaps, in many instances, sincerely attached to the Romish church, but at heart many of them still venerate the inti (sun). They are strong and hardy, and are very numerous in places, when they have avoided connections with Whites and Negroes; for this, after all, appears to be the great secret to preserve them from destruction.

FOURTH EPOCH.

	YEARS	
12th Scyri, Toa the Caran, and Duchicela the Puruhá	70 „	1,300 to 1,370
13th Scyri, Autachi Duchicela	60 „	1,370 to 1,430
14th Scyri, Hualcopo Duchicela	33 „	1,430 to 1,463
15th Scyri, Cacha Duchicela	24 „	1,463 to 1,487

FIFTH EPOCH.

16th Scyri, Paccha and Huayna-Capac, 13th Inca of Peru	38 „	1,487 to 1,525
17th Atahualpa, son of the above	8 „	1,525 to 1,533
18th Hualpa-Capac, his son	0.2mo	1533
19th Rumiñahui, the Usurper, from December, 1533 to May		1.533

SIXTH EPOCH.

The Spanish Conquest, about 300 years.

SEVENTH EPOCH.

The present Republican form of Government.

The coast of Equador was discovered by Pizarro, in 1526.

In 1812, the country declared against Spain, and the battle of Ayacucho, 9th of December, 1824, closed the war of Independence.

POPULATION OF EQUADOR.—Whites, descendants of
Europeans 601,219
Indians, descendants of the Conquerors . . . 462,400
Negroes 7,831
Mixture of Negroes with Whites and Indians, as Mulattos,
Zambos, Mestizos or Cholos 36,592

                                                                   1,108,042
Eastern savages from Chinchipe to the Putamayo . . 200,000

                                                                   1,308,042

According to an official report, the population in January, 1858, was 1,040,371, having augmented, since the previous year, 19,919; born 41,008, deaths, 21,089.

The revenue of Equador in 1856 was 1,372,000 dollars; expenditure, 1,858,498.

ETHNOLOGY OF EQUADOR.[1]—The races are, the European, Negro

---

[1] Translated principally from Geografia de la Republica del Ecuador, por Villavicencio, New York, 1858.

and American. The mixture of these three, form sub-races, distinguished by the names of mulatos, zambos, mestizos or cholos. The first are from the union of the Negro and Indian; the second, the Negro and White; and the third of the White and Indian.

The American race is subdivided into families.

QUITU FAMILY.[1]—These Indians constitute the greater portion of the native population, and have been improperly called Peruvians. The Quitus were powerful and organised, when they were conquered by Huayna-Capac, Inca of Peru, who governed them thirty-eight years. The language of the Quitus (Cara-Quitus) had affinities with the Quichua. Thus Huayna-Capac said, "These kingdoms must have been established by two brothers;" but he had little foundation for this opinion.

I have said, at p. 79, that it was probable the Caras came originally from the coast of Peru; if so, they may have brought a language having some connexion with Quichua, and would account for the Cara—Quitu being understood by the Incarial invaders. Now this Cara language introduced the o, which was a prominent vowel in the Quichua, into the Quitu. The Puruha's and other nations south of Quito became allied to the Scyris of Quito, but of their languages we knew very little. Velasco,[2] says, at the period of the Conquest of Quito by the Incas, in the intermediate country the Quichua was not spoken; thus I suppose that the Quichua, which formed a part of the Cara-Quitu, was brought by the Caras from the coast of Peru in early times. Still, as the Incas had been advancing north for a long period, the Quichua of Cuzco, which was rigorously imposed on the conquered nations, crept onwards and also communicated by them to the Cara-Quitus, who had been extending their dominions towards the south.

The general character of the Quitu family is, that of having the cheek-bones large, narrow forehead, large ears, hair straight and thick, of a copper colour, and but little beard. Those Indians who are free from consecutive labour are better made than the gañanes, conciertos, or hired persons, such are nearly black; they include shepherds, &c., who are exposed to the burning sun of the tropics, or to the frozen temperature of the Paramos or Andean regions, and who go about naked. It is generally said that the Indian is astute and suspicious; but, if so, let us do him the justice to say, that we have, in many cases, abused his confidence.

---

[1] See Ludewig 159.
[2] II., 52.

The Lojanos are as bronzed as the Cañazes, but the latter are more intrepid, robust and taller, and generally have large cheek-bones, and bent (roman) nose; the Puruhás or Chimborazos are somewhat whiter than the preceding, more robust, and the American type is strongly marked in them; the Tacungas are rather white, active, and their physiognomy approaches the Caucasian; the Quitus proper, are distinguished from the Tacungas by their activity and liveliness; they are generally enterprising and brave: the Imbabureños are as white as the Europeans, their females, particularly those of the Cotacaches, have expressive and beautiful features.

The Napos, Canelos, Santo Domingo, Intags, Nanegales and Gualeas speak the same language as the Quitu, which we will add to this family; specifying that these tribes are distinguished from the Quitus, in being taller, more agile and muscular, of agreeable countenance, bent nosed, and the cheek-bone not much developed. These Indians are generally known as Yumbos, adding to this the name of the province they live in, as those of the Napo; they are called Yumbos of the Napo.

CAPAYA FAMILY.—These differ but little from the Yumbos; they are not so tall, but have the cheek-bones somewhat larger. They preserve their primitive idiom, which is guttural, but they all speak the general language or Quitu; they live in a state of liberty and independence, and only allow the Romish priests and whites to be amongst them during their feasts, and for trade.

COLORADOS FAMILY, are to be found in the forests to the east of Quito; their language is nasal, but the greater portion speak the Quitu. These three had settlements, but they have begun to disperse and form others, as Palenque-alto, &c.

JIVARO FAMILY.—This great nation is found between the rivers Chinchipe and Pastassa; composed of numerous and large tribes, taking the names of the rivers on the shores of which they live, as Moronas, Pautes, Zamoras, Gualaquisas, Upanos, Pindos, Pastassas, Agapicos, Achuales, Cotapasas, &c. All these speak the Jívaro language, which is clear and harmonious; easy to learn and energetic. This last quality emanates from the warlike and proud character of the Jívaros. The Incas of Peru tried in vain to conquer them; the Spaniards succeeded in reducing them, founding cities in their country; but a rising in one day destroyed the work of many years. Since then, some attempts have been made to subdue them, but without success.

They are active and muscular, have black eyes, small and very animated; they show a bold front, are bent nosed, thin lips, and have teeth as white as ivory.

Many of them are whitish and bearded: it is believed this comes from the Spanish women they stole when they rebelled in 1599.

They use the lance with great dexterity and manage the shield well.

Although the Jivaros are of so unbending a character, some of the tribes approach the conquered settlements, entering into relations with them, as has occurred in Canelos, with some of the Jívaros of the Pastassa, and they have even learnt the Quitu language. Other tribes have crossed the Cordillera, and have entered the towns, seeking peace and trade, inviting them to open roads.

ZAPARA FAMILY.[1]—This is less numerous than the Jívara, and inhabit the upper waters of the Pastassa and Napo; they are divided into many independent tribes, taking their names from the rivers near to which they live, as the Mueganos, Curarayes, Tupitinis, Matagenes, Yasunies, Mautas, Shíri-punos, Nushinos, Andóas, Rotunos, &c. All speak the same language, which is simple in its grammatical construction—nasal, guttural, and abundant in burlesque phrases.

This family is more pacific than the Jívara, less cunning in war, but more skilful with the lance. They are particularly active, attached to the white man, and hospitable to him. Their civilization would be easy.

Between the Záparo and the Jívaro, there is a great difference in their customs. The Záparo is generally indolent; thus only a few of the tribes have small plantations of maize and yuca; the majority supporting themselves by the chase, fish and wild fruits, their only dress being the bark of trees. The Jívaro, on the contrary, has a fixed residence, cultivating with care large portions of land with plantains, yuca, maize, mani, maudi, potatoes, beans, vegetables, &c.; they also breed large numbers of swine, trading them in Canelos, Macas, and with tribes on the Amazon; they weave cotton clothing, which they dye with pleasing colours.

The Záparo live in well-constructed assemblages of ranchos, where only are found hammocks, serving them for beds and seats, whilst the Jívaro build strong houses with doors, closed inside at night by an upright bar on an angle; he sleeps on a bedstead, and his principal apartment has wooden chairs around it.

---

[1] See Ludewig, 207.

In appearance the Záparo is somewhat like the Chinese: of middle stature, robust, round face, small eyes placed angularly, and very knowing; nose flat and broad at the end, lips rather thick, and slightly bearded. Those who live on the margins of the rivers maintain themselves by fishing: they are copper coloured; but those who reside in the interior and in the shades of the forest, are lighter coloured, and the women have an agreeable and expressive countenance

ANGUTERA FAMILY.—Inhabits the central and lower portions of the Napo. They appear to be a branch of the Putumayo Indians, with whom they have identity in language, customs and appearance, and live in friendship with them. The Anguteros have fixed residences, cultivate the plantain and yuca, also the yuca-brava, a poisonous root, this property it loses by fermentation, into which they put it to make bread, their principal food, as well as chicha, from the same root: both are pleasant and nutritious.

The countenance of the Angutero is not an agreeable one, being rather ferocious; he has black eyes and large eye-brows, his nose bent and broad, hair thick and long, of dark copper colour, and many have a blueish complexion. Their arm is the lance. These Putumayos are those Indians dreaded by travellers, who, when coming up stream, attack them at night, robbing them of their tools of iron; but their most frequent frays are with the collectors of sarsaparilla. They are beginning to sell provisions, hammocks and sarsaparilla.

ENCABELLADA FAMILY.—This is a small one, and is found on the lower part of the river Aguarico. Their numbers are much reduced, and, although wild, have lost their former ferocity. They are in appearance somewhat like the Anguteros, but different in their customs, and much given to fishing for the manati (sea-cow), charapas or tortoises, with which their river and lakes abound. They supply travellers with meat and fat.

OREJON FAMILY[1]. These join the Anguteros, and inhabit the country at the mouth of the Napo. The name of Orejones (big-eared) comes from the custom they have, after having bored their ears, to introduce daily pieces of wood, one larger than the other, until the size of a foot in diameter is attained, the size of the wheel that is within the lobe of the ear.[2]

---

[1] See Ludewig, 139.

[2] This was a form of an order of chivalry of the Incas, or, perhaps, the custom existed even before their time.

Their language is guttural and nasal, somewhat confused by its precipitate utterance; it differs from that of the Anguteros, as these latter, independently of theirs being very nasal, accent the last syllable with a peculiar and unpleasant sound.

The Orejones have broad faces, which are almost square, large cheekbones and thick lips; they are in communication with the Ticunas, and prepare the Orejon poison for their arrows. They are not so wild as the Ticunas, and trade in poisons, hammocks and provisions, bartering for iron implements, &c.

AVIJERA FAMILY.—This family inhabits the southern shores of the Napo, at its mouth, and in front of the Orejones or Payaguas.[1] They appear to be allied to the Yquites and Mazanes, for their language and customs are the same; they consist of many tribes, speaking the same language, but with different accentuation.

They are like the Anguteros in feature, but are darker, the nose wider, very large faces, and the cheek-bone well developed. These tribes live by fishing and the chase; they have some plantations, and supply provisions to the traveller.

Next to the Avijeros, and in front of the Anguteros, are the Santa Marias, formerly a branch of the Anguteros. These are pacific and more industrious than the Anguteros; they cultivate large portions of land with maize and yuca-brava, collect sarsaparilla, and make hammocks for sale. The Santa Marias dress as the Anguteros, in a long narrow tunic, very clean, painted with various colours and fanciful figures.

COFANES FAMILY.—These tribes live on the head waters of the river Aguarico, between it and the Azuela, and near to the foot of Cayambé. This family, once so dreaded by the Spaniards for the blood they shed of the missionaries, have much diminished, and are losing their wildness; they now leave their forests and visit the neighbouring settlements. The Cofanes speak a guttural rough language; they are very united amongst themselves, and occupy an advantageous position for defence, in case of being attacked.

Independently of the families already described, each one speaking a different language, there are small tribes of savages living between the Amazons and the territory of the Jivaros, each having a particular dialect. There are also other inhabitants, as the Mulattos[2] of

---

[1] See Ludewig, 78.

[2] These have their origin from run-away negroes, who appear to have killed the male Indians of this district, taking possession of their women.

Esmeraldas, and the Mangaches of Palenque-alto, who, although they speak Spanish badly, have a particular language, which appears to be a dialect of the Colorados de Santo Domingo.

The wild nations of Equador, as the Jivaros, Záparos, Anguteros, &c., believe in a good and evil principle: this faith somewhat governs them. They suppose that the good principle is more powerful than the evil, the former being shared in by the virtuous. All the savages of the eastern districts believe in the metempsychosis, and suppose that the brave are transformed into the most beautiful birds; cowards and traitors, into unclean reptiles.

POPAYAN, now a portion of New Granada, was so called from a great chief of that name, and who ruled over many large tribes.

The first Spaniards, in a very short period, founded twenty-one cities, seven towns, villages and settlements. These were furiously attacked by the natives. Velasco[1] thinks that nearly all these nations of Popayan were descendants of Caribs of the Antilles, on account of their barbarous proceedings and analogous vices, particularly that of eating human flesh. There were, however, some tribes who appear to have had other and more noble origin. If there were ferocious and inhuman ones, as the Pachanchicas, Masteles and Abades, there were others kind, sociable and humane, as the Yuncales and Sanquampúes: if there were stolid, brutal and rude, as the Guanacas and Paes, there were others clever and of noble ideas, as the Antagaímas and Coyaimas. If there were weak, cowardly and unwarlike, as the Timanáes and Nievas, there were others formidable for their valour and military spirit, as the Noannamáes, Chocóes, Andaquies, Pijáos, and particularly the Barbacóas.

The continuous and sanguinary wars of the Spaniards, destroyed, in a short space of time, so large a portion of the native population, that, for working the gold mines, Negro slaves had to be imported.

It is difficult to give a correct list of the various nations that inhabited Popayan. In the N.W. there were fourteen, including the Chocóes; in the N.E. there were twenty-three, including the Anatagaimas and Pijáos; in the W. there were five, including the Barbacóas; in the E. there were eight, including the Andaquiés, Coconucos, Niêvas, and Timanáes; in the S.W. there were eighteen.

---

[1] III., 37.

In the S. and S.E. there were twenty-six, including the Mocoás.

QUITO.—This great kingdom[1] comprised the following nations, said to have had each a different language, with the number of dependent tribes who spoke dialects. The Alausi, eight; Angamarca, two; Cañar, twenty-five; Canelo, one; Cara, seven; Caran-quin, eight; Cayambé, two Chacayungo or Jaen, ten; Chimbo, five; Cofan, five; Esmeralda (Tacamez), twenty; Guancavelica, sixteen; Hambato, four; Huaca, three; Hamboya, two; Lapuná, two; Latacunga, sixteen; Maca, eight; Manta, ten; Mocha, five; Mocoa, five; Otavolo, nine; Pacamores, twelve; Palta, four; Pinnampiros, five; Poritaco, two; Paruhay or Riobamba, thirty; Quitu, twenty-nine; Quijo or Canela, twelve; Lucumbio, five; Tiquizambiz, one; Tijanes, one; Jibaro, thirteen; Yaguarzongo, twelve; Yumbos, Zarza or Lonja, eighteen; besides others the names of which are not known.

Thus we see that there were about forty nations who spoke distinct languages, and more than 300 tribes who had dialects. Of the tribes more than forty were extinct before 1789. The greater portion of the forty mother tongues are lost, and the dominant ones are Peru-Quiteño and Spanish.

The Huancavilca, Jibaro and Pacamoro nations, for their indomitable valour, may be classed with the Araucanos of Chile. The Huancavilca and Cofan nations had a well-regulated government, the more so that of the monarchial Pacomores. The Chimbos and Mocoas were weak and cowardly. Some were well inclined, pacific and friendly to the Spaniards, as the Mocoas, Yumbos, Macos, Huamboyas and Canelos; and others indomitable, as the Tortolas, Jivaros and Lapunás.

Some 100 nations are spoken of as having inhabited the Marañon, and 140 more on its tributaries; many of these nations and tribes are extinct.[2]

EQUADOR LAND COMPANY.—Being anxious to support every undertaking calculated to develop the inexhaustible resources of S. America, I readily co-operated in the formation of the Equador Land Company, being invited thereto by the Chairman, Mr. Gerstenberg.

The Equador government had issued land warrants to the amount of £560,000 to British creditors in part payment of arrears of interest at the conversion of their debt in 1855. The committee of bondholders commissioned Mr. George Pritchett to proceed to that country, to

---

[1] Velasco, III., 175.

[2] See Valley of the Amazons by Markham, Hakluyt Soc., 1859, for principal tribes of the Amazons.

choose lands suited to European immigrants and for commercial purposes. He selected five districts: the Pailon, Atacames, Molletura, Gualaquiza, and Canelos, in all about four and a half millions of acres, at the average price of 2s. 5d. per acre. The land warrant of £100 being however only worth £5, the marketable value of the acre is little more than one penny.

The holders resolved, upon Mr. Pritchett's favourable report, to form a company under limited liability, subscribing one share of £2 in respect of every land warrant they hold, thus furnishing the means of sending out a first expedition to the port of Pailon. The promoters agree to surrender £1000 land warrants each to the company, to enable the same to take immediate possession of the Pailon.

The amount required for that purpose is £60,000, but it has been considerably exceeded, and the subscriptions now amount to nearly £100,000.

On the 25th of March of 1859, the company was duly incorporated, under limited liability, after a unanimous resolution of support and co-operation on the part of the land warrant holders, passed by a public meeting at the London Tavern on the preceding day.

The allotment of the two eastern districts, the Canelos and Gualaquiza, being made the pretext for hostilities on the part of Peru, the Equador Land Company took a warm interest in the unprovoked quarrel, pleading the just cause of Equador, not only by the press, but also in a memorial presented by a deputation to Lord John Russell. The Secretary of State for Foreign Affairs at that interview made the important statement that the blockade was irregular and should be enquired into. Shortly afterwards Lord John Russell sent a reply to the directors conveying the gratifying announcement that his lordship was fully alive to the great importance of the question involved, and had requested the naval officers stationed on the west coast of S. America to obtain the fullest information on the subject; meanwhile a British man-of-war being ordered to the coast of Equador to watch British interests.

The Equador Land Company have proceeded vigorously with their preparations. Being possessed not only of a large amount of land warrants but also of sufficient funds, they purchased the yacht "Kittiwake" of 250 tons, to convey to Equador, as pioneers, a commercial representative and his staff; the important post of geologist and engineer, has been confided to the well-known Australian and Californian explorer, Mr. J. S. Wilson, whilst the offices of surgeon, botanist, agriculturalist, &c., are filled up by practical individuals.

The immediate objects of the expedition will be to establish a small colony at the Pailon, and make arrangements for future immigrants. From the paucity of serviceable ports on the west coast, the new port of Pailon will be useful to navigation generally.

The next step will be to construct a road to Ibarra and Quito, as the landholders on the line and the government of Equador have offered their assistance and co-operation, volunteering labourers and a pecuniary guarantee of 10 to 15 per cent. on the outlay of capital. Along the road, the most favourable spots on the rising ground and table-lands will be selected for settlement of European immigrants and the cultivation of the various products best adapted to the different zones, such as cocoa, cinchona, caoutchouc, coffee, sugar, cotton, maize, wheat, &c., and for the exploration of the varied mineral riches of the country.

This road will enable the rich provinces of Esmeraldas, Imbabura, and Quito to send their abundant supplies of valuable produce to the Pailon for shipment, whilst they are at present almost entirely lost, owing to the difficulty and great expense of transporting them first to Quito, and thence round Chimborazo to Guyaquil.

Afterwards the road from Ibarra is to be continued to the Canelos, thus reaching, by the river Napo, the Amazons, and establishing a practicable and inexpensive route for merchandize from the Atlantic to the Pacific.[1]

Not only colonization and commercial establishments are the objects of the company, but also scientific researches, and they will represent various scientific societies in England and on the Continent.

In September, 1859, Peru declared war against Equador; one complaint is, that Equador has given up lands to the British bond-holders, belonging to Peru. A few words on the boundary question may not be uninteresting.

---

[1] It is stated by a Belgian paper, that M. T. Lois has accepted the invitation of the Brazilian government to navigate the whole of the Amazon river with sixty-four companions.

BOUNDARY QUESTION.

Villavicencio[1] says " Equador is bounded on the N. by New Granada, on the S. by Peru ; on the E. by Brazil; and on the W. by the Pacific. The exact limits with neighbouring nations are not yet determined. Those I have given on my map appear to me to be the most natural ones, although Equador has rights over the province of Mainas, situated S. of the Marañon, and the space between the rivers Putumayo and Caquetá, and where foreign maps generally run the boundaries."

Herrera states that the old coast line was from Buenaventura (3° 45′ N.) to Paita (5° 10′ S.), or about 200 leagues.

Seemann,[2] in his route from Piura north, came to the R. Ana-cara, in about 4° 30′ S, 80° 00′ W., which, he says, is the south boundary line of the two Republics, and that the River Mira is the north boundary with N. Granada; but which of the mouths to take is the question. Those who wish to join N. Granada say the channel flowing south of Point Mangles is the one intended; while the Equadorians maintain the Tumaco branch, about twenty miles to the northward, is the true one. In a late map, the boundary line is moved to the River Patia, sixty miles north of Tumaco, falling into the sea, just north of Point Guascamo.

The latter end of 1859, Castilla, the president of Peru, sailed from Callao with a large force, making himself master of Guayaquil ; and, as civil war was raging in Equador, this precluded any opposition.

Castilla, on taking possession of Guayaquil, placed General Franco in power there. However, the disturbed state of Peru, coupled with the approach of the rainy season, obliged Castilla to make his way back to Lima to watch the movements of the Echenique party, which he had turned out, and the chance of a difficulty with Bolivia.

Castilla concluded a treaty of peace with Franco, who only commands in Guayaquil. Peru not to be identified for cost of Castilla's expedition, estimated at seven millions of dollars. Two years from date of treaty allowed for Equador to prove her right to the provinces of Quijos and Canelas, and, failing this, to surrender them at the expiration of that time to Peru. British bond-holders to have lands assigned to them in exchange for lands in the above mentioned provinces.

The head government in Quito refused to ratify this treaty, and Franco, aided by Castilla, proposed to march against Quito to compel its recognition.

---

[1] Geografia de la Republica del Ecuador, 27.

[2] Voy. of Herald 1., 60, 72.

Translation of Names in the Work and Map of "Geografia de la Republica del Ecuador," by Villavicencio.

The names of plains, mountains, rivers, lakes, &c., some of which have their origin in the ancient idiom of the Quitus—of these we are ignorant of their etymology—others are of the times of the Schyris and the Incas; of these some have been preserved in their purity, as Allapaca, caqui-bamba, chuqui-pata; others have been altered, as cajas-bamba (cajabamba), chimbu-razu (chimborazo); others have been translated, half in Spanish, half in Quichua, or Verde-cocha, Limpio-pungu, Frances-urcu; and others into Spanish, as Rioblanco, Laguna-grande, Monte-negros; but the Indians still call these Yurac-yacu, Hutun-cocha, Yana-urcu.

We give a list of some of the words met with in our work and map, so as to facilitate a knowledge of places, inasmuch as the names given to localities by the Indians, signify the relation as to figure, colour, the abundance of animals or fruits in the mountains or forests, rivers, lakes, and places.

Allcu-chaca	bridge of the dog	Caniro-cocha	river of the Canero (a little dog, very carnivorous
Allcu-chupa	tail of the dog		
Allcu-cocha	lake of the dog		
Allcu-quiro	tooth of the dog	Casha-yacu[1]	river of thorns
Allpa-chaca	bridge of earth	Casha-urcu	mountain of thorns
Allpa-rupahsca	earth, burnt	Caspi-cocha[2]	lake of poles or sticks
Angas-cocha	lake of Ancon	Chaca-yacu	river of the bridge
Angas-quingrai	vuelta (turns) of Ancon	Chaca-yungas	bridge of the warm country
Añango-yacu	river of ants		
Ata-hualpa	chicken, handsome	Chalhua-cocha	lake of fish
Balsa-yacu	river of the balsa (float)	Chalhua-bamba	plain of the fish
Balsa-urcu	mountain or forest of the balsa	Chahuar-urcu	mountain of the cabuyos
		Chambira-yacu	river of the chambira (palm)
Caballo-guañusca	dead horse		
Cachi-loma	hill of salt	Chaqui-bamba	plain of the feet
Cachi-llacta	land of salt	Chaqui-maillana yacu	river to wash the feet
Cachi-yacu	river of salt		
Cajas-bamba	elevated plain	Chaqui-ñan	footpath
Cajas-cocha	lake on elevated plain	Charapa-cocha	lake of the charapas, (tortuguilla)
Cajas-ñan	road on elevated plain		
Cajas-urcu	mountain or forest on elevated plain	Chonta-yacu	river of the chonta (palm)
Callana-yacu	river of Callana (also earthen vase)	Chonta-cocha	lake of the chonta
		Chonta-urcu	forest of the chonta

[1] Caparurar (or snow mount.), the mountain of El Altar.—Stevenson.
[2] Caspi-cara was the name of an Indian sculptor in Stevenson's time.

Chiri-yacu	cold river	Huama-urcu	forest of the huama (large cane)
Chiri-urcu	cold mountain		
Chimba-yacu	river in front	Huama-yacu	river of the huama
Cocha-pata	foot of the lake	Huasca-yacu[2]	river of cords or ropes
Chuqui-pata	foot of the hill of the chuquis (dancers)	Jahua-urcu	forest of the jahua (fruit of a palm)
Chimbu-razu	snow of Chimbo (the province of Chimborazo)	Llusca-loma	a slippery mountain
		Lulun-bamba	plain of eggs
		Imba-bura	the fish preñadilla, breeding-place (a species of small vagre)
Cocha-yacu	river of the lake		
Chuqui-poyo	springs of chuqui		
Churu-urcu	mountain of the shells	Maillana-yacu	river to wash in
Chini-playa	shore (or dry sides of a river) of Ortiga	Manduro-yacu	river of achiote
		Mapa-yacu	dirty river
Cundur-hatu	meeting of the cundures (condor)	Mapa-cocha	dirty lake
		Mauca llacta	ancient country
Cundur-huacbana	the condor's nest	Mulli-pungu	easy narrow pass
Cunchi-bamba	plain of the swine	Limpio-pungu	clean narrow pass
Cunuc-pata	foot of the hot hill	Libro-urcu	mountain like a book
Cunuc-yacu	hot river	Morote-urcu	mountain or forest of morote (fruit of a palm)
Curi urcu	gold mountain		
Curi-yacu[1]	gold river		
Cusni-tambu	cottage of smoke	Nina-caspi	wood used as a candle, fire
Cusu-bamba	plain of the cusu (larva of the beetle)	Nina-yacu	river of the candle or fire
Cuy-cocha	lake of the cuy (a species of hare)	Paccha	cascade
		Paccha-yacu	river of the cascade
Danta-yacu	river of the danta (the great beast)	Pacha-mama	cobija madre[4]
		Pacay-yacu	river of the huaba (fruit of the mimosa indica)
Huacamayo-urcu	torrent of the parrots (a species)		
Huachi-yucu	river of the huachi (flower of the cane)	Palanda-yacu	river of the plantain
		Palu-urcu	forest of serpents
Huachi-cocha	lake of the huachis	Palta-urcu	forest of the paltas or ahuacates (a fruit)
Huaicu-huasi	house of the ravine		
Huaicu-yacu	river of the ravine [name	Paña-cocha	lake of the pañas (a little fish with strong teeth)
Hushua-lluma	bald-headed boy, a nick-		
Huahua-Pichincha	young Pichincha		
Huahua-yacu	river of the boy	Paushy-yacu	river of the pauji
Huagra-uma	head (herd) of cattle	Papa-urcu	mountain of the potatoes
Huagra-urcu	mountain of the cattle	Papa-llacta[5]	country of the potato
Huagra-yacu	river of the cattle	Pasu-urcu	forest of the pasos (fruit)
Huaira-pungo	door of the wind		
Huaira-urcu	mountain of the wind	Pindu-urcu	forest of the pindos (flower of the wild cane)
Hatun-cocha	large lake		
Hatun-taqui	large drum or tambor		
Hatun-yacu	large river	Pindu-yacu	river of the pindos
Hatun, chalpi-yacu	large river of chalpi	Piscu-urcu	forest of the birds
Huarmi apacyacu	river that takes the women	Puca-allpa	red earth
		Puca-cocha	red lake

[1] Curi-urcu, golden male.—Jameson.

[2] Cimpu-chaca, bridge of ropes, or rather tresses (cimpu).—Stevenson I. 421.

[3] Mundi-yacu (water).—Jameson.

[4] Probably Head-waters.

[5] Papa-llacta, papa, potatoe; llacta, village.—Jameson.

Puca-huaico	red ravine	Tiu-pullu	sand, fine as mist
Puca-loma	red hill	Tuni-curi	nugget gold
Puca-rumi	red stone	Turu-bamba	plain of mud
Puca-urcu	red mountain	Turu-yacu	river of mud
Puca-yacu	red river	Tuta-pishco-yacu	river of the bat
Pucará	fortress	Uchuc-cocha	small lake
Pucará-cocha	lake of the fortress	Uosha-tambu	thatched resting place
Puma-chaca	bridge of the lion	Ucsha-huasi	thatched house
Puma-cocha	lake of the lion	Uma-urcu	mountain of head waters
Puma-llacta	country of the lion		
Puma-yacu	river of lions	Uma-cocha	lake of the head waters
Pungu-cocha	ravine of the lake	Uma-yacu	river of the head waters
Quinua-loma	hill of the Quinua (chenopodium)	Upia-yacu	river, or water to drink
		Urcu-siqui-yacu	river at foot of mountain
Quingrai-ñan	zig-zag road	Urpi-urcu	forest of pigeons (palomas)
Rio-bamba, Ric-bamba	plain on the journey		
		Inga-chaca	bridge of the Inca
Rucu-pichincha	old pichincha	Inga-ñan	road of the Inca
Rumi-chaca	stone bridge	Inga-pirca	walls of the Inca
Rumi-ñagui	face of stone	Inga-chungana	play of the Inca
Sara-yacu	river of maize	Yahuar-cocha	lake of blood
Sara-urcu	mountain of maize	Yana-cocha	black lake
Sigse-yacu	river of the sigsi (flower of a grass)	Yana-urcu	black mountain
		Yana-yacu	black river
Sigsi-bamba	plain of the sigsi	Ichu-bamba	or Uchuc-bamba, little lake
Supai-urcu	mountain of the devil		
Supai-cocha	lake of the devil	Yahuar-Zongo,	a heart of blood
Supai-yacu	devil's river	Yunta-pungu	ravine of the Yuntas
Suru-bamba	plain of the Suru (canes that entwine with each other)	Yurac-yacu	white river
		Yurac-campañia	white country
		Verde-yacu	green river
Tiu-cajas	sandy heights	Verde-cocha	green lake
Tiu-bamba	sandy plain	Zapota-yacu	river of the Zapota (a fruit)
Tiu-cocha	sandy lake		
Tiu-loma[1]	sandy hill		

When Quito was conquered by the Incas their language, the Quichua, became the general only in those provinces subjected by them. A mixed language was spoken in Quito of Quitu, Cara, or that of the Scyris and Puruhuá. When the Incas took Quito more Quichua was introduced, changing in that of Quito the g for the c; b for p; u for o; and sometimes o for u.

In Pastos, to the N. Quitu is not spoken, neither in Guayaquil, excepting a few words of old Schyri.

The pure Cuzco Quichua was introduced into Maynas by the missionaries.

COLLECTED FROM VELASCO.

Here we have a mixture of Quitu, Cara, Puruah, &c., and Quichua.

Rumi-nahui	face of stone	Umiña	the emerald, goddess of health, a deity
Colta-cocha	lake of wild ducks		
Colay-cocha	lake of punishment	Inga-rirpo	looking glass stone of the Inca
Pugilli	red potter's earth		
Quispi	rock crystal	Quillay	iron ore

---

[1] Tiu-puyo, springs in the sandy deserts.

Quichua	English	Quichua	English
Titi	lead	Papa	potatoe
Chuya-cullqui	mercury	Sara	maize
Cullqui	silver	Caspi caracha	itch tree[2]
Tumbaga, puca-curi	alloy of gold and copper	Ahuara, vagra	danta, a great beast, tapir
Curi	gold	Llama (Quichua), Llausa (Quito)	animal, beast, is tame
Llambo-cullqui	tin		
Copé	mineral pitch, used as building cement	Paco	alpaca, is tame
		Guanaco	is wild
Cui, chunchulli	intestines of the cui or guinea pig	Vicuña	is wild
		Puma, pagi	lion
Huayacan	holy wood	Puca-puma	leopard
Machacui-huasca	rope of the serpent bejuco	Yana oryacu-puma	water lion
		Otorongo	tiger
Saire	tobacco	Vinchinche	large tiger
Supai-huasca, shilento	devil's rope	Ucumari, iznache	bear
		Atuc	wolf
Sinchi-caspi, shinvilto	wood that gives strength, or its infusion	Yuca-atuc	red wolf
		Yana-atuc	black wolf
		Yacu-atuc	sea wolf or seal
Uttcu or ucuiba	cotton	Alleu	dog
Macnu	cochineal insect, the grain	Yuray-taruga	deer, white
		Puzuc-taruga	deer, coloured
Indaco, añil	indigo	Rucu (old), Uuicho	deer with small horns
Maguaci, cabuyo	yelda, the pulqui		This yields the Bezoar stone
Mate, vingos, pilches	calabash		
		Ucuhue-lluicho	small deer
Rumí	saffron	Zoche, chita	wild goat
Cauchuc	india rubber; in the Esmeraldas it is called jebe	Tumla	hares, rabbits
		Cushillo	monkey
		Añango	fox
Cangi	gum arabic tree	Quiriqui	armadillo
Alquintara	dragon's blood tree	Quillac	the sloth, lazy
Ispingo	flower of the Canelo tree (cinamon)	Ucucha	rat
		Mashu	bat
Lulam (Quito), Ruru (Peru)	cocos of the palms	Cuntur	condor
		Llecama	royal eagle
Chonta, rúro'	palm tree (Euterpe, Spruce)	Huanga	common eagle
		Huaman	falcon
Angas, chonta	date tree	Ullahuanga	Gallinazo
Anana	pine apple	Curi-quingui	the Inca's bird, spotted with gold
Cacao	chocolate tree		
Chirimuyu, chirimoya	fruit of the cold pips	Rinavi	crow
		Atallpa	peacock
Inchic	mani	Urpi	pigeon
Palta	ahuacate	Cullcu-urpai	dove
Tanda	plantain	Mama-yuta	large partridge
Tanda-asua	plantain chicha	Tucan	the preacher
Tocte	Quito almond	Shicunga, guacamayo	parrot[3]
Batata	camote, or sweet potato		

---

[1] Chonta, pulp or fruit of a palm. Jameson.

[2] Mandi, root of arum. Jameson.

[3] Huaca-maya (El Guacamayo), the sacred river. There is a mountain called El Guacamayo, covered by an impenetrable forest, and clothed in mist. Jameson.

Tuyuya	pelican	Coniapuyara	amazons or good women
Cayma	cayman, crocodile	Quitu	chief of the Quitus
Apashiru	iguana	Caran Scyri	chief of the Caras
Ucullucuy	lizard	Huaracu	sling
Hambatu	frog	Condorazo	chief of Puruhá
Picupicu	toad	Tumbalá	chief of Puná
Tuclliu	small frog, spawn of frog	Huanca-hatun, taqui'	war drum, gong
Machac, amatu	serpent	Tola	a tomb
Huancoyru	bee	Taravita	a swinging bridge
Cucuyos	fire fly	Barbacoa	ditto ditto
Inti-mama	mother of the sun, fire fly	Larcas	aqueducts
Pilluutu, taparoco	butterfly	Vircus	secret aqueduct
Chuspi	fly	Inti-cusi	joy of the sun
Tancayllu	horse fly	Huallpa	young turkey cock
Sullacura	species of horse fly	Atahuallpa	turkey cock
Uru, paccha	spider family: cochineal insect belongs to this family	Rumi-iñahui / Quisquis	face of stone / barbarian } names of chiefs
Añall	ant	Popayan	name of chief
Isuli	large ant	Calarcá	chief of the pijaos
Pilis	head lice	Imbabura	from the fish, imba, or prenadillas
Usa	body lice		
Nina-curos	glow worms	Iña-Quito	plain north of Quito
Manati, lamatin	manati, sea cow	Cara-huiraso	volcano of
Cuchi, chalhua	pig fish	Cuspi-pamba	beautiful plain
Harmi-machacuy	the serpent's mother, a river fish	Chandui	S.W. wind, name of a mountain; this may be an old Quitu word
Punuy-sigui	sleeping fish		
Rumi-chalhua	stone fish	Yaguar zongo	heart of blood
Toa	black fish	Paititi, or Yurac-guasi	palace, or white house. Paitite, a fabulous kingdom in Peru
Charapa	small tortoise		
Churu	shell or shell fish		
Galapagó	land turtle, terrapin		
Tumba	fresh water shell	Tio-puyo (Tiu)	springs in the sand or desert
Tumba-llimpi	mother of pearl		
Tumba-maru	pearl	Huampu	balsa, or raft
Cui	guinea pig species of rabbit	Paccha-chire	waterfalls
Tarigatanga	one in three, three in one	Curi, mullinvino-maca	snake, shining, spotted like a tiger
Chambo	small copper axe		
Jungada	balsa, float or raft		

NAMES OF ANIMALS INTRODUCED BY THE SPANIARDS INTO QUITO, FROM VELASCO.

Horse	huihua, or domestic animal	Goat	chita, as being like a native animal
Ass	huihua	Pig	chuchi
Bull	Uagra, as having horns	Dog	Alleu
Sheep	llama	Cat	Misi
		Perecote, Rat	Uchuca

[1] The warriors of the Incas were armed with estolicas; these are flattened poles, a yard long and three fingers broad. In the upper end a bone is fixed, to which an arrow is fastened. At fifty paces they never miss. "Valley of the Amazons," 80. Hakluyt, Soc., 1859.

WORDS USED BY THE COCAMAS ON THE UCAYLI, from Velasco.

Caquire tanú Papa, caquere ura Dios ica, totonare. God be with courageous man, God protect thee and give thee long life.

FROM JAMESON.

The Indians of Archidona call Agami (psophia crepitans) a bird domesticated by them

Pauxi (crax alector) do. associated with the poultry

The Záparos call the blowpipe Bodaquera, made of chonta, five yards in length, and three quarters of an inch in diameter.

FROM STEVENSON. Words used about the coast.

Achote	small tree (bixa orellana) gives a red dye, used as a spice or colouring matter for food	Pilcay	cochineal insects, from cochinilla or old sow
		Kiebla	the fermented liquor of the yuca
Ceibo	balsa wood	Puichin	the spirits of this liquor
Huachapeli	cedar (?)		
Caoba	mahogany	Sorbetana, bodejera	
Ahi	sloth, ahi from the noise it makes		thehollow tube through which is blown the poisoned pua or dart
Allullas	cakes		
Copulies	wild cherries	Chautisa	small fish, resembling a shrimp
Huasi-cama	house servant		
Huadhuas	bamboo, contains between the notches sometimes as much astwoquarts of water	Moracumba	wild cocoa
		Jebe	Indian rubber, caoutchouc

ADELUNG III, 522. From Hervas.

	Quiteño.	*Quichua.*		*Quiteño.*	*Quichua.*
Hair	accha	chuccha	Leg	changa	chaki
Soul	aya	songo	Below	urae	urapi
Animal	ususa	llama	Eye	amsa	tulayasca
Light	ancha	illan			

G. Osculati, Esplorazione delle Regioni Equatoriale, &c., Milano, 1850, gives lists of the Quichua of the Incas and Quiteno, but not the date of the vocabulary from which he extracts, as—

    The Banana, gives the Palandra, ayu, or chicha
    The yuca, do. Lumo, ayu do.
    The yuca, do. Tziaspha do., blanca or white
    Wito, gives a black colour
    Roucou, red dye of the bixia orellana. Gives Zápara grammar and vocabulary

FROM SEEMANN.

Achira	canna discolor	Matapolo	loranthus destructa
Aroihtocta	composita	Matico	piper
Canchalagua	gentianea	" (riobamba)	eupatorium glutinosum
Capuli	prunus capulin	Melloca	ulicus tuberosus
Chuqui-ragua	chuquiraguer	Pigonil	festuca quadrientata
Chussalonga	eupatorium glutinosum	Quinquina de loja	cinchona cond.
Contra de vivora	raunolfia	Seraja	sonchus
Cuichunchuilla	jonidiun	Ullco	ulicus tuberosus
Joyapa	maclenia	Zauco	cestrum

PERU AND BOLIVIA.

War between Atahualpa and Huasca—Conquest of Peru by Pizarro—Fate of the Conquistadores—Viceroys and present rulers—Origin of name of Peru—Geography of Peru and Bolivia—Cinchona—Traditions of the Incas—Incarial history—Lima—Population—Pizarro—General Castilla—Literature — "Mercurio Peruano"—"Lima por dentro y fuera"—Zodiac of the Incas—Chincha Islands—Guano—Arica, tombs, cave in the Morro—Pintados—Pisagua—Province of Tarapacá—Iquique—Nitrate of Soda—Huacas—Journey into the interior—Pintados—La Noria, Nitrate of Soda works—Discovery of Borate — Matilla—Engraved rocks—Condors—Andes, and Volcano of Isluga — Mamiña, Aymara town—Quichua — Aymara — Indian revel, &c.

We left Francisco Pizarro at Tumbez, where he became impressed with the certainty that his conquest of the country was not far distant. He marched south in 1532, and erected the fort of San Miguel at Piura. The fratricidal war then raging between Atahualpa, the Scyri or King of Quito and his brother, Huasca, Inca or Emperor of Peru, was most favourable for the invaders.

In 1531, the armies of Atahualpa and Huasca met at Huamachuco, 7° 40′ S., 78° 10′ W. The battle was against Huasca. In 1532, Huasca was made prisoner near Cuzco, and was killed, it is said, when attempting his escape. Pizarro marched upon Cajamarca, 7° 5′ S., 78° 30′ W., seized Atahualpa and executed him.

Cuzco, the capital of Peru, was far away in the interior to the S.E.; the city of Quito, next in importance, was in the N., and the coast region to the S. was densely populated, particularly at Pacha-camac, near to which Lima was founded.

Peru, the long looked-for prize, being attained, dissensions commenced amongst the conquerors. The first dispute was in consequence of Pizarro dealing ungenerously with Almagro, who, however, went to the conquest of Chile, but returned abruptly to Cuzco, where he met with his death by order of Pizarro. In 1541, the conqueror of Peru was assassinated in Lima by the Almagro party, on Sunday, the 26th of June; he was sixty-five years old. Young Almagro was declared governor, but his power was of short duration: he was beheaded in Cuzco. Gonzalo Pizarro elected himself to supreme power, when Spain appointed, as viceroy of Peru, Nuñez Vela. Gonzalo Pizarro gave him battle in Quito in 1546, where Vela was slain.

Gonzalo Pizarro was now absolute master of Peru, but considered by the king of Spain as a rebel. The politic La Gasca was now sent from Spain to arrange matters in Peru as he thought best; he fought Gonzalo Pizarro at Huariña, on the eastern shores of Lake Titicaca, which was fatal to the rebel, who was beheaded and buried in the convent of La Merced, at Cuzco, where lay the bodies of the two Almagros.

Ferdinand Pizarro was imprisoned in Spain for twenty-three years; and, when released, was completely broken down by advanced age and suffering.

From Francisco Pizarro, the conqueror of Peru and first viceroy in 1530, to La Serna, the last, in 1821, there were forty-four viceroys.

From 1821 to 1860, there have been twenty-one rulers of the Republic, the present one being General Castilla. These have taken the following titles:—Protectors, Presidents, Supreme Delegates, Dictators, Supreme Chiefs, &c.

Peru was formerly divided into Upper and Lower: the former is now known as Bolivia.

The origin of the name of Peru is involved in obscurity.[1] On Pizarro's first journey across the Isthmus of Darien, the name of Biru, a chief, is mentioned.

Andagoya, one of the Conquistadores, on asking an Indian the name of a spot not far from Panamá, received the word Biru as the answer.

Garcilasso says pelu means a river; this is denied by Montesinos: mayu and yacu is river in Quichua.

The capital of the Puru-huá nation was, where now stands Riobamba, 1° 40′ S.

---

[1] Yucatan comes from tectetan, or I do not understand you, the answer given to the Spaniards, when asking the name of the country.

There is a Virú, Birú or Birué, in 8° 35′ S. on the coast, and the district is sometimes called Birúquete, which in ancient times was ruled over by the chief Birú.[1] Under the Incas, however, Cuzco was their capital and called Ttuhanti-ntin Suyu, or th fcour parts of the empire—that to the South Colla-suyu, colla south; suyu, district; that to the north, Chincha-suyu, from the great Chincha nations of the coast—this is sometimes called Tahua, four, suyu; that to the east Anti-suyu, anti from a nation of that name on the eastern slopes of the Andes, and not from anta, copper—neither from Andes, which comes from the Spanish word andenes, steps. The first Spaniards called the terraced gardens and plantations in the mountainous regions Andenes; to the west, Cunti-suyu—cunti may mean west. Cuzco, or Ceuzco, probably means centre or navel, or from Coscos heaps of earth which had to be levelled before the capital could be built.

GEOGRAPHY OF PERU.[2]—Under the Incas the line of coast was from about 2° N. to theriver Maule, 35° 30′ S., in Chile. During the Spanish domination, several territorial changes were made, but at present the former possessions of the Incas are divided into the republics of Peru, Equador, Bolivia, Chile and a portion of the Argentine Provinces.

A sandy desert runs along the whole extent of coast from Tumbez to Loa. Although generally barren, this desert is crossed by valleys watered by streams that rise in the western cordillera. The sandy waste on the coast is from thirty to sixty miles in width, forming extensive plains and arid ranges. The Andine portion, or Sierra, succeeds the western Cordillera.

The western Cordillera is ascended by rugged paths to an elevation where the frozen Andean plains or paramos are found, out of which rise the colossal peaks of the Andes, many covered with eternal glaciers.

The territory between the western and eastern Cordilleras is varied in aspect, climate and productions. It contains considerable ranges of the Andes, many paramos, the table lands of Titicaca and Bombon, ravines and valleys, some hot, others temperate.

From the eastern Cordillera extends the transandine country, or Montaña, where run innumerable rivers, some of the largest in the world. Vegetation is most prolific in the impenetrable forests. These and the extensive grassy plains are inhabited by wild Indians.

The mighty Cordillera of the Andes traverses Peru and Bolivia with

---

[1] Velasco, His. Quito, ii., 73, the river Birú origin of name.

[2] See Ledesma's Geografia del Peru, translated by me, Geogr. Soc. Journal, 1856, Mercurio Peruano, i. 1, 290, iv. 9, 19, Lima 1791. Skinner's "Present State of Peru," London, is a translation of the more important papers of the "Mercurio Peruano."

its mountain knots. There are many lakes, that of Titicaca being the principal one. The rivers belong to three hydrographical regions—the Pacific, that of Titicaca, and the Amazons. There is every gradation of climate, from the burning heat of Egypt to the icy cold of Siberia. Earthquakes are disastrous, particularly on the coast. As to natural productions, it is one of the richest countries in the world. In the valleys of the coast, and those of the interior, all the species of quadrupeds and domestic birds known in Europe are now bred. The plains and mountains of the interior are covered with herds of oxen, sheep, llamas and alpacas. In the Cordilleras are large herds of vicuñas and guanacos.

The transandine territory is distinguished by the great variety and number of its birds, many of beautiful plumage; also of animals, reptiles, and curious insects; the rivers afford many species of fish.

Peru produces, in its various climates, all the fruits, grain and vegetables cultivated in different countries, independently of those which are indigenous; the latter including many of exquisite flavour, such as the chirimoya pine and palta.

The transandine region is most interesting for the abundance of its productions. In its immense forests are ornamental woods in great variety, also the Peruvian-bark tree,[1] cocoa, coffee of fine flavour, coca, sarsaparilla, vainilla, &c.

The mineral kingdom of Peru is celebrated for placeres and mines of

[1] CINCHONA.—From Markham's Notes on the Culture of Cinchonas.—I have already alluded to the species found in New Granada and Equador.

From CARAVAYA.—1, C. Calisaya (var. Vera), the most valuable and richest in quinine. It grows on declivities and steep rugged places of the forest-covered mountains, 5000 to 6000 feet above the level of the sea. The tree grows best where there are heaps of fallen trees, forming layers of manure, one to three feet thick, and between 13° to 16° 30' S. It flowers in April and May.

2. C. Calisaya (var. Josephina), a shrub six and a half to ten feet high, with a slender branched trunk, from one to two inches thick. It grows in the warm pajonales, or open spaces at the edge of the forests, and at a greater height than the tree calisaya. Weddell is of opinion that, under favourable circumstances, the shrub might grow equally well with the tree, as its appearance varies very much according to the situation in which it grows..

3. C. Ovata (var. Vulgaris), found between 9° to 17° S., from 6000 to 7000 feet above the sea. It grows in warm forests, and is often found at the outer margins of the woods. It flowers in May and June.

4. C. Ovata (var. Rufinervis), a valuable species; found with the above. Flowers later than calisaya.

5. C. Micrantha; grows in the moist forests of Caravaya, not unfrequently near the banks of torrents. Flowers in May and June.

The other cinchonas of Caravaya are the scrobiculata, pubescens, amygdalifolia, Boliviana and caravayensis: but they are of inferior quality.

gold, mines silver, mercury and copper; some lead, sulphur and coal is met with, as well as quarries of various marbles. Important are the gold washings of Carabaya, the silver mines of Pasco, Puno, Gualgayoc and Guantajaya;[1] the mercury mines of Guancavelica and Chonta; the salt, nitrate of soda and borax beds of Tarapaca;[2] the salt pits of Huacho and Sechura. The guano deposits on the coast is a source of considerable revenue.

The population of the republic is about 2,200,000. Lima, its capital, is one of the most opulent and beautiful cities in Spanish America, containing more than 80,000 souls. Lima is in 12° 3′ S.; but from the recent observations of Moesta, of the Chilian observatory, Lima is 5h. 8. 8. 6, and Callao 5h. 8. 37. 3 of Greenwich.[3]

Amongst the other cities, besides Lima, remarkable for population and importance, are Cuzco, Cajamarca and Arequipa. Its principal ports are Callao, Payta, Trujillo, Cañete, Pisco, Camaná, Islay, Ilo, Arica and Iquique.

The population is a mixed one, including the descendants of the old Spaniards. The aborigines are numerous; the Mestizos also, who are a mixed race, uniting the aboriginal with more or less Spanish blood. There are Negroes also, their descendants mixed with the other races.

The number of each class is thus estimated: Whites, 240,000; Mestizos and dark, 300,000; Indians. 1,620,000; Negroes, 40,000, including 12,000 Negroes who have lately been given their freedom.[4]

The Spanish language is principally spoken: the Quichua and Aymará in the mountains. The Indians of the transandine territory speak various dialects.[5]

From HUANUCO.—C. Nitida, found in about 10° S. It grows in exposed situations.

C. Glandulifera, one of the finest kinds of cinchonas. Flowers in March.

C. Uritusinga, found at Chicoplaya; another valuable species, known as hoja de oliva; probably the C. Nitida of Pavon. Flowers in May.

Mr. Hill, in his "Peru and Mexico," I. 301, when on his way from Cuzco to Puno, gives some account of the Chunchos Indians and the cinchona bark country of the Macapata mountains. Very little is known of these Indians; they were neither conquered by the Incas or by the Spaniards. They were formerly the terror of the Peruvian bark collectors, and used to shoot them down with poisoned arrows. Friendly relations have at last been entered into with them, and they now assist to discover the position of the bark trees.

[1] Proceedings of Geological Soc., II., 1838, on these mines, by me.

[2] W. Bollaert's papers, Geographical Soc., on Southern Peru (first series), 1851. Essay Soc. Arts, 1853. British Association, Aberdeen, 1859, (second series), Geography, &c., of Peru.

[3] Geographical Soc. Journal, 1858, for Moesta's paper, which I translated.

[4] A new element is being introduced—viz., Chinese as labourers.

[5] W. Bollaert's Obs. on the His. of the Incas and Indians of Peru, Ethnological Soc., III., 1854.

The republic is divided into thirteen departments : Piura, Amazons, Libertad, Ancas, Lima, Junin, Guancavelica, Ayacucho, Cuzco, Arequipa, Puno, Moquegua.

The religion of the State is Roman Catholic. The government of Peru is republican, founded on the principle that the sovereignty resides in the people, its power delegated to the legislative, executive, and judicial bodies.

GEOGRAPHY OF BOLIVIA.—This Republic[1], anciently Charcas, known formerly as Upper Peru, lies between 6° 46' E. and 6° 16' W. of Chuiquisaca, La Plata, or Sucre, is in 19° 14' 50'' S., 66° 46' 30'' W. of Paris. Pentland makes it 19° 3' S., 64° 47' W. of Greenwich. Of this vast territory, seven hundred miles in length by five hundred broad, three-fourths of a most fertile land, is still a wilderness.

Bolivia is bounded by Chile on the S.W., on the S. by the Argentine provinces; S. E., by Paraguay; E. and N., by Brazil; N., by Peru; and on the W., by the Pacific.

The divisional line, between Bolivia and Chile, is said to begin at the Rio Salado, in 25° 39' S. Dalence says the line was formerly more to the S. The Chilians are encroaching on Bolivia.[2]

The divisional line with Peru begins at the river Loa, then by the Cordillera, and in a N. direction across the Lake Titicaca, then by a curved line to the E. of the snowy range of Apolobamba, up to 9° 30' S.

The Government is republican, the religion of the State is Roman Catholic.

The Cordillera enters Bolivia on the W., in 25° 39' S.; in the interior in 27° 38'. Between 21° and 22° it divides into two great systems: the western approaching the Pacific, the eastern declining towards the E. The elevated peaks begin between 17° and 19° S., where arise, including Tata-Sabaya, Cancoso, and Choja, about 20,000 feet (on the boundary with Peru), and Sajama, 22,350 feet. The eastern, or Cordillera real, is composed of five parallel chains. E.S.E. of La Paz, 16° 37' S., is seen the peak of Ilimani, forty leagues round; the S. peak 21,149 feet above the sea. The great table land is 180 leagues in length, and thirty to thirty-five broad, and about 13,000 feet above the sea.

Bolivia has every modification of climate; as Puna-brava, the region

---

[1] See Geografia de Bolivia, de José Maria Dalence, Chuquisaca, 1851. Delence died 1851.

[2] It is not easy to discover the course of this river Salado, of Dalence, or where it enters the sea, for 25° 39' S. is about Lavata, Bay of Fitzroy; and, when I came along the coast, I saw no stream or valley in that latitude. Hueso Parado, in 25° 39', was shown me as the boundary. Moesta makes the river Salado enter the Pacific in 26° 2' S. at Chañaral.

of perpetual snow, about 17,000 feet. Here are found plants, as the resinous yareta, valerians, and gentians; the vicuña, huanaco, llama, and alpaca, the viscacha, chinchilla, and condor. Puna region, here potatoes, ocas, quinua, cañagua, barley, and pastures grow, between 11,000 and 13,000 feet. Cabezera de valle, from 9,000 to 11,000, wheat, and some maize, also European vegetables. Medio Yunga or Valley, between 6,000 and 9,000 feet, maize, wheat, and European fruits yield in abundance. Yunga, commencing at sea-level to 6,000 feet, where the coca, cocoa, sugar cane, plantain, and pine apple grow.

Bolivia is divided into nine departments: 1. Atacama, having Cobija as its port, in 22° 23′ S. The Cordilleras are not difficult to pass, and contain many Potreros or farms, where cattle are reared. The country to the west forms the great desert of Atacama. The valley of San Pedro yields maize, wheat, and fruit. The rich copper mines (barilla, or native copper) of San Bartolo are to the north of San Pedro. There are also the villages of Chiuchiu, Calama, Tocanao. In the desert of Atacama, at Imilac, in 23° 49′ S., 69° 14′ W., Dr. Philippi places the position of the Meteoric Iron of Atacama.[1] Near Rosario, are ancient gold mines; at Olarios, nuggets have been found of eighteen to thirty-seven ounces. Copper and gold is worked at Conche; silver, iron, alum, sulphur, salt, some borate of lime, and probably some nitrate of soda. Guano is found particularly at Angamos, Port San Fransisco, 21° 51′ S., on the coast.

D'Orbigny says: the natives of Atacama were called Olipes or Llipes. Philippi estimated the population of San Pedro de Atacama from 5,000 to 6,000. The greater number are Indians, who speak a peculiar language, very harsh and gutteral.

Don Vicente Pasos, in his letters on Buenos Ayres and Peru, in 1819, observes that the higher portion of Atacama is cold, and its productions peculiar to such a climate, as farinaceous grains and roots. The province had nine small towns, the population being 30,000.

The mines of Conche supplied Potosi with copper hammers for the miners.

2. Potosi: the city is in 19° 35′ S., 13,330 feet above the sea. The summit of the Silver mountain is 15,200 feet; its population, as early as 1611, was 170,000 souls. Up to 1846, the quantity of silver extracted from its mines was £330,544 311.[2] Lipes is a cold climate, has rich silver mines; gold and copper veins are numerous; also large

---

[1] See my "Southern Peru:" Geogr. Journal, 1851-5; also my paper to Meteor. Soc. 1859.

[2] See my translations from M.S.S. "Anales de Potosi,' Belle Assemblee, Oct., 1851.

salt plains and lakes. It is said that the emerald, topaz, opal, lapis-lazuli, jaspers, and marbles are also found. Chichas is also a mineral region, but a more fertile soil than Lipes. Porco : from its mines the Incas drew much silver, and wines are produced in this province. Chayanta, or Charcas, has abundance of timber and pastures. Gold, silver and tin mines are scattered about. The silver mines of Aullagas, after having been abandoned sixty years, are again being profitably worked.

3. Tarija : is divided into the provinces of the Cercado, Concepcoin, and Salinas. The territory is fertile and climate fine. The Coca and Paraguay tea tree grows here. Fossil bones of Mastodon and Mammoth are found in various places. Gold and silver is said to be met with in the mountain of Polla, which district has not been explored on account of the wild Chirihuano Indians. It would seem that the Jesuits, in former times, extracted much gold from this part of the country.

4. Chuquisaca: Dalence says, is from Chuqui-caca—bridge of gold. It was called La Plata by Pizzaro. However, in Quichua, ccuri, is gold, cullqui is silver, bridge is chaca, and chuqui is a lance. This place is celebrated for its universities, colleges, and the number of persons enriched by the neighbouring mines.

Yampara has a fruitful soil. There are silver mines at Huallas; copper and tin exists; Cinti, wines are produced; also rum from sugar cane. The gold lavaderos on the river San Juan, it is supposed, if worked properly, would yield equal to those of Tipuani.

5. Cochabamba: this department was formerly called the granary of Peru. Its mineral and vegetable productions are in great variety. Choquecamata yielded much gold.

6. Santa-Cruz : in 20° S.; rice, cotton, honey, indigo, cochineal, sugar, coffee, cocoa, and tobacco are produced. The precious metals are said to exist. Chiquitos is a tropical country, but little inhabited. Gold, mercury, and iron, have been met with. Guarayos, in the mountain of Caparrus, there are veins of fine gold.

7. Beni: an extensive and fertile district; its three provinces are Caupolican or Apolobamba, Yuracaré, and Mojos. In olden times this region was called Gran Paititi, Gran Mojo, and Empire of Enin. It has every sort of climate and production. In the warm portions varieties of cinchonas grow.

Twenty-six leagues north of the confluence of the Itenes commence the cachuelas or falls; they are seventeen in number, five in the Mamoré, the remainder in the Madera. The last fall is in 8° 48' S., distant from Tamandua thirty leagues. From this point to the Atlantic there is no obstruction for navigation.

8. La Paz:[1] In 16° 35', is in a deep ravine. When the Indians rose, in 1780, fourteen thousand strong, the city suffered a siege of 140 days. The Cercado has every variety of climate, and in short distances. Chuquiaguillo is famed for gold washings, a nugget of 172 ounces was once found. In 1681, lightning struck and dismembered a portion of the summit of Ilimani, when large quantities of gold was collected.

Yungus de Chulimani: Of this province, D'Orbigny says "the magnificent vegetation of Rio Janeiro is reproduced here, but in greater luxuriance and splendour," including the calisaya cinchona. In the sands of the rivers gold is found; but the climate is prejudicial to human life. In the province of Larecaja, are the famous gold washings of Tipuani. In Muñecas, at Curba and Charansis, live the Indian herbalists, or travelling doctors of Peru.[2] Omasuyos,[3] in this province, tradition makes Manco-Capac first appear. Its climate is cold. However it produces some potatoes, ocas, beans, quinua, cañagua, barley, vegetables, and a few flowers. There is mountain pasture for sheep and the llama family. There we have great Lake Titicaca. Gold and silver mines were formerly worked in this district; and at Guariña or Carbiza, one of mercury. In the province of Pacajes, many silver mines were worked, in Berenguela alone 700; these are now abandoned, on account of their being in water. Much native copper (barilla) occurs at Corocoro. In the mountain of Ancora, green stones, like emeralds, are said to be found. The mines of Sicasica have produced much silver, as have those of Inquisivi of gold and silver.

9. Oruro: has a cold climate, its capital, of samename, is in 17° 57' S. So opulent was this place, that it competed with Potosi. In 1678, it had a population of 76,000. It has ten districts of mines, principally of gold, silver and tin; copper, iron, lead, bismuth, antimony, &c., are met with. Carangas has silver mines; Paria also, including one of gold, another of bismuth.

The population of Bolivia is estimated as follows: whites and others, 1,373,896; wild Indians, 760,000.

The races inhabiting Bolivia are the Spanish, Indian, some few African, and many Guarani,[4] who have come from the other side of the Paraguay and settled in the Cordilleras of Caiza.

---

[1] La Paz. I have deposited in the British Museum what I suppose to be a very ancient Aymará stone idol, from this district; it is about ten inches long, much like one figured at p. 197, Trans. Amer. Ethno. Soc. III., part 1., from the West Indies.

[2] See my account of these in Medico-Botanical Soc. Journal, 1831,

[3] Uma, or water, in Quichua, country of waters, or Lake Titicaca. The province is on the east shores of the lake. Markham says, water is pronounced Unu in Cuzco, Yacu in Ayacucho.

[4] Ludewig 75. The most extended nation of Southern Brasil, Argentine Republic, Paraguay, and Uruguay.

Dalence observes: it appears to him that America has been peopled from various sources, and at several periods; the ancient monuments the variety of human figures, represented in stone, and the difference in architecture seems to justify this opinion. Indeed, those who knew the Chirihuanos[1] or Guaranis, cannot believe them to belong to the Quichua or Aymará races, or to class the latter with the North American tribes. The Guarani family are comparatively white, robust and intelligent.

The Gnarayos[2] and Sirones[3] are descendants of those Spaniards who, deserting from their chiefs, went in search of the kingdoms of Patiti and Mojo; some are dark, others white and bearded; the former hospitable and kind, the latter wild and ferocious.

The Quichua and Aymará races preponderate, and are in about equal numbers. Then follow the Guaranis, Mojos,[4] Chiquitos;[5] Yuracares,[6] the latter say they are the only men in the world, the rest are men-lice.

Yuraccari is a quichua word, said to mean white man.

Their imports, in 1846, of foreign goods, amounted to 2,457,781 dollars; articles from Peru, Chile, and the Argentine provinces, 1,315,030.

The exports were Peruvian bark, copper, tin, wool, chinchilla, vicuña skins, &c., 491,767 dollars; the difference, 3,281,114, was paid in gold and silver, the produce of the Bolivian mines.

The roads from the interior to the coast of the Pacific are very bad, and over deserts. Advantage might easily be taken of two great outlets, one by the Pilcomayo, Paraguay, and thus to the river Plate also by the Mamoré, Madera, and Amazons.

TRADITIONS AS TO THE ORIGIN OF THE INCAS.—1. A man appeared at Tia-Huanacu; the mention of this most ancient spot induces me to think that the Incarial race may have sprung from one of the old Aymara nations. I have sometimes thought that the first Inca may have come from one of the great nations to the east of Bolivia: perhaps there is as much foundation for the opinion that the first

[1] Ludewig 75, 162, 418. Bollaert's Incas of Peru. Ethno. Soc. Journal, 161, 1854.
[2] Ludewig 75, 77.
[3] Ludewig 77. I have deposited in the British Museum an idol of the wandering Sirionos, found to the north of Santa Cruz. It is merely an upright pillar about ten inches long and nearly three inches at the base. The label I had with it was as follows:—"This object is composed of the dung of fish, and a particular sort of earth." It appears to me to be of stone.
[4] Ludewig 126. Moxa, Mossa, their language allied to the Maipure Indians of the Upper Orinoco.
[5] Ludewig, tribes on the Upper Paraguay.
[6] Ludewig, inhabit the eastern slopes of the Andes.

Inca may have come from some of the nations of the coast of the Pacific. Tschudi, in Rivero and Tschudi,[1] says it would appear that three distinct races dwelt in Peru before the foundation of the empire of the Incas, as the Chinchas of the coast, those of the vast Peru-Bolivian elevations, which D'Orbigny distinguishes by the name of Aymaraes; and the Huancas, who inhabited the country between the Cordillera and the Andes, 0° and 14° S. This man divided the land into four parts amongst the chiefs, Manco, Colla, Tocay and Pinuah: this name of Manco appears early on the threshold of Incarial history, but its meaning is very obscure. Manco went to the north and founded Cuzco. Colla may have gone south. Of the other two we know nothing.

2. In the beginning of the world, four men and four women, brothers and sisters, appeared at Paucartambo, 13° 25 S., 70° 35 W.: they came out of openings in some rocks. The men were Manco, Ayar Cachi Ayar Uchu, and Ayar Sauca. Manco founded Cuzco. Paucar signifies beauty, Ayar a corpse, Cachi anything white or resplendent, Uchu the andean pastures.

3. At Pavec-tampu, shining dormitory or house of veneration, eight leagues south of Cuzco, appeared three men—Ayarache, Ayaranca and Ayramanco,—and three women—Mama-coya, Mama-cuna and Mama-raña. Mama I believe to be the Spanish word for mother; for woman in Quichua is Huarmi, old woman paya. Coya is queen or empress. These persons were clothed so beautifully that they were called tocabo, or royal. They had a golden sling, which was endowed with peculiar virtues. They had abundance of wrought silver, assumed the government of the country, and built Pavec-tempu. Ayarache having got possession of the sling, overturned by its power mountains and gained such a superiority that his brothers became jealous and sought to destroy him. They persuaded him to enter a cave for a precious vessel which they had left there and pray to their father, the sun, to assist them in the conquest of the country. Ayarache entered the cave, when his brothers blocked up the mouth with stones; upon which a violent earthquake was felt, overturning mountains, entombing hills, woods and rocks in the bowels of the earth. Ayarache was then seen flying in the air with painted wings, and a voice was heard telling the two brothers not to be afraid, for Ayarache was going to found the empire of the Incas. Ayarache then discovered himself to his brothers, desiring them to build a temple where Cuzco now stands, in which the sun should be worshipped. Ayra-maneo was chosen Inca or emperor, from Inti, the sun; Intip-churi, child of the sun; the sun is also called Ppunchau.

[1] Antiguedades Peruanas, 26.

After which Ayarache and Ayranca were converted into stone statues. Ayra-mano and the women founded Cuzco, the man taking the name of Manco-Capac. Capac or supreme chief—Capac-apu, master, lord, ruler.

4. The following is a clumsy and modern piece of invention, first found in Stevenson,[1] also in Miller's Memoires. Rivero and Tschudi,[2] however, observe that the traditions of the Indians and the opinions of historians relative to the origin of the Incas differ much; some there are which by their simplicity and verisimilitude, cannot fail to satisfy, while there are others, which, by their silliness, arbitrary assertions and historical improbability, do not deserve the slightest credit. Such as, for instance, the one which makes an English sailor the legislator of Peru. A Peruvian prince, Cocapac, who chanced to be on the sea-coast, met a white sailor. On asking him who he was, he replied "an Englishman," a word the prince repeated Ingasman. Cocapac took the white man to his home, where he had a daughter, and she became the wife of the stranger. They had two children, a boy and a girl, and then the Englishman died. The boy was called Ingasmau-Cocopac, the girl Ocllo[3]. From accounts given by the stranger of the manner in which other people lived, and how they were governed, Cocopac determined on exalting his family. He took the boy and girl to Cuzco (some 4° from the coast! through sandy deserts and over the Cordillera!) where one of the largest tribes of indians resided, and informed them that their god, the Sun, had sent them two children to make them happy, and to govern them. He requested them to go to a certain mountain on the following morning at sunrise and search for the children. He moreover told them that the Huiracochas children of the sun (sometimes spelt Viracocha; Montesinos says, this means on account of extraordinary actions, but Vira or Huira is fat or scum, or such like matter that floats on water, also sacrificial oil, cocha is a lake or sea, or that these children came from the sea) had hair like the rays of the sun. In the morning the Indians went to the mountain Condor-urcu and found the young man and woman, but, surprised at their colour and features, they declared the couple were a wizard and a witch. They sent them to Rimac-Malca, the plain on which Lima stands, (only 6° of distance!) but the old man followed them, and next took them to the vicinity of Lake Titicaca, or among the Aymaras, (8° back again!) where another powerful tribe resided; Cocopac told these Indians the same tale, and requested them to search for the Viracochas at the edge of the lake at Sunrise; they did so, and found them there, and immediatly declared

---

[1] I. 394.
[2] Antiguedades Peruanas, 68.
[3] May be from Aclla, a maiden.

them to be children of their god, and their supreme governors. Cocopac to be revenged on the Indians of Cuzco (probably Quichuas,) privately instructed his grand-children in what he intended to do, and then informed the tribe that the Viracocha Ingasman Cocopac had determined to search for the place, where he was to reside; he requested they would take their arms and follow him, saying that wherever he struck his golden rod or sceptre into the ground, that was the spot he chose to remain at. The young man and woman directed their course to the plain of Cuzco, and the Indians surprised by the re-appearance of the Viracocha and overawed by the number of Indians that accompanied them, acknowledged them as their lords and the children of their God.

Stevenson thinks there is an analogy between this and a story he heard in Brazils, in 1823, that before the discovery of that country by the Portuguese, an Englishman who had been shipwrecked fell into the hands of the Coboculo Indians. He had preserved from the wreck a musket and some amunition, with which he both terrified and pleased the Indians, who called him Camaruru, the man of fire. He was alive at the conquest of the country, and was carried to Portugal, when King Emanuel granted him a valley near Bahia.

He then alludes to the white man with a beard, who appeared in the plains of Cundinamarca, called Bochica, with his wife, Chia. This has as little foundation as Quatzalcoatl, of Mexico, having been a bearded white man. Of the same negative value is the reported tradition that Manco Capac, Bochica and Quatzalcoatl having predicted the arrival of bearded men, and the conquest of the different countries by them.

5. The "Memoiras Peruanas" of Montesinos[1] is worth referring to by the student of ancient Peruvian history. He visited Peru a hundred years after the conquest, travelling fifteen years through the viceroyalty. His favourite idea was that Peru was the Ophir of Solomon, and that America was peopled from Armenia.

Five hundred years after the Deluge (4004 B.C.) begins the catalogue of the monarchs, whose names are quoted by Montesinos, amounting to 101, previous to the conquest of the country by the Spaniards. I have been unable to learn how or in what manner he obtained his materials

---

[1] Rivero and Tschudi, 51. Also T. Compans, translation of Montesino's Ancient His. of Peru. The Anales Peruanas, by Montesinos, are in MSS. and devoted to the conquest. Dalence, in his Geografia de Bolivia, says—"Bolivia formerly Charcas, was a populous country existing before the empire of the Incas." According to Montesinos, the historian of the Gran Colla, was equal in civilization to Tlascala (Mexico). At present Charcas, the capital of that ancient state, is only a miserable village annexed to the parish of Chayanta.

for the "Memorias."[1] With the learned reviewer of Rawlinson's "Herodotus," (in the January volume, 1860, of the "Edinburgh Review,") as applicable to the Montesinos Memoirs, I think that we ought to be curious to learn how much truth is hidden under romantic disguise. But for this the student in Peruvian history has no hieroglyphics or written language. There were the Quipos, but the Quipocamayos, or readers of the knotted strings, have passed away and left but a very small key to *their* wonderful art. It would be worth while to ascertain, if possible, the real meanings of the names of the Incas as given by Montesinos, as also of the names of the months given in brackets by Rivero and Tschudi; for instance, Raymi. in Quichua, stands for December—also, a solemn dance. But we have also Sassippunchau, not very clear; sassi may have some relation to huasi, a house and the sun is sometimes called Ppunchau—thus it may mean the sun's place or house in December. A critical examination and comparison of the first Quichua, Aymará, Chincha-suyo, Quitu, Guarani, and other vocabularies and grammars would be of service.

I give a few extracts which may be found useful as far as some of the names of Incas, things and places are concerned:

His 1st Peruvian ruler was Pishua-Mauca. Pishu is a bird in Quichua; macana is a sort of sword, also the morning star.

2. Manco-Capac. Capac is lord, ruler, emperor. People came from the side of Arica and Colla (probably Aymaraes) to beg land from this chief, which he gave them in the north.

3. Huaina-evi-Pishua (huayna, handsome youth). During this reign the use of letters was known and the art of writing on plantain leaves.

5. Inti-Capac-Yupanqui (yupanqui, capable of great deeds.) He gave them the institution of the year of 365 days.

6. Manco-Capac II. caused the priests of the sun to live in cloisters, and edifices to be constructed for the virgins of the sun. During his reign appeared two comets and two eclipses of the sun. Can this be verified?

12. Ayartaco-Cupo. Giants entered Peru settling at Huaytara Quinoa, Punta de Santa Helena and Puerto Viejo, and built a sumptuous temple at Pachacamac, near Lima. These places are principally on the coast of Equador, thus they came by sea. As to their being giants, that is fabulous; but doubtless there came, invading nations by sea from the north, others retreating from their enemies. Here we see that the temple of Pacha-camac (maker of the earth, sometimes

---

[1] Prescott, Conq. Peru, for observations on Montesinos, ii. 50.

called the unseen god, is not of Incarial origin, and appears very early in Peruvian history.)

13. Huascar-Titu (Huasca, a rope or chain; Titu, liberal) died at the period when it was proposed to make war upon the Chimus (Kings) of Trujillo, on the coast.

21. Manco-Capac-Amauta (amauta, learned) was addicted to astronomy. He convened a scientific meeting, when it was agreed to that the sun was at a greater distance from the earth than the moon, and that both followed different courses. He fixed the beginning of the year at the summer equinox.[1]

31. Manco-Avito-Pacha-cuti, (Pacha, earth or the world; cuti to change or "change-world,") began the year with the winter equinox.

32. Sinchi-Apusqui, (Sinchi, valiant; Apu, lord; died 2070 after the Deluge. He ordered that the Piruha (the Puruhá was one of the southern nations of Quito) gods should be called, Illatici-Huiracocha.

34. Ayar-manco, divided the month into thirty days, and the week into ten days, calling the five days at the end of the year, a small week. He collected the years into decades, or of one hundred years, which formed one sun or century.

38. Capac-Raymi-Amauta. (Raymi, a solemn dance; December the first month.) He knew which was the longest and the shortest day of the year, and when the sun reached the tropics. His people, in honor of him, gave the month of December the name of Capac Raymi.

42. Toca-Corca-Apu-Capac, founded the university of Cuzco. (Toca may mean regal.)

44. Hina-Chiulla-Amauta-Pachacuti, the 5th year of his reign corresponds with the year 2500 of the deluge. (Nina, fire.)

It is observed by the authors of the "Indigenous Races" (p. 197) that the rock-caves with their fantastic relief are of Buddhust origin, more chaste a style than the idols of the present worshippers of Shiva; and belong to a period of Indian history classical for art and poetry, from 500 B.C. to about 300 A.D. By a strange coincidence, it is the same period in which Phidias Praxiteles and Lysippus, and the Roman artists of Agustus and Trajan, flourished in Europe. If we follow Montesinos, this was about the period of Peruvian history.

51. Yahuar-Huiquiz, (Yahuar, blood; Huiquiz, to weep,) he intercalated a year at the end of four centuries.

55. Huillca-Nota-Amauta. He gained a victory at Huilca-Nota (Vilcanota) over hordes from Tucuman, who had invaded his country.

---

[1] See further on for Peruvian Zodiac.

(The eighth Inca Viracocha, according to Garcilasso went to Charcas, where he received an embassy from the King of Tucma or Tucuman[1].)

60. Manco-Capac III.[2] reigned in the year 2950 after the Deluge, consequently at the time of the birth of Christ.

64. Titu-Tupanqui-Pachacuti V. Irruptions of hordes from Brazil and the Andes. He was killed in battle. Ludewig says, the Brazilians, or rather Tupis, were once a numerous and mighty people. Eight different dialects are enumerated by Vater. Martius divides the Tupis into north, south-east, west, and central, naming, besides these, 245 different tribes as living within the Brazilian Empire.

65. Titu. Civil wars caused the loss of letters.

77. Topa-Cauri-Pachacuti VI., the ninth of his reign, corresponds with the year 3,500 after the Deluge. He prohibited the use of the quellca, a species of parchment of plantain leaves to write upon, but introduced the use of the quippos.

79. Arantial-Cassi. He commanded that in the tomb of his father should be buried his wife and favourite concubines.

82. Tocosque. During his reign the country was invaded by savage hordes from Panamá, some from the Andes, and some from the port of Buena Esperanza. These nations were cannibals and lived like brutes. (were these of the widely-diffused Carib race?)

86. Chinchirocca. They began to make golden idols (Sinchi, valiant; rucu, aged. In Garcilasso's list, this, his second Inca, is said to have been the first to be served in vessels of gold and silver).

90. Inti-Capac-Maita-Pachacuti VII. During his reign, was completed the fourth millenary cycle since the Deluge. Mama Ciboca, by artifice, raised to the throne her son, Rocca, so handsome and brave, that he was called Inca, which means cid or lord. This title of Inca was adopted by the successors to the throne of Peru.

91. Inca Rocca, came from the ridge of Chingana, near Cuzco, and presented himself as a child of the sun. He married his sister, Mama Cora (coya, empress). On the day after his marriage, more than 6000 were married. He declared war against neighbouring princes, who refused him obedience and would not acknowledge him as a child of the sun. He conquered the king of Huillcas. He commanded that the sun should be the principal god.

94. Inca-Capac-Yupanqui. His brother, Putano-Uman, formed a conspiracy against him, but the Inca, forewarned of it, caused the

---

[1] Ludewig, 243 for Catecismos, Gramaticas, &c., of the various languages of Tucuman.

[2] The first Inca, Manco-Capac, according to Garcilasso, began to reign A.D. 1021.

traitor to be interred alive, and threw the other conspirators into a ditch filled with serpents, jaguas and pumas.

97. Inca-Huiracocha. He made a campaign to Chile, conquered the Cañar Indians, those of Quito, the Chonos of Guayaquil, the chiefs of Puná, and those of Chimu. He repaired the temple of Pachacamac. During his reign there were two great earthquakes, and two irruptions of the volcanos of Quito.

98. Inca-Topa-Yupanqui II. He reduced the Chimus to obedience, who had rebelled anew, forbidding the use of water for the irrigation of their fields.

99. Inca-Inticusi-Huallpa, called also Huayna-Capac, on account of his beauty and prudence. He almost annihilated the nation of Palcas. He reduced to obedience the Indians of the river Quispe, commanded by a woman called Quilago. After a severe battle, he routed the Prince Coyamba (Cayambé) on the banks of Lake Yahuarcocha.

100. Inca-Inticusi-Huallpa-Huasca. Montesinos says, that the name of Huasca was given to this Inca by his foster-mother, and declares to be apocryphal the story of Garcilasso and other historians, touching the chain of gold, made in honour of his birth.

101. Inca-Huaypar-Titu-Yupanqui-Atahuallpa. Montesinos deduces the surname from atahu, virtue or strength; and alpa, good, gentle.

It has always appeared to me, that the small number of twelve to fourteen Incas, given by Garcilasso and some others, were too few in number to have built the edifices attributed to them; at the same time, the list of 101 rulers and Incas, according to Montesinos, is most questionable. I offer the following as the least defective or the more probable history of the Incas who commenced their dynasty at Cuzco.

1. Inca-Manco-Capac (capac, emperor), the ninety-first Inca-Rocca, according to Montesinos, reigned forty years, died 1062, A.D.. His wife was Oclo, Ocallo (virgin), Huaca (sacred), Capac-Coya (royal lady, empress). He is said to have appeared on the shores of Lake Titicaca. I have supposed that the Incas may have been of Aymará origin; if so, the said to be secret language of the first Incas was probably a dialect of the Aymará, and not known to the early Quichuas.

Cuzco then, it is said, was commenced by Manco; his dominions extending on the north to the river Paucartambo, on the east eight leagues, on the west to the river Apurimac, and nine leagues on the south to Quequesama. Manco was called Huac-chacuyac, the friend and protector of the poor; Yntip-churni, child of the sun. He gave to his people laws, brought them into communities, and then ascended to his father, the sun.

2. Inca-Sinchi-Roca, son of Manco, reigned thirty years, died

1091, A.D. Herrera says, Chinche: can this have any relation with the Chinche nations of the north? His wife was Oello Coya. He was the first to be served in vessels of gold and silver.

3 Inca-Lloqui-Yupanqui. (Lloqui, left-handed; Yupanqui, capable of great deeds.) He was the son of Roca; reigned thirty-five years, died 1126, A.D. Coya Cava or Anavarqui was his queen. He subjected the Canas and Ayaviri, and built fortresses. The Collas (mountaineers), a nation composed of many tribes, were conquered by him, as well as the Chucuytus; then towards the Lake Titicaca, the Hillari, Challu, Pamata and Cipita nations were joined to his kingdom. He was the first Inca who invaded the coast territory belonging to the Chimu or Chincu, whose capital was at Trujillo; but it was only under the ninth Inca, Pachacutec, that the Chimu of his day was induced to yield allegiance to him, at the Chimus palace and fortress of Paramonga, five miles from Patavilca, 10° 50' S. He conquered the populous country of Hurin-Pacaca (this may be about Pachacamac; Lurin is there also).

4. Mayta-Capac, son of the preceding, reigned thirty years, died 1156, A.D. His wife was Coya-Cuca or Coca, the name of a graceful plant, the leaves of which are still chewed by the Peruvians. He went to the south of Lake Titicaca, and subjected the people of Tia-Huanacu. In the village of Tia-Huanacu are the ruins of a palace of Mayta-Capac; also walls built by the Incas thirty miles long, reaching from the top of the Cordillera to the Lake of Titicaca.

These ruins must not be confounded with the very ancient ones there. The name of Tia-Huanacu is comparatively modern (the original name of the spot is lost, and we are ignorant as to who were the builders of these wonderful remains), and was so called in consequence of one of the Incas being there and receiving important news brought by a messenger who had travelled with great speed, when the Inca said to him, in praise of his exertion, "Tia-Huanacu; rest thou, Huanacu;" thus comparing his celerity to the fleetness of that animal.

Mayta conquered the Cacyaviri, Mallanca, and Huarina, 16° 45' S. 69° 30' W., on the eastern shore of Lake Titicaca. In the west his army was victorious, particularly over the Cuchuna. Having made himself master of the districts of Llaricassa, Sancavan, Solla, and all the tribes from Huaycha to Callamarca, 17° 48' S., 68° 35' W., Mayta went twenty-four leagues further to Caracollo and the lake of Parca (Paria 19° 20' S.), through the country of the Chaccas; thence, turning east, entered the lands of the Antis, a nation remarkable for cruelty to their prisoners. Valera says: they were cannibals, and never conquered by the Incas. Ludewig[1] calls the Antis, " Brazilian Indians on the eastern slopes of the Andes." Some nations in this direction submitted to the Inca, even to the valley of Chuquiapa. He threw a swinging bridge over the Apurimac to the west of Cuzco, and having traversed the desert of Conti-suyu, he subjected the peaceful people of Tanima, Gotahuaci, Parihuana-cocha, Puma-tampa, Arum-Callahua, unto the valley of Arcypa or Arequipa[2], 16° 17′ S., 72° W. Mayta was succeeded by his son.

5. Inca-Capac-Yupanqui, reigned 41 years, died 1197, A.D. His wife was Curyllpay. His first conquests were over the Yanahuara. The extended country of the Aymará nations about Lake Titicaca fell under his sway, where eighty tribes in vain assembled to oppose him. The Aymará country was called by the Incas Uma-Suyo, land of waters, that is, of Lake Titicaca and its rivers.

He sent an army, under his brother Auqui-(prince)-Titu, to Colatampa and Colana, south-west of Cuzco, inhabited by a portion of the Quichua nation, which was conquered. This same army entered the country of the Huamanpalpa, and the lands of these tribes on both sides of the river Amancay, also of Quichua origin, and conquered them.

The valleys of Huacari, Uvina[3], Camaná, 16° 12′ S., Carivillé, Pietaquellca, as well as the valleys of the Pacific, submitted to his arms.

The Inca went himself against the people of Lake Paria. He traversed the districts of Tapac-ric and Cocha-pampa, 18° 20′ S., and entered the country of Chayanta, 18° 55′ S., 67° 30′ W., where the curacas, or chiefs, hastened to do homage. Covered with glory, the Inca returned to Cuzco, whilst his son, Roca, conquered the countries of Curahuari, Amancay, Sura, Apucara, Runcana, and Hatunrucasca; from whence he descended to the coast, subjecting the valley of Mansaca, as well as the country between it and Arequipa. Capac Yupanqui made a statue of gold, and called it Inti-lapi.

6. Inca Roca, reigned fifty-one years, died 1249, A.D. His wife was Coya Micay. He went against Chinchasuya, Tacmara, Quinullai, Cochacaca, and Curumpa. He was also successful in Anta-hualla, inhabited by the Chancas. He went to the east of Cuzco, reducing

---

[1] Langue des Antis (Echoratos), vocab. 16, pp. 290, 291, of Castelnau, vol. v. Appendice.

[2] Arequipa is at the foot of its volcanic mountain. Earthquakes are severe and frequent.

[3] In 1600, occurred the very great irruption of the volcano of Guaynaputina, in the curacy of Omate (probably the Uvinas of Pentland); ashes fell more than ninety miles distant. The earthquakes were very severe.

the small nation of Challapampa, and took possession of Havisca and Tuna. His last expedition was into Charcas, where he reduced the Picunca, Muyamaya, Misqui, &c., to Chuquisaca.

7. His son, Inca Yahuar-Huacac succeeded him. He reigned forty years, and died 1297, A.D. His wife was the Coya Chichia. His brother Mayta conquered Colla-suyu, which is between Arequipa and Atacama. The Inca's eldest son, afterwards known as Viracocha, gave him much trouble, when he was exiled to Chita, where he remained three years. About this time, the Chancas, Uramarcas, and others, rebelled against the Inca, and marched upon Cuzco. The Inca retreated to Colla-suyu, and the people of Cuzco fled from the city; when some of them met Viracocha, informing him of the revolt, as well as the flight of his father, whom he succeeded in joining, and persuaded all the Incas of royal blood, amounting to four thousand, to return with him to Cuzco, where he formed an army of ten thousand men. The Quichuas, Aymarás, Catacampas, Cotanecas, and others, twenty thousand strong, joined the standard of Viracocha; battle was given to the Chancas, who were defeated at Yahuac-pampa, or field of blood. Viracocha now took the government of the empire into his own hands, and sent his father to a place of retirement at Muyna. It would appear that Viracocha had some share in this rebellion against his father.

8. Inca Viracocha, from the phantom king he said had appeared to him when in exile. He reigned sixty-three years, and died in 1338. His Queen, was Coya Runta, fair or as white as an egg. The Inca Ripac is sometimes alluded to, who may be the same as Viracocha, and that he conquered Tucuman. The Inca Urco, son of Viracocha, was deposed after eleven days, being incapable of governing. Viracocha built a palace in the valley of Muyna. He resolved to subject the country of Carama, Uullaca, Chica, and Llipi (Lipes), 21° 40' S., 68° 45' W., giving the command to his brother Palmac-Mayta, or, he who flies. The Inca proceeded to the north of Cuzco, making himself master of Huaytara, Pocra, and Huamanca (Guamanga), 13° S., 74° W. He cut a canal from the mountains of Parcas to Rucanes. He then went to Charcas, where he received an embassy from the King of Tucma (Tucuman), 27° S., 65° W., who became subject to him. Hualla, a chief, not contented with the government of Viracocha, persuaded many to emigrate with him, which they did, and probably went in an eastern direction. The chief of Charcas also retired two hundred leagues from his own country; and Viracocha ordered other nations to take possession of the vacated lands.

The tomb of Viracocha was in the valley of Xaxahuma, six leagues from Cuzco; it was opened by Gonzalo Pizarro, who plundered it of its riches. Garcilasso, who saw the bodies of Viracocha, Yupanqui, and Huayna-Capac, says that the first must have been very old when he died, for his hair was as white as snow.

9. Pacha-cutec (change world) succeeded his father, Viracocha. He reigned sixty years, and died 1400, A.D. His wife was Coya Anavarqui. His first conquests were over the Huama, and the country of Sansa or Jauja, 11° 50′ S., 75° 10′ W.; also over the wandering tribes Churcupu, Amarna, and Huayllas, 9° S., Pisco-pampa, Chuncuca Huamachaca (Guamachuco) 7° 45′ S., 78° 10′ W. The victorious army then entered the country of Cassa-marca, 7° 10′ S., 78° 30′ W., and Yauyu. In the third war, the people of Ica, 14° 10′ S., and Pisco, 13° 45′ S., on the coast, submitted without opposition. The Chinchas, about 13° 25′ S., also, after some resistance. The Inca's army marched into the valleys of Runahuac, Huarca, Malla, and Chilca, 12° 30′ S., where the chief, Chuqui-Manca, after a siege of eight months, was conquered.

The valleys of Pachacamac, Rimac-Malca, Chancay, and Huaman, composed a State under Quis-manca, who became the ally of the Inca.

Quis-manca had a temple at Pacha-camac, and another in honour of the oracle Rincac of Rimac.

This Inca's army entered the country of an old enemy, that of the powerful Chincu or Chimu, who possessed the valleys of Pumunca, Huallmi, and Huarapa (Trujillo), 8° 10′ S., near Guambacho, the Inca defeated the last Chimu of Trujillo.

The Quichua language was now becoming pretty generally known among the conquered nations; but the Chinchasuyo of the coast, and the Aymará of the Collas, Paiquinas, &c., were still spoken by large numbers; indeed, the Aymarás held the Quichua language, of Cuzco, in contempt. It is said by some writers that the Incas had a secret language of their own, which is supposed to be lost; as I have supposed the first Inca may have been of Aymará origin, his language is what has been called a secret one, was probably one of the Aymará dialects.

10. Yupanqui, son of Pacha-cutec, reigned thirty-nine years, died 1439. His queen was Chimpu Ocallo. (Chimpu is a coloured thread or fringe, the redness of the sky, the halo round the sun or moon.) The Musas became his allies, he marched against the Chirihuanos (of the Guarani family), but was not successful. He then projected an inroad into Chile, about 1440, giving the command of the army to Sinchicura, who marched over a portion of the desert of Atacama, and subjected the Copayapenicas (Capiapo), the Cuquinpu (Coquimbo); and his army went as far as the river Maulli (Maule), where the Puru-

macuas, Antalli, Pienca, and Canquis (Araucanos) formed a coalition, and, after much fighting, forced the Peruvian monarch to fix his somewhat problematical boundary at the river Maule. He was succeeded by his son

11. Inca Tupac-Yupanqui (the brilliant). He reigned thirty-nine years, and died 1439. His wife was Coya Ocllo. He sent expeditions against the Huacrachuca, Chuchapuya (Chachapoyas) 6° 15' S., 77° 10' W., and other places in that direction; also against Huanucu 10° S., 75° 40' W.; the Canuaris, their capital, was in 2° 57' S., where Cuenca now stands, and Tumipampa. He gave the command of an army, for the conquest of Quito, to his son, Huayna Capac.

12. Inca Huayna Capac (the youthful). It is said that he had four wives — 1. Pileu (a wreath of flowers); 2. Huaca (sacred); 3. Rava Ocallo, the mother of Huasca; 4. Paccha, the daughter of the conquered Scyri of Quito, and mother of Atahualpa. He reigned fifty years, and died in 1525, A.D.

This Inca added to his empire Quito, and lands to the north; the country between the Chimus and Ympris (Tumbez); the neighbouring tribes of Chunana, Chintuy, Collonche and others, became his vassals, as well as those of the island of Puná, whose chief was Tumpalla. Lastly, he turned his arms against the country of Manta, inhabited by the Apechique, Pichusi, Sava, Pampahuaci, Sarumisa, and Passau.

In the Equador section, I have noticed some of the more salient points of the history of this Inca, as connected with his conquest of Quito. Huayna-Capac, being at Tumipampa, in Quito, the news was brought to him of the appearance of the Spaniards on his coasts. He died shortly afterwards. The kingdom of Quito was given to Atahualpa; the empire of Peru to Huasca.

13. Inca Inti-Cusi-Huallpa, or Huasca,—this last word means a chain or rope. Tradition relates that to commemorate his coming of age, a golden chain was made long enough to go round the great square Cuzco. He reigned eight years, when he became the prisoner of his brother Atahualpa, by whose order, it is supposed, he was killed, in 1533, at Andamarca.

14. Inca Atahualpa. He reigned eight years, including one year and four months over the empire of Peru; and was strangled by order of Pizarro, the 29th of August, 1533. Like most of the incarial family, he is said to have been handsome. His manners were elegant, and his perception remarkably quick and clear. Brave and active in war; he was also sagacious in politics.

15. Manco Capac II., brother of Huasca, killed by some of Almagro's followers, about 1544.

16. Inca Toparpa, brother of Atahualpa, died on his way from Cuzco to Cajamarca.

Manco-Capac II. was succeeded by his three sons, Sayri-Tupac, Cusi-Titu-Yupanqui, and Tupac-Amaru, who reigned with a slight shadow of royal dignity. The last was beheaded, in 1571, by order of Toledo, fifth viceroy of Peru.

The most eminent period of the dynasty of the Incas is the reign of Huayna-Capac.[1] The warlike and civil works of so noted a sovereign deserves to be recorded by an eloquent pen; and his biography,[2] compiled with the necessary circumspection, would throw more light upon the ancient Peruvian history, than all the memorials, relations, and commentaries, which embrace so many indigestible folios filled with contradictions, errors, and fables.

Under the dominion of Huayna-Capac, the empire attained its greatest height and prosperity; extending from the river Andasmayo, north of Quito, to the river Maule, in Chile, embracing a distance of eight hundred leagues (which surpassed by some degrees the greatest extent of Europe), and, bounded in all its western extent by the Pacific Ocean, extended to the pampas of Tucuman, on the south-east, and to the rivers Ucayali and Marañon on the north-east. This vast empire contained ten or eleven millions of inhabitants, a number which rapidly diminished after the conquest, as, in the year 1580, the census, made by order of Philip II., by the Archbishop Loaiza, does not show more than 8,280,000 souls.

The population diminished in the course of time to less than one half; and, in the main, we may admit, that the valleys of the Peruvian coast contain positively but the tenth part, or even less, of what they contained in the time of the Incas. The valley of Santa, for instance, held 700,000 souls; and, at the present day, the number of its inhabitants does not amount to 1,200.

According to Father Melendez, there were found, shortly after the conquest, in the parish of Aucullama, of the province of Chancay, 30,000 individuals paying tribute, that is, men of more than eighteen or twenty years. At present they number 425 inhabitants, and among them 320 negroes.

For a period of three centuries Spain received hoards of gold and silver from her American possessions, produced principally by forced Indian labour. During such a lapse of time, some progress, we might expect, would have been made in the position of the native inhabitants of the

---

[1] Rivero and Tschudi.
[2] Some good materials for this history of Huayna-Capac will be found in Velasco's His. de Quito.

soil, if only in the more useful arts; but no such change occurred; all was stultified by the tyrannous, cruel, and exacting character of the Spanish rulers, the gloom of the cloister, and the wickedness of the Inquisition.

With the distracted political position of Spain at the commencement of the present century, the South Americans, aided by the Indians, also assisted from England principally with loans of money and men, threw off the yoke of the Spanish tyranny, erecting the vice-royalties into republics.

There have been occasional risings of the Indians in Peru. That of Tupac-amaru, in 1780; he wrote from Tinta a long letter to the Visitador Areche, in which the sufferings of the Indians are stated in a calm, manly way, and remedies suggested; but no ear was given to the appeal of humanity. Tupac-amaru was betrayed and cruelly butchered with his family, and the greater part of his followers. There was another rising under Puma-cagua, in 1814; the Indians were beaten, and their chief shot, 11th March, 1815.

If the origin of the Incas is involved in fables and traditions, still more difficult is it to give an idea of the Pre-Incarial, and of contemporary nations with the Incas. The Inca Peruvians, or those of Cuzco, were taught by their regal and theocratic rulers, that the first Inca and his sister wife, had been sent from the sun to govern them. We are told that, before the arrival of these children of the sun, Peru was divided among several nations, wandering and fixed, rude and ferocious, ignorant of all industry and culture, more resembling brutes than the human race. This character may have been that of some of the nations; but there were others who lived in large cities, and had a civilisation, religion, and language different from that of the Incas. I will only instance here that there must have been a very ancient nation, the builders of Tia-Huanacu, of whom we know nothing. There are ruins on the shores and islands of Lake Titicaca as old perhaps as those of Tia-Huanacu; and the Incarial city of Cuzco may have been built on the ruins of a nation passed away ere the Incas appeared. There is another spot in this direction, that which holds the considerable ruins of Ollantay-tambo; by some it is supposed that a chief who ruled here, was contempory with the Inca Pachacutec who reigned in Cuzco in 1400, A.D., but the date goes farther back than this, not for the builders, but for the last independent occupiers.

Tradition has preserved the circumstances connected with a precious dramatic composition, said to have been performed before the court of Huayna-Capac, of the play of "Apu Ollanta," the lord of Ollantay, whose ancestors, probably, built Ollantay-tambo. The story of

Ollantay's love for Cusi-Collur (joyful star), the daughter of the Inca, Pachacutec, bears the title of "Ollanta, or the severity of a Father and the generosity of a King." A portion has been elegantly translated from the Quichua by Mr. Markham,[1] in his interesting work, the pages of which shed fresh charms over the history of the worshippers of the brilliant Inti. Allied to Ollantay is the Usca-Paucar, or the loves of the golden flowers; the Yaravies or melodies, and the Cachuas or songs, we may look upon as Incarial.

Turn we to old and enigmatic Huanuco, in 9° N., with its six stone portals, one inside the other; said to have been conquered by the Inca Tupac-Yupanqui.

Descend we to the coast, to the country of the Chimu-Canchus, whose principal city was in the valley of Trujillo. It took the ninth Inca a long period, and with large armies, to make them his allies. In this region is found a peculiar civilisation, architecture and language.

Coming south along the coast, we find other nations, such as those governed by the Cuiz or Curys-Mancus, rulers of Runa-huauac (the present Lunahuana), about where Lima now stands; their ancestors, the originators of the celebrated temple to Pachacamac, the creator of the world, which, when the later Incas conquered that part of Peru, found it prudent not to demolish, but rather to erect a temple to the sun by its side. South again of these were the Chincha nations, the Chuqui-Mancu rulers, living about the vicinity of Cañete.

Between these and the commencement of the nations of Chile, were some Aymará tribes, who appear to have descended from the Andean regions, the present province of Tarapacá being still inhabited by them.

In my paper to the Ethnological Society,[2] in May, 1852, I entered into an examination of some points of Peruvian history. I opposed such writers as Marco Polo in olden, and Rankin in modern times, and who have spoken so decidedly as to the Asiatic origin of the Peruvians in the thirteenth century; they asserting that Manco-Capac was the son of Ghengis Khan, and came with elephants![3] and that the term Inca comes from the Mongol word Ungut! also, that Montezuma was the grandson of Askam, a noble of Tangut! More than one author has written on the identity of the people of America with the Tyrians.[4]

---

[1] Cuzco and Lima, London, 1856.

[2] Obs. on the History of the Incas, &c., vol. III., 1854, in Ethno. Journal.

[3] I have already, at p. 80, adverted to the supposed elephant's bones (which are fossil) found in various parts of America.

[4] Ancient American History, by George Jones, London, 1824. See European Colonization of America in Ante-Historic Times, by Zestermann, of Leipsic, with Critical Obs. by E. G. Squire, Amer. Ethno. Soc., April, 1851.

I also dwelt on the view that the Inca dynasty was rather modern, and adverted to the Pintados or Indian Pictography observed by me, in the province of Tarapacá, South Peru, in 1827.

The reader will now please to go with me south, along the coast of the Pacific from the green shores of Equador, and in sight of the sandy desert of Sechura. In about 8° S. we pass the country of the Chimus; Lima and the ruins of Pachacamac in 12°, where the Curys-mancus were the rulers; and in 14° S., the Chincha country, formerly governed by their Chuqui-Mancus, which region has become so interesting, as yielding such vast quantities of guano.

I have to make a few observations on Lima, the Guano Islands, &c.; I shall then explore the Indian tombs of Arica, proceed to Tarapacá, in South Peru, examining into its antiquarian, ethnological and other matters.

Lima is in about 12° S., six miles from the port of Callao, from which there is a railway to the capital. It has a population of some 55,000, composed of descendants of the Spaniards, Indians, Mestizos, Negroes, Mulattos, Quarterones, Quinterones, Zambos, &c. Since the separation of Peru from Old Spain, foreigners of all nations have settled in the country; there are many Chinese as servants and labourers.

In 1600, there were 14,262 souls; 1700, 37,259; 1790, 52,627; 1820, 64.000; 1836, 54,618.

The first good account we have of Lima and Callao, its port, is by Frezier, 1712-1714. Lima is built on a plain in the valley of Rimac, the name of a noted Indian oracle, whence by corruption, says Frezier, and through the difficulty those people found in pronouncing the letter R as harshly as the Spaniards, came the name of Lima. I would observe, that it is more likely that the Inca or Quichua people found a difficulty in pronouncing the R of the nation they subdued here, ruled over by the Curys-mancus. Pizarro, when he founded Lima, called it the City of the Kings, from the King and Queen of Spain. In 1682, when the Duke de la Palata made his entry as viceroy, one of the principal streets he had to pass through was paved with ingots of silver, valued at £16,000,000. The Inquisition was established in 1569, its name giving terror everywhere. First, the informer was reckoned as a witness; second, the accused knew not their accusers; third, they were not confronted with witnesses.

In 1735-40 we have, in the "Brothers Ulloa's Voyage to South America," another good description of Lima. Stevenson also gives interesting details. A small annual volume, the "Calendario y Guia de Forasteros," is a useful reference. In 1839 appeared the "Estadistica de Lima," by Urrutia, in which there is much recent information given by a native. The last is that by Mr. Markham, in his "Cuzco and Lima," published in 1856, to which work I must refer my readers who wish to be initiated into particulars as to the present political and social character of Peru. It will be seen that Lima has often been well described; still I will mention a laconic idea of it, that it is the heaven of women, purgatory of men, and hell of jackasses—or that the Limeñas are beautiful, the men enslaved by them, and the donkeys are cruelly cudgelled by the negroes. In ".Heylin's Cosmographie," 1654, England is called the paradise of women, purgatory of servants, and hell of horses.

I must confess that I was struck with the peculiar, fascinating appearance of the Limeñas, added to which were feet of from $4\frac{1}{2}$ to $5\frac{1}{2}$ inches![1]

Let the unsuspecting youth, particularly if he be a foreigner, beware in particular of the Calle del Peligro, the street of danger—not from the stilletto, but from sparkling eyes, beautiful figures, and small feet; and, if he understands Spanish, he will be enchanted with the Syren song of the Limeña.

Stevenson[2] says that portion of the Plaza allotted to the flower sellers is appropriately called the Calle del Peligro; for here the gentle fair resort, and their gallant swains watch the favourable opportunity of presenting to them the choicest gifts of Flora. This locality, at an early hour in the morning, is truly enchanting. The fragrance of the flowers, their beauty and quantity, and the concourse of lovely women, persuade a stranger that he has found the muses wandering in gardens of delight! The charming climate near the coast[3], the vicinity to the mountains, where all climates may be found, from the ever-during snow to perpetual sunshine, send their abundant and rich produce to this cornucopia of Ceres and Pomona.

I here found the famed chirimoya in its greatest perfection. It takes its name from chiri, cold, and muhu, seed—or cold-seeded. It is a species of anona. They may be seen at times weighing as much as two pounds, and contain about seventy black seeds. This is called the queen of fruits by some; by others as having that happy mixture of sweetness and acidity, with delightful scent, which forms the perfection of fruits. Mr. Markham denominates it as "spiritualised strawberries." The flowers most in use by the Limeñas are those of the chirimoya, the scent being exquisite.

---

[1] The very small feet (in Chile) are sometimes attributed to mixture with Indian blood. "Smith's Chile and the Auracanians," 245.

[2] I. 227.

[3] Maximum temp. 78°, minimum 62°.

Pizarro founded Lima on Monday, January 18th, 1535, which proceeding was confirmed by Charles V. 7th December, 1537. The conqueror of Peru built himself a residence about two hundred yards from the river Rimac, opposite to where the Palace of the Viceroys was built. The remains may yet be seen in the Callejon de Petateros, mat-maker's alley.

Prescott[1], who follows the Spanish writers, says, Pizarro received a wound in his throat, and reeling sunk on the floor, when a stroke more friendly than the rest put an end to his existence, and, in a note, Borregon struck him on the back of the head with a water-jar. In the "Estadistica de Lima," p. 140, 1839, it is mentioned: it appeared to Juan Sanchez Borregon, that Pizarro was not dead, so he smashed his face in (desbarató la cara) with a water-jar that stood on a table. His body, begged as a favour, was wrapped in a coarse frieze, and after having been tied it was carried on the back of a negro, by the false door, known as that of the fish-market, to that spot in the cathedral called the Naranjos (where criminals were buried), when he was deposited in a hole, and covered with earth. Years afterwards his bones were put into a vault, and subsequently placed under the high altar in the cathedral. At page 68 of the Estadistica, when describing the cathedral, it says: "Under the choir is the Panteon where are preserved the remains of archbishops, canons, and the *head* of the conquistador Pizarro."

When in Lima, I failed to get admittance to what is called Pizarro's tomb, a larger sum of money being demanded by the sacristan than I cared to give, particularly as it was very uncertain that the *body* was there. However, parties are made up to visit the said tomb, and a friend of mine told me that he explored the vaults, and saw the so-called body of Pizarro, dressed in Spanish costume, when one of the visitors purloined a button from the vest; at another period, among other things taken from this body, was one of the little fingers. It is admitted on some authority, that the head is there, but as to the body, it is most questionable.

In the Museum of New Granada, is the banner with which Pizarro led on his band[2] when he entered Cajamarca.

In June, 1859, General O'Brien (who had been aide-de-camp to General San Martin) showed me in London, the large and rich umbrella-formed canopy, which was held over Pizarro when he went abroad in state; this was given to O'Brien when the patriots entered Lima as conquerors.

---

[1] Conq. Peru ii., 117.
[2] Holton's New Granada, 159.

Perhaps a few lines may not be out of place regarding the present ruler of Peru, General Don Ramon Castilla. He is the son of Pedro Castilla, of Tarapacá, who lived principally at the amalgamating works of La Tirana, and worked the llampos and gransos (refuse silver ores) of the mines of El Carmen. He discovered the class of ore called lecheador (chloro-bromide of silver).

Yesqueros, a sort of tinder-box, were not in general use, and, as Pedro Castilla was a great smoker, he used to carry a lighted piece of dried mule dung from La Tirana to the mines. The present president of Peru was his father's leñatero or wood-cutter; he enlisted in the royalist army and attained the rank of sergeant. When the war of independence broke out, he received a commission from the patriots. In 1826 I found Don Ramon Castilla as Intendente of his native province of Tarapacá, and under his auspices Mr. George Smith and myself surveyed the province.[1] I did not again see him until 1854, in Lima, when he was on the eve of upsetting President Echenique.

In 1846 Castilla was elected president of Peru and restored peace after a long period of anarchy and civil war. He retained power until 1851, when General Echenique became president. In 1854 Castilla, assisted principally by Elias, after several encounters and extensive marchings, beat Echenique at the battle of La Palma, near Chorillos, entering Lima in triumph in January, 1855. Castilla abolished the capitation tax on the Indians, and put an end to slavery.

LITERATURE.—Of modern Peruvian authorship, I will first allude to an extraordinary work "A Defence of Governments against the pretensions of the Court of Rome," in six volumes; there is also a "Compendio,"[2] in one volume, both by the priest Dr. Francisco de Paula Vigil; he was excommunicated for this, by Pius Nono, in 1851; but the Peruvian government ignored the papal document, "Ad perpetuam rei memoriam." Vigil had been in ill health for some time, however, when the excommunication was fulminated against him, he regained his health and answered the "Beatissimo Patri," in a most temperate manner: his reply is a fine specimen of sound reasoning, and most eloquent are his words. I had the pleasure of Dr. Vigil's acquaintance, in Lima, where he quietly superintends the national library, beloved by all who know him.

In the chapter "Proyectos y Decretos," among the latter are the following:

---

[1] See my Southern Peru, Geographical Soc. Journal, 1851.

[2] "Defensa de la Autoridad de los Gobiernos, contra las pretensiones de la Curia Romana, por Franscisco de Paula G. Vigil." Lima, 1852.

Sundays only to be recognized as feast days. No ostentation at funerals. Bishops not to publish their edicts or pastorals without permission of the government, nor ordain more priests than absolutely necessary. A bishop's income to be two hundred pounds, paid by the State; as also that of the priests. Charges for marriages and burials, one half the present prices. No ecclesiastical immunities. Those leading a monastic life, not to vote at elections. Monastic life, conditional only. Neither monasteries or convents to inherit property. Marriage to be a civil contract. Married men and widowers to be preferred for public employment. The father who has six children, to pay half taxes; he who has nine, a third; he who has twelve, none. In mixed marriages, or between Catholics and Christians not Catholics, should the Ordinary object to give permission, the marriage can take place before the civil authorities. The nation recognizes as lawful the marriage of priests. A Father, requiring the assistance of a son, such not to enter monastic life. Third article of the Constitution to be thus read:—The religion of the State is that professed by the Roman Catholic Apostolic Church; the public profession of other religions not to be excluded. The dead to be buried in one burial ground, which in future need not to be consecrated.

Colonel Espinosa is the author of an interesting political work, published in Lima, 1851, "La Herencia Española," or what Spain has bequeathed to its colonies, namely, indolence, pride, and love of show; The origin of bad government in South America is, that Spain is the worst governed country in the world—that the Spanish Americans believe themselves to be a very superior people, and will not acknowledge their sad inferiority in comparison with the people of Europe.

The legal works of J. S. Santistevan,[1] particularly his "Derecho Peruano," have earned for him the name of the Peruvian Blackstone. Mariano Paz Soldan published, in New York, in 1853, an important report on the penitentiaries of the United States, as applicable to Peru. Manuel Bilbao has most eloquently written the biography of the unfortunate General Salaverry, who became a victim of civil war in 1836. Bustamante[2] must not be forgotten, his contribution is a literary curiosity; the record of his wanderings in various parts of the world, and rather original observations thereon.

The Peruvians are much given to pamphleteering and verse making; but the poetry of Marquez, particularly the "Flor de Abel," is much prized. It is in defence of innocence and charity, in a heroic combat

---

[1] Derecho Peruano, Piura, 1853.
[2] Apuntes y observaciones, &c. Paris 1849.

against the worldly selfishness that devours us. A brother poet is Althaus; his most important composition is in prose, "To a Mother," many poems, including the "Canto Biblico," said to resemble some of the Hebrew melodies of Byron, and has the advantage that the Spanish is a more suitable language than the English for the lamentations of the Captives of Babylon.

In 1851, was published, at Vienna, the very important "Antigüedades Peruanas," by M. E. de Rivero and Dr. Tschudi, in folio, with a large atlas of coloured plates. This work has been translated into English by Dr. Hawks, of New York. It is indeed a most valuable acquisition to ancient Peruvian history; and truly, they say, in their dedication to the Sovereign Congress of Peru, "centuries have passed without the possession by Peru of a collection of such of her ancient architectural monuments, as have escaped the ravages of time, avarice, and superstition. These silent, yet eloquent, witnesses reveal the history of past successes, and demonstrate the intelligence, power, and grandeur of the nation once ruled by the Incas."

I will now make a few observations on the "Mercurio Peruano" and "Lima por dentro y fuera." One of the first newspapers that appeared in Lima was the "Diario Economico," by Jayme Bausate; but, in 1791, commenced the publication of an important periodical, the "Mercurio Peruano." About the same time was established the Academical Society, which offered gold and silver medals for various researches. The Mercurio was only allowed to continue some three years, issuing three volumes annually. This learned work met with great opposition, more especially from the church, on account of the freedom it introduced into the discussions of the variety of subjects of polity, &c.

By the capture of the Spanish galleon, "Santiago," in 1793, from Lima to Cadiz, by the English, a collection of the Mercurio came into the possession of a Mr. Skinner, of Tottenham, who gave extracts in the Monthly Magazine, 1797-8. In 1805, he translated the more important papers in a quarto volume, with plates, entitled "The present state of Peru," from which I here give the heads only of the principal subject matter.

General idea of Peru, including produce of the mines. Ancient monuments, where it is stated that the ruins of Tia-Huanacu are unquestionably anterior to the times of the Incas; in Chachapoyas is a stone building with unwieldly busts. Geography. Botany. Zoology, describes the Llama family. Alludes to the fossil bones at Manta, Tarija, and Chichas. Account of a giant in New Granada, Pedro Cano, over seven feet five inches. Basilio Huaylas, a Peruvian giant, more than seven feet two inches, his limbs out of all due proportion (a drawing is given). Mineralogy, condition of the miners. Commerce, in 1780, including the galleons, 16,375 tons of shipping belonged to the port of Callao; 2000 quintals of cinchona bark annually exported. Contraband trade. Description of Lima, statistics, coffee houses established in 1771, maté or paraguay tea had previously been used. Customs and manners. Calle del Peligro, or the promenade of beauty. Complaint of a husband of his wife, and hers also, shows what were the peculiar domestic relations. Indians, their ideas of religion. Indians of the Pampa del Sacramento and of the Andes. Negroes of Lima. Province of Guamalies. Valley of Vitoc. Biographies, that of Father Menacho, born in Lima, 1565; at six he could read, write, cipher, and draw; his statue was prodigious; at seven he appeared to have attained his fifteenth year; at five and twenty he had grown to such proportion that there was no person in Peru whom he did not, like Saul, exceed from the shoulder upwards; at seventeen he entered the Jesuits' college; he became professor of theology at Cuzco; he had a wonderful memory, he died in 1626. Antonio L. Pinelo, an indefatigable writer on jurisprudence and history; he was appointed principal chronologist of the Indies. Fray Castillo, a poet: one of his modes of versifying was to touch a guitar, and at the close of the day to recapitulate what he had done, heard, or discussed, without omitting any of the circumstances, which he constantly realized with grace and ingenuity. Lopez: he possessed more than a common share of mathematical knowledge, and having heard that the Paris Academy had offered a considerable premium to him who should discover, for the benefit of the longitudes at sea, the quadrature of the circle, he began to draw lines, make calculations, forming tables, circles, and filling reams upon reams of paper with figures—in a word, he became crazy. He died in 1790, after having toiled uselessly for fifty years. Castro-Monte, of Huaraz, died at 133 years of age. He had never tasted wine or strong liquors. Earthquakes; Missions of Caxamarquilla; Explorations of the Huallaga to the lake of the Gran Cocama, with a map; Of the Marañon and Ucayali to the tribes of Manoa; from Huanuco into the mountains, 1631; from Jauja by Andamarca, 1673; from Huanta, 1671; from Chachapoyas to the junction of the rivers Mayobamba and Huallaga, 1560 to 1685; Descent of the Marañon from Tomependa to the town and lake of Cocama; Descent by the Marañon to Tefe, a Portuguese colony; entrance into the mountains of Huamalies; from Pataz to Caxamarquilla; Itinerary from Chavin to Chicoplaya—these explorations appear to be worthy the attention of modern geographers.

Some years since a copy of the curious sarcastic poem "Lima por dentro y fuera," by Simon Ayanque (a fictitious name), fell into my hands. I intended at that period to have given some account of it, but my copy was stolen. When lately in Peru I procured another copy, printed in Madrid, 1836. On making inquiries as to the author I was informed that his real name was Atnraya an Andalucian. He was a lawyer, and had visited all the Spanish colonies. Having made money in Mexico, he went to Lima, but, in the over-enjoyment of pleasure in the luxurious capital of Peru, became poor, and, suffering for his past conduct, wrote the work about 1790-5. My informant's father procured a MS. copy of the work, taking it to Spain about that period. It is thought the poet died about 1795, and it is said that after his death in Lima, his voluminous MSS., principally severe critiques upon manners and customs in the Spanish colonies were destroyed by order of the then viceroy of Peru.

The only notice I have met with of this work is in the "Estadistica de Lima," 1839—"that Taralla occupies himself in pourtraying vicious people, a class he probably belonged to, if one may judge from his observations." This is not quite fair: what he did was to draw Lima and its people too true to life; and as he had been victimised and ruined, surely retaliation was no more than could be expected from poor human nature.

The following is the title: "Lima inside and out, being economical, salutary, politic and moral; which one friend offers to another, the latter having decided to leave the city of Mexico for that of Lima. A jocose and diverting work, in which, with witty conceits are described, with other things, customs, usages and artifices there and in other parts, by Simon Ayanque, for the warning of some and the amusement of all. Madrid, 1836; with an amusing address to the reader, in which, among other observations, it is stated, that if the pernicious customs of the New World are satirised, similar cases occur in the Old." The work is divided into eighteen parts; containing the will of the author, made fifteen days before his death; his epitaph and notes, 144 pages, 16mo.

He begins by asking his friend what his country has offended him in, why he leaves beautiful Mexico for Lima, an absurdity, most notable excess; to leave a glory for a well known hell, light for darkness, life for death, joy for torments, or

> Por una sombra, una luz,
> Por un eclipse, un lucero.
> Por una muerte, una vida,
> Y un gusto, por un tormento.

The voyage from Acapulco to Paita is described, also the burning desert of Sechura; that he will see many nobles in Trujillo, and alludes to their Quixotic character; that in the market flour and meat are bartered for eggs and bread; also, cats for dogs.

Now you are in Lima at last; I tell thee no falsehood, here will be the last of you, like unto many others. Speaks of the tambo (inn) of the Sun, where the sun (its sign) can be seen at all seasons; for in winter the atmosphere is so misty, that the sun is seldom observed. Of the Calle del Peligro, in a note it is said, in front of the cathedral is a path, on each side of which are Indian women who sell fruit and flowers, called the path or street of danger, on account of the risk the unguarded run from the beautiful women who promenade there.

> Que pasas por un café
> Y dices acá fé? niego;
> Porque acá fé no se halla
> Ni en uno ni otro sexo.

You pass a café (coffee-house), and you say, acá fé (is there good faith here)? I deny it; because acá fé (good faith here) is not to be found in man or woman.

Lima is described as a dirty city; the gutters in the streets pestiferous, broken conduits, dunghills, heaps of mud, myriads of flies, wet mist, the people pale and melancholy, fleas in abundance in summer; the dogs so lazy, that they will not get out of the way of carriage wheels. Señas or tokens were used at shops. The puchero or bunch of flowers, wrapped in a plantain lealf, is alluded to, as the gift of the Tapada, who has her face covered, one eye only seen; the codeo, or self-invitation to take ices, &c.—

> El artificioso meneo
> Que de voluntades Conquista,

the artful wagging walk, the cause of many a conquest.

Describes the want of domestic management. The young miss wishes for roast meat for her breakfast, another, criadillas; another, pigs'-feet: this boy asks for nuts, another cakes, pastry; the Negress for panal, the Negro, brandy; the Mulatto, meat; the coachman, bread and sweets; the lady of the house demands milk, the master, toast. This system goes on for awhile, but the day arrives when bread is wanted, and their goods are pawned or sold.

The stranger gives a supper to the family who had invited him to dinner. This is a codeo, or loafing on a grand scale. The said family invite their relation, friends, acquaintances and hangers-on; as, their cousin, the priest; the collegian, a relative; the officer, a brother; the tradesman, a brother-in-law; the lawyer, an uncle; the father-in-law, a notary; the captain, a godfather; the doctor, a grandfather; the professor, a relative; the miner, a comrade; the neighbour, a musician; the priest, a relative; the landlord of the house, the stepfather; and the stranger is the host. Then follows what all these ask for at the café, after which, they take their victim to the fonda or hotel, where they sup, and, having got all they can out of him, they quarrel with him, call him swine, miser, wretch, savage, donkey, "Chapeton grosero," or vulgar Spaniard.

Our hero falls in love, and having been well swindled by the lady, is turned out of the house, and, under plea that he is persecuting her, he is banished from Lima by the authorities. He is advised to beware of the Moscardones, loafers or false friends of the most ungrateful stamp. General pillage of servants. Married life—the Limeñas treat their European husbands badly, marrying them for a home only and because they are industrious, not like the Limeños, who are indolent. The Limeñas' dowry of fifteen thousand dollars is amusing: value of a sofa and chairs, one thousand five hundred dollars; other articles of furniture and dress of similar fictitious value, and to obtain which, a lawsuit is necessary. If there be any children, the boy is more especially alluded to, as being the mortal enemy to every European; but, when it suited any particular purpose, that they were descended from pure Spanish blood, as, my father was a gallego, my mother born in Spain; my great-grandfather was an Andalusian, my grandfather from Asturias, my uncle from Zaragosa, my kinsman from Barcelona, I have property in Toledo, I have an uncle a cardinal, another a councillor of state, another mariscal de campo, who wrote to me by the last mail: all I have of Creole, is that of having been born here.

> Pero soy mas Español,
> Que los mismos Europeos.

But I am more of a Spaniard than they themselves. Alludes to those who call themselves white:

> Que investigando el natal
> La estirpe, y el nacimiento,
> O hai *pasas* en la cabeza,
> O *chicha* en los pies corriendo—

or that they have Indian or Negro blood. That you will see many good and men of talent poor, abandoned and wretched.

PERUVIAN ZODIAC OR LUNAR CALENDAR.—Although this interesting monument was found at Cuzco, still, as it came into the possession of

General Echinique when President of Peru, I introduce it here. The following is from my paper to the Royal Society of Antiquaries, in January, 1860:—

Mr. Markham, when in Lima, made drawings of the objects I am about to describe. He says,[1] "I have seen a golden breastplate or sun; it is of pure gold, and the figures upon it are stamped, being convex on the outer side." I. This, I suppose, may be a lunar calendar or zodiac, the only example I know of.

Mr. Markham observes,[2] "In one part of the convent of the Virgins of the Sun there was a space set apart for artificial flowers, imitated in gold with the most wonderful skill." II. One of these is a model of a circular fruit in gold. Diameter of the outer ring 3 inches, the two middle rings $2\frac{6}{10}$ inches, inner ring $2\frac{3}{10}$ inches. III. The model of the leaf of a plant in gold, $12\frac{7}{10}$ inches long, including the length of stem $5\frac{1}{2}$ inches, breadth of base of leaf $3\frac{1}{10}$ inches. IV. is a fillet or llautu of gold, worn round the head; its length is $18\frac{1}{4}$ inches. V. is a pin or tupu of gold, profusely ornamented; length 5 inches, breadth at base $2\frac{1}{2}$, at end $1\frac{3}{10}$; when entire was about 8 inches long. The figures are cut on its flat surface (B.)

The important figures here are what we know as the Maltese cross. This sort of cross was supposed by the Spaniards to denote a connexion with Christianity: however, this form of ornamentation was well known in early times among many nations in the old as well as in the new world. It may have meant, as regards the Inca Peruvians, the planet Venus (Chasca), for the Amautas or astrologers noted its movements and venerated it as a page of the sun, (Chasqui-Coyllur). The pin has some thirty-three of these stars on it; also some other figures. There are three circular compartments, the upper containing five stars, the centre a large star, the lower four small animals round a circle. This may have been the *tupu* or pin for fastening the mantle of a priestess of a temple or altar to the planet Venus.

The Incas had in Cuzco a similarly formed cross of white and red marble, three-fourths of a yard in length, which was held in great veneration. In the ruins on the island of Coati, in the Lake of Titicaca, are several cruciform figures on the walls. It is also seen on vases. The stone pan-pipes found in a tomb at Cuzco (pan-pipes were also made of cane) had twelve Maltese crosses. It would be erroneous to deduce from these crosses any inference as to a connexion between the religion of the Incas and Christianity. The cross is a figure so simple and easily represented in design and sculpture, that it exists as an ornament amongst all nations.

THE ZODIAC (A).—I will now describe what I suppose to be an incarial lunar calendar or a zodiac; it is of gold, and on a circular plate. The outer ring is $5\frac{3}{10}$ inches in diameter, the inner ring 4 inches. There are apparently four holes on the inner ring, so as to fasten it on the breast of an Inca, priest, or amauta

---

[1] Cuzco and Lima, 107.
[2] Cuzco and Lima, 123.

Bollaert's Antiq: S. America.

Inca Zodiac, of Gold.
found at Cuzco.
5 ⁷⁄₁₀ Inches diameter.

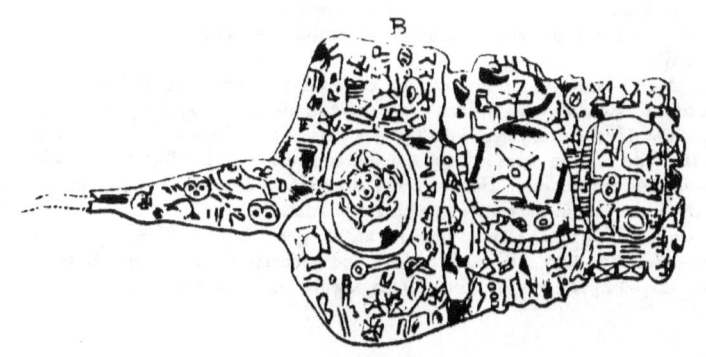

Gold Tupu, or Pin,
found at Cuzco.

(astrologer or learned man). There are apparently twenty-four compartments, large and small, including three at the top, a triangular gateway, on its right a small space with two circles and three lines; on the left three lines, and two upright ones joined. At the bottom are two spaces; figures were probably here, but looks as if worn away.

I will advert to the centre portion first. It is surmounted by the prongs of a trident, (our Aquarius is sometimes represented with a trident); on each side are four small circles; there are other four on the nose, and two more on the sides, at the base of what may be intended as pillars or ears; the circles may represent the bases of the stone pillars used as gnomons by the Incas for determining the solstices. Two large eyes, teeth showing the canines, and eight angular points; the last may be intended for the sun's rays; the whole figure represents the face of the sun.

Underneath the eyes are two faces; these may represent the first Inca and his sister-wife, the reputed children of the sun.

Description of the Zodiac in connexion with the Lunar Months of the Incarial Calendar.

1. *December.* (Raymi, a solemn dance.) The first month; it began with the winter solstice. In the space is a face or sun, a small diamond-shaped figure underneath it, and another to the right. In this month was held one of the four principal feasts of the year. The Inca Peruvians counted the months from the 20th, 21st, or 22nd, according to the solstices, until the same day of the following month, so that December included twelve days of January, or from one new moon to another.

2. *January.* (Huchhuy-poccoy, from small, and to ripen, because the corn began to form small ears.) Here is a space with an oblong figure, a quarter of a moon, and four small circles.

3. *February.* (Hatun-poccoy, from hatun, great.) The corn began to increase in size. There is a ladder-like figure, two straight and two waved lines.

4. *March.* (Paucar-huaray: paucar, beauty of flowers; huaray, figuratively, to unfold a carpet of flowers.) Here are two small spaces, one with three strokes, a half-moon figure and two circles: in the other, a square oblong and two circular ones.

5. *April.* (Ary-huay, or an ear of corn with grains of various colours.) In this month began the grain harvest; there was dancing, and deep libations of chicha. Here is a face with an angular projection, and an oblong figure difficult to describe.

6. *May.* (Aymuray, because of the conveyance of the corn to the public granaries.) Here we have the sun's face and two diamond-shaped figures.

7. *June.* (Inti-Raymi, from inti, the sun, and raymi, dance.) In this month was the third solemn feast. They rested from labour, giving themselves up to pleasure and enjoyment. Here is a sun, diamond underneath it, a diamond on left side; a square in the corner enclosing two small circles.

8. *July.* (Anta-asitua: anta, copper; asitua, great dance.) This began the summer solstice; they cultivated the land and prepared it for sowing. Here is a pear-shaped figure, a curved line, and an angular one, and three strokes.

9. *August.* (Capac-asitua: capac, powerful.) They sowed corn, potatoes, &c. Here are two longitudinal lines, and two cross lines; also, a pear-shaped figure, a curved line, an angular one, and three strokes.

10. *September.* (Umu-Raymi: umu, head.) In this month took place the enrolling of those liable to be taxed, and the verification of the prior register. It was also called Coya-raymi, for now the coyas, or princesses, and others married. Here are two small spaces, one with two diamond-shaped figures, the other with a diamond, quarter of a moon, and two curved lines.

11. *October.* (Aya-marca: aya, a corpse, and marca, to carry in arms.) Now was celebrated the feast of the dead. The potters made large vessels for the chica. In each house this beverage was made and drunk at the feasts of the following months. Here is a different sort of face of the sun, and a quarter of the moon.

12. *November.* (Capac-raymi: capac, rich; raymi, to dance.) This space is similar to the first month. Dancing and drinking were carried to great excess. They represented tragedies and comedies composed by the Amautas. The Haravec or poet composed the haravi or melodies, and cachuas, songs.

One of the dramas has been preserved; A portion will be found translated by Mr. Markham. It is called "Ollanta, or the Severity of a Father and the Generosity of a King," composed in Quichua about the beginning of the fourteenth century. The following is part of a speech by the Huillac-Umu, or high-priest of the Sun:—

"O living Sun! I watch thy course,
As it moves downwards in the heavens;
For you are now preparing
A thousand sacrificial llamas.
Their blood shall flow for thy glory.
For you, too, is gathered the herbs of the field.
Glory to thee, O living sun!"

The small compartments on either side of the triangular gateway at the top, as well as those at the bottom of the Zodiac, composed of a diamond and two lines, and two lines and two circles, may be intended for the Puchucquilla, or fourths of a moon, remaining.

We know that the Inca Peruvians divided the year into months, or quilla-huata, (moon-year); the solar being called inti-huata, (sun-year). As their lunar year fell short of the true time, they verified their calendar by solar observations, made by means of a number of cylindrical columns raised on the high land round Cuzco, which served them for taking azimuths; and by measuring their shadows, they ascertained the exact time of the solstices.

The period of the equinoxes they determined by help of a solitary pillar or gnomon placed in the centre of a circle, which was described in the area of the great Temple of the Sun, and traversed by a diameter drawn east and west.

The constellation Hyades in Taurus they called the jaw-bone of the Tapir. The Pleiades and Southern Cross were known to them.

The Mexicans had an elaborate Zodiac; the Muyscas of Bogota had a curious

---

[1] Cuzco and Lima, 174.

lunar calendar; of the other nations of America I have been unable to find that they had any such astronomical representation except this of the Inca Peruvians, and the first I have seen or heard of. The learned in ancient Peruvian history may be able to give other information regarding this, to me, curious monument of antiquity.

It has been suggested to me, that what I consider to be a zodiac may be a talisman. The Peruvian Indian had his piripiri or charms, equal to the talisman. They consisted of the Bezoar stone (biliary calculi of the llama family); yairuvies, or small black and red seeds, worn as preventives against colds and coughs; loadstone, worn by either sex, to attract lovers and keep off evil spirits; there were charms against wizards, and witches, also against poisons. The idea that this object is a talisman I do not consider of much value, but rather think that it was attached to the breast of an Inca, or principal priest of the sun, when performing his sacred duties.

GUANO.—The most important deposits are on the Chincha islands; these lay in 13° to 14° S., and twelve miles from the land. Its extraction and sale is a government monopoly, and a most ready-money source of revenue. The political party who may have possession has the command of almost any amount of funds; thus guano has become a curious political element. As an instance, in 1853-4, when General Castilla, Elias, and others succeeded in turning out President Echenique and his party, this revolutionary state of things was known as the Guano War, and the possession of the Chincha islands was the prize.

Guano, or huanu, means dung, as huanacu-huanu, excrement of the huanaco; pishu-huanu, birds' dung. Tschudi kept one of the guano birds, the sula variegata, and found its daily weight of excrement to be 3¼ to 5 ounces. Formerly, the great flights of sea birds on the coast of Peru used to astonish me; since 1841, when the first cargo of guano was sent to England from Paquique, in the "Charles Eyes," the haunts of the birds have been so disturbed by the collectors, that their numbers have much diminished.

When I lately visited the Chincha islands, there were more than two hundred vessels lading guano; the work of excavating and loading the ships was done by Chinese, said to be smuggled out of China, and brought to Peru as labourers.

Some say there is guano only for a few years; others, for a hundred years. In an article on the "guano diggings," in "Household Words," 1853, the writer estimated there were 250,000,000 tons on the Chincha islands alone, and that it would take one hundred and eighty years to clear them; so that, at the present selling price in England, £12 per ton, would give £3,000,000,000!

Mr. Geo. Peacock[1], well known on the west coast in connection with the Pacific Steam Navigation Company, his researches in the Chile coal districts, also for his surveys of the islands and coast containing the Huaneras, reported, in 1846, the following as to quantity:

On the Chincha group	18,250,000
At Chipana	280,000
Punta de Lobos	1,460,790
Huanillos	1,912,505
Pabellon de Pica	2,975,000
Puerto Ingles	1,292,500
Lobos Islands, Guanapes, &c.	7,000,000
Tons	33,170,795

This at £4 profit per ton to the Peruvian government, shows a sum of £132,683,984. From the commencement in 1841, to June, 1858, it is estimated that 2,608,659 tons had been shipped from Peru, which at £4 per ton gives £10,600,000.

Guanos are divided into three great varieties: those which have suffered little by exposure to atmospheric action, as the Peruvian; those which have lost a considerable portion of their soluble ingredients, Chile, some of the Bolivian, and the Ichaboe; and those which have lost all their ammonia.

The early shipments of Bolivian guano were about equal to the Peruvian, and were collected from near the surface. I am informed that recently very large quantities of a hard rocky material have been met with on the Bolivian coast, containing much less organic matter than the surface guano, but a great increase of phosphate. This we may look upon as the result of very old deposits.

In 1847, a curious stone slab[2] was discovered in the N. Chincha, under eighteen feet of guano; now, if we suppose this stone had been buried two hundred years, this would give a deposit by the birds of about one inch per year. It is said that guano is found from thirty to one hundred feet thick; and the general opinion is, that it has been accumulating for thousands of years.

TROPICAL SUNSET.—In the region of the Chincha islands, even at sea, it is very hot during the calm portions of the day; this is tempered by the daily cool south winds, and by the cooler land breezes at night. The sky is deep blue and clear, and hereabouts is the real Pacific Ocean.

---

[1] Official correspondence of Service, &c. Exeter, 1859.

[2] I have given a drawing of the Chincha Islands, and of this stone to "Illustrated Times," March 5th, 1859.

The sunsets at times are magnificent, and the colours so brilliant. On one occasion, in particular, the day had been cloudless, and the sun shining vividly; from a gentle breeze it became calm; and it now required, but a slight stretch of imagination, to fancy that we were sailing through a sea of the most glistening ultramarine; and, as the sun was setting, the western sky was as if on fire, causing the sea to glow with its glorious reflections. The other half of the heavens was composed of light rose and lavender colours, blending harmoniously into one another; then the change was so rapid. One sees all this wonderful beauty—in a moment it is gone, and one has to call upon a traitorous recollection for a faint description.

Arica is in 18° 20' S. Frezier, who visited the coast in 1712, thus describes the Huacas, or ancient tombs at Hilo and Arica their bodies are entire, with cloths on, and often found with gold and silver vessels. The graves are dug in the sand the depth of a man, and enclosed with a wall of dry stones, covered with wattles of cane, on which there is a layer of earth and sand; such I saw during my first visits to Arica, in 1825. In 1854, I again came here, when a railway was in construction to Tacna, and a portion of the Morro or headland was being excavated to fill up ground on the shore; by this operation, as the loose ground on the side of the Morro was broken up, an ancient cemetery was discovered in the debris, resulting from the rock of the Morro. The graves were near the surface, lined with stone, and some closed with a stone slab. The bodies were in a sitting position, completely dessicated (not embalmed), and wrapt in woollen and cotton mantles: sometimes a dog is found in the graves. The weather was extremely hot, and, whilst examining these tombs, I became ill with fever and ague, very common here, and of a bad sort, so that I could not continue my researches with the care and attention I had anticipated. Wherever a stream of water from the Cordillera comes to the coast, dense vegetation is seen just were the water may run; the decomposition of this vegetable matter produces terciana or ague.

I made a collection from these tombs, the objects are now in the British Museum; they consist of cotton and woollen cloth of various colours and patterns, ordinary pottery, small wooden idols (some gold figures of men, animals, and ornaments, I saw in the possession of a native), double pandean pipes (huayra-puhura) of cane, some other articles, and a golden coloured semi-transparent object, which has been at last determined to be the eye of the cuttle-fish; these eyes were not introduced into the head of the mummy, but deposited in the grave as something rare, beautiful, or as a huaca (sacred).

Rivero found in other parts of Peru thin plates of gold and silver painted of different colours to represent the eye, and introduced. I may here advert to what Rivero and Tschudi state, that in the mouths of some Peruvian mummies is found a rodaja (round disk) of gold, silver or copper; had we any information respecting the existence of a Peruvian Charon, we might suppose this disk was intended for the obol.

Mr. Fariss, who lately returned from the north of Peru with a collection of antiquities, informs me that, at Atequipa, 15° 35′ S., he has seen such disks of gold, with a human face on them, in the mouths, ears, and nostrils. At Huamanchuco, he found these rounded pieces of metal loose in the graves. Stevenson says, any small piece of gold which was buried with the bodies, at Huara, is generally found in their mouths.

The Crania, at Arica, were generally like those described by Tschudi, as Aymarás; but I saw two, one with a deep hollow across the centre,[1] the other nearly square.

The Morro, or headland, of Arica, is five hundred feet above the sea; its base is of gneiss, succeeded by porphyries, then horizontal layers like basalt, its flanks deeply covered with debris. An interesting feature about the Morro is the existence of fissure caves, probably formed by earthquakes. Mr. Geo. Taylor, an old resident, informs me that, in 1827, he was accompanied by a friend on a treasure trove expedition into the great cave El Infierno or hell.

They were inside a long time, and travelled about one thousand fathoms; the air was bad, and their lights would go out; at times very cold, with gusts of wind. They did not get to the end. They found large numbers of gallinazos, or turkey buzzards' nests, and much of their ordure. There is a smaller cave, which can be traversed in an hour; in this, people, when in "difficulties," political or otherwise, hide themselves.

I examined another cave at the sea-level, known as the 'Infernillos' or little hell; this is a frightful looking place, and may communicate with the others in the Morro. There is an account of a balsa being upset here by the heavy surf; the balsa was washed into "little hell," and never seen again; the man who was paddling managed to escape by clinging to the rocks.

It is probable that the great cave may have been used anciently as a place of burial, for at its mouth are painted small red figures of men, animals, &c.; and I think I observed the " Mano Colorado," or red hand:

---

[1] Ethno. Soc. Feb. 1860. "On the deformed skulls found at Wroxeter." It was thought that the general deformity of some Peruvian skulls had been produced by some outward cause after interment. What I observed at Arica may have been thus caused, as the Peruvians generally buried their dead in a sitting position.

the colouring matter of these is either oxide of iron or cinnibar. Mr. Miles,[1] in his paper on "Demigods," and in the chapter devoted to the "Mano Colorado," says, it is found in caves in Australia, in other parts of the world; and that Stevens found it in Yucutan, not drawn or painted, but stamped by the living hand.

Gilliss[2] observes, that ten miles from Arica is a place supposed to be full of Huacas. A friend wrote to him, that near Tacna is an old Indian cemetery, on the bare face of the sloping mountain, at whose base these tombs are; he noticed huge characters traced in the sand; they can be perceived and could be read with the unassisted eye, if one understood them, at a distance of ten to fifteen miles. The whole side of the mountain is covered with them. They appear to be written as are Chinese characters, in vertical lines. Some must be ten to twelve hundred feet in length, that is, each character is of that size, and looks as fresh as if just made; they are ancient Indian records, gigantic picture writing, and probably allied to the Pintados of Tarapacá.

PROVINCE OF TARAPACA.

Camarones is one of those deep and narrow ravines running from the Cordillera to the coast: this is the north boundary of the province of Tarapacá. Indian tombs are met with here, near the sea. Pisagua is another of these ravines; the stream is found generally a league from the port; but, during the rainy seasons, or the melting of snow in the Andes, it occasionally reaches the Pacific. Here, and at Alcaparosa, two leagues north, are tombs and Indian ruins. Much nitrate of soda is shipped from Pisagua.

IQUIQUE, 20° 12′ S., 70° 30′ W., var. 11° 20′ E., in the department of Moquegua (Moquingoa). This district, in the twelfth century, was included in Coya-Suyu, probably Colla-Suyu, and was starved into subjection by Maita Capac, fourth Inca. The Incarial armies, when going south to Atacama and Chile, passed through the province, and knew of its mineral riches.

In 1538, the following was communicated by Pizarro to the court of Spain: "Its inhabitants are the Cacique of Tarapacá, whose name is Sanga, including the fishermen of the coast. There are villages, called Pachica, Pinchuca and Guaviña, which are in the valley of Cato, under the Cacique, Opo. In the valley of Carvisa is the village of Camiña,

---

[1] Ethno. Soc. Journal. London, III., vol.
 United States Astronomical Expedition to Chile, I., 144.

where Ayviro and Taucari are the Caciques. There is another town called Comagnata under Ayvire; another town, Diayapo, under the Cacique, Chuqui-Chambi, with 900 Indians."

Almagro having seen the greater number of his followers on their way from Chile, across the desert of Atacama (when Tarapacá was discovered), he went by water along the coast in a vessel commanded by Nogueral de Ulluoa, and took Cuzco by surprise in 1538.

Iquique is the principal port for the shipment of nitrate of soda. It is dug up and refined some leagues distant in the interior. In 1830 only 900 tons were exported, but in 1859, 78,700 tons.

The present population of the province is about 18000, the greater portion occupied in the manufacture of nitrate of soda; then follows the agricultural, which is but limited, in consequence of the general arid character of the country; still some alfalfa or lucern, as food for cattle, conveying the nitrate to the coast, produces 100,000 dollars; the wine of Pica, 84,000; some figs, other fruit, and a little wheat are grown; however, provisions are principally brought from Chile and other parts of Peru.

The mercantile portion, including many foreigners residing at Iquique, pay 200,000 dollars or more annually to the Customs, mainly on flour. About 84,000 dollars duty were paid on wines and spirits in 1858. The Post Office of Iquique yielded in 1859, 3,130 dollars.

From 1st January to August 1st, 1859, 281 vessels entered Iquique; in all 74,420 tons.

Tarapacá, far away in the interior, is the capital, and the residence of the authorities.

The climate on the coast is temperate, owing to the cool southerly winds. In the nitrate districts the heat is great during the day, cool at night in summer, but cold in winter. In the Cordilleras, to the east, there is every gradation of temperature. Pica and Tarapacá are very hot during the day, and agues common, but generally the province is healthy.

This province was first celebrated for the rich silver mines of Huantajaya;[1] the La Fuentes alone paid in duties to the Spanish crown more than a million sterling. They sent a mass of native silver, weighing nearly thirty-three hundred weight, as a present to the king of Spain; it was rolled by hand from the mines and then allowed to fall by its own weight down the sandy side of the mountain range to Iquique; a portion of the track it made is seen to this day.

At present the province of Tarapacá is well known as producing vast quantities of nitrate of soda. In 1827, at the request of General Castilla, then Intendente of the province, Mr. George Smith and myself

---

[1] See my paper to Geological Society, 1838.

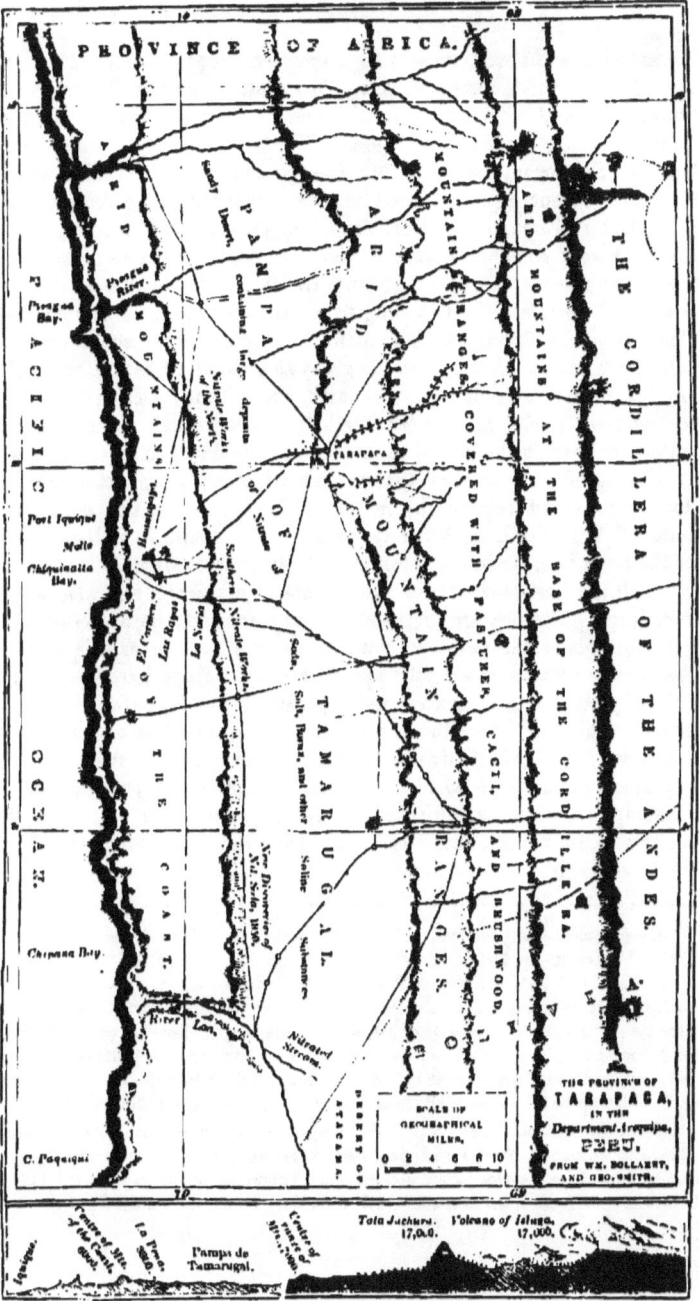

examined the district, presenting survey and report to the Peruvian government; this I extended in my Observations on the Geography of Southern Peru,[1] with map. In the notes reference is made to further information by myself and others. Whilst these pages were going through the press, my friend, Mr. George Smith, has forwarded to me the most recent account about nitrate, printed on an elaborate plan, published in Lima, of the localities in the province of Tarapacá, where the nitrate of soda and borate of lime are found, with the positions of the principal oficinas or works, and the ports the nitrate is shipped from.[2] I translate the following from his observations on the plan:—
The Pampa de Tamarugal is a plain, having a rise of about one per cent. from east to west. There is great abundance of salitre or caliche (native nitrate of soda) on the north, about Tana; also in the south to the river Loa. In the far north it is not worked, there being no water; neither in the south, on account of the distance from the coast. It is generally considered that the nitrate of soda producing ground does not extend beyond the ravine of Camarones on the north, nor south of the river Loa; however, some say it is found in Bolivia, south of the river Loa, far in the interior and distant from water. Mr. Smith gives all the positions whence the nitrate is extracted, and also where very large quantities are pretty well known to exist; he likewise notes the spots where the borate of lime is met with. He calculates that the nitrate ground covers fifty square leagues. There have been single square yards of ground that have produced nearly a ton weight of nitrate, the layer being three yards thick. If we allow only one hundred pounds weight of nitrate for each square yard, we shall have the enormous quantity of 63,000,000 tons; so that, at its present rate of consumption, there is sufficient for 1,393 years. The opinion in the country is, that the nitrate is formed from the waters that come from the Cordilleras.

---

[1] Geographical Soc. Journal, 1851; "Southern Peru," United Service Journal, 1848; "Essay on the Origin of Salt, &c.," Journal Soc. Arts, 1854; "Examination of the Nitrate of Soda and Borate Districts," British Association, 1859; P. of Tarapacá, by J. H. Blake, Silliman's Journal, 1818; "Darwin's Geological Obs. on South America;" "Source and Supply of Nitrate of Soda," by P. Pusey, Journal Agricultural Soc., 1853, map; "Williamson Obs. sobre la Industria de Tarapacá," Lima, 1859; "Trade in Nitrate of Soda," Steam Shipping Gazette, Sept. 19, 1859; "Obs. on P. of Tarapacá," by Don M. B. de la Fuente, Geographical Soc. Journal, 1856.

[2] Plano de las localidades de la P. de Tarapacá en el Departamento de Moquegua, adonde se encuentra Nitrate de Soda y Borato de cal con las oficinas principales y sus caminos á los Puertos habilitados para su embarque, por Jorge Smith, F.R.G.S. Dedicado á S. E. El Gran Mariscal Dn Ramon Castilla, Prusidente del Peru.

There are about forty nitrate works and nine shipping ports, including Iquique

At the Soronal (its lowest position), the nitrate is found at 2,593 feet above the sea, and thirteen miles inland; its most elevated is 3,724 feet, and at twenty-three miles. The borate is found as high as about 3,600 feet, and as low as 3,211, at the Noria.

In 1826, when I first lived at Iquique, it had a population of fishermen, in all about one hundred souls; subsequently my friend, Mr. George Smith, became one of the principal nitrate of soda refiners and exporters; and now Iquique boasts of a well-built and flourishing town. Water for drinking is distilled from sea-water, and sells for about three halfpence the gallon, at which price £40,000 worth is used. Its importance as a port is only second to that of Callao, its population being about 5,000.

There is one amalgamating establishment for separating the silver from the ores of Huantajaya, two iron foundries, a candle manufactory, steam bread making machines, and gas is projected.

Guano was taken from its island in ancient times; in modern, the deposit was 800 yards in length, 1,200 in breadth, and was cleared in twenty-five years. Iquique has always been a fishing place, and will account for the number of Huacas found here, as also at Molle, a few miles off, and other points of the coast.

In this district, as it seldom or ever rains, the bodies would soon be dessicated and remain so for ages; also, being preserved by the saline and very dry surface soil which covers the whole country, plain and mountain, up into the very Andes.

I think, with Rivero and Tschudi,[1] that if embalming was practised in Peru, it was a very uncommon proceeding, and only used for the Incas and principal chiefs, and, as I have observed, the heated saline soil of the coast was sufficient to dessicate the bodies;[2] they observe, that in the interior the pure cold air and dry winds would do the same thing; they note that in the tracks, such as from Islay to Arequipa, and from the latter to Lima, there are numbers of mummies of animals, which serve as land-marks to show the road. I may also state that Iquique, La Noria and other nitrate works are perfect Golgothas, and the tracks over the province are densely strewed with mummies of mules and asses; these are brought principally from the Pampas of Buenos Ayres, some 8000 annually; one-half die on the desert tracks for want of food

---

[1] Peruvian Antiquities, 208,9.

[2] E. M. Rivero Antiguedades Peruanas, 1841; Tschudi, Travels in Peru, 504.

and water; whilst they can work, they are mainly fed on barley from Chile.

I have placed in the British Museum articles from the Huacas of Iquique and Molle, consisting of wooden combs, bones used as awls, spines of the cactus, pierced at the thick end for needles, copper fish-hooks, stone arrow-heads, coloured woollen cloth, yellow, brown and red mineral pigments, heads of indian corn (a rare species, zea rostrata), &c.,[1] and the crania of Aymará type, with the Ethnological Society of London. Morton[2] gives four forms of crania among the old Peruvians, produced by artificial means: first, the horizontally elongated; second, conical; third, flattening the forehead; fourth, vertical elevation of the occiput: these had their names, as Caito, Oma, Opalla, &c.; and describes a very conical head from Chuichuic or Atacama baja, on the western edge of the desert.

When I was last at Iquique, a Huaca, containing some 500 bodies, was discovered a short distance from the town; the bodies were in a sitting posture, wrapped in woollen mantles of various colours. There were found pieces of ordinary pottery, fishing utensils, mummies of dogs and birds, maize and coca in the hualqui or long bags.

Not long since, in cutting a water-course in the valley of Quilliagua, on the river Loa, images of gold were found, one in the shape of a heart, weighing 1¼ ounces, with a hole through it, so as to be worn; huacas were then discovered with their mummies, also finely wrought reed baskets, in various colours, capable of holding water; arrows of tamarugo (acacia), bows, slings, vessels filled with coca and maize, some chicha in a jar, mantles of various colours, netting, and some small granaries.

In my papers to the Geographical Society, and the Ethnological, in 1852, I gave some account of those curious ancient Indian remains called "Pintados," or Indian Pictography, found in the province of Tarapacá; and I described those I had examined in 1826 in the valley of Pintados, in 21° S., at the foot of the Andes, consisting of representations of Indians, llamas, dogs, and other forms, on the side of the desert ravine, some of the figures being thirty feet or more in height, cut, or rather scraped out in the sandy soil, the lines being twelve to eighteen inches broad, and six to eight inches deep. I was then informed they were the work of "Indios Gentiles," or old pagan Indians, and I thought that the Pintados had been done by ancient and modern Indians

---

[1] Tschudi says, he found ears of maize in tombs, belonging to a period anterior to the Incas, and of two kinds.
[2] American Journal of Science, 1846.

for amusement; but I have now reason to believe, that some of them mark burial places, places of worship, and to preserve memorials of the past.

At Las Rayas, south of the mines of Huantajaya and Santa Rosa, Mr. George Seymour gives me the following description of one: the sides of one of the barren mountains is laid out, as if for a garden, with a large double circle in the centre, and paths branching off dividing the ground into compartments. The loose stones having been picked off the paths, which are rendered hard apparently by the feet of people, it is supposed that rites and ceremonies were and are still performed here.

Long after the conquest the Indian continued secretly to render homage to his religion on the summit of mountains in particular. In some provinces they had the custom of taking their dead into the rocky fastnesses, and among the snows, burying with them food, gold and rich apparel: thus I think it most probable that many of the Pintados of Tarapacá mark the position of Indian tombs, as well as of places of worship.

We will now make an excursion easterly towards the Andes. The western chain is the Cordillera, the eastern the Andes. Mounted on a sure-footed mule, the saddle-bags well stored with provend, booted, spurred, and ponchoed according to the fashion of the country—no turnpike to pay, or hotel-keeper with heavy charges to annoy—having generally for one's resting place at nights the sand of the desert[1], the bright, starry heavens for a canopy, with generally for my companion my old friend, Don Jorge Smith. And a better desert traveller cannot possibly exist, he wending his way calmly and stoically over the burning[2] sandy, saline, desert plains, when I would fain have been elsewhere; and the fearless manner he would go up and down the Andean laderas, or steep places, was rather astonishing.

Leaving Iquique and its sandy, shelly, and saline plain, the escarped porphyritic coast range is ascended by a steep cuesta, its summit 1,761 feet, when undulating desert land in the mountains is traversed. To the left are the Pintados of Las Rayas, already described; to the right, on the side of a barren mountain, are others, consisting of

---

[1] Garcilasso, Book ii. How to make a horse fast in the sandy desert. Dig a hole, fill a bag with sand, put it into the hole, and press down; to the end of the bag attach the cabresto or rope.

[2] On one of our trips in January, 1854, the thermometer stood as follows: at La Noria, 3213 feet above the sea, 5 a.m., 64°, 1 p.m. 83°, 10 p.m. 63°. In the sun at noon 92°; on a heap of sand 128° Faht.

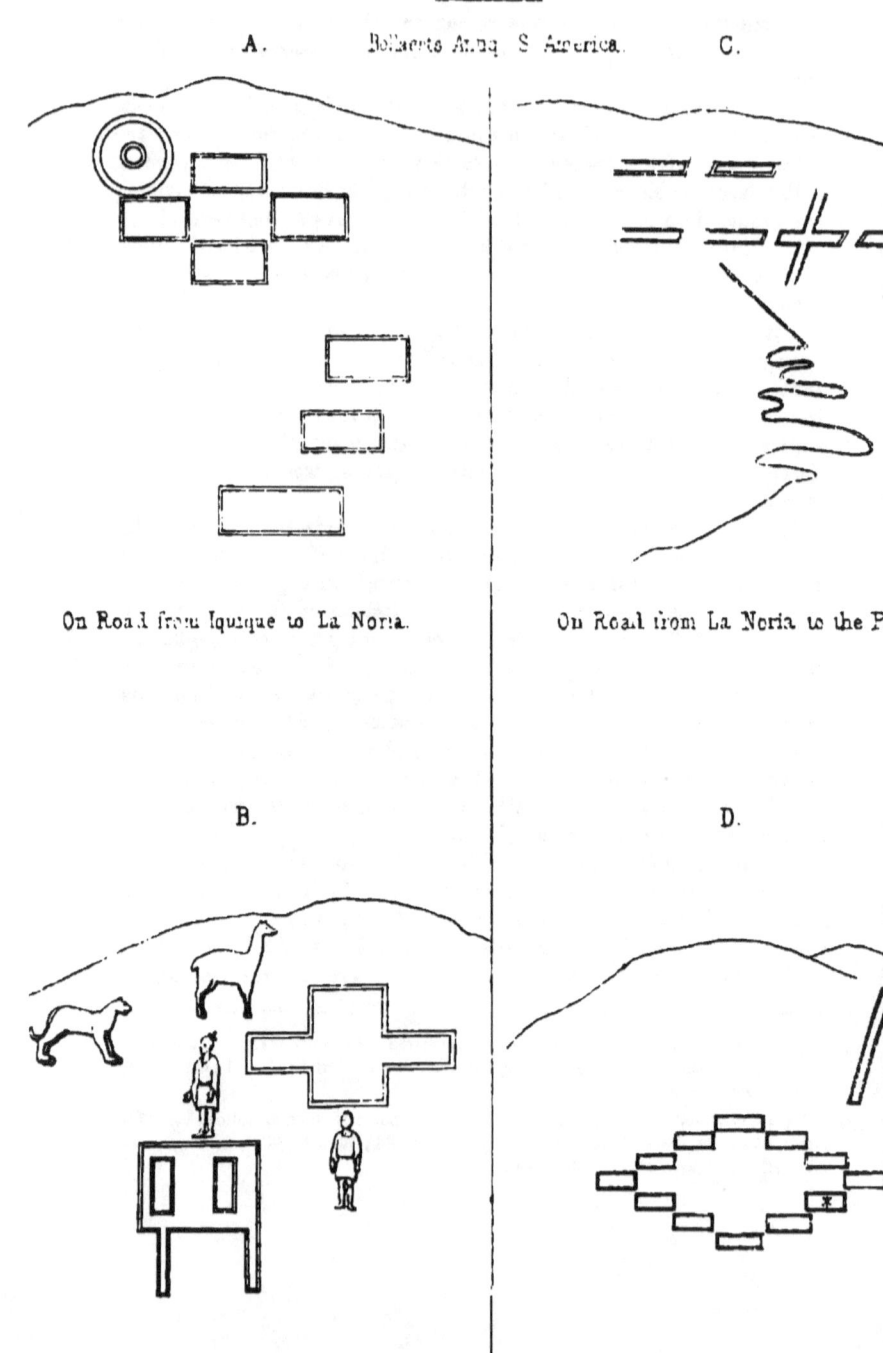

four paralellograms, a cross-like figure, the commencement of another parallel form and a zig-zag track running down the mountain (c). These figures are of large size, and well seen from the road below, formed by the disintegrated pieces of rock and sand having been scraped and picked off inside the outline.

At the salitre or nitrate of soda works of Cocina, huacas have been found containing mummies, arrow heads of silicious stones, stone clubs, or huactans, 14 inches long by 5 broad; also a dozen globular objects of black stone, inserted into the quills of condors, the use of which I do not know. Among the mountains of the coast are many huacas of the "Gentiles," where, independent of other objects, weaving apparatus and small perforated stones, have been met with.

Having rested at La Noria, a town built of salt, and the largest nitrate of soda quarry and refining works, our track is now S.E. towards the Pampa de Tamarugal, and one league on this track to the S., on the side of a mountain, is another pintado (A), consisting of a large circle, with a smaller one in the centre; then four oblong spaces, and three more underneath. The desert mountains about here are very wild and rocky. The track leads into the Pampa de Tamarugal, over grounds containing nitrate of soda and much common salt. We now come upon two small towns, Las Tisas, the origin of which is interesting. Some years since a chalky-looking substance was met with, which was called Tisa. On examination it was found to be a mineral of Borax. Subsequently a box of minerals was sent to me by Mr. Smith, in which was enclosed some small specimens of the tisa. This was examined, and proved to be a new boracic-acid mineral.[1] Mr. Smith came to England, and on his return I begged of him to examine the locality for borate. This he did, and found the district to be very rich in the mineral, as well as various other parts of the Pampa de Tamarugal. It has also been found in the northern part of the desert of Atacama. Preparations were made to work the borate grounds, but the Peruvian government having been led to believe that it was too valuable an article to be exported, except under similar conditions as the guano—viz., a government monopoly—the working of it is interdicted. Some portion has been extracted, and the greater part smuggled out of the country. Permission has occasionally been given to a favoured few to export small parcels, which brings about £30 per ton in the English market.

If allowed to be exported under favourable circumstances, there would

---

[1] Hydroborocalcite or hayeecine. A specimen examined at the Museum of Practical Geology, gave water, 27·22: sul. acid, 1·10; lime, 14·32; soda, 8·22; potash, 0·51; chlo. sodium, 1·65; sand, 0·32; boracic acid, 45·66; nit. acid, 1 = 100, with traces of iodine and phos. acid.

be a good demand, and it would be applied to numberless uses in the arts. I have deposited in the Museum of Practical Geology in London, a large nodule of this new boracic-acid mineral; also specimens in the British Museum. Pickeringite and Glauberite occur with the borate. Iodic and chromic salts are found with the native nitrate or soda.

In my second series of observations on "Southern Peru," read at British Association, 1859, I have given details of this borate formation, and its connection with the nitrate of soda deposits in the province of Tarapacá. The first series on this subject will be found in Journal of the Geographical Society for 1851.

South of the Tisas five leagues, are the mountains of Pintados where, for the space of a league, it is covered with figures of llamas, squares, circles, and other forms; and farther south still, is the Pintado of a large Puma; indeed, these peculiar remains are met with in many other places in the province. There is the "Cerrito Pintado," three leagues south-west, from Messrs. Geo. Smith's Salitres at the Soronal.

North of Las Tisas, on the road from Iqique to Tarapacá, is another collection of Pintados; the principal one composed of irregular designs, a puma, a llama, and two Indians. (B).

The most interesting Pintado is east of the Salitre works of Zavala, and near La Peña (D). There is a straight line, a calle or street; but the main figure is made up of fourteen compartments, joined by their edges of a rhombic form; one of these compartments my friend, Don Lorenzo Zeballos found to be a huaca or grave, paved with stones; in the grave was a mummy of an Indian female in a dress of feathers, with a well-made straw helmet on, under her head a jar containing two small bones.[1] Here we have an instance that some of these Pintados are ancient graves. A few years since a huaca was found near Quilliaga, the body was in a horizontal position, dressed in penguins' skins neatly sewed together; at its side was a bow and quiver full of arrows, the arrow heads of cornelian.

Near La Peña is the hill of Unita, where there is a colossal pintado of an Indian, the guardian of some supposed hidden treasure; and, it is said, the Indians of Atacama, taking treasure for the ransom of Atahualpa, when they heard of his death, buried it here. There are also figures of llamas, birds, arches, circles, and other forms.

---

[1] Rivero and Tschudi, 205. In imitation of the Egyptians, the Peruvians drew out the brains through the nostrils, thus explaining the want of the small bones which separates the eyes, and the fracture made in the suture. The bones mentioned as found in the Pintado, could they have been of this character?

An old Indian road runs from the hill of Huara (which also has Pintados) to the town of Tarapacá, the stones having been merely picked off the track.

The desert hill of Huara is a Bramador, roarer or bellower, sometimes called the musical mountain; also Retumba de los cerros, rumbling of the mountains. Darwin describes such a one near Copiapo. The mountain of the Bell, in Arabia, is of this character. Mysterious sounds are heard in the morning at the statue of Memnon, "a low, sad monotone—the music of Memnon, in harmony with the changeless sunshine and the stagnant life of Egypt."

Mr. Seymour gives me the following which may have been a Pintado, at Pisco,[1] it is on the north side of the peninsula of Parracas, 13° 52′ S. It is of considerable dimensions, and most probably the work of the natives before the conquest. The central prong of this trident looking figure is two hundred feet long, and the lines ten yards broad. It is annually visited by Indians, who " scour " away the sand that may have accumulated, having a Fiesta or holiday; the lower portion I suppose to be a huaca or grave. I find that Gilliss says, it is apparently made of white stones set in the face of the rock, by whom, or for what object this huge emblem of the Christian truth (?) was constructed, no one can tell. A Priest said that Christ had wrought it in one night, during the rule of Pazarro, and as a warning to the sun worshippers; also, that, annually, the devoutly inclined go with the priests from Pisco to the cross, its conclusion smacking more of " earth earthly " than " heaven heavenly."

Sculptures on rocks, and of various periods, are not uncommon throughout America;[2] but the existence of this class, viz., the Pintados of Tarapacá, I do not find noticed, except in England—in Berks, Wilts, and Bucks—the " White Horses " in the two first counties, and the " White Leaf Cross " in the latter is one hundred feet high. Near Oldbury Castle, in Wilts, is a white horse, carved out on the slope of a hill, supposed to be a memorial of Alfred the Great's victory over the Danes at Eddington, or may even be of higher antiquity, as the white horse of the Celts, which was of religious origin. Triennially the people assemble to " scour the horse," or clean away the turf.[3]

A huaca was discovered, in 1830, at the entrance of the valley of Tarapacá; it was surrounded with stones; in the centre was buried an

---

[1] *Pisco* and *Pichui*, bird.

[2] For drawings of some, see L'Univers Pittoresque, Bresil, 1837; Wallace, travels on the Amazon, 1853; see also Humboldt, Schomburgh.

[3] See my Antiquarian researches in Tarapacá, Peru, Antiq. Soc. Lond., 1857.

Indian female under these stones; at the four corners, under a pile of three stones, were male Indians. Amongst other articles deposited was a stone figure of a female, the face of silver.

Two leagues from Mamiña is the cross of St. Marcos; here is a gigantic Pintado of an Indian idol.

Starting from La Noria, entering the great Pampa of Tamarugal, and resting at La Tirana, where good water is procured from wells, and where formerly much silver ore of Huantajaya and Santa Rosa was amalgamated, either by being trod out by the feet of men or subjected to heat in boilers. The journey is continued in an easterly direction to the foot of the Andes. In the summer it is intensely hot during the day, and oftimes clouds of saline dust and sand envelope the explorer. There is no shade to protect from the ever scorching sun, and the mirage or delusive appearance of water, the espéjo or looking glass of the Spaniards, is most tantalizing to the thirsty traveller. This very arid district is a portion of a great desert which, with little intermission, extends 1,500 geographical miles, from Coquimbo in Chile, to Payta in Peru.

About south-east are the rather large towns of Pica and Matilla, where the vineyards are nourished by waters of irrigation. The church of Matilla is an imposing building, erected by an Indian architect.

We now progress by Tambillo and the pretty Indian farm of Manuel Cruz, with its gigantic algarobo tree (Prosopis horrida) and its andenes or step-like hanging fields and gardens; we ascended a very rough, dangerous cuesta and laderas, to some 10,000 feet above the sea. We soon descended to the Indian village of Macaya, 6,278 feet, which is in a deep ravine. Near Macaya, are the "Minas del Inca," yielding copper, formerly worked for the use of the Incas.

On the way to the rich copper mountain of Yabricoya, and one league from Macaya, I observed an interesting monument in the Pampa del Leon. It is a large, isolated block of granite, 12 feet square, called the "Piedra del Leon," it is covered with very old Indian sculptures. The centre group consists of a man wrestling with a puma, holding the animal with one hand; in the other is a stone as if defending himself. There is a smaller puma; also figures of llamas, guanacos, circles, serpents, &c. These figures are not chiselled, but picked out with some pointed instrument. A cross has been cut subsequently on this stone. I suppose this to be very ancient Aymará work.

In this region the docile llama and alpaca flourish, droves of wild vicuñas and guanacos are seen, also many chinchillas and biscachas. This animal I have seen as high as 14,000 feet in the Andes. The puma occasionally roves about here, as well as the ostrich. Pariñas, or

flamingos[1], and then the mighty condor that builds its nest higher than 15,000 feet, and was seen by Humboldt wheeling in circles at an elevation of 22,000. Condor, cuntur, called huitre by the Spaniards. The English Cyclopedia says the condors are to be seen in groups of three or four, but never in large companies, like the vultures. This is hardly the case. My friend, Mr. George Smith, and myself were attacked by rather a large flock of condors, on the heights of Iquique, in 1826. I saw, in 1854, a group of fifty condors, near the cuesta of Iquique. They are to be seen at times, as many as a hundred or more, hovering over the farms in Chile. In 1820-3, when there was whale fishing at Coquimbo, the offal would float on shore, when as many as two to three hundred condors were to be seen in company ready to gorge on dead whales. I once was exploring with Mr. Smith the Mountain of Molle, above the Noria nitrate works, on the summit of which is an abandoned silver mine. Having entered it to rest and get out of the heat of a scorching sun, we very soon had to make our exit in consequence of being covered with condor lice. Such a spot is called the "Alojamiento," or resting place. On another occasion, exploring some high mountains overlooking the Pampa de Tamarugual, on a rocky crag we found a deposit of their excrement. From such a spot the condor watches for dead and dying mules and asses in the tracks, particularly to and from the nitrate works.

The condor was an object of worship by some of the Peruvian nations.

I am informed that at Mani, in the south, there are, sculptured stones with the sun, moon, and stars, Indians, and animals; and that, at Huatacondo, are many huacas, in which have been found objects in gold and silver; that in the valley of Sipuca, 7 leagues S. of Mani, in the huacas there, small stone figures were found.

Between Arequipa and Uchumayo are sculptured stones; the spot is known as the "Campanas del Diablo."

The Indians of the province of Tarapacá are Aymarás, and speak that language. They may be said to be partially Christianised; some, however, still practise ancient ceremonies, such as bowing to the rising sun and certain mountains.

In the Pass or Abra of Pichuta, I noticed a pile of stones with quids of coca on it. It would appear that the mastication of coca when going to great elevations facilitates the ascent, and these piles of stones are called apachitas or cotorayarumi. The Mercurio Peruano for 1794 says these piles of stones were adored as deities, they are found in all the

---

[1] A specimen of this bird, a new species, I have deposited in the British Museum.

mountain roads, and appear to have had their origin among the early Indians; for, when they ascended a mountain, or passed over a dangerous track laden, they put the load down, and, as a sign of gratitude offered the first thing they got hold of (which was generally a stone) to Pacha-camac, saying "Apachecta," which means "To him who has given me strength."

In the pass of Pacheta I found a pile of stones which takes its name from the Apachitas.

Ascending the ravine of Pisagua, which runs through the mountains of the coast and northern part of the Pampa de Tamarugal, the large Indian town of Camiña is attained, where maize, alfalfa, olives, grapes, and other fruits grow. The llama and alpaca are also reared. This may be called one of the entrances to the Cordillera. Ancient Indian graves are met with containing objects in gold and silver, also pottery with designs in alto-relievo. The track now goes easterly up the cuesta of Parasuya to the pass of Pichuta. Maymaga is near a marsh; at sunrise in November the thermometer was at 26°. This is one of the many solitary spots in the Andes called estancias or llama farms. We come next to the pass of Pichuta, 15,000 feet at least, where it generally blows a piercing gale of wind from the S.E.

From here the Volcano of Isluga is seen, as well as many snow-capped peaks and ridges; from Anquaje five openings in the volcano are observed. Isluga is an Indian village 14,000 or more above the sea, with a stream coming from the colossal mountain of Carabaya, 18,000 feet high, which runs into the lake of Isluga, where there is an ugly-looking fish, the suchi. In the hollows among the mountains a few potatoes and quinua are with difficulty grown.

The volcano of Isluga is not very conical, but occupies some extent. In winter it is covered with snow to its base. Loud rumbling noises are heard in its vicinity and earthquakes often felt. I give as the height of the volcano, the approximate elevation of seventeen to eighteen thousand feet above the sea. Mr. Smith and myself were the first, I believe, to describe this volcano. To the east of Isluga commences a salt plain, extending to near Potosi, varying in breadth from three to eight leagues, the salt being from five to ten inches thick.

South-west from Isluga is Chiapa, 9000 feet above the sea. From this Indian town Mr. Smith and myself ascended the beautiful looking mountain of Tata Jachura (see p. 10 for tradition) in the month of June. We left Chiapa at noon, by ridges, stony cuestas, and at sundown camped for the night under the lee of some huge rocks. The following morning, at sun-rise, it blew strongly from the east and very cold. We travelled onwards with our mules as long as the rugged track

permitted, when our Indian guides begged to be left behind in charge of them. To this we were obliged to agree, and continued our ascent on foot. We soon left the large cactus below us, and the only plants seen were the ichu pasture, stunted tola bushes, and the resinous yareta (Bolax). Our ascent was over steep broken rock (probably porphyry), until we came upon thick ice. We bled a little at the nose, had an unpleasant singing in the ears, headache, dimness of the eyes, caused by the puna, soroche, or attenuated state of the atmosphere; the body was benumbed by the extreme cold. However, at one p.m., after a painful and laborious struggle, we reached the summit over broken rock and ice, there being glaciers below us. I give the elevation of this peak over 17,000 above the sea. It blew a piercing gale from the east, and so cold was it, that the water in a gourd was frozen, and a piece of roasted meat was as hard as a brick. Our fingers were so stiff and cold that we could scarcely use our surveying instruments; there was not sufficient power in them to strike fire wherewith to light a cigar, and we could scarcely hear each other speak.

From the summit there was a glorious view of the Andes; many peaks must have been from three to six thousand feet higher. We saw to the north some high mountains, most probably the volcanic group, sixty to seventy miles off, containing the Gualtieri, 22,000; Parinacota, 22,030; and the Sebama, 22,350 (Pentland). The cloudless sky was of a very dark indigo colour, and the icy peaks and ridges showed a bold and well defined outline. Humboldt observes, that in the Andes the azure is less blended with white, because there the air is constantly of extreme dryness. I am informed that the Andes of Atacama is so dry, that picture frames are made of salt An interesting phenomenon was, that stars were visible as if it were night. I am told that at Copiapo, the sky is so clear, that a planet has been seen at one p.m.

Our descent did not occupy much time; we soon regained our guides, and entering Chiapa at sun-set, the bells of the church were set ringing, and a good meal awaited us, including the callapurca, a savoury stew, kept hot by large heated pebbles put into it, and old oily chicha, in honour of our having been the first, in all probability, who had ever gained the summit of Tata Jachura.

Mamiña is a large Indian town, and where the Aymará only is spoken. Above the town are seen several tiers of small doors; they look like the port-holes of a ship-of-war. These are the doors to caves in the rock, and used by the Indians as store-houses, and are probably of aboriginal origin. The doors are fastened by wooden padlocks, opened and shut by a skewer-like key.

According to D'Orbigny, the Quichua is spoken from the equator to

28° S. (interrupted at 15° S. by the Aymará people), consisting of 934,707 pure, and 458,572 mixed. The Aymarás are from 15° to 20° S., round Lake Titicaca and ruins of Tia Huanacu (surrounded by Quichuas) 372,397 pure, and 188,237 mixed.

QUICHUA.—We are told that the Incas had a secret language of their own, and the general tradition is they first appeared about the Lake of Titicaca; if so, it would be very old Aymara. If they came from the country to the E. it might have been the Calchaqui; or, if from the coast of the Pacific, the Chinchasuyu. However, the language spoken by the early Incas is lost; but it is said that a few words have been spared. I have not seen them particularised.

In that admirable work of Ludewig's on the literature of the American aboriginal languages, it is stated that the Quichua is the language of the Peruvians. I will admit that the Quichua was spoken by people inhabiting Cuzco and its vicinity; but to have so fine a language, they could not have been the barbarous tribes so stated by historians. They were most probably the remains of a once powerful nation, brought again together by the Incas. That Quichua was spoken by the nations the Incas first conquered is easily understood; also, that it subsequently got mixed with the language of the Chimus of Trujillo, sometimes called the Lamano, with the Chincha about Lima, the Calchaqui of Tucuman, with the Cara-Quitu, Aymará, &c., &c., which has given rise to the idea that these and other languages are dialects of the Quichua.

Before the conquest of the various nations by the Incas, each most probably had its separate language, and when in proximity, affinities with each other; and, ere the Incas over-ran the country, I conceive that each nation had its own language, and even at the present time they should not be called dialects exactly, but corrupted by the Quichua, the language of their Incarial invaders.

To get at any knowledge, and of, perhaps, only a few words of the various pure languages spoken from Quito to the Chile, we must go back to the earliest MSS. and printed vocabularies and grammars arranged by the Spaniards.

AYMARA.—Ludewig classes the Aymará race as Indians of Bolivia, the N.W. provinces of the Argentine Republic, and Southern Peru. I found the Aymarás to be of a brown olive colour, but darker in the Andes; the hair black and straight, sparely made, and may be called a small race of people. The Aymará Indian population of Tarapacá is about 6,000. La Paz, in Bolivia, is about the centre of the Aymará country, which anciently included, among others, the Canchis, Casnas, Collas, Lupacas, Pacases, Carancas, and Charcas.

The following may not be deemed uninteresting to philologists. It is from the Spanish preface to the Gospel of St. Luke, translated into Aymará by the late Don V. Pazos. The Aymará language has a labial dental and guttural pronunciation peculiar to it. The first is designated as pp, being pronounced by emitting the respiration with force against the lips united as ppia, a hole; ppampaña, to bury. The second, with tt, is done by the tongue being placed against the teeth, as ttanta, head, but which, if pronounced with force, would mean something knavish. The third, ck or k, are pronounced in the throat, with this difference, that the first is more guttural, as choka, tree; kollke, money. The w has been introduced because the Spanish v and u do not give the sound of w, but which in Aymará is the same as in English—thus: acawa, this; acanwa, here. The other letters have the same value and sound as those in Spanish.

Rivero and Tschudi say, the Aymará language is very much like Quichua, and doubtless came from the same root. Very many words in the two idioms are identical, and even in the grammatical structure there is a striking resemblance.

Under Yahuar-Huacac VIII. Inca, Colla-suyu, or the country between Arequipa and Atacama, was brought under his rule; this would include the province of Tarapacá. At Mocha resided, in 1826, a noble Indian family named Quispe Sugso, descended from the Incas.

Being at Macaya during the feast of "our lady of Candelaria," there being no priest, the cacique read prayers in the chapel, and as the sun was setting and throwing its rich golden light on the mountains, just under the cacique's house, on a dais, a cloth was spread. To the sound of the merry Cachua songs, of tambourines, pan-pipes, and pipes, women brought earthen vessels containing rich stews, condimented with aji or red pepper.

The cacique and the men seated themselves at the dais, being served by the women with savoury dishes, potatoes, beans, maize, &c. The women afterwards sat on the ground in groups to their meal. The young girls now handed about the chicha to the men, who drank copiously, after which, and as night approached, the festal party retired to a large building to sing haravis[1], or mournful and other melodies, dance, laugh, and whoop as the Indian can when under the influence of his beloved chicha[2], recite traditions as that of Tata Jachura (p. 10), or recall scenes from the play of the Death of Inca Atahualpa. Could there then be any good feeling for the Spanish invaders? The times of

---

[1] From Harivicus, the Indian poet, who composed dramas, wrote idyls and odes in particular.

[2] See my paper on "Indian Corn," Hogg's Instructor, July, 1852.

Tupac-Amaro, Puma-cagua, and other Indian patriots would be recalled. There were a few pretty girls, and when the excitement of the dance chased away the usual melancholy that pervaded their features, they then looked interesting. For the matrons I cannot say so much, for the coca-chewing does not add to fading beauty. In the middle of the carousing there occurred a sharp shock of an earthquake, commencing with its rumbling noise, then an undulatory movement, and then the shake. This broke up the Indian revel.

It is at such times the Indian plays the game of pasa. It is one of great antiquity, and seems to be the only one of this sort. Pasa means a hundred, as he wins who first gets that number. They play at it with two instruments: one a spread eagle of wood with ten holes on each side, being tens, and are marked with pegs to denote every man's gettings; the other is a bone in the manner of a die, cut with seven faces, one of which has a particular mark, called guayaro (huyaru). The other five tell according to the number of them, and the last is a blank. The way of playing is to toss up the bone, and the marks on the upper surface are so many got. But the guayro goes for ten, and the like number is lost, if the blank side appears.

In Ulloa's time the Indian had the reputation of a belief in fortune-telling, and that they employed artifices, supposed charms, and strange compositions, in order to obtain some visionary happiness. In Southern Peru I found no ghost stories; however, now and then one hears of sayings approaching superstitious belief. On asking why the silver mines of El Carmen, near Iquique, are not worked, the answer was that a white mule had foaled there, which caused the mines to stop yielding.

CHILE.

Geography—Chango Indians—Atacama—Huacas—Ruins of Lasana—Copiapo—Huacas—Antiquities—Musical Fish—Huasco—Coquimbo—Valparaiso—Santiago—Antiquities—Supposed existence of Nitrate of Soda and of Gold in Copper from Atacama—Nitrate of Potash in Equador—Valparaiso and Santiago Railway—Coal mines of Lota and Coronel—Araucanos—Indians of Tierra del Fuego.

CHILE[1] is a beautiful and fertile country, situated between the Andes and the Pacific. It extends from the desert of Atacama to Cape Horn; in some parts it is thirty, in others seventy leagues wide. It is bounded on the north by Bolivia, on the east by the Argentine Confederation, on the south by the Southern Ocean, and on the west by the Pacific.

This country, it is said, was called Chile by the aborigines, and to have originated from the notes of a species of thrush, or from the Quichua word chiri, cold; as being a colder land than Peru. Its population in 1854 was 1,439,120; foreigners, 19,669, and thirty-one Negroes. In 1843 there were about 15,000 Araucanos, but in the middle of the last century Superunda gave 50,000.

The inhabitants consist of Chilenos and Indians; the first occupy the greater portion of the territory, and are descendants of the Spaniards; the latter are divided into independent tribes, speaking the same language, which is abundant and harmonious. Some reside in the Andes, to the south of 33°, as the Pehuenches, Puelches and Huillches; these are wild and barbarous. The brave Araucanos occupy the lovely country south of the river Biobio.

Chile may be called a rugged inclined plain from the foot of the Andes to the Pacific. This space has three chains of mountains parallel to the Cordillera with their fruitful valleys, particularly in the southern portion. The mighty Cordilleras run north and south through Chile, being 120 miles or more in width, with its numberless icy peaks and volcanos, the mountain of Aconcagua being, according to a recent calculation, 23,910 feet above the sea.

There are many rivers and torrents; they rise in the Andes and run into the Pacific, about 120 in number. Some are navigable, as the Sinfondo, Bueno, Chaivia, Valdivia, Cauten, Tolten, Biobio, and Maule

---

[1] See Lastarrias Jeografia de Chile, Valparaiso, 1857. Gaye, His. de Chile, maps. Essai sur le Chile, par V. Peroz, Rossles, Hamburg, 1851, maps.

Many hot springs are found in the Cordilleras, as Colina, Cauquenes, Panimavida, and Chillian. There are salt lakes towards the sea, as those of Bucalemu, Cohuel, Vicuquen, and Bolleruca. Lakes of fresh water, as those of Ranco, Villarica, and Llanquihue.

Very many are the ports on its long line of coast, the principal ones being Valparaiso, Talcahuano, Huasco, Coquimbo, and Caldera.

There are several islands, including those of Juan Fernandez, Quiriquina, Santa Maria, Mocha, Chiloe, and Chonos.

The greater portion of the year the atmosphere is fine and clear. Meteors are often seen traversing the heavens in various directions. Southern auroras are occasionally observed.

The climate is healthy and benign. The more northern portion partakes of the arid character of the desert of Atacama. The principal productions are silver, copper and some gold; wheat and other grain, also much timber.

Silver and copper are found in the rich mines of Copiapo, Huasco, Coquimbo and Aconcagua.[1]. Wheat is produced in all the territory, from the valley of Aconcagua to Arauco. Timber for building comes from the banks of the Maule, also from Valdivia and Chiloe. The principal vegetable productions are wheat, barley, maize, beans, potatoes, and other vegetables. Amongst the fruits are some chirimoyas and lucumas; pear, apple, peach, figs, oranges, melons, watermelons, almonds, nuts, and a small species of coco-nut in abundance. Wheat yields a hundred for one, maize and barley the same. The hemp and flax are very good in quality. The vine flourishes and yields good wine. The maju, yuca, potatoes, quinua and madi are indigenous aliments; the frigol or bean, and aji or pimenta is grown in abundance; silk can be produced, also tobacco of good quality; herbs of various sorts, including medicinal ones, and others useful in the arts. Some portions of the Chilian soil will produce cotton, pine-apple and sugarcane. Of trees, its magnificent forests produce, pines, cypresses, alerces, laurels, cedars, oaks, lumas, litres, &c. Coal[2] also has become an important article of extraction and export.

The animals imported from Europe have increased extraordinarily, as the horse, horned cattle, sheep, pigs, &c. There are indigenous animals, as the vicuña, the chillihueque (llama), huanaco and huemul (a deer), the Chilian lion (puma), and a species of jagua; the cunning fox, the terror of the hen-roost. No serpents or venemous animals have been

---

[1] See R. A. Alison's admirable observations on the Geology of Chile, Mining Journal, Aug. and Sept. 1859.

[2] See my paper on Chile coal, Geogr. Soc. Journal, 1855.

observed in Chile. Among birds is the gigantic condor. Fish and shell-fish is abundant on its coasts.

Chile has been free from Spanish domination since 1818, when it became a republic, and is most prosperous.

In 1855 the amount of imports and exports were more than 37½ millions of dollars. 841,842 tons of shipping entered its ports, 820,024 left. In 1857, exports and imports were nearly forty millions of dollars. General instruction is spreading rapidly. At Santigo is the university and national institute; there are schools all over the country; also schools of arts and agriculture.

The territory of the republic is divided into thirteen provinces and two territories: Atacama, Coquimbo, Aconcagua, Santiago, Valparaiso, Colchagua, Talca, Maule, Nuble, Concepcion, Arauco, Valdivia; colonies of Llanquigüe and Magellan.

CHANGO INDIANS.—In 1828, when at the Bolivian port of Cobija, 22° 28' S., on my way along the coast of the desert of Atacama,[1] I first saw a few Chango fishermen. I left Cobija in an open boat, bound south for Paposo, sailing during the day (beating to windward), rowing at night, along a most wretched, sterile and mountainous coast. On the ninth day I saw a few Chango fishermen on shore; they understood a little Spanish, but their own language is probably a mixture of Atacama and Aymará. The following day, three came off in a seal-skin balsa out of Caleta de Cordon, bartering their dried congrio fish for flour and coca. On the twelfth day, three more Changos came off from El Rincon (a fishing cove), and on that day I anchored in Paposo, where I found a few families, people of Copiapo, who were here to barter for dried fish with the Changos.

At Punta Grande were three or four families of Changos, and at Agua Dulce half a dozen more, who had a few goats and asses. Having traversed the dangerous Mal Paso, I came to Hueso Parado, 25° 30' (this spot was shown to me as the divisional point with Bolivia). At Salinas I found four or five families of Changos; and as they had just then been supplied with wine by the purchasers of their dried fish, wild dancing and singing continued all night. It was a sort of wake, in consequence of the death of two children: the bodies (angelitos) were about being taken to Copiapo for interment. Thus some of these Indians may be called partially Christianized.

The Changos move from one cove to another; they told me they belonged to the district of Copiapo, but paid no tribute. They go

---

[1] See my trans. of Philippi's Researches in the Desert of Atacama, Geogr. Soc. Journal, 1855.

occasionally with asses laden with their dried fish (charquicillo) to San Pedro de Atacama, across a long angle of the desert, also to Copiapo. They are called Changos, but I could not discover that they constituted a distinct tribe; and I look upon the term Chango (given to them probably by the Spaniards) rather as something to do with their miserable condition and occupation. I saw about one hundred, I allow fifty more fishing north of Cobija, and another hundred travelling in the interior, would make two hundred and fifty souls.

Acosta speaks of a nation of Changos north of Cuzco. In 12° 20′ S. in the interior, in some maps, is a spot marked Changos.

D'Orbigny says these are a distinct tribe, and gives their population at 1000 souls. From having visited them, I gave at most 250. He speaks of a "Chango nation," and says they were "once powerful"— if they lived on the desert coast of Atacama, they had no means of becoming powerful; he also says that Cobija was the centre of this family, but nothing is known of their government and religion. Their huacas opened at Cobija, in 1830, the sexes were found buried separately and lengthways; that they may be a transition from the Aymarás and Quichuas towards the Chilian races, for, long after the conquest, there was a large Indian population in the valley of Copiapo. Their huts, I observed, were generally made of whales bones covered with seal-skins. Fish is their principal food, and their dried fish, the congrio, they bartered with the Indians of the interior for maize, coca and stuff for clothing. They generally congregate a league or so from streams, so as to avoid ague and mosquitos; they oftimes supply themselves with water from springs in the mountains. On asking them about their history, their reply was merely, "Si, señor," and "No, señor" —Yes, sir,—no, sir. They fish in the seal-skin balsa, which is safe in any surf. A few years ago the Changos suffered severely from small pox and measles. They can imitate the bark or cry of the seal, by which means they get them to approach, and easily spear them.

In my "Southern Peru,"[1] I give some particulars of the coast of Atacama and presumed positions of the Atacama meteoric iron. Since then, Dr. Philippi, by order of the Chilian government, has examined the great desert of Atacama,[2] and determined one of the positions of the said meteoric iron to be at Imilac, in 23° 49′ S., 69° 14′ W.[3] He speaks of the Changos as inhabiting the coast from Huasco to Cobija, and as being an indigenous population. The men fish, the women tend small flocks of goats. This sort of life requires

---

[1] Geogr. Soc. Journal, 1851.
[2] Geogr. Soc. Journal, 1855.
[3] See my paper on the Meteoric Iron of Atacama, Meteor. Soc. Journal, 1858.

that they should frequently change their abodes as fish is scarce or plentiful, or as the desert pastures are abundant or not. They live in miserable huts formed of the bones of whale or cacti, covered with sealskins, rags or sea-weed; and, as the occupation of the men is different from that of the women, they live but seldom together.

ATACAMA.—D'Orbigny says, "the natives of Atacama were called Olipes or Llipis, and inhabit the western declivity of the Cordillera, from the 19° to the 22° S.—viz., Tarapacá and Atacama." My observations show, that Tarapacá has been, and is still inhabited by Aymarás.

Philippi estimated the population of San Pedro de Atacama, from five to six thousand; the greater number are Indians, who speak a peculiar language, very harsh and guttural, but they understand Spanish.

Four days journey from the port of Cobija is Calama, and two days' more is Chiu-Chiu, in the desert of Atacama, an ancient Peruvian burial place. Here Dr. Reid[1] found in an extensive half-moon, in a sitting position, men, women and children, five to six hundred in number,[2] all in the same attitude and gazing vacantly before them. They still sit immoveable in the dreary desert, and like dried mummies by the effect of the hot air. There are cooking vessels beside them full of maize. Near here is the old Peruvian fortress of Lasana,[3] built on a tongue of land, between the two arms of a small river. The style of building is similar to that of old German fortresses, the walls being of coarse masonry, and the small rooms, holes, and hiding places, endless and indescribable. No room is more than eight feet square, many scarcely five; door, two feet in height; windows few in number, and those not larger than one's fist; and with all the whole town (a hundred or a hundred and fifty families might have dwelt here) built like one room, in which the greater part had to pass through from ten to fifteen rooms to get to their own apartment,[4] we literally stand and walk on skulls and bones. Every corner is full of them.

CAPIAPO.—Molina says, according to Indian tradition, owes its name to the great quantity of turquoises found in its mountains. I have already mentioned the existence of antiquities near this district, viz., those of Lasana, in the desert of Atacama, which are Incarial. I now come to the valley of Copiapo, which rises in the Cordillera, crosses nearly the whole breadth of Chile and runs into the Pacific a little to the south of the now flourishing port of Caldera, from which so much silver and copper is shipped.

---

[1] Chamber's Edin. Journal, March 8, 1851.
[2] A male and female, is now in the museum at Ratisbon.
[3] Probably Caspana, and south-east of Chiu-chiu.
[4] Such as the Inga-pirca or palace at Cañar, in Equador.

From Caldera there is a railway to the city of Copiapo, and branches even farther in the interior. It is in contemplation to carry this line over the Andes into the Pampas, from whence there will be but little difficulty in reaching Buenos Ayres and Europe.[1]

As to the antiquities of Chile, I am not able to say much; but on the Ethnology there is something more to communicate, particularly as regards the Araucanos.

From what we know of the Indians of Chile, they appear to have been, and in the south still continue a roving race rather than a fixed one. Those tribes who anciently inhabited the valleys of Copiapo, Guasco, Coquimbo, Quillota, and the beautiful country where now stands the capital of Chile, cultivated the land, and had their habitations. I find no account of ancient temples or other buildings of stone among the Indians; they had a fine climate and prolific soil, and scarcely required such, as did the Incarial nations of the elevated plateaus of Peru; and this may be one reason why we do not find monuments of antiquity among them.

Yupanqui, tenth Inca of Peru, projected the conquest of Chile. He organized an army of ten thousand men, about 1400, A.D., which passed the desert of Atacama; he gave the command of this army to Chinchi-cura. The Incarial force came to the country of Copayapu (Copiapo), but there met with determined resistance. The Inca reinforced Chinchi-cura with ten thousand men, when the Copayapenicas found it prudent to obey his laws, and receive the religion of Inti.

The Peruvians descended into the valley of Copiapo by the ravine of Paipote, where now is seen a rill of water, with a little vegetation, and even a few algaroba trees.[2]

The Peruvians, reinforced by a third army, then traversed the desert track to Huasco and Cuquimpu (Coquimbo), conquering to the river Maulli (Maule), but at this line the Araucanos successfully opposed them. When Almagro arrived at the valley of Copiapo, the Indians gave him vessels of gold valued at 2,000,000 ducats, equal to £400,000.

When I first visited Copiapo, in 1828, I sought for ancient ruins and huacas; I heard of the existence of some of the latter, but could find no one to further my views of exploration.

Being in Valparaiso, in 1854, my old friend Mr. Bridges, the botanist, handed me several pieces of huaca pottery, from Peru and Chile, to bring to England; amongst these were six specimens from Copiapo, now in the British Museum; one of them, a painted drinking cup.

---

[1] Proposed railway across the Andes from Caldera to Rosario, viz., Cordova. By W. Wheelwright, Esq., F.R.G.S., read to Geogr. Soc., January, 1860.
[2] Darwin Nat. voy. 359.

Mr. Abbott, of Copiapo, gives me the following account of huacas opened in 1843:

In consequence of the great development of mineral wealth in Copiapo, it was necessary to build houses and amalgamating works, and in doing so, many Indian tombs of the Copayapenicas were cut into. These huacas were large and small, built up from the surface like a mound, some twelve feet high and twenty to thirty in length. One examined contained the skeletons of a man and a woman, no clothing was found, as in the Peruvian mummies; and the skulls were of good form.

With the skeletons were several pieces of pottery, as large jars for holding water, others for chicha, and others for boiling water in; also, ornamented vessels for holding and carrying water or chicha, silicious arrow heads, copper pins, upper and lower stones for grinding maize, and maize in earthen pots.

An interesting object was found about 1832 at Copiapo, in a huaca, by Dr. Adrian Mandiola. It was of fine gold, as thin as paper, in the form of a small coco-nut shell, and open at top; when blown into gave a whooping sound; it bent on being pressed by the hand, but resumed its shape, the pressure being removed. This was presented by Mandiola to the National Museum. So much was this gift valued by the government, that he was sent a colonel's commission.

At the time of the Peruvian inroads into Chile, the district of Copiapo must have been well populated, as huacas are found throughout the valley. Dr. Echeveria, when building on the hill at the old port of Copiapo, found many huacas containing skeletons. For such a state of things, there must have been more land under cultivation, by reason of there being more water in the river, and, perhaps, more frequent rains. At present the stream is insignificant and rain uncommon; indeed, it may be called a desert country. To account for so dry an atmosphere at present, there must have been some change in the carrying power of the vapour of water and duration of winds.

About 1544, Valdivia sent emissaries from Chile to Peru by land, to give an account of his doings, which were not successful, Monroy, Miranda, six companions and an escort of thirty horse, they were attacked by the chief of Copiapo and killed, excepting Monroy and Miranda, whose lives were begged by the chief's wife, to teach her sons the management of the horse. Being out one day with one of their pupils, Monroy fell suddenly on the young chief, mortally wounding him, whilst Miranda, turning upon the officer in command of the guard, wrenched from his hand a lance, and, breaking from the Indians, they escaped and fled to Cuzco.

In 1548, the Indians of Copiapo rose on the Spaniards settled in the valley of Coquimbo and destroyed the city of La Serena.

Towards the Cordillera from Copiapo, and near Punta Gorda, are some old Indian ruins. Darwin[1] says, he observed Indian ruins in several parts of the Cordillera: the most perfect were the Ruinas de Tambillos (or little Tambo or Tampu, a resting place), in the Uspallata pass. Tradition says they were used as halting places by the Incas, when they crossed the mountains. At first, Darwin supposed these buildings had been places of refuge, built by the Indians on the arrival of the Spaniards. He is inclined to speculate on the probability of a small change of climate.

In the northern part of Chile, within the Cordillera, old Indian houses are said to be especially numerous. By digging amongst the ruins, bits of woollen articles, instruments of precious metals, and beads of indian corn, are not unfrequently discovered: an arrow-head of agate was found, and of precisely the same form as those now used in Tierra del Fuego.

In the valley of Punta Gorda, the remains consisted of seven or eight square little rooms, which were of a similar form with those at Tambillos, but chiefly of mud, which the present inhabitants cannot, either here, or, according to Ulloa, in Peru, imitate in durability.

Silver mines of Tres Puntas. Gilliss (1, 2, 3, plate VIII) gives a description of Indian antiquities found near the Incas road, including a cast copper axe, weighing about 3¼ lbs. He observes, that the old Chilian Indians do not appear to have worked in metal. Pottery was also met with, two specimens being glazed. I may observe, that salts of borax exist in the desert of Atacama, which may have been used for glazing.

In the atlas to Gaye's large work on Chile,[2] are two plates of Chilian antiquities, consisting of a sort of chopper in metal, a quiver for arrows, metal star-like war implements, &c.

MUSICAL FISH.—Gilliss (I., 270) speaks from report, of musical fish in the bay of Caldera; they were heard from January to March, 1852, but not since then. His informant says, he went out in a boat, and lay with his ear to the bottom of the boat, when he heard certain well-defined sounds, which he calls musical. Singing shells are mentioned as existing at Ceylon, and a species of snail at Corfu is said to emit an audible and not unmusical sound.

My friend, Mr. J. S. Wilson, late Geologist to the North Australian Expedition, gives the following on the subject of musical fish, in his

---

[1] Nat. Voy. 356.
[2] Historia fisica y politica de Chile.

paper to the Geographical Society (vol. xxviii., 1858, 149). The cat-fish in the Victoria River makes a singular trumpeting noise, while it is in the water and after it is landed. It is armed with a strong sharp spine, 2 to 2½ inches in length, standing perpendicularly from the back; and if the fingers get pricked with this, it causes a stinging sensation. I think I have heard this trumpeting sound when fishing in some of the rivers of Texas, where the cat-fish abounds.

Naturalists observe, that to some fish is accorded the faculty of ruminating, which is an error; that they possess a voice—another mistake. It is possible they may make some noise with their movements.

HUASCO.—At the conquest this valley had a chief named Marcandie, who, with the ruler of Copiapo and twenty-eight Indians, were burnt by Almagro for the killing of three Spaniards: this was the first Chilian and Spanish blood spilt in Chile.

COQUIMBO.—At the time of the conquest, the name of the nation who occupied this pretty and fruitful valley, was called the Cuquimpu. Whilst I was there in 1828, the guest of the hospitable and kind David Ross, who for many years has been Her Majesty's Consul at Coquimbo, he had occasion to repair a wall, when a huaca was met with, containing bones of its ancient people and a painted vase.

My friend, Mr. Alison, informs me, that in the port of Coquimbo, huacas with bodies have been found; also at Herradura, under a block of sienite of some five tons weight, three bodies were found. In the vicinity was much broken pottery.

At Andacollo, huacas have been met with, also a bronze chisel, fourteen to fifteen inches long. There are gold mines here.

Leaving the rich mining districts of the north, I remained some time in Valparaiso, the emporium of the west coast. The best idea I can give of its rapid progress is, that in 1825 the population was under 10,000, in 1854 more than 80,000, including a large number of English, Americans, Germans, French, &c., as merchants, shopkeepers and artizans.

Independent of its theatres, other places of amusement, colleges, hospitals, it has scientific and literary institutions; indeed, when perambulating its gay streets, lined with fine shops and houses, and examining its picturesque bay full of ships, an Englishman can scarcely realise the idea that he is so far distant from home, and in a locality, not long since possessed by the jealous Spaniard.

A beautiful ride of thirty leagues brings one to the capital. One ascends (formerly on horseback, now in a gig) the granitic mountains of the coast, covered with shrubs, cacti and palmetto, and, in the season, multitudes of pretty plants, including the calceolaria. A gallop of a few leagues brings the traveller to Casa Blanca; then over the interesting scenery of the mountain ranges of Zapata and Prado, where the pass is 2,394 above the sea. The descent is to the table-land of Mapochó, on which stands Santiago de Chile, founded by Valdivia in 1541.

From the hill of Santa Lucia, there are commanding, extensive and lovely views, comprising not only the large and populous city, with its suburbs and promenades, but the fertile valley, broken here and there by detached hills, and bounded on the east by a long line of Cordillera, clothed in perpetual snow. On the hill of Santa Lucia we find the National Observatory ably conducted by Moesta. The city is well built, many of its houses may be called palaces; its population is hospitable and refined. I became the guest of my old friend Mr. George Bingley, unto whom I am under great obligations for his unremitting attentions.

Santiago now boasts of a good University, one of its professors being the learned and amiable Domeyko, who is a considerable contributor to the scientific "Anales de la Universidad," and has a very fine collection of the minerals of the country, including a huge mass of the meteoric iron of Atacama; whilst the Museum is ably superintended by Philippi, the explorer of the desert of Atacama. I had not the pleasure to see Señor Pissis, who is conducting an elaborate survey of the country. The National Library is extensive, containing several thousand volumes formerly belonging to the Jesuits, also curious manuscripts relating to the Indians. There are some antiquities in the Museum, most probably the handy-work of the Peruvians during their ingressions, and a few Auracano weapons. An interesting relic of the conquerors is Valdivia's house.

Some old Indian ruins appear to exist near the gold mines of Yaquil, south of Santiago. On the Cerro de los Incas, near Lake Taguatagua,[1] are the remains, probably, of a fortress, said to be erected by the Promaucaes, the tribe which drove Almagro from the country.

On the Maipu, at San José, ancient human remains have been found, also implements of pure copper, as chisels; also a knife like the modern one of the leather-cutter.

Darwin saw one of the perforated stones used by the old Indians; these were fixed on the ends of sticks, and formed a rude agricultural instrument. These stones are of a circular flattened form, five to six inches in diameter.

---

[1] Mr. Smith, H. M. Consul at Santiago, gave me specimens of mastodon's bones from this spot; Professor Domeyko has lately sent to the Paris Museum similar specimens, also large horns of fossil deer.

To the north of Valparaiso is the port of Zapallar, and a few miles inland is the hacienda of Catapilco; between these places there is a considerable Indian cemetery. About 1850, these huacas, or ancient tombs, were discovered, and found to contain very large quantities of sea-shells; they were extracted, burnt into lime, and sent to Valparaiso. I have not been able to obtain particulars as to the state in which the bodies were found, or as to the objects buried with them.

Whilst in Peru, I was invited by my esteemed friend, Henry F. Fox, of the firm of Messrs. Ravenscroft, to visit him in Chile, and examine some saline bodies from the desert of Atacama, said to contain nitrate of soda, with a view of establishing nitrate works in that district. I went to Chile, examined the minerals, but they turned out to be merely common salt and sulphate of lime, and useless. I do not wish it to be understood that nitrate of soda does not exist in the desert of Atacama: I think that in the northern part it will be met with. I am aware that the borate of lime has been found in this direction.

I assisted Mr. Oxley, of Valparaiso, in the careful assay of native copper from San Bartolo, in Atacama, purporting to contain a large per-centage of gold; we did not find the slightest trace.

On my way from Guayaquil to Lima, I made the acquaintance of Señor Moncayo, then going from Equador to Peru as minister, he kindly ordered a copy of Velasco's Historia de Quito to be sent to me, also samples of the saline products of Imbabura, in Equador; I found these to be nitrate of potash, in various stages of purity, extracted from surface soil. There is much salt in the vicinity of this nitrate formation. Were there a direct road from Imbabura to the coast—say to the port of the Pailon, where it is the intention of the Equador Land Company of London to commence a settlement (see p. 103)—this nitrate might become a valuable export.

During my stay in Chile, a serious question arose, as to the direction the line of railway ought to take from Valparaiso to Santiago. Allan Campbell projected it, along the coast to Concon, Quillota, &c. To Viña de la Mar there was no objection, but from thence by the coast, it was soon discovered, that in consequence of very light sandy soil and back water at times, from rather heavy rains, it would be difficult to have a permanent way; thus it was necessary to look for another line. Mr. Lloyd, the engineer, requested me to accompany him and his staff; my department was to examine the country gone over for lime, as this substance would be required in large quantities.

After due investigation, Mr. Lloyd decided upon altering Campbell's line, and go up the valley of Viña de la Mar to Limache, and thus avoid the almost quicksands of the coast. From Limache we crossed the pass of the Dormida, 4,526 feet (July), where we found Snow, to the gold mines of Tiltil. We returned to Limache by the copper mines and pass of Caléo: near to the pass are some gold mines and washings; lower down are the gold mines and washings of Ocoa. The rock of the country is granitic with quartz veins, coloured with oxide of iron, resulting from the decomposition of the sulphuret. On this trip, I only met with granite yielding sand, and rocks yielding sandy clays; except near the village of Alvarado, there is a silico-calcareous rock, which may be useful. A similar formation exists at the Calera, near to Santiago, and in some few other localities.

At the request of Messrs. Cousiño and Garland, of Valparaiso, I went and reported on the coal mines of Lota and Coronel. My observations were read before the University of Chile, and will be found also in the Journal of the Geographical Society of London for 1855. This coal belongs to the tertiary formation, and appears to be in abundance. There are thirty-four mines at Lota, employing nearly 3000 workmen. In 1859, Lota alone extracted 39,807 tons.

After examining this coal district, I could not resist another visit to Arauco, celebrated by Ercilla, in his poem, "La Araucana," and by Oña, in his "Arauco Domado."

As early as 1828, I had been in this region, with Mr. George Smith, of Iquique, on a survey of the Island of Quiriquina and vicinity for coal.

Accompanied by a friend, both well mounted, with our thick woollen ponchos to protect against rain, we went by the cuestas of Colcura and Villagran; on the summit of the latter, there is an interesting view of Colcura and the country of the coal mines of Lota and Coronel. We forded the river Chivilingo, but had to swim our horses over that of Laraquete, whilst we crossed on foot over the bridge—namely, a long pole. There had been heavy rains, so the tracks were perfect quagmires, generally obliterated; we were lost for awhile, but came up with a rancho, the mother and daughter only within; the latter, a little girl, at our request, jumped up behind my friend, who was very tall, his large tarpauling hat, long Indian poncho, huge boots all over mud, with the descendant of the Lautaros and Guacoldas in half-Indian costume—her good-natured face, and long black hair, flowing freely in the wind—made a good picture.

Onwards we went, through mud and streams, to another rancho, where we procured a guide in his picturesque guaso costume, who conducted us over the Vegas, down the river Carampangui, which we crossed in a launch, and, after a smart gallop, arrived at the famed fort of Arauco, at the entrance of which I was shown a hole that held the pole on which had been placed the head of one Zuñiga; he was of the rebel party, headed by General Cruz, and thus disposed of just before the bloody battle of Longomillo.

I found a considerable town in formation outside the walls; on a former visit there were only a few huts within. Now coal mines are being opened, corn and timber mills established; indeed, a busy and increasing population.

At the house in which I stopped, I saw some Araucano women; they were of small stature, the head large and covered with thick black hair, round features, a red tinge on the cheeks, seen through the copper colour; nose flat, eyes bright, small feet and hands, and habited somewhat like the Indian women of Peru, with the choñi or blue shifts, without sleeves; the yquella or mantle, fastened by the large silver topo or pin, broad girdle, the end having tubular tin ornaments; round the neck a silver-mounted collar, from which hung a breastplate of beads, the neck part studded with two-rial pieces, and in the ears large silver rings or oupelles.

Subsequently I saw parties of Araucanos on horseback; they were thick-set men, had large heads, broad faces, their black hair bound by the red llautu or fillet; the under clothing or macun, then a sort of waistcoat and short trousers, and the never-failing poncho. They were armed with the lance and some had sabres, and men who looked as if they were not to be trifled with; they also use pikes, axes, darts, arrows, slings and lassos. The favourite and death-dealing weapon of the Araucanos, at the time of their terrible wars with the Conquistadores, was the macana, said by some to be shaped like a long sword, by others, a club. They still paint their faces with red and black pigments.

The earliest notice we possess of the aborigines of Chile, have descended to us from the Peruvians. Ercilla and Oña follow, Molina copies from them. Stevenson, in 1825, gives his observations. English and American missionaries have made reports, particularly the late Captain Gardener; much is to be found in Gaye's History of Chile; and, lastly, E. R. Smith's "Araucanians," published in New York, 1855, is the most recent account we have of a tour amongst them. From this work I make some extracts.

The aborigines of Chile and of a portion of the present Argentine Republic, were of one race, and spoke but one language; they called themselves Alapu-che, children of the land. They were distinguished as Pehuenché, people of the east; Moraché, people of the west; and Huillehé, far-off people living in the south. These were divided in'o provinces, as the Purumancians; and then into districts, and lived as separate tribes; the most important was the so-called Araucano, a name given to them by the Spaniards.

Mr. Smith tried to discover whether the Araucanos retained any traditions of times anterior to the Spanish conquest, especially of the encroachments of the Peruvian Incas, but he was surprised to find that their historical recollections did not extend farther back than the wars of South American Independence.

The Mapuchés appear to have no idea of their origin, but assert that they always lived in the same place and manner as at present; nor have they any traditions respecting a deluge.

Valdivia is said to have met with certain rudely-carved figures on the Cauten, at its confluence with the Damas, bearing some resemblance to the double-headed eagle.

Mr. Smith observed, between Cholchol and Cautin, graves marked with a single post, rudely fashioned and ornamented at the top; some by a figure resembling the European hat; others, by what might by one so predisposed, be constructed into a double-headed eagle. What this latter carving was intended to represent we know not. Mr. Smith thus describes the grave of the Huilyichés: over each is planted an upright log, ten or twelve feet high, rudely carved to represent the human figure. The chief—for such he must have been—stood in the centre of the group with a hat on and a sword; while on either hand were ranged his wives. These were the only carved representations of the human figure, or of any other animate object met with among the Mapuchés; for they have no idols, neither do they mould earthenware vessels into forms of men and animals, as was customary among the Peruvians. There appears to be an Araucano Charon, sometimes a few beads or money deposited in the grave, as was done at the burial of the Mapuché chief, Cari-coyan (the green oak). Tempulagy is their She-Charon. They dread magic and are very superstitious.

I have already referred to the custom of the ancient and modern Peruvian Indians—that of making offerings of apachitas, being a stone, coca or other object, when they had arrived at the summit of a mountain or elevated pass. I find that the Araucanos have something similar. At the entrance to one of the narrow defiles in the Cordilleras, in which they are often overtaken by violent storms, there has been observed a large mass of rock with small cavities upon its surface, into which the Indians, when about to enter the pass, generally deposit a few glass beads, a handful of meal, or some other propitiatory offering to the genius supposed to preside over the spot and rule the storm.

As to the language of the Araucanos, I must refer to Ludewig, who gives copious lists of grammars and vocabularies of Chile. He says the aborigines call themselves Auca, Moluche, or Chilidugu, and are divided into Pikunche or Puelche; Pehuenche, to which the Auca or Moluches proper belong, and Huilliche. D'Orbigny distinguishes them by the sedentary (Araucanian) and roving (Auca) tribes.

I trace in the Chilian language some almost pure Quichua words, probably left by their Peruvian invaders; as, Anti, the sun; Anti-chéo, Albatross of the Sun, the name of a chief; Epu-namun, god of war—this is from Apu, lord or master; Apo-ulmenes, chiefs or lords; Piri-mapu, Andes: Chiri would be the frozen Andes in Quichua. Yquella, mantle, lliclia; topo, pin, from tupu; llantu, fillet round the head, same in Quichua; also maçana, a club; &c.

The Guarani,[1] to which the Chilian attaches itself, and which manifests a great grammatical development, was spread throughout the south and east of South America. The Pampean or Moxo belongs to the Carib family.

Araucania[2] formerly extended from about the river Biobio, in 36° 44' S., to Valdivia, in 39° 38'; Concepcion bounded it on the north, the Llanos or plains of Valdivia, on the south. The Cordillera formed its eastern limits, and the Pacific its western. It was divided into four parallel strips or uthal-mapus: first, Laugen-mapu, the maritime country, including Arauco, Tucapel, Ilicura, and Boroa: Second, Lel-bun-mapu, the plain country containing Encol, Puren, Repoura, Maquegua, and Mariquina: Third, Mapire-mapu, the foot of the Cordilleras, as Malsen, Colhue, Chacaico, Quecheriqua, and Guanague: Fourth, Pire-mapu, the valleys of the Andes. These were again divided into allareques provinces, and reques districts. This form of division existed before the arrival of the Spaniards. Each uthal-mapu was governed by a Toqui, who had under him Apo-ulmenes and Ulmenes. There was also the Grande Toqui, the head of all, and who presided at their councils.

The Supreme Being was called Pillian, or the invisible Toqui. Epu-namum, the god of war; Alooc, the devil. No Temples, idols, or religious rites were observed by Stevenson; but they believed in witch-craft, divination, omens, flights of birds, and dreams.

The following I obtained regarding the present position of the Araucanos. They are divided into Costeños, or those of the coast who trade with the Chilians, exchanging cattle and horses, principally for

---

[1] "Indigenous Races," 83.
[2] See Stevenson, I., 47. Historical and Des. Narr. of Residence in S. America, London, 1825.

silver, indigo and beads: gold they call copper.[1] These Costeños trade with other Indians inhabiting the country between the coast and the Cordillera, and these latter with those of the Andean valleys, who cross the mountains to rob or barter with the Indians on the Mendoza side, passing their booty of horses and cattle to the Costeños, who sell to the Chilians.

The Araucano of the interior will not part with his land, but the Costeños are sometimes induced to let land; and such, when near the Chilian frontier, is considered as sold.

Captain Gardener says,[2] although frequently confederated, they are not strictly federal, each tribe being independent of the rest and distinguished by a particular name, as Huillches, Moluches, and Picuntos, on the western; Pehuenches, Puelches,[3] and Chuelches, on the eastern side of the Andes.

With the exception of the Chuelches, who are reported as distinct in language from the rest, but one common tongue is said to be spoken by all.

Their habitations are generally oval. At Piligen, in every house was observed two spears hung up to the beams across the roof, with their points directed towards the entrance ready for use; they are sixteen feet long, and headed with a narrow steel point. They manufacture a coarse woollen fabric, make reins for bridles, stirrup leathers and saddle girths. Indigo is in general demand for dyeing; other dyes are also employed, and some that are peculiar to the country, which are chiefly required for the bordering of their ponchos; each tribe, like the Scotch clans, have a distinctive colour.

The Picuntos are distinguished by a red bordering to their ponchos; the Huillches, by a party-coloured fringe, yellow, red, blue, white and green. They have neither whiskers nor beard. The heads and feet of both men and women are always uncovered. Infants, when put to

---

[1] Smith, "Araucanians," 181. Gold is not seen in their possession, in all probability from the difficulty of procuring it by their own labour. Silver, which they use in large quantities for their spurs, bits, stirrups, head-stalls, saddle ornaments, ear-rings, breast-pins, &c., is drawn from the currency of the country, probably to the amount of £40,000 annually. According to Molina, the copper mines of Payen, in the Puelche country, furnished pure copper containing half its weight in gold. The mines of Curico yielded a similar alloy.

[2] "Indians of Chile," London, 1840.

[3] Puenche or Puelche, is applied to those Araucanos living east of the Cordillera, or, perhaps, amongst the mountains east of the plain (of Chile). The name signifies pepuen, pines and che, people; probably from the forests of the Araucano pine, found at the foot of the mountains. Puelche, in the sense of east, or wind from the east.—Smith's "Auracanians," 64.

sleep, are confined by bandages to a sort of wooden trough. The women are employed in cultivating the ground, preparing the food, and other family offices. The men attend to the cattle, fell timber, train horses, and prepare their weapons, and have as many wives as they can maintain.

The present frontier system of the Chilenos is based upon the ephemeral principle of expediency: the peace they cannot ensure by their arms, they maintain by bribes; especially by the introduction of cider, to effect unequal sales, and thus by gradually intermixing with them whenever allowed, to push forward their frontier to an indefinite extent.

Their form of government is patriarchal, each community acknowledging a chief of the particular district, who is styled Ulmen; all the chieftains are hereditary, and although they differ in power, according to the strength of their respective tribe, none are permitted to exercise independent control over the whole tribe, excepting in time of war; but even this temporary dictatorship of the Toqui is elective.

They have neither priesthood, temples, nor idols, but regard the sun, under the name of Anti, as the supreme being; some pay a veneration to (kayan) the moon; and their devotions do not amount to anything more than occasional offerings to propitiate their favour in cases of sickness, or on the approach of war.

Frezier informs us, that the Araucanos, to keep account of their flocks and preserve the memory of particular affairs, make use of the Quipo, the science and secret of which parents do not reveal to their sons until they are about dying.

Stevenson gives the following as regards the Quipo: in 1792, a revolt took place near Valdivia, and, on the trial of the accomplices, Marican, one of them, declared that the signal sent by Lepitrarn was a piece of wood, that it was split and found to contain the finger of a Spaniard; that it was wrapped round with thread having a fringe at one end, made of red, black, blue and white worsted; that on the black were tied by Lepitrarn, four knots, to intimate that it was the fourth day after the full moon when the bearer left Paquipilli; that on the white were ten knots, indicating that ten days after that date the revolt would take place; that on the red was to be tied, by the person who received it, a knot, if he assisted in the revolt, but if he refused, he was to tie a knot of the blue and red joined together; so that, according to the route enjoined by Lepitrarn, he would be able to discover on the return of the messenger, how many friends would join him; and if he dissented, he would know who it was by the place where the knot uniting the two threads was tied. Thus it would appear that the

Toquis of Arauco may preserve records by means of a sort of Quipo, which they may have had originally from Peru.

Their important meetings wind up with a lengthened scene of drinking, called Cahouin Touhan, their beverage being chicha of maize, apples, and from the berries of the huinan (schinus molle); from this last is prepared a sort of honey and vinegar; the gum of it is used medicinally, and a decoction of the bark dyes a brown colour.

The apple tree has been said to be indigenous: I have always had my doubts on this point; and Smith,[1] in speaking of an apple orchard, judging from the age of the trees and the regularity with which they were set out, says they must have been planted by the Jesuit missionaries. The apple abounds in Southern Chile, and found growing wild throughout the Indian country; yet, that it is not indigenous, but owes its introduction to the Spaniards, seems proved also by the fact that the Indians call the fruit manchana, a corruption of the Spanish manzana or apple.

Three leagues south of the fort of Arauco, is the river Tubul. The hills of Colocolo are of recent sandstone, and bear evidence that their bases were not long since washed by the sea, although now half a mile inland. The river Tubul is a tidal stream, and at its mouth is a bar; the port was formerly two miles inland, and there are the remains of an old ship-yard there; this would show that the elevatory process is going on rather rapidly. The shores are thickly strewed with large mussel and other shells. Sea birds, flamingos and green parrots are in abundance; the hills and valleys covered with pastures, shrubs, trees, and flowers, including the Copique (Lapageria rosea), gorgeous with its crimson blossoms; the Indian revelling in the more secluded forests and where grows the beautiful Araucano pine or pehuen. This tree is said to grow to the height of two hundred and sixty feet; the seeds are called piñones; they are nutritious, and in flavour resembling the roasted chesnuts; when boiled, they are eaten hot or cold. Mr. George Smith, of Iquique, made an elaborate drawing of the tree in 1828 (the first accurate one), which the late Mr. Lambert introduced into his great work on pines.

In the beginning of 1859, some of the Araucanos were induced to aid the movement headed by the Gallos; however, the Montt government was the strongest, and the Gallos were beaten after some sanguinary fights in the north and south. The government seriously propose to attempt the settlement, even by force of arms, of that portion of Arauco near the Chilian frontiers.

In August, 1859, the Araucano chief, Maguil, organised a force of

[1] The Araucanians, 267.

13,000 Indians. In December the Chilenos pushed forward, when Mariñan, with sixty Mocetones, came to the city of Arauco, sent by Lepin and other chiefs, asking why the Chilenos were attacking their frontiers; the answer was, because the Indians were assisting the enemies of the government, and for this must be punished. A few days afterwards, the Chilenos went in search of stolen cattle, when several Indians were killed. This has been followed by other fights; but the conquest, or even pacification of the Araucanos is a very serious question.

On a late occasion an Indian, mounted and with his lance, came out on the plain and challenged any Chilian to single combat, when Casimiro Anquita accepted the defiance with sword in hand. The fight was of some duration and severe, when at length the Indian's lance was dexterously parried by the sword of the Chileno, and he with his other hand seized the Indian by the hair of his head, cutting his throat with his sword, when the victim fell to the ground.

A German colony has been established near Valdivia, and appears to be progressing.

I visited the island of Juan Fernandez, but found no indication of native inhabitants. The island was discovered by a Spanish pilot named Juan Fernandez; it was occasionally occupied by the buccaneers, and immortalised by Defoe in his Robinson Crusoe.

INDIANS OF TIERRA DEL FUEGO.—In 1825, whilst chemical assistant in the laboratory of the Royal Institution, I accepted an appointment connected with mining operations in Peru. I proceeded to Buenos Ayres, but the passes of the Andes to Chile being closed by winter snow, I took my passage round Cape Horn.

I had to remain some days in Buenos Ayres; and, amongst many others, I have to thank Sir Woodbine Parish, then our representative there, for much kindness. I was informed that a large mass of the meteoric iron of Otumpa was deposited in the arsenal, and obtained permission to inspect it, and even to cut a small piece off, which I sent to my friend, Professor Brande. Years afterwards, when going through the British Museum, I was indeed gratified to see the same mass presented by Sir W. Parish. It weighs about 1,400 lbs,[1] and the largest specimen of meteoric iron in any collection.

I sailed the 1st of July in the brig "Cherub," bound to Valparaiso; we had bad weather, but having got to 58° S., 69° W., hoped to have weathered Cape Horn. However, on the 6th of August at noon land was seen. We thought ourselves to have been farther to the west. It came on to blow hard from the S.W., when, at eight p.m., we found

[1] See Buenos Ayres, &c., by Sir W. Parish.

ourselves among the rocky inlets of York Minster, where we passed a fearful night. From two a.m. the following morning to daylight, we were prepared to be dashed upon a lee-shore. At this critical moment the gale abated, and, by judicious management, we rounded False Cape Horn, and got into Nassau Bay. Here we intended to wood and water, and the time thus employed, gave me an opportunity of examining this but seldom visited portion of South America.

8th. Landed up a sound, probably that of Tekenika, when a native and a dog was first observed; the man hallooed and beckoned us to approach; he kindled a fire on the beach; other natives appeared, saw some canoes on the shore, and a grass-covered hut and females peeping at us through the bushes. We landed, approaching the men, who had squatted round the fire, and whose shoulders only were covered with a seal-skin. They rose to receive us, when we gave them some presents; we proceeded to the wigwam, but found that our visit was not wanted in that direction. In rambling about, piles of dead whale flesh were found; this was the winter stock of food of the natives, who, from our charts, were called the Red Magellans: on the other side of the bay was placed the Black Magellans. On the pile of whale flesh was a trap of whalebone for catching birds. I gave a young Indian boy a red "comforter;" in return, he stripped himself of all he had on and gave me, namely, a seal-skin, and a bracelet made of pieces of small birds' bones. The tallest man here was not above 5 feet 4 inches; they appeared in good condition and well greased with whale fat, to protect themselves somewhat from the cold. One of the men had three streaks of red paint across the face, others two. They repeated what we said to them correctly, but rapidly; we danced and sang to them, in which they joined. One of them had a strip of a check shirt round his head, showing that such had been received from whalers or sealers, who came into these waters.

9th. Blowing a heavy gale from south-west. The mountains at the head of the bay seen, very well defined.

11th. The Indians procure fire by rubbing iron pyrites with hard stone, letting the sparks fall on dry moss. I tried to gain admittance to their principal wigwam, but was refused. I gave them salt beef and biscuit; the biscuit only was liked. The canoes were of bark of trees, fastened by thin strips of whalebone. About the shore were ferns and many pretty sorts of trees; the rock of the country granitic.

12th. Went up the bay on foot; wood is in abundance, including the winter's bark. Saw much wild celery: it would appear that this useful anti-scorbutic was introduced by early navigators; we procured a quantity of the seed for our pea-soup. Few land birds, but sea fowl in abundance, including penguins. Returned to the wigwam, and was allowed to enter. What a scene of misery! a small rude grass hut, four feet high, sunk two feet in the ground, filthily dirty. There sat an old man and woman in tears, the smoke from the fire of green wood giving them much pain; the party consisted of fourteen men, two women, and three children; their only clothing a small piece of seal or other skin. The day was fine, the small birds were chirping, the sun was bright, clouds clearing away, so that we could see well the majestic scenery of this region.

They had some rude cutting instruments of iron, doubtless made from iron hoop given to them by whalers. They make neatly-platted baskets, skin bags for holding water, food and fat; their arms are the bow and arrow and sling.

14th. We got under weigh, when a canoe came off to bid us farewell.

15th. Passed False Cape Horn at noon. Three p.m., the south point of Cape Horn seen. We now ran to more than 60° S.; the lowest temperature observed was 20° F. We reached Valparaiso on the 24th of September. I found no vestige of carving in wood or stone, or monument of any kind in Nassau Bay. The occupation of the natives is in fishing, catching seals and otters for food, using the skins as raiment; and when a dead whale might float on shore, they would remain at the spot until it was consumed. They may have a few edible roots, but they have several varieties of wild fruits. I thought if the potato was introduced, it would be a great boon. Doubtless the scattered population of the archipelago of Tierra del Fuego communicate with each other, and originally have come from the main land. I have again to advert to this people when on my passage through the straits of Magellan.

Having concluded my engagement at the mines in Peru, I returned to Chile on my way to England.

On the 11th of February, 1830, I embarked on board H. M. surveying vessel, "Adventure," Captain P. P. King, who kindly allowed me a passage.[1]

On the 16th we arrived at Juan Fernandez; Dr. Bertero, the botanist, had come with us; he found many new plants. The Chilian family of Larrain was renting the island from the government, for breeding cattle. Large quantities of fish, langosta or lobster and seals caught in these waters.

17th. Made one of a party to go goat hunting, had some good sport. The highest spot on the island is the Yunque or anvil, about 3000 feet.

[1] See Narrative of Surveying Voyages of the "Adventure" and "Beagle," 1826-36.

It was supposed that sandal-wood grew on this island, which does not appear to be the case.

We sailed on the 22nd for Talcahuano, arriving the 3rd of March. On the 6th I started for the fort of Arauco, saw Indians there making purchases; returned to Concepcion by the Molino delas Cruzes, so called from stones found here, having a cruciform appearance. Captain King had an interview with the Araucano chief, Pinoleo.

15th. Left Talcahauno for the straits of Magellan.

In 45° S. is the Chonos archipelago, inhabited by rude tribes, who maintain themselves by fishing.

We had rough weather on the voyage south, but having passed Cape Pillar and entered the straits on the 1st of April, we had smooth water.

2nd. Anchored at Playa Parda, on our route passed much rocky scenery, and some glaciers. Guanacos have been seen on the Fuegian side.

5th. Got under weigh; noon off snowy Sound, some glaciers seen. A canoe came along side with two men and two women. The painter or boat rope, was of platted reeds, the fishing spears had bone barbs, knives of obsidian, had supply of iron pyrites for obtaining fire.

6th. Canoes with Indians came from Port Gallant, and nearly naked, and in this cold climate; we bartered for spears, bows and arrows, obsidian, pyrites, slings, combs (of the jaw-bone of the seal), necklaces of small pearly-looking shells, cups made of the bark of trees, baskets, red paint, (oxide of iron.)

Went on shore to wigwams. There can be no doubt that some of the whalers and sealers treat the natives badly.

The Indians of Port Gallant are like those I had seen in Nassau Bay. They object much to part with a lock of their hair; a lock of hair having been cut from a woman, half of it was returned, which they immediately burned; an old man held his hands over the smoke, when they all uttered "Picheray," and looking upwards. Fitzroy thinks it may mean "give me." They were anxious to possess the other half; I halved it again; one of the men warmed his hands, rolled the hair up and swallowed it: they cut some of our hair, going through the same ceremony.

7th Accompanied a party from the "Adventure" to replace Bourganville's papers on the summit of the mountain of Santa Cruz, left by him there in 1766; they had been examined by Cordova in 1786, and by the "Beagle." The papers, with some by Captain King, were put up in a lead case; two metal plates were deposited also, containing the names of the officers of the "Adventure."

We began the ascent at 9.20, a.m., through fallen trees, then over mossy ground, and through shrubs, arriving at second peak, 2,300 feet, at 12.15, p.m. We dug a hole a yard deep, depositing the papers.

8th. Many canoes came off to us. Here I picked up the following words: yab-skooler, probably means to eat, or something to eat; sherro, ship, boat or canoe; kaib, no, or if disappointed; chox-pitit, little child; jar, jar, yes; uxchuca, water, probably from the Spanish, agua.

They use some few Spanish words, as capitan, perro (dog), canoa, huanaco, cuchino for cuchillo, knife.[1]

For some trifling offence, one of the men nearly laid open his squaw's skull. They have no fish-hooks, but pull the fish up when the bait is down its throat; also spear them. At times the men are painted from head to foot, red, white and black: we had seventy to eighty Indians about us.

11th. Off Cape Froward; anchored in French Frigate harbour, where there is a creek, and much celery.

12th. Went to Port Famine. The berberries in season, and very good.

14th. Visited the Sedger river, saw a fuschia in flower.

15th. Walked into the interior: grass in abundance.

16th. The transit instrument put up.

18th. Day fine, breezes from south-east; nights beautiful and clear. The comet, though now small, is near to the Magellan clouds.

20th. Went to Port Piedra: there have been Patagonians here lately.

21st. Fine and clear: saw peaks of the celebrated Mount Sarmiento seventy miles distant, 6,800 feet high. Nine canoes full of Fuegians took up their quarters near us. On Captain King's landing, found an old man with stones in his mantle, as if ready for the sling. Captain King showed him a musket, the Indian threw the stones down. I went on shore to live in the marquee, where the transit instrument was.

22nd. Indians bartered with us. As we had clothes out drying, and the instrument up, a line was drawn round us and a sentry stationed; the Indians pretended they did not understand us. At noon I went on board, and returning at one, p.m., heard a musket fired down at the meridian board, and learnt that Captain King, when showing his telescope to the Indians at the lines, one pulled and broke it; he ordered them to go away, this they did, but getting near the meridian board, broke it down, and prepared their slings, putting themselves on the offensive; a musket was fired, and the Fuegians made off round St. Ann's Point. Two boats went to see what they were about, and when returning, a volley of stones from the slings were directed against our men, who fired a few shots, just to frighten them.

---

[1] See Vocabularies in Voyage of "Adventure" and "Beagle," in 4th vol.; also in Weddell, Snow.

23rd. Indians very saucy to us, but kept their distance.
27th. The Indians came near the watering place, shouting "Osa, osa."
2nd of May. Broke up our camp and went on board.
3rd. Our tender, the "Adelaide," arrived.
6th. Left Port Famine; 7th, noon, near Cape Gregory, saw a party of Patagonians on shore with their horses; arrived at Monte Video 23rd May.

Many attempts have been made to civilise the inhabitants of Tierra del Fuego, but they have failed; the last information is up to March, 1860, and as follows:

The "Allen Gardner" (Patagonian missionary schooner), Captain Fall, which sailed from the Falkland Islands for Woolga, Tierra del Fuego, October 7th, was taken by the natives at Woolga, Beagle Channel, on the 6th of November, and the master, mate, five seamen, and Mr. Garland Phillips, the catechist, murdered, one man only escaping. The "Nancy Smyley," with extra hands and weapons on board, had sailed from the Falkland Islands to recover the schooner.

Captain Snow, in his Cruise off Tierra del Fuego, 1857, says the Fuegians are divided into seven tribes: 1. Oensmen; 2. Yapoo; 3. Tekeenica; 4. Alikhoolip; 5. Chonos; 6. Pecherey; 7. Irees.

June 2nd. Invited to accompany the officers of the tender, "Adelaide," to Rio de Janeiro, the "Adventure" in company. 25th. Arrived at Rio, and in England 14th of October, 1830.

PATAGONIA is that country south of the frontiers of the River Plate and Chile, and of a most uninviting aspect; the principal trees are a few willows on the banks of the streams. Mineral matters have not been met with. Some guano has been found on the coast; huanacos and pole cats are the principal animals.

Among the Patagonian tribes are sometimes included the Molucos, Puelches, Puenches, Araucanos, Tehuelches, and others; but they may be divided into three classes, as Araucanos, Indians of the Pampas and the Patagonians to the south; these last are a dirty, indolent race; they are wanderers, and go where they may meet with food and good climate; they clothe in guanaco and pole-cat skins in winter, and also use the poncho. The Patagonians or Pehuenches are tall men.

PAMPA INDIANS are not so rude as the Patagonians; they have some permanent tolderias or villages, have property and ideas of traffic; they obey a chief and clothe themselves; the horse is their companion in peace or war. The territory occupied by them may be considered as belonging to the Argentine provinces. Lately Urquiza went against Buenos Ayres, having as his allies some 2000 of these Indians, and mainly for fear of their pillaging Buenos Ayres, the inhabitants came to terms with Urquiza.

PRE-INCARIAL, INCARIAL, AND OTHER MONUMENTS OF PERUVIAN NATIONS.

IN preceding pages I have brought together particulars concerning the antiquities of New Granada, Quito and Chile. Popayan and Pasto, to the north of Quito, were once well populated lands, but I find little as to the existence of ancient ruins in these districts; should any be discovered, they may partake of the Muysca character, or even that of an older period.

Generally speaking, the antiquities met with in Peru are assigned to the Incas; however, the Conquistadores were told that some ruins were much older than the Incarial times. Then come the pure Inca remains, and, lastly, the contemporaneous. It is not my object to describe the antiquities of Peru in detail, but rather to separate them somewhat into their particular periods, adding, at times, new matter regarding them.

PRE-INCARIAL MONUMENTS.—I will commence with the very ancient ruins of Tia-Huanacu,[1] in 16° 42′ S., 68° 42′ W., 12,930 feet above the sea, and near to Lake Titicaca. The principal remains are the sculptured monolythic doorways, one ten feet high and thirteen wide; pillars seven yards high, partly cut, partly rough, placed in lines at regular distances; it is thought that these were never finished; masses of hewn stone, some thirty-eight feet long by eighteen broad, whilst at Cuzco there were none nearly so large. Gigantic idols of stone and various sculptures are alluded to by old writers; Cieza de Leon particularly describes some stone figures, the length of the head of one, from the point of the beard to the top, being three feet six inches; in the upper part were wide vertical bands, in the lower, symbolical figures with human faces; from the eyes descended a band terminating in a serpent.

In 1842, an idol was excavated and taken to La Paz, 3½ yards in length and half a yard in width.

In 1846, further excavations were made, when some idols were met with, and some sculptured masses of large dimensions; some were ten yards in length, six in width, and more than two yards thick, and were so cut, that when resting on each other, their junction formed a

---

[1] See Rivero and Tschudi, Antig. Peru.

channel between them. One proof to me that these statues are not Incarial is, that their ears are not enlarged like the Inca Orejones. It would seem that two different sorts of sculpture are met with: one example is the portion of a statue, the face in particular naturally designed; others, as the centre figure in the large monolythic doorway, which is grotesque and of a much older date, but neither have the enlarged ears. The 4th Inca, Mayta Capac, was at this spot, but we do not know if he lived here for any time; if he did, the naturally-designed work may be attributed to him; if not to him, then there is the probability of there having been two pre-Incarial epochs at Tia-Huanacu. I have sometimes considered the remains in this locality to be very old Aymará, but, in truth, no date can be assigned to them.

In plate XLVI. of Rivero and Tschudi, is a drawing of the great broken monolyth doorway; on the right, in the upper part, are nine lines of heads, six of these have five heads each, three have four heads; the same number on the left, also two more heads, under the large figure, in all eighty-six heads. Can this collection of heads represent the number of chiefs who may have ruled here, belonging to a particular dynasty? if so, then the number of one hundred and one chiefs and Incas of Peru, according to Montesinos, may be worthy of further investigation.

In the frontispiece to the "Antiguedades Peruanas," containing the large figure in the centre, there are ten human figures to the right at top, and as many on the left; then a similar number with heads of birds; then follow below the same number of heads as above; in all, forty human figures, and twenty with heads of birds. No explanation is given by Rivero and Tschudi.

Dr. Latham observes, as to the ancient skulls found in this region, 1. that they are flattened in front, behind or laterally, with the surture obliterated; 2. the present inhabitants are not in the habit of flattening the skull; 3. the old race of the flattened skulls, is the race which appears to have been the executors of the oldest portion of the Peruvian architectural antiquities, and as such, civilised or semi-civilised.

Neither tradition or history have handed down the original name of this most ancient site. Garcilasso sometimes calls these ruins Chiquivitu, but under the Incas the western border of the Lake of Titicaca was called Chucuito, the eastern Umasuyu: this latter word means land of waters.

The origin of the term Tia-Huanacu is as follows: One of the Incas, probably Mayta Capac, being here, and receiving important news brought by a rapid foot messenger, who had travelled with great speed, said to him, in praise of his exertions, "Tia-Huanucu," sit or rest thee, Huanaco," comparing his celerity to that of the fleet Huanaco.

In Incarial times, this portion of Peru was also known as Colla, or the mountain region, and was inhabited by various tribes called Collas, or mountaineers, including the most populous one, the Aymará; but these were not the builders of Tia-Huanacu.

When Cieza de Leon examined these monuments, he asked of those who dwelt there, if the Incas had built them; the Indians smiled at such a question, and told him they were centuries older than the Incas, that they had once the idea of residing there, so as to take advantage of the buildings, but changed their mind, went to Cuzco and built it, something after the style of Tia-Huanacu.

Latham, in his "Migrations of Man," says—"the present occupants of the country of Tia-Huanacu and Titicaca wonder at the ruins around them, just as a modern Greek thinks of the Phidian Jupiter and despairs." I believe that the Incas also looked with wonder on these monuments; and it is more than 700 years since Mayta Capac beheld Tia-Huanacu with astonishment.

Humboldt thus generalises: "Throughout Mexico and Peru the traces of a great degree of civilisation are confined to the elevated plateaux. It can only have been men of a northern race, who, migrating from the north towards the south, could find delight in such a climate." I may observe, that old and enigmatical Tia-Huanacu is 12,930 feet above the sea; but there were great nations on the tropical coasts of the Pacific, as the Caras, governed by their Scyris; the country of Trujillo, by the Chimus, at Lima, and to the south the powerful Curys-mancus and Chuquiz-mancus ruling the Chincha nations.

The latitude of Tia-Huanacu is about 16° S., but what surprises, is the fact of its height of 12,930 feet above the sea. From my own experience of this sort of region, such an elevation is not propitious to the respiratory organs for man or animal; very few trees or shrubs grow, maize and wheat in any quantity is out of the question. In the summer months, some quinua or millet may grow, but this last would hardly give sustenance to the builders of Tia-Huanacu. The Collas had no maize to make their chicha from, but used the quinua for this purpose, and gave llamas in exchange for fuel brought from the lower country. This elevated region, in summer, may have fed on its rough pastures the domestic llama and alpaca (but these did not yield milk), also the wild huanaco and vicuña. We may also include a few deer, biscachas, chinchillas, and guinea pigs; there was also water fowl and some species of fish in the Andean lakes and streams. Maize and other vegetable productions may have been provided from the valleys below.

I have already referred to the quinua plant as affording grain; and Tschudi speaks of the maca, a tuberose root (probably a Tropæolum). It was in such a region the potato may have grown in the summer, but was frozen in winter; then it was called chuño and pagi, the starchy part being changed into saccharine[1]. Still it is a matter for wonder to find so large a collection of ruins in now a generally frozen desert. Similar and other monuments are also met with around Lake Titicaca, which is only 135 feet lower than Tia-Huanacu.

Buckle[2] is not quite correct in stating that the original civilisation of Peru was seated in a hot country. Tia-Huanacu, the site of some of the earliest architecture, is almost in a continual frozen region.

Weddell[3] went from La Paz (which is in a ravine, 12,226 feet, its upper part, or alto, 13,560 feet above the sea), by Tia-Huanacu, to Arequipa; he first traversed a stony desert; there were some spots, here and there, capable of cultivation, but without verdure. Innumerable piles of stones, formed by clearing the ground of them, show the difficulty the Indian has to put it into a state of cultivation, say for quinua and the maca. After passing Laja, the stony plain was covered with a more recent soil, and another plain, on which stands the ruins of Tia-Huanacu, is of a similar formation: the ruins are on an eminence, which formerly may have been a small island. Other heights about here show lines of water level, and this same appearance is perceived even to the shores of Lake Titicaca.

Pentland tells us that the extent of the great lake is decreasing even within the historical period, that its waters washed the walls of Tia-Huanacu in 1634; whereas, it is now 135 feet above the level of the lake, and twelve miles from it. It is 30 to 60 miles broad by 400 miles in circumference.

We now come to the valley of the Desaguadero: it drains Lake Titicaca, in a south-easterly direction, into the Lake Aullagas. It would seem that the waters of Lake Aullagas are kept at lower level than the Desaguadero by atmospheric evaporation, and the probable filtration through the earth and by fissures; for as yet no outlet, either to the east or west, has been discovered. The Desaguadero valley, in the south, is cold and unproductive, there are no trees, rushes only are seen; in the north some barley and potatoes are grown, but only in sheltered situations.

Lake Titicaca is, according to General O'Brien, 160 miles in length, and 50 to 80 broad. Pentland gives it an elevation above the sea of

---

[1] Buckle's His. Civilisation in England, 1., 100.
[2] His. Civilisation, I., 86.
[3] Voy. dans le Nord de la Bolivie, 1853.

12,846 feet: he sounded in 120 fathoms, but supposes it deeper. Much tortora or rush grows on its shores, there is water fowl and seven or eight sorts of fish. Pentland says its shores are cultivated, producing corn, barley, potatoes, and even indian corn, and this at an elevation of 12,846 feet! Later travellers add, that around Lake Titicaca, for eight or nine months of the year, the sky is cloudless and the earth arid: in winter it is cold, but the months of September, October and November are temperate. General O'Brien says the west side of the lake is navigable for 160 miles, but barren of all productions, excepting silver and copper and the gold washings of Carabaya. Parts of the east side has corn, fruits and timber, and round the lake alone the population exceeds a million.

As to the position of Tia-Huanacu and its elevation, we see that the waters of Lake Titicaca have retired from its walls not more than 220 years since; this appears to show, that at that period there must have been more rain and other systems of winds than at present, and thus the climate has changed in this respect. Still the rarity of the air would be about the same, but the temperature may have been higher. The wonder, however, remains, that the seat of an ancient legislation should have been placed at such an elevation, and is a subject of speculation and inquiry, as to what was then the nature of the climate and soil, to have produced sustenance for the builders of these extensive and interesting monuments. I do not think we can bring to our assistance the upheaval of the country, to cause this cold and arid character. Darwin tells us, that at Valparaiso, within the last 220 years, there has been a rise of 19 feet, and Lima has been upheaved 80 to 90 feet within the Indio-human period; but such small elevations could have but little power in deflecting the moisture bringing atmospheric currents. Mr. A. Taylor has computed that all existing causes would produce an elevation of only three inches in ten thousand years.

Cuzco is in 13° 36' S. The building of this city, I will suppose, originated with the 1st Inca, 1100, A.D.; its elevation is 11,378 feet. Sometimes the soil is called moderately fertile: the little stream of Guatani is dry for nine months in the year. The Spanish conquerors found it very cold, but well supplied with provisions, the vegetable portions of which must have been brought from such temperate valleys as Yucay; for there pomegranates and other European fruits grow; it was one of the country retreats of the Incas: indeed, the first Spanish settlers wished to remove from Cuzco to Yucay, in consequence of the inclement climate of the capital of the Incas.

Cajamarca, in 7° 8' S., and 8,840 feet above the sea; its name implies, place of frost, but Humboldt calls it a lovely and fertile plateau. This portion of Peru was conquered by the Inca Pachacutec about 1400, A.D., and became the second city of the empire, and must have been much enjoyed by the Incas, for its fine climate; and we can easily conceive the love Huayna Capac had for Quito, in 12' S. at about 10,000 feet above the sea, its mean temperature being about 60° F.

There is no cause for surprise to find the Muisca seat of civilisation at Bogotá, in 4° 36' N., at an elevation of 8,190 feet, and where the mean temperature is 58° F.

Continuing onwards, we find climate propitious: Yucatan had a table-land little elevated above the sea, and Guatemala at 5000 feet.

The city of Mexico, in 19° 25' N., is at 7,468 feet above the sea on the table-land of Tenochtitlan, one-tenth of its surface covered with lakes, and its mean temperature 62° F. It had its mountains or cold countries, and its lower or tropical, and was thus supplied with productions of every climate.

Many of the ruins on the islands and shores of Lake Titicaca may be as old as those of Tia-Huanacu. On the island of Titicaca, or of the Sun, are very ancient terraces and ruins.

Dalence[1] speaks of ruins like those of Tia-Huanacu at El Fuerte, in the province of Chuquitu, where there are statues and sculptures.

Cieza de Leon alludes to ruins of very ancient and large edifices, also stones with writing on them, on the banks of the river Vinaque, near Humanga, which, according to tradition, was built by a bearded people, long before the Incas came here and made this their home: Herrera says "white and bearded." In Chachapoyas, to the east of the Marañon, are very ancient ruins, too far from Cuzco, and too old to be Incarial. Chacha means brave. The people of this country worshipped the condor in particular, and bowed down before reptiles. Llavantu was the name of their capital. Some of these monuments are of a conical form, with large statues, and may have been the tombs of chiefs: the ruins of Cuelap, in this direction, appear to be extensive, consisting of chambers, tombs, and walls. At Concon, half-a-day's journey from Lima towards Pasco, are ruins of an ancient place, surrounded by walls: nothing is known of its history.

Curumba, seven leagues from Andaguaylas, is an old square fortress, sometimes called a pyramid; it is of solid masonry, and was probably erected by an independent nation previous to the conquest of this part of the country by the Incas. The Chulpas are seen on the hill bathed by the lake of Clustoni, in Puno: they may be tombs, they have sculptures of lizards, serpents, and other objects. Here also are the ruins

---

[1] Estadistica de Bolivia.

of Hatun-Colla, said to have been the residence of a chief, the Gran Ccoya, whose palace and town was covered by the waters of the lake; also that this was the capital of the old Collas (most probably Aymará's), who lived principally around Lake Titicaca, and who courageously opposed the Incas.

D'Orbigny mentions the existence of a colossal statue at the entrance of the cemetery of Santiago de Guato.

Ollantay-tambo, 13° 15′ S., 72° 18′ W. This strong position, and the singular construction of its edifices, induce the supposition, that it dates its origin from remote centuries; that some of the later chiefs of this territory were independent and contemporaneous with the first Incas, and was only conquered by them in later times. Here are the remains of a strong fortress, palace, walls, and galleries or terraces. Mr. Markham,[1] who visited this place in 1852, speaks of them as remarkable for their enormous size, and the accuracy with which the stones are cut; some at various angles, to receive the dove-tailings of their neighbours. Bustamante[2] supposes there were three periods of architecture at Ollantay-tambo. The construction of the first appears most perfect, the stones are large and built with taste and symmetry. In the second the same care is not observed, the stones are smaller and unequal: the third inferior to the second, and may be of a period not long before the Spanish conquest. Guaraconda is in the vicinity, and has similar ruins.

Hill,[3] a recent visitor to this place, calls it Ottantaitambo and Attantaitambo, and composed of ruins of dwellings cut in the solid rock, at the height of fourteen or seven hundred feet; there are also numerous terraces formed of irregular stones, which once supported a productive soil, where now all is barren. Innumerable stone buildings are seen everywhere in the most thorough confusion, as if an earthquake had distributed them.

Osery, the companion of Castelnau, observed on the top of a mountain near Ollantay-tambo, a monument, supposed to be for astronomical purposes, composed of a square building, each side having three windows: unfortunately his murder on the Marañon by his guides prevents us deciding if the position of the twelve windows corresponded with the sun's risings, during the twelve months of the year.

Old Huanuco, in 9° 58′ S., 75° 40′ W.: these ruins are interesting, from the six stone portals one within the other. Another object there is called the "look out," but may have been a place of sacrifice. The

---

[1] Cuzco and Lima.
[2] Apuntes, &c., Paris, 1849.
[3] Peru and Mexico, I., 286, 1860.

architecture here is singularly distinct from other edifices built in the time of the Incas; but as this place was taken by the Incas, some of their works are also found. In Huaytara, province of Castro-Vireyna, is an edifice similar to old Huanuco, also sculptured stones. In Guamalies it is reported there are ancient ruins.

I will now come to the monuments of the coast nations, commencing with the very extensive ruins of the Chimus or Chincus; their capital was at Trujillo, 8° 8′ S.

We know very little concerning the history of the Chimus: the first mention of them is by Montesinos, who states that Huasca-Titu, his 13th chief of Peru, died when he was about to make war upon this nation. The next account is by Garcilasso: that the 9th Inca, Pachacutec, sent an army of 30,000 men to conquer the Chimu-Canchu or Canchu, known also as the Gran-Chimu, or king of Manseriche. Stevenson states that at Eten, 6° 50′ S., the Indians speak Chimu, which is the original language of (this part) of the coast of Peru, and so different from the Quichua. Rivero and Tschudi inform us, that the works of art of the Chimus, and those found in Cuzco, are much more perfect and correct than those which are seen in the Sierra and on the coast of Central Peru.

Don Mariano E. Rivero visited Trujillo, and described the ruins in a work published in Lima in 1841, and subsequently re-published in London.[1] They are found in the valley, but there is no data to fix with certainty the period they were erected. When the last Chimu was conquered by the Inca's troops, by the advice of his chiefs, he offered to worship the sun and abandon the idols of his country, which consisted of the representations of fish and other animals. The ruins covered a space of three-quarters of a mile, exclusive of the great squares, the walls of which are of small stones joined together with mortar, and were probably used as fields.

From the village of Mansicho or Manseriche, we begin to see the walls of adobe, and the vestiges of this once great city. The dimensions of the great squares vary from 200 to 270 yards in length, and from 100 to 160 in breadth; their number may be seven or eight. The walls which surround these edifices are formed of adobes, often of twelve yards long and five or six broad in the lower part of the wall, but diminishing until they terminate in a breadth of one yard at the top. Some of the squares contain huacas or tombs, and the walls of large apartments or halls. Each of the palaces was surrounded by an exterior wall of stone and mortar and adobes.

---

[1] See Rivero and Tschudi for drawings, &c.

In the first palace there is a square, in which are found apartments made of small stones and mortar; it is supposed these were tombs, or, perhaps, apartments for the concubines of the Chimu. The building of the walls is simple and elegant, consisting principally of sculptured panels and ornaments.

The second palace contains various squares and buildings. At one end is the huaca of Misa; this tomb is traversed by small alleys and has some large chambers. Mummies, cloths, pieces of gold and silver, *iron*? (if so, probably meteoric), an idol of stone, with small pieces of mother-of pearl, were found.

Among these ruins are many artificial eminences; these are huacas, and frequently curiosities have been taken from them illustrative of the ancient inhabitants. In 1563 and 1592, the king's fifth of the gold found amounted to nearly £61,000. In 1550, Don Antonio Chayque, a legitimate descendant of the Chimu-Canchu, showed to the Spaniards a huaca called Llomayoahuan, upon condition that they should give a part of the treasure obtained for the relief of the Indians; but after having taken from it much wealth, the agreement was violated by the Spaniards.

It is certain that there have been obtained from the huaca of Concha much gold, also some fetters supposed to be of copper. The huaca of the bishop is the largest, but as yet has yielded nothing.

In the "Mercurio Peruano," vii., 80, is a notice of various curiosities taken from the huaca of Toledo; one was the body of an Indian with a veil and a crown with four tassels; on the neck was a sort of broad cravat; in one hand was something like a nail, in the other a symbol which was unintelligible; the outer robe was a tunic.

A Temple of the Sun is described as existing near here, which is most probably of Incarial origin.

I have deposited in the British Museum specimens of red pottery from Trujillo, including a vase representing the head of an animal, a whistling jug, also a beautiful specimen of modelling, perhaps one of the finest produced from South America, and as seen in the frontispiece to this work.[1] It is a vase, being the head, most probably, of a Chimu ruler; it has the lobes of the ears enlarged by the insertion of a wheel of gold, silver or wood, ornamented with small circles, and would

---

[1] The authors of the "Indigenous Races of the Earth" say, that Tschudi (in Rivero and Tschudi) compares his Peruvian vase to any Etruscan pottery; but if we must dissent from his view, we may study the high proficiency of Peruvian art, when we behold two exquisite heads in the British Museum, found at Titicaca: the male head compares advantageously with the Egyptian and Etruscan.

be called in Peru an Orejon or great ears, indicative of high rank.[1] The head here has not the Llautu or Incarial fillet, but a cap or casque with, seemingly, a bat's head in front, and two circular ornaments at the side.

The Otolicnians had "such very large ears, that they do sleep upon one, and cover themselves with the other."[2] If we refer to the size of the metal or wooden wheels introduced into the gristle of the ear of the Orejones, or large-eared chiefs, among the Peruvians, we have an approach to these Otolicinians.

At Pativirca or Pati-Huillca, near the coast, are to be seen large walls of adobe, the remains of an ancient structure of the Chimus. Five miles distant are the ruins of Paramanca, probably of a fortress and palace; and it is the general opinion that the Chimus erected the fortress as a frontier post against the Peruvians. Sculptures in porphyry and basalt are said to have been met with here.

Chaix[3] states, that from Lima to Piura was inhabited by Chimus, sometimes called Yungas, and are of foreign origin; that they came to Peru on rafts, bringing with them a green idol,[4] called Llampellec, from which Lambayeque: their language is distinct from the Quichua. In 1644, forty thousand Indians spoke this language, but in 1791 it was nearly extinct. After their establishment, they had their Chimu rulers, who were as powerful in the plains, as the Incas in the mountains. Their country extended 200 leagues in length: their civilisation was probably of an older date than that of the Incas, and their monuments are first seen at Supe, in 11° S.

Mr. Farris lately returned to England from this part of the country with an interesting collection of antiquities extracted from huacas: a portion has been purchased by the British Museum. A brief notice may not be out of place. From Trujillo, pottery with figures of men,

---

[1] The reigning Inca pierced the ears of those of royal blood with pins of gold, which they wore until the aperture was large enough to hold enormous pendants, peculiar to their order, which consisted of wheels of gold or silver.

The Botucudos of Brazil enlarge the ear and under lip. The Apangis of same country have the ears pierced and loaded like the Peruvian Orejon. The inhabitants of Easter Island, when Captain Cook visited it, men and women, had an oblong slit in the ear. The statues on Easter Island show no ear perforation, and were probably the work of another race.

[2] See Rawlinson's Herodotus, Edin. Review, Jan. 1860.

[3] His. Amer. Merid. I., 213.

[4] The natives of Manta had the goddess of health, Umiña; the face was of an emerald.

women, animals, and plants; mantles, large silver breast-plates, with embossed figures of men, animals, fish, and plants. The tombs of Huarman, Manseriche, Ascope and Chocope have yielded pottery with various figures. Beruć or Virú, much ornamented and painted pottery; one in particular is a globular vase (A.) (this is in the British Museum), with a circular handle, at the top of which was the spout. It has paintings of two figures with wings, probably the god of war of the Chimus (B.): it holds a club in one hand, a shield and arrows in the other. There are four compartments in the body of the figure, containing something like hieroglyphs. The figures are painted red on a yellow ground (in the drawing they are in black), and the first I have seen with wings. The painting on this vase is Etruscan-like, and may be considered unique.

I cannot make anything out of the hieroglyphs, but as to the figures, they may represent the god of war, and probably flying over a wooded mountain: there is an insect flying, something like a figure on the Athenian vase of Electra at the tomb of Agamemnon.[1]

Santiago de Cao ornamented and figured pottery. Huamanchuco, 7° 50′ S., 78° 10′ W.: this country was conquered by the 9th Inca, Pachacutec; pottery and a fine collection of copper and stone axes and other implements of war, copper chisels, ornaments and tupus or pins, nippers for extracting hair from the face, also two stone heads, called "ornaments from the palace of the great chief, Marco Huamanchuco," Mr. Farris tells me, that one of these was one of eight heads set round a stone pillar, in the centre of a large apartment of the palace, which was also a fortress; the other head is of an old man, and has the ears enlarged like the Orejon; it is from a doorway.

An oracle existed in the province of Huamanchuco, called the Huaca Catequilla, which predicted to Tupac-Yupanqui the result of the campaign which he was going to undertake against a brother, who had rebelled, that he, Yupanqui, should die in battle; and this was verified. The son of Tupac, irritated at the death of his father, destroyed the temple of the oracle; but the priests resolved to place the idol in safety, and carried it to Cahuana, where they built another temple and continued its worship.

A monk of the Augustine order, in describing the superstitions of Huamanchuco, alludes to a custom, that does not appear to have found imitators in other countries: when a young man asked for a young woman to be his wife, her father told him all her defects, so that he might not be dissatisfied afterwards, should she turn out wanton or

---

[1] Birch's Ancient Pottery, II., 124.

lazy: "Take her," the father would say, "and if she is good-for-nothing, do not blame me, for I have told you the truth about her."[1]

Viracocha-pampa: pottery, implements of war in copper and stone. Amaro: pottery and stone hammers, round at both ends. Tayabamba: east of the Marañon, 8° S., 77° 25' W.: pottery and other objects. From Buldeburé, Parcoi, Pataz, Amaro, Tuscan, Nañac, various descriptions of pottery. One of these pieces of terra-cotta pottery is that of an Indian bearing a small load, as they had to do in the presence of the Inca, so as to show their humility. In this collection were many objects like spindle twirls of stone and clay. From Sacrificios, in Mexico, many such have been taken from tombs; it has been thought that they served as buttons.

Chancay, a league from the sea: the huacas have yielded household gods of terra cotta, different from that of the Chimus, or similar works of art from the interior of Peru: for specimens, see plates XVI., Rivero and Tschudi.

What I have to say of Supe and Huacho, I am indebted to Stevenson.[2] Supe is south of Pativirca, and between it and Huara is the extensive plain or pampa del medio mundo (of half the world), which before the conquest was under irrigation: vestiges of old canals are visible, and bear witness of the enormous labour of the ancient inhabitants, as well as of their skill in conveying water to great distances. The principal canal here, took its water from the Huara river, and winding round the foot of the mountains, conveyed it to the distance of ten leagues, irrigating in its course some very beautiful plains, which are now sandy deserts.

Near Supe are the remains of Indian towns, one built on the side of a rock, galleries being dug out of it, one above another, for the purpose of making room for their houses.

Stevenson says, he was fully convinced that the Indians buried their dead in the houses where they had resided, as he dug up many of them; they were buried with whatever belonged to them at the time of their death: he found bodies of women with their pots, pans and jars of earthenware, some of which were curious; one had two Indians upon

---

[1] Huamanchuco is between the Nevada of Huaylillas and the River Marañon, from Maran-i-obbo or river of the Marans. The Maran tree yields the balsam of Copiaba. —Schomburgh. Velasco says, the Marañon derives its name from the circumstance of a soldier, who was sent by Pizarro to discover the sources of the Piura river, who, beholding the mighty stream, and astonished at a sea of fresh water, exclaimed, "Hac mare an non." At p. 414 of the Arauco Domado, the Licentiate Marañon, visitador and oidor of Quito, is spoken of.

[2] Narrative, I. vol.

it, carrying a corpse on their shoulders, laid on a hollow bier; when the vase was inclined backwards and forwards, a plaintive cry was heard resembling that made by the Indians at a funeral. Long pieces of cotton cloth, calabashes, maize, quinua, beans, leaves of plantains, ostrich feathers, dresses, spades of palm wood, lances, clubs, jars of chicha, small dolls of cotton; their dress similar to that worn at present by the females of Cajatambo, rings and small cups of gold, the latter beat out very thin, and their size that of half a hen's egg-shell; it is supposed they were worn in the ears, for a small shank is attached to them; slips of silver, about two inches broad and ten long, as thin as paper, also frequently dug up. The body of a man was found whose hair grew from his eye-brows, or rather he had no visible forehead; a great quantity of dried herbs had been buried with him, some small pots and several dolls: the Indians who saw him, said that he had been a wizard, diviner, or a doctor.

Huacho is an Indian village in the valley watered by the Huara. It contained in 1815, four thousand Indians, who cultivated their farms, cut salt at the salinas, caught fish, and made straw hats of fine rushes, or of macora, the produce of a palm tree. They were kind and hospitable, but timidity and diffidence made them appear reserved and sullen. The Indians on this part of the coast of Peru are of a copper colour, with small forehead, the hair growing on each side from the extremities of the eye-brows; they have small black eyes, small nose, the nostrils protruding like those of the African; a moderately-sized mouth, beautiful teeth, beardless chin, except in old age, and a round face; their hair is black, coarse and sleek, without any inclination to curl; the body is well proportioned, and the limbs well turned, and they have small feet; their stature is rather diminutive, and they are inclined to corpulency: the perspiration from their bodies is acetous, which some have supposed to be caused by a vegetable diet. In the colder climates, although in the same latitude, the complexion of the Indian is lighter; however, the Araucanos, who live in a much colder climate, are of a dark copper colour.

At Huacho, Stevenson saw one of the ancient Indian rites—the ñaca feast. A child never has his hair cut till it is a year old; the friends assemble, and, one by one, take a small lock and cut it off, at the same time presenting something to the child. This ceremony among the Peruvians, was practised at the naming of the child, and the name was generally appropriate to some circumstance which occurred to the child on that day. The 7th Inca was called Yahuar Huacar, weeper of blood, because on that day drops of blood were observed falling from his eyes; and Huasca, the 13th Inca, was so named, because the nobles on this day presented him with a golden chain or huasca, after the ceremony of the ñacas.

Near Chancay are ruins of subterranean depositories for food, called colcas, built by the Chimus during their wars with the Incas. Shortly after the Spanish conquest, in the parish of Ancallama, a population of 30,000 paid tribute, at present there are only 425 inhabitants, 320 of whom are Negroes. Guarmey, 10° S.: here is an old Indian fortress. Lima, 12° S., six miles from the port of Callao: in 1740,[1] there were two Indian suburbs at Callao called old and new Pitipiti. The great number of Indians who inhabited this valley before and at the time of the conquest, were reduced to the few inhabitants of Pitipiti, and had only two caciques, and these in such low circumstances as to teach music at Lima for subsistence. Lima is built on the river Rimac, the banks of which are covered with ruins of ancient towns and tombs. One tomb, 1¼ miles south of Lima, is nearly 200 feet high. Three leagues from Lima, Darwin[2] visited the ruins of one of the old Indian villages, with its mound-like or natural hill in the centre. He observes, the remains of houses, enclosures, irrigating streams, and burial mounds, scattered over this plain, cannot fail to give one a high idea of the condition and number of the ancient population. The burial mounds or huacas, are really stupendous; although in some places they appear to be natural hills incased and modelled.. Rimac comes from the word rimay, to speak, from an oracle that was here. Stevenson states that its ancient inhabitants called the valley Rimac Malca, or the place of witches; it being the custom among the Indians who lived in its vicinity before they were conquered by the Incas, to banish to this valley those who were accused of witchcraft. Its climate was bad, having marshy ground; thus fevers generally destroyed in a short time such individuals as were the objects of this superstitious persecution. It is said, that when Manco Capac and his sister, Ocollo, were presented by their grandfather to the Indians living at Cuzco, and were informed by him, that they were the children of the Sun, the fair complexion of the strangers, and their light-coloured hair, induced the Indians to consider them as Rimacs, and they were exiled to this spot.

This territory was anciently governed by various powerful chiefs, the principal one being the Curys-mancu, his dominions extending from Pachacamac to Barranca. We know but little of these coast rulers or their origin. The Incas, particularly the 8th and 9th, descended from the Andes as conquerors to the country of the Curys-mancu, who had

---

[1] Ulloa, II., 43.
[2] Nat. Voy. 368.

a temple erected to the invisible god, Pachacamac; he was incorporated into the Incarial family of Pachacutec, whilst other chiefs were severely punished for their opposition to the Incas.

Three leagues north-east of Lima, in the valley of Guachipa, are standing walls of a large town; the streets are narrow, the houses of mud, and each house consists of three small apartments. There is one house larger than the rest, probably that of a chief. This spot is known as "Old Cajamarca." The walls, as well as similar ones in the district, have no foundations, and have withstood those violent earthquakes which overthrew the more solid buildings of Lima and other towns.

The ruins of the great temple to Pachacamac (Pacha, the earth; Camac, participle of Camani, I create) and city of the Curys-mancus, are some seven leagues south of Lima. There are many descriptions of this celebrated locality, but I will only briefly refer to the observations in Wilkes' United States Exploring Expedition, to Rivero and Tschudi, and Markham.

According to Wilkes, the temple is on the summit of a hill having three terraces; some of the walls are of unhewn blocks of rock; these were cased with adobes or sun-dried bricks, then covered with plaster and painted red. A range of square pilasters projected from the upper wall, evidently belonging to the interior of a large apartment: no traces are found of doors or windows. Some graves were observed south of the temple, but the principal burial ground was between the temple and the town. The skulls were of various characters, the majority presented the vertical or raised occiput, the usual characteristic of the old Peruvians, while others had the forehead and top of the head depressed. The bodies were wrapped in cloths of various qualities and colours: various utensils and other articles were found which seemed to denote the occupation of the individual, as wooden needles and weaving utensils, netting, slings, cordage, baskets, fragments of pottery, maize, cotton seeds, wool, gourds, shells, &c.

Rivero and Tschudi give a large drawing of the ruins, and describe them as much dilapidated. On a conical hill, 458 feet above the sea, are the ruins of the Temple of Pachacamac; at the foot of the hill are the decayed walls of the edifices intended for strangers who came on pilgrimage; the whole was surrounded by a wall of adobes, nine feet in width. The material of the fabric is not of stone, as in Cuzco, but of sun-dried bricks, easily crumbled. In the most elevated part is the temple, which, when first visited by the Spaniards, they found the door to be of gold, inlaid with precious stones; the interior was obscure; this being the spot where the priests had their bloody sacrifices before an idol of wood, the worship of which succeeded the pure abstract adoration of the invisible Pachacamac. At present there remain of this temple some niches, which, according to Cieza de Leon, contained representations of wild animals: fragments of painting of animals are observed on the walls.

Outside of this edifice there was a temple to the Sun, palace and house of Virgins of the Sun; monuments erected by the Incas, Pachacutec and Yupanqui, after their conquest of this great coast nation.

Ruins of vast extent still remain, with saloons twenty to twenty-five yards in length, and six to eight in width, of mud walls, forming narrow streets, all indicating that here was once a large population. Two miles off shore, are three barren islands, supposed to have formed part of the continent, but separated by the terrible earthquake of 1586.[1]

Mr. Markham, in his "Cuzco and Lima," speaks of Pachacamac as a city of the dead: the roofs of the habitations are gone and the dwellings filled with sand. The ruins of the temple consist of three broad terraces, twenty feet high, in parts of which the vermillion paint, that once coated the whole, is still seen. Above the terraces there is a level platform, where once a splendid fane arose in honour of Pachacamac, the creator of the world, the supreme god. The great silent city, which does not contain one solitary inhabitant, is spread out immediately beneath the hill.

The valleys of Pachacamac, Rimac-Malca, Chancay and Huaman composed the state of the Curys-mancus or Quis-mancus.[2] Montesinos observes, that under the Peruvian Emperor, Ayartaco-Cupo XII, the giants that came to Peru and populated Port Santa Elena, built a

---

[1] A very severe earthquake commenced in the morning of the 19th of April, 1860; one shock lasted eighty seconds, the heaviest since old Callao was submerged. On the 22nd the ground shook violently for fifty seconds, doing great damage to Lima and its vicinity, also destroying several estates at Cañete. In Manta trees were rooted up, and one of the mountains close by was rent in two, and produced a volcano of hot fetid water. Up to the 27th, twenty-eight shocks had been counted; they commenced with oscillation of the ground, then heaving, followed by subterranean noise. A chasm, nearly a mile long and several feet wide, has been opened in the ground near Lima.

[2] The Estadistica of Lima, 1839, mentions, that the department of Lima in ancient times was governed by many chiefs, the principal ones being the Curys-mancus, whose dominions extended from Pachacamac to the town of Barranca. The origin of this nation is so remote that it is not known whether it was not older even than the Incas; history only tells us that the conquering arms of the Incas, having arrived at the frontiers, and discovering that the Curys-mancu had a temple erected to the invisible god, Pachacutec, the 10th Inca, confederated with and incorporated him into the Incarial family.

sumptuous temple at Pachacamac. It is sometimes said that the Yuncas (another name for the people of a portion of this country) built this temple. There must have been various buildings farther south; but as these were most probably composed of adobe, they have mouldered down level with the earth; however, the huacas or graves are abundant as at Cañete, in 13° S. (founded in 1559, near an ancient fortress and palace), formerly the country of the Chuqui-mancus, who ruled over the beautiful valleys of the Guarcu, and may have been occupied by one of the great Chincha nations of the coast. At Chincha-baja there is a fortress called the Inca's palace.

Cañete, in the province of Yauyos, extends from the coast towards the Cordillera. The inhabitants are distinguishable by their faces and figures, and also by their language, from other Indians of the coast and mountains; their language, the Cauqui, contains many radical words of the Quichua. Here rich huacas have been opened. I have placed in the British Museum, from this spot, large silver-gilt ear-rings, a pair of scales, the beam of bone and netted bags to serve as scales, and some very thin pieces of silver, an inch square, each having holes at the corners, probably to attach to dresses; a sling of very fine workmanship, and some sweet-smelling resin, probably used as incense.

Rivero and Tschudi say that, under the collective names of Canopa or Chanca, the Peruvians designated their minor deities, and they mention in a note that the Quichua word, Canopa, deserves the attention of antiquarians; for, by the word Canopus or Conobas, the Egyptians denominated a beneficent spirit or tutelar god, representing it under the form of a bird or human head. Chanca, I can understand to be a Quichua word, but Canopa looks to one as if it had been introduced by some Spanish antiquary. In the "Extirpation of the Indians of Peru," Lima, 1642, by the Jesuit, Arriaga, who travelled in that country from February, 1617, to July, 1618; he says he confessed 5,624 people, imposed penance on 679 ministers of idolatry, removed 603 principal huacas, 3,418 Canopas (household gods), 45 Mamazaras, deities of indian corn; 189 huancas, masters of the field; and 617 mallquis or bodies of ancestors.

The Chincha coast race, with the Aymarás and Huncas, appear to have been the three great nations of Peru existing before the Incarial times.

In an interesting paper in "Fraser's Magazine," 1844, on the state of the Peruvian Empire previous to the arrival of the Spaniard, by General Miller, is the following:—"To the summons of Capac Yupanqui, brother to the Inca, Pachacutec, who died 1400, the chiefs of the densely peopled country of the Chinchas gave the following reply: 'We do not want to have the Inca for a king, nor the sun for a god; we already have a god whom we adore, and a king whom we serve. Our god is the ocean, and every body may see that it is greater than the sun, and that it besides yields to us an abundance of food; whereas the sun does us no good whatever: on the contrary, he oppresses us with too much heat in our sultry region, and we have no occasion for it, as they who live amidst cold mountains, where it may be right to worship him, because he is useful there . . . The Inca had better return homewards without entering into war with the lord and king of Chincha, who is a most puissant ruler.'"

Arequipa, 16° 50' S. Under Mayta Capac, 4th Inca, the country of Arequipa or Arceypa, was subjected. Plate xxix., Rivero and Tschudi, is a head of red pottery, very different from the figures from the coast and the interior, being so much more perfect: the eyes are apparently of gold.

In the province of Canas there is a fortress on the mountain of Molloccahua, where the Caneños defended themselves successfully against Huayna Capac, who, being unable to subject them by force of arms, went to the court of the Ccana or ruler of the country, asking for his daughter to be the Inca's wife, and thus the Ccana was allied.

In the district of Chota are many subterranean works and tombs, and in the court-yard of the farm of Mamoy there formerly stood a high stone tower that had sculptures in basso-relief of various figures of animals. This monument has been destroyed.[1]

PERUVIAN POTTERY.—I do not find any account of the employment of the potter's wheel or table, in Peru; still, as they made globular and circular vessels, they may have had some approach to this useful invention. The Maypures of Colombia form the clay into cylinders, and mould the largest vases with their hands. The American Indian appears to have been unacquainted with the potter's wheel (which was familiar to the nations of the east in the remotest antiquity); and as they did not use the oven, they generally placed twigs around the pots, baking them in the open air.

Several sorts of terra-cotta pottery are found in the Peruvian tombs: black, various tints of red, yellow, brown, and some of a blue colour; the black is generally modelled, the red modelled and painted: as to moulding, this requires further examination. None of the old Peruvian pottery I have seen is glazed. Mr. Squier, in his Archæology of Nicaragua, states, that the pottery made there is formed by the hand, without the aid of the potter's wheel, baked, and when intended for

---

[1] Guia de Forasteros, 1840.

purposes requiring it, is partially glazed; and in a note alludes to Edwards' Voyage up the Amazon, who says that the glazing (varnishing rather) there is produced by a resinous gum, gently rubbed over the vessels, previously warmed over a bed of coals: this description applied equally to the modes practised in Nicaragua. I have seen no glazing on ancient Peruvian pottery.

I have supposed that the Huaqueros or sacred vases, found in the Inca Peruvian tombs, were made under the superintendence of the priests. The household pottery was made by working potters, who were called Sañu-camayoc, the earthen vessels, Manca; stone vases were used, also vessels of gold, silver, and copper. The greater portion of Peruvian pottery may be called terra-cotta; many hold water, and liquids can be boiled in them. From the north of Peru I have seen clay figures, "characterised by a prurient indecency."

Mr. Birch,[1] alluding to ancient vases of the old world, with white ornaments, mæanders, &c., says, they much resemble those found in the tombs of the early Peruvians, and may be regarded as displaying the first attempts at decoration. He gives a drawing[2] of a double cruze of glazed ware from Egypt, united by a band: many of the Peruvian vessels are double, quadruple, sextuple, and octuple. Some of the double ones, when filled with liquid, the air escaping through the opening left for that purpose, produce musical sounds, or as that of birds and animals.

After the conquest, Spain supplied earthenware to its colonies; China a considerable quantity by way of the Philippine Islands; and in our own times, England principally manufactures for South America.

At p. 89, I mentioned the existence of potter's clay in Quito, having a delicate fragrance. Molina[3] gives the following of a similar clay found in Chile, near the capital, called Buccari; it is fine and light, of an agreeable smell, of a brown colour spotted with yellow. In many of the convents they manufacture from this clay, jars, bottles, cups, &c., which they paint, gild, and varnish. These vessels communicate a pleasant smell and flavour to the water put into them, which proceeds from some bituminous body in the clay. I have some of this pottery, and it appears to me that the fragrance has been given to it by cloves, vanilla, or such like bodies.

---

[1] Ancient Pottery, II., 253.
[2] Ancient Pottery, I., 55.
[3] His. Chile, I., 53.

INCARIAL MONUMENTS.

Generally speaking, the formation of those wonderful roads in Peru have been awarded to the Incas: still I consider that before their times many were in existence, but were extended by them. Those travellers who have examined these roads say that, even in the existing state of our knowledge, and with modern instruments of labour, they would be deemed worthy of the most civilised nation.

According to Sarmiento, some of these roads passed over terrific sierras, while the only means for their construction were fire and a tool for picking. Cieza de Leon describes roads, some over the Andes, with their tambos or lodging places and depositories, also one along the coast, probably commenced by the IX. Inca and completed by Huyana Capac XII. This was a broad road. On each side it had a wall, while in parts the road was shaded by trees. Velasco notices well preserved spaces in Quito twenty-one feet wide, parts cut out of rock, and, to equalise the surface, it was covered with a cement of bitumen. Humboldt examined some of these roads, and states that they do not fall behind the most imposing Roman ways. Rivero and Tschudi tell us that the upper road from Cuzco to Quito was from eighteen to twenty feet wide and about twelve hundred miles in length; the lower road a foot wider and nearly 1600 miles.

Almagro, when going from Cuzco to the Conquest of Chile, during the first part of the way profited by the great road of the Incas, which stretched across the table land far towards the south. On his return, his army crossed the desert of Atacama and through the province of Tarapacá. Here I observed broad tracks cleared of loose stones, so as to allow of easy transit: these are considered as ancient roads. I will here only allude to the bridges, some of stone, others swinging or suspension: their acqueducts, one made by the Inca Viracocha, 450 miles in length along the steepest sierras, nourishing the andeneria or terraced gardens; tunnels, quarries, fortresses, arsenals, obelisks, theatres, schools, temples to the sun in particular, houses for the virgins of the sun, and as to palaces there were above two hundred from Cuzco to Quito. These and other forms of building, combined with their peculiar form of government, render the Incarial race a most interesting people.

The Incarial monuments are square, oblong and cyclopean; of granite, porphyry and other stone: at Lunatambo stones of spherical form are seen, but adobes or sun-dried bricks were used in the more rainless portions of the empire. The lintel is sometimes narrower than the threshold, but the architecture characterised by simplicity, symmetry and solidity. The present houses of Cuzco are built of stone, the lower part being usually constructed of the massive and imposing buildings of the time of the Incas, while the upper, roofed with red tiles, is a modern superstructure.

The principal ruins in Cuzco are the following: the great temple to the sun, on the site of which the church of Santo Domingo is built; the Sacsahuaman,[1] or great fortress, with underground communications, which took fifty years to build; Colcampata, the palace of Manco-Capac; palace of Inca Roca; Ab. Uahuan, or residence of the Virgins of the sun; palaces of the Incas Yupanqui and Huasca; ruins within the Convent of Santa Teresa and monastery of San Francisco; Cyclopean constructions in the street of Marquez-Intipampa or square of the sun; gardens of the temple of the sun; Coricancha or square of gold.

In the Yacha-huasi, or schools founded by the Inca Roca, are serpents carved in relief on stones, and the same designs are to be seen on a stone lintel on the walls of the palace of Huayna Capac, and on other Incarial buildings.

There are four figures in relief on large slabs in a house occupied by the Inca Garcilasso de la Vega: on the two upper slabs are the figures of two monsters with the heads of women and bodies of birds, resembling the harpies of Virgil, and on the lower slabs are monsters with scales and long tails coiled up behind their backs. The walls generally were built of huge stones, with recesses and doors at certain intervals, the sides of the doors approaching each other at the top and supporting stone lintels. The side walls were pierced with small square windows, and the whole was thatched with Ichu or mountain grass. The interiors consisted of spacious halls, with smaller rooms adjoining, and the interior walls were adorned with animals and flowers in gold and silver; mirrors of hard stone hung on stone pegs; while in the numerous recesses were utensils and household gods in gold, silver or terra cotta. The couches were of vicuña cloth, and the tianas or seats used by the Incas were covered with gold.

The temple of Cacha, on the banks of the Vilcamaya, built by

---

[1] Bustamante, in his apuntes, says Sacsay-Guaman means, gloat thyself, eagle, and that the Peruvians buried much treasure here, to save it from the Spaniards.

Viracocha, is described as having been something very beautiful; it was square with a door on each side, and in the centre was the statue of a spirit in long flowing robes, leading some strange animal by a chain.

In the valley of Yucay, four leagues from Cuzco, is Tambo-toco, where there are considerable ruins, said to have been built by Manco Capac: still it is generally believed they are of greater antiquity. Garcillasso says that it is not known who built the great walls of Cuzco.

Although I have given a list of Inca ruins, there are many more, as at Cajamarca, 7° 8' S. 78° 32' W.: this was the second city of the empire, built in all probability on the ruins of the capital of the Chimus, of Chicama, the last being subjected by the Inca Pachacutec. The approach to Cajamarca from the coast was guarded by fortresses of masonry. The Spanish conquerors describe the city, with its white houses glittering in the sun like a sparkling gem on the dark skirts of the Cordillera: it was a league in length, and contained 10,000 people; the houses were generally built of clay hardened in the sun, the roofs thatched or with timber. Some of the buildings were of hewn stone. There was a house for the virgins of the sun and a temple to the same, hidden in a deep grove; there was a square of large size, containing capacious halls of stone and dried brick, with wide doors, probably used as barracks. At the end of the square was a stone fortress; there was another fortress commanding the town, with spiral winding walls, this was of great strength. The Inca Atahualpa's quarters was an open court-yard, a light building with galleries was around it; the walls were covered with shining plates, white and coloured, (red) and before the edifice was a bath fed with hot and cold water. There was a large stone building with a serpent sculptured on its walls (the hall of the serpent).

Benzoni states that when Pizarro first saw Atahualpa, he was adorned with golden wreaths and beautiful feathers of various colours, dressed in a shirt without sleeves, and a band of cotton round his middle, a tassel of fine red wool on the left side of his head shaded his brow, and his shoes were almost apostolical. He was of moderate stature, wise, energetic, and desirous of empire: his sister Pagha (Pacha) was his wife. The Peruvian nobles had a fillet round the head, and a woolen tassel hanging from the left ear.

Atahualpa's palace[1] was built of large sun-dried bricks, containing many large apartments; on its site was afterwards built the cabildo, chapel and prison. Only one unroofed room of the Inca's palace

---

[1] Guia de Forasteros, 195, Lima 1858.

remains, twelve yards long by eight wide, and where Atahualpa was imprisoned; until lately could be seen the mark the Inca made on the wall of the height the treasure should be piled for his liberation.

The stone on which the Inca received his death was one and a-half varas in length and two thirds of a vara wide, called penna, and is now used in the altar of the chapel.

The rapacious Spanish invaders disorganized a population of ten millions of people, who had a length of more than a thousand leagues of coast, and from thirty-five to ninety in width; they robbed their palaces temples and tombs, polluted their altars, and committed every species of enormity upon an unoffending race.

We have sketches and plans of some of the Peruvian monuments, but these have not generally much architectural value, as few are to scale; thus, no very critical comparison can be made with the ruins of such other countries as we have truthful views and plans of. However, let us hope that the period is not distant when the monuments I have referred to, will be more carefully examined and properly described.

HIEROGLYPHS AND QUIPPUS OF THE PERUVIANS. — Some early writers tell us that the ancient Peruvians used a specie of hieroglyph engraved on stone and preserved in their temples, and that there appeared to be a similarity between them and those found in Mexico and Brazil. Tschudi states, that among the Indians of the river Ucayali, on the birth of a child the name of an animal is given it; the witnesses of the ceremony mark with a wooden pencil some hieroglyphical characters on two leaves, which are carefully preserved, and, on the death of the Indian, deposited in the grave with him.

The Peruvians had no manuscript characters for simple sounds, but they had a method by which they composed words and incorporated ideas, which consisted in the dexterous intertwining of knots and strings so as to render them auxiliaries to the memory, namely, the Quipu.

It was generally of twisted wool, consisting of a string or cord as the base of the document, and of threads, more or less fine, fastened by knots to it. These threads include the contents of the Quipu, expressed by single knots or intertwinings.

The size of the Quipu is very different, sometimes the base cord is five or six yards long, at others, it is not more than a foot: the pendant strings or branches rarely exceed a yard in length.

The different colours of the threads have different meanings; thus, the red signifies a soldier or war; the yellow, gold; the white, silver or peace; the green, wheat or maize, &c. In the arithmetical system, a single knot means ten; two single knots joined, twenty; a knot doubly intertwined, one hundred; triply, one thousand: two of the last united, two thousand, &c.

Not only is the colour and mode of intertwining the knots to be considered, but even the mode of twisting the thread, and particularly the distance of the knot from the junction of the thread with the base of the cord, are of great importance to a proper understanding of the Quipu.

It is probable that these knots were at first applied to purposes of enumeration only; but, in course of time, this science was so much perfected that those skilled in it attained to the art of expressing by knots historical relations, laws and decrees, so that they could transmit to their descendants the most striking events of the empire; and thus the Quipu might supply the place of documents and chronicles.

Whenever a Quipu came from a distant part it was accompanied by a verbal commentary to indicate the subject matter of which it treated. The officials had certain signs at the commencement of the mother thread, or base cord, which had a meaning intelligible to them only.

Repeated attempts made in our day to read the quipus have proved failures, because of the great difficulty of deciphering them. In effect, each single knot represents some notion or thought, while there is wanting (for a meaning) a quantity of conjunctions or links. Besides there is another greater impediment in the interpretation of the Quipus found in the huacas, and that is the want of a verbal commentary to explain the subject matter of the document. Rivero and Tschudi think there are still, in the south of Peru, Indians who know very well how to decipher these intricate memorials, but they guard their knowledge as a sacred secret, inherited from their ancestors.

The "Mercurio Peruano I., 206," observes, that the Peruvian letters, of Madame Grafigny, caused Prince de S. Severino, a member of the Acadamy of La Crusca, as well as an Italian duchess, to write on the quipus; after detailing what Garcilasso had said on the subject, the authors describe, with too much assurance, the grammar and dictionary of the Quipus, and would lead one to believe that they were Quipu-Camayus, (record readers) of the Incas!

In the "Westminster Review," XI, 1829, there is an article by T. Perryonet Thompson, on "A prospectus of the Quipola, or an explanation of the Quipoes, now open for public opinion, London, printed by J. Phair, 69, Great Peter Street, Westminster, 1827, 64-mo. p.p. 18." It would appear that a ship carpenter, Alexander Strong, purchased this Quipo in a box from the mate of a merchant brig, Robert Baker, for £10. Baker said the Quipo had come into the possession of a native of Lyons named Rosenberg Vestus, who got it from the family of a chief in Chilo of the Guarcos, who considered himself a descendant of the Incas, who had fled from Peru to avoid the Spaniards. Vestus was married to one of the chief's daughters, but after a time he left the Indians, came to Buenos Ayres and sold the Quipo and box to Baker. It would be interesting to know where the Quipo may be now deposited.

The secret language of the Incas is lost. They conquered the Quichuas, and the language and dialects of these nations, were the more general ones spoken in Peru;[1] however, the Aymará, with its dialects, was extensively known. I have sometimes thought that the Incas were of Aymará[2] origin, or from one of the great nations to the East of the Andes, such as the Guarani, Tupi or Brazilians.

Montesinos (not a good authority) says, that during the reign of the III. sovereign of Peru (according to his list of 101) the use of letters was known, and the Amautas or learned men taught astrology and the arts of writing on leaves of the plantain; that under Titu-Yupanqui, the 64th sovereign, civil disturbances caused the loss of letters, and that the 78th sovereign, 3,500 years after the deluge, prohibited his people from making use of the Quillca, (a species of parchment of plantain leaves) but introduced the Quipo, or knotted coloured strings.

According to Acosta, p. 51, the Peruvians had symbolic paintings, for, at the Conquest, the Indians made their confessions by paintings and characters, which indicated the Ten Commandments, &c.

In many parts of Peru, chiefly in situations greatly above the level of the sea, are vestiges of inscriptions on stone very much obliterated by time; one Tschudi found near Huara; also other engravings on granite, representing animals, flowers and fortifications on the heights of Caldera near Arequipa, and he says, these may tell of events anterior to the dynasty of the Incas.

On another stone he found engraved a flower, a fortress, and what may be a river; the Cross looks as if placed after Christianity had been introduced. Ancient Indian sculptures are figured in Rivero and Tschudi.

In Huaytaca, province of Castro Vireyna, Bradford notices that in

---

[1] Dialects of the Quichua.—1. Of Cuzco, or Quichua proper. 2. Lamano or Lamissa, round Trujillo. 3. Chinchaisuyu. 4. Calchaqui in Tucuman. 5. Quito. —Ludewig.

[2] Aymará, spoken in Bolivia, the N.W. provinces of the Argentine Republic, and in Southern Peru bears a close resemblance to Quichua. Dialects of the Aymará, spoken by the Kanchis, Kasnas, Kollaguas, Karankas, Charcas, Pacases and Lupakas. —Ludewig.

an edifice similar to Old Huanuco, are coarse engravings on a mass of granite,—also a stone pillar with marks and inscriptions.

At end of Vol. I of Molina, are supplementary Notes from an anonymous work on Chile, printed at Bologna, 1776. In the description of the province of Cuyo, it is stated that, between Mendoza and La Punta, upon a low range of hills, is a large stone pillar, one hundred and fifty feet high, and twelve feet in diameter. It is called the Giant, and contains certain marks or inscriptions, resembling Chinese characters. Near the Diamond river is also another stone, containing some marks which appear to be ciphers or characters and the impression of a man's feet with the figures of several animals. The Spaniards call it the stone of St. Thomas, from an account which they pretend the first settlers received from the Indians, that a white man, with a long beard, formerly preached to their ancestors a new religion from that stone, and, as a proof of its sanctity, left upon it the impression of his feet and the figures of the animals that came to hear him. This man they suppose to have been St. Thomas, from a tradition of his having preached in America. Cuyo was peopled by the Guarpes, thin, brown and of lofty stature; they were subdued by the Peruvians after they had conquered northern Chile. On the road over the Andes, from Cuyo to Chile, are still to be seen some small stone edifices, erected for the accommodation of the officers and messengers of that empire.

The Allentiac and Milcocayac, (Chilian languages) are spoken by the Guarpes Indians of the province of Cuyo, which word means sand; the general character of the soil is arid. There is an extensive succession of valleys running north from Uspallata, through which it is said, that an ancient road of the Peruvians is to be traced at the present day, nearly to Potosi. The Inca's bridge is on the road from Mendoza to Chile, which, according to Darwin, is composed of a crust of stratified shingle, cemented by deposits from neighbouring hot springs.

In Southern Peru, there are the Pintados of Tarapacá; some of these may be of hieroglyphic character. The engraved granite stones, particularly that of the Pampa del Leon, are pictorial at least.

In Rivero and Tschudi, (plate XLI) is represented a stone two feet broad, from Huara in the department of Junin, the country of the ancient Huancas. A portion of the engraving may have some analogy to No. 7, or Cuhupqua, the ear or snail-shaped granaries of the Chibchas; there is a figure of this character on a slab of stone, from Timaná, New Granada, supposed to represent some astronomical subject.

In plate XXVI is a Canopa, or sacred vessel, in shape of the human figure, they suppose to be a priest offering sacrifice, which has on a mystic belt; they do not give the locality from whence this was obtained. It looks to me like the pottery from Pachacamac, in latitude 12° S. The belt is curious, but we know not what is meant by the hieroglyphic writing. The priest may be drinking the sacred chicha and imploring a good harvest. Plate xx. is a double vase, with symbolical signification of sun, moon, &c. Plate xxi. are two vases, one with mystic figures. There is a female figure from Peru, in the British Museum, something like the one described above, with hieroglyphs above its head, composed of angles principally. I may add, that on the head of a statue found at Tia-Huanacu, are some hieroglyphical characters, a drawing of which is given in "L'Univers Pittoresque."—Bolivie, 1843.

Gilliss (ii. 138) gives a drawing of an approach to the hieroglyph, worked in a coca bag or chuspa.

CON, PACHA-CAMAC, THE SUN. — As there is some confusion in regard to the history of the Peruvian deities, I will here offer a few remarks thereon:—CON, is first heard of as the Supreme power,—the invisible and omnipotent spirit in Quito, under the Scyris, and in Peru, long before the times of the Incas. Con was a spirit without bones or flesh; he made the world, and flying rapidly from north to south in America, caused the mountains and valleys to appear; he then formed man, giving him every species of food and pleasure. Man offended Con and was chastised by having the previous abundance of food taken from him; the land became a desert and the human race was changed into ugly cats, and other black animals.

PACHA-CAMAC is generally looked upon as the son of Con; he had pity for the degraded position of the human race, took the government of the world into his hands and created all things anew, including that of the present form of man and woman.

We then find that temples were raised to this new power, one particularly on the coast of Peru, south of Lima, called after him Pacha-camac.

Montesinos informs us, that under Ayartaco-Cupo, his XII ruler of Peru, giants came to the coast and built a temple to Pacha-camac, using instruments of iron (?) As they were very wicked, divine wrath annihilated them with a rain of fire, although a part of them were enabled to escape by going to Cuzco. Ayartaco-Cupo went out to meet them, dispersing them about Lima-tambo. He also states that the 97th ruler of Peru, the Inca, Topa-Yupanqui, also called Huiracocha and Viracocha, repaired the temple of Pacha-camac. This Inca is the 8th, according to Garcilaso, and died about 1340, A.D.

It would appear that many nations, even from distant parts of Peru, came to this temple, making rich offerings: their sacrifices on the altar and adoration were simple and pure, to this great deity. They entered the sacred place barefooted; in invoking his name, they prostrated themselves to the earth. There was no image to represent this deity, as he was considered to be there in spirit only. This idea of supreme power, and preserved for a very lengthened period, was corrupted by the Incas and his cushipatas or priests.

THE SUN.—The history of the worship to this luminary is as follows: Montesinos calls his 1st ruler of Peru, Pishua-Manca; he was the youngest of four brothers, he shut one up in a cave, threw another into a deep hole, and caused the third to fly to a distant country. The fratricide consoled his four sisters, telling them that they must consider him as the only child or son of the Sun, and obey him as such; he is said to have built Cuzco. Following Montesinos, his 5th ruler, Inti-Capac-Yupanqui, was very zealous for religion and the worship of the supreme gods, Illatici-Huiracocha, and the sun.

If we follow Garcilaso, the 1st Inca, Manco Capac, only appeared about 1022, A.D., telling the people that he was a child of the sun; also that Con and Pachacamac had been children of the sun like himself; that the sun had sent him on earth to teach and govern them; that he was the offspring of the sun and moon.

It must be admitted that the worship of Con and Pachacamac was widely extended long before the Incarial times, and it was only under the 9th Inca, that the country of the Curys-mancus, whose capital was at Pachacamac, was conquered by the Incas of Cuzco, and the intrusive religion of the sun was in danger from the older and purer one of Pachacamac; however, after much negociation, it was arranged that Pachacamac should retain his temple, and that another should be built there to the sun, as the father of the 1st Inca and Pachacamac. After a time the Incarial priests erected a statue of wood to represent the formerly-invisible Pachacamac, and invented oracles. Faith in the immortality of the soul was one of the fundamental ideas among all the Peruvian nations; and, first, Con, then Pachacamac, and, lastly, the Sun, were the judges of the human race. Supay, the evil spirit, is found early amongst this people, and in some places children were sacrificed to it.

QUESTIONABLE TRADITIONS AS TO A GENERAL DELUGE.—Tierra Firme had a tradition that their progenitors, with some animals, had been saved in a vessel; of having sent a bird out to see if the rains had ceased, which did not return, and then another bird, which did return with a green branch; and then the people came out and settled on the earth for a second time.

QUITO.— The tradition there was of a very ancient deluge, that a few were saved in a house of wood on the top of Pichincha. This deluge was for the punishment of three of the sons of the first man or god, called Pacha; these not having whom to subdue, went to war with a great serpent, who, being wounded by arrows, revenged itself by vomiting so much water as to deluge the earth: that Pacha, with his three sons and their wives, built a dwelling on the summit of Pichincha, wherein was put animals and food: after many days, a ullaguanga (a bird like a raven) was put out, which did not return, having remained behind to feed on dead animals: another bird was sent, which returned with green leaves: that Pacha descended from the mountain with his family to where Quito now stands, and whilst building a home, they could not understand each other's language; they separated with their wives, locating in different parts of the country. The history of the same tradition is also said to have occurred in another place from whence their fathers came, which was by sea to Cara; and they explain this, that some of them were descendants of the primitive Quitus, others from the strangers who first established themselves in Cara.

CUZCO.—The tradition of the Inca tribes or Peruvians, of a deluge, was as follows: all mankind was drowned, except a few whom the sun hid on an island in lake Titicaca, or in the cave of Pacaritambo; after a time a Viracocha or grand personage, came forth with his family, when, after having built Tiaguanaco, went to Cuzco, and then the human race multiplied again.

PACHACAMAC (Lima). Those of this district (the subjects of the Curys-mancu) and neighbouring ones, many centuries ere they were conquered by the Incas, had the tradition that there had been a deluge of rain and the earth was submerged, except the top of a high mountain, where a few people built a house, with windows high above the ground, and well secured, storing it with animals and food: after it had rained for a long time, two dogs were put out, these returning wet and not covered with mud, showed that the waters had not subsided: some time afterwards, two other dogs were sent, these returned dry; this showed that the waters had subsided. The inmates of the house on the mountain descended and commenced re-peopling the earth.

There is a general idea that nearly all the nations of South America have traditions of a deluge. An examination of the various accounts leads me to think that the hand of the Spanish priests can be seen in the arrangement of these deluges, taking as the original that of Noah, or, as Prescott says, the story of the deluge is told by different writers with many variations, in some of which it is not difficult to detect the plastic hand of the Christian convert.

CONCLUSION.

I now offer some remarks upon what is likely to be the fate of the Red man of the new world, which does not present anything cheering; also, some observations on the present populations of the South American republics, and their system of government.

MEXICO.—Von Tempsky[1] speaks thus of the Indians of Mitla (vale of the dead) and its ruins: The faces of the idols are true types of the spirit of Indian religion,—awful, terrible, and hideous countenances, calculated to influence their worshippers with fear, the only feeling an Indian acknowledges. Nearly all the American Indians sacrifice but to power of darkness; the good spirits, they think, need not be propitiated, so they pay reverence but to the one they fear.

Unhappy, ill-fated America! how all thy children seem to have been doomed to fall, until they are fast disappearing from the face of the earth. They first built altars to their own bloody gods, and were afterwards dragged before similar tribunals the white man brought from the east; and now the powerful vices and diseases of Europe are raging amongst these helpless creatures. Such fate befalling whole races, nations that were numbered by millions! is awful to contemplate.

Squier[2] tell us that the conquest of Nicaragua was effected with no less violence than that of Mexico and Peru; ship loads were annually taken to Panamá and Peru, and sold there. Las Casas says, half a million Indians perished in the wars of the conquest. . . . The present quiet of the Indian may be that of the slumbering volcano, and its continuance may depend very much on the judicious encouragement of white emigration from the United States and Europe.

The foregoing remarks, which express my own feelings, and over which I have often pondered, with some experience of the Indian both in North and in South America, open a painful field of enquiry. We are accustomed to brand the name of the Conquistadores as murderers and robbers, but had the handful of men who made these wonderful conquests been of any other nation, the chances are that history would have had to chronicle very nearly the same results. Oppression causes

---

[1] "Mitla," in 1843–55.
[2] Trans. Amer. Ethno. Soc., 1853.

resistence; and this is met by fresh efforts of power; and, as the white man, although numerically so far inferior to the red, yet he had arms of steel and the command of gunpowder, moreover, well trained warriors in the science of European warfare.

The Red man in the United States is still an enemy to be feared; and should political difficulties occur between the North and South, the Indian might join one side or the other, or even oppose both; the slave might even join the Red man; for awhile the scalping knife and tomahawk would have severe vengeance; then would come the retaliation of the white man, and the unerring rifle would take fearful retribution, and the consequences be fatal to the Indian and negro.

It is very difficult to even semi-civilize the Red Man; you may modify his religious and moral ideas to some extent, but he is adverse to change from the hunter to the farmer; he loves to roam over his prairies, he hates the subjection of cities; he has occupation enough for his wants in the wilderness, and he becomes bewildered and uneasy in community with the white man. Thus he remains in the savage state, warring with his own race or revenging himself on the white intruder.

The mixed population of Spaniard, Indian and Negro, in Mexico, drove the old Spanish government from that country: since then, civil wars have succeeded. Not long since, we saw citizens of the United States, "revelling in the halls of the Montezumas;" and ere long, the more judicious of the Mexican people may find it suit them to federate with the United States

Another point. It is well known that in the Republic of Guatemala, although the European press eulogized the important and scholastic work of Don M. M. de Morentin, "Estudios Filologicos; Dificultades Principales de la Lengua Espanola." This work has been declared by the Padres Jesuitas there, "to be prejudicial to youth and highly scandalous and heretical." This censure was given in consequence, that in the said work they found the celebrated composition, in verse, of the "Ejercicios de San Ignacio, ó la Penitencia de los Teatinos," and other select pieces which gave some particulars of the history of the "meek" followers of Loyola.

VENEZUELA AND NEW GRANADA. — In this region much of the Indian element is subjected; still there is a large proportion in the savage state, but broken up into small tribes; thus there is but little union, and, whilst they remain so, they are powerless. The Spaniards did what the English and some other nations refrained from: namely, that he married the native woman, and subsequently the negro was introduced,[1] producing mixed races; these assisted in upsetting Spanish despotism in several of the colonies. Republics have been the result, but these have generally been governed by military chiefs, and with few exceptions civil war has continued to rage in these States—thus putting themselves in the position of becoming a prey to any powerful foreign invader; and, secondly, the Indians might join such to revenge themselves on their present rulers; then the Indian in his turn would in all probability get into difficulties with the foreigners.

Romanism is the religion of New Granada (as in all the South American States), but a late President there confessed to me his bias for Protestantism—his enmity to the Jesuits—and his wish to have the religion of the Bible in his country.

EQUADOR.[2]—The Indians of Cuenca and all those of Equador speaking Quichua, have changed but little since Pizarro's invasion. They are aware that they have been the lords of the country; and they are often heard to say, that if they steal anything belonging to a white man they are not guilty of theft, because they are taking what originally belonged to them. That the Indians entertain a hope of freeing themselves from their oppressors, by "driving them into the sea," seems to be a well-established fact. Whether they are sufficiently united to act in concert for carrying out their plan is difficult to determine; but it has been ascertained that there is an alliance between all the Indians speaking Quichua, called Los Gentiles by the Spaniards, and the more barbarous tribes living in the fastnesses of the primeval forests. Should they persevere in their intention, they will find it every day more easy, unless the face of the interior of Equador and Peru is greatly altered; for the white and mixed population since immigration has ceased, or at least been less numerous, is decreasing; while the Indians, wherever they have kept themselves free from intermixture with other races, are steadily increasing. Equador presents a vast field for enterprise, and if the tide of emigration which has now set in with such force towards North America and Australia, could be directed somewhat to Equador, the political and social condition of the country would be altered in a short space of time. It is now so thinly peopled, and inhabited by so limited a number of whites, that about 12,000 immigrants would effect surprising changes. They would not only exercise a most salutary influence upon the elections, by

---

[1] In 1859, there were fearful negro insurrections in Venezuela, a war of race and colour. A judge was assassinated.

[2] Seemann Voyage of "Herald."

placing the Supreme power in the hands of superior men, and they would have no difficulty in keeping in order the negroes and Zamboes of Guayaquil, the chief promoters of most of the revolutions that have disgraced the annals of this republic.

PERU.—Here civil war has repeatedly been on an extensive scale; also serious doings with its neighbours, Quito and Bolivia. The mixed element of White, Indian and Negro, has great difficulty in settling down. Should the Anglo-American element in particular find it at any time convenient to locate—say on the Amazons—and get the Indian to assist, the result is not very problematical as to who will become masters of the country.

The following is from the "Spirit of the Times," New York paper, of August 1854, as regards Huacho in Peru.

In no better place can be studied the various traces of the Spanish, Indian, and negro admixtures, for although the Indian trace predominates, the cunning mestizo, and zambo occupy a marked proportion. The head belongs to the pyramidal type, somewhat rounded by the oval of the European, or distorted by the maxillary peculiarity of the African. A pretty mestiza face may sometimes be seen—the hair is ever black, the eye ever soft and melancholy, the skin pleasingly bronzed, and the teeth as perfect as health and assiduous care can make them. A single drop of Indian blood contains the elements of all that is, ossifically, perfect, so that our pretty creole girl will have the smallest hand and foot, the neatest figure, if not too adipose, and among the crania that fell to my lot (taken from an Indian huaca), I have yet to find caries of a single tooth. Many huacas (the ancient receptacles for the symbols of life and death, rather than the mere graves of the dead), are scattered over the vale. It is said that the Indians object to opening them. And it is thought—moving fact—that even after so many years of captivity, the patient Quichuas still indulge the hope of an ultimate political regeneration—hence, their sacred care and jealousy of relics.

BOLIVIA.—This is a very rich country, the seat of gold and silver mountains, with mighty streams wending their way to the Atlantic. I have heard from the lips of an ex-president, that he had quelled more than thirty revolutions in seven years.[1] Here the romanized Indian is almost the slave still. The Indian is still powerful in this country; and he has not forgotten the bloody acts of the times of the Pizarros, or the

---

[1] In 1859, the republic of Mexico had been in existence thirty-eight years; during which time there had been fifty-six changes of government, nearly all produced by revolutions.

severe punishments inflicted both in this country and Peru, when he has risen against the Spaniards. It would not require a large foreign force to steam up the Amazons and its tributaries, and "settle" most advantageously portions of Equador, Peru and Bolivia.

ARGENTINE PROVINCES.—Here we have the old story of civil war, and the unfortunate consequences of the facility of arriving at supreme power. Lately one of the republican chiefs was assisted by a large body of Pampa Indians to settle his differences with Buenos Ayres.

CHILE.—Has had its civil wars and turmoils; but here we have an industrious people much given to agriculture and mining; the great majority being occupied with more important affairs than the eternal and fatal "politica," and are progressing in a wonderful manner.

The European element has increased very much in Chile—not the Spanish, but English, German, French, also North American, many of whom have married Chilenas. The son of an Englishman, by a Chilian mother, has been a minister of finance; many others of such descent, having government appointments, are in the army and navy; others occupied in commerce, mining, &c.; and it is a curious question to speculate upon the part this new race may play.

In the south of Chile, the Araucanos and confederated tribes require to be cautiously dwelt with. It is in contemplation to invite European emigration on a large scale into Arauco, which, if accomplished with sufficient numbers, as it must to protect itself against the Indians, who will oppose as long as possible, but his weakened numbers in the end will be driven into the Andean fastnesses, where it will not rapidly increase; and, if they attempt to descend into the Pampas, they will meet with fresh enemies in the Buenos Ayrians.

Looking at the various forms of government (as an Englishman), I see no better, for the practical affairs of life, than a constitutional monarchy, such as Britain may boast of. "Liberté, fraternité, egalité," is a mere banner, unfurled to suit the artful demagogue; who, when placed in power, becomes the despot, as we see if we look about us. Far be it from me to recommend monarchy to republican South America; but perhaps the best political move they can make is to patronize for their presidents civilians, and not military men.

APPENDIX.

Abstract of First Series of observations on the Geography of Southern Peru, including Survey of the Province of Tarapacá and route to Chile by the coast of the Desert of Atacama. By W. BOLLAERT, F.R.G.S. (*From Journal of the Royal Geographical Society of London, Vol. XXI.*, 1851, *with Map.*)

LEAVING England, visiting Buenos Ayres, being some days with the Indians of Tierra del Fuego, and rounding Cape Horn, I made an interesting tour through some of the Gold, Silver and Copper Mining districts of Chile; including an examination of the coast of Concepcion for coal, which was found at various spots and is of a tertiary formation. In concert with my friend Mr. George Smith of Iquique, the island of Quiriquina was carefully surveyed; its geological formation at surface is sandstone debris containing coal; then follow shistose rocks.

I then steered my course north to Peru in the month of December (the summer of this region), with the usual southerly wind, which, during the night, veers towards the land, forming the terral or cool breeze from the Andes; thus, depressing the temperature of the air, dew is formed, and, as but little falls on the land, will account in some measure for the arid and desert character of the coast of Peru.

In winter, namely from May to July, the winds are from the north, the air is charged with much vapour, called garua, camanchaca, cerazon, and Llovizna, enveloping the mountains of the coast, and where an occasional cactus and a few bulbous plants appear. This period is known as the Tiempo de Flores, when Ihuanacos may be seen roaming about these elevated flower spots in the desert.

A residence of some years in Southern Peru, particularly in the province of Tarapacá, commencing in 1826, during which time I was engaged at the celebrated mines of Huantajaya, afforded me the opportunity of examining this but little frequented portion of Peru.

As Arica is approached, barren undulating land is seen, and in the rear, ranges of rocky sterile mountains, and further east, in the back ground, peaks of the Andes towering majestically above all.

ARICA.—All around is a desert, save where the stream may run; this gives rise to vegetation, increased by irrigation and guano; the principal productions are cotton, wine, aji or red pepper, oil, maize, fruits and vegetables. The rock of the country is porphyritic; in the hollows and plains there is much debris and saliferous matters.

As to its ancient history, Acosta says, "Ica and Arica sailed westward thither upon sea-wolves skins, blown up like bladders."

A desert route of thirty-five miles brings one to Tacua, a pleasant and pretty town, 1800 feet above the sea, and supplied with water by a fair stream, originating in the Andes. Earthquakes are common in this district, and the ruins of houses and walls bear witness to this agency. As it seldom or ever rains in these latitudes, and there being no vegetation, the surface of the country has remained desert, and may do so for ages, in the same state. The mean temperature of Tacua is 64° F. Tacora, east of this, is volcanic, capped with snow and 19,000 feet above the sea. At Santa Rosa de Chaca, gray copper is found in abundance.

ISLAY.—This port is about 100 miles north of Arica, and, although in a desert, has, since 1827, superseded Quilca, being free from terciana or ague, in consequence of there being no water in the vicinity but that which is conveyed to it by an aqueduct.

The track, from Islay to Arequipa is, first, over stones mixed with sand and white volcanic ashes; water is met with, at the olive grove of Guerrero: then, up a ravine which runs through the mountains of the coast, to the great Pampa, an elevated desert plain, 3000 feet above the sea, covered with sand and volcanic dust; bounded on the west by the mountains of the coast, and on the east, by the Andes, with the volcano of Arequipa as a landmark, generally emitting smoke.

In these desert plains are seen the Medanos, or moving semi-circular sand hills, the concavity generally towards the north, on account of the winds being from the south. In case of heavy winds these Medanos shift and are blown about, and travellers have been overwhelmed and lost in them. They are of all sizes, from that of an ant-hill, to hundreds of feet. Here the mirage is seen in great perfection. It is burning hot during the day, and at times very cold at night.

Having passed the Pampa, a distance of thirty miles is gone over, composed of volcanic rocks, sandstone, and here and there a little dark granite, and their debris, when the vineyards of Tiabaya appear; and a few miles further is Arequipa, at the base of the volcano anciently called Misti. Arequipa is a most picturesque city, first visited by the Spaniards in 1533, and founded by Pizarro in 1539.

It is some sixty miles from the sea, and may contain 50,000 inhabitants. According to Haenke, who visited the summit of the volcano in 1794, the circumference of the principal crater was about 1380 English feet; a second crater was 440 feet in its largest part, and 120 in its least.

Mr. Pentland makes the elevation of the volcano of Arequipa 18,300 feet, and the city 7,788 feet above the sea. Nearly the whole of the year, the summit of the volcano is covered with snow. All around is composed of lava and ashes.

Arequipa has often been visited by earthquakes; those of 1582, 1600, 1604, 1660, 1667, 1687, 1715, 1725, 1738, 1784, 1785, may be particularised from their ruinous effects. In 1667 there was a violent eruption of the volcano of Arequipa.

Garcilasso speaks of an eruption (probably of the volcano of Arequipa), when it rained ashes for twenty days, the ashes being found in places one-and-a-half yards thick.

In February, 1600, there was a great eruption of the volcano of Omate, south-east of Arequipa (probably the Uvinas of Pentland), accompanied by severe earthquakes, which destroyed many villages with their inhabitants; ashes were carried to great distances from the volcano: I have been informed that they fell even in the province of Tarapacá, 240 miles off.

The mountains of the coast, from Arica to Islay, as well as those to the north, have not the elevation of those to the south, neither are they so well defined, but sufficiently elevated to receive moisture from the garuas in the winter months, which gives life to a few cacti, a little pasture, and some flowers on the lomas or summits.

PROVINCE OF TARAPACA.

The first account we have of South Peru is in 1450, when the Inca Yupanqui established his court for a time in Atacama, intrusting the command of an expedition to Sinchi Roca against the Copiapinos: this chief went as far as the fruitful plains of Maipu. Tarapacá was the most distant and extensive province of Peru, but so uninhabited and without the means of cultivation, that it was almost disregarded by the discoverers, who, when they were questioned concerning it, replied— "that its tracks were over rocky mountains, sandy, uninhabited, and rainless deserts, covered with salt and without water; excessive heat during the day and cold at night." However, Oña, in his "Arauco Domado," says—

> "Su nombre es Don Alonzo aquel de Vargas,
> Aquel de lengua breve y manos largos,"

called the Señor of Tarapacá.

The physical features of this province, which will generally apply to the southern portion of Peru, may be described as follows:—1st. The arid mountains of the coast are porphyritic, running north and south, rising at times abruptly from the sea, from 3000 to 6000 feet, and some thirty miles in width, having extensive hollows and undulations, destitute of vegetation, and the greater portion of their surface covered with sand, salt and nitrate of soda. When they are found mixed, they are called Caliches. The origin of the salt in particular is not clearly made out; it has been called a saliferous alluvium, by some supposed to be washed out of the mountains; by others to have been left there by the ocean—neither of which opinions are of much value. In this range the rich silver mines of Huantajaya, Santa Rosa, El Carmen, Chanabaya, and others, are situated. 2nd. The Pampa, or great plain of Tamarugal, 3000 to 3500 feet above the sea, running north into the province of Arica, and south into the desert of Atacama, about thirty miles wide. Much of it is covered with sand, salt, nitrate of soda, particularly on its west margin, and other saline bodies.[1] Water, derived from the mountains to the east, is found at various depths. Some Tamaugos, Algarobos, and a few other plants grow in the Pampa.

---

[1] Lately, salts of borax have been found in abundance.

3rd. Thence rises a desert range of mountains of some 7000 feet elevation above the sea, and twenty miles in width.

4th. An elevated district follows, much broken; and here, for the first time, are seen coarse pastures, brushwood, and large cacti. The pastures improve as they get higher, until, by the severity of the climate, they diminish, and finally disappear at an elevation of 16,000 feet.

5th. We are now at the base of the Western Cordillera, in which are very high mountain ridges, including Lirima or Chuncura, 19° 47', 69° 12' W., supposed by Mr. George Smith to be 24,000 to 25,000 feet above the sea. Ille, in Aymará, is snow; hence Illi-rima, from whence Lirima. Crossing high passes, and descending a little—

6th. Is an elevated undulating region, known as the Puna, Paramo, or Sierra; this comprises a great extent of country, north, south, and east, and is sometimes called the mountain knot of Potosi; in it appear high ranges of mountains, including the snow-capped heights of Lipes, and, far to the east, Ilimani and Sorata. There are considerable depressions in this elevated region, where there are lakes, containing fish; pasture is found, and quinua grown. This great mountain knot, or rather the Peruvian Andes, may be looked upon as one of volcanic elevation, containing at present many active and numberless quiescent volcanos—the Thibet of Peru.

In the province of Tarapacá, the two Cordilleras are not so well defined as farther to the north, where they may be truly called the Peruvian and Bolivian ranges. We know, however, but little of the geography of this great mountain knot in the district under consideration, but doubtless the seat of much volcanic action: indeed, the Indians say that the greater number of the mountain peaks have been formed by volcanos.

A survey of the province was made by Mr. George Smith and myself in 1828, at the request of the Peruvian Government, and published by the Royal Geographical Society; introduced by Arrowsmith into his maps for the works of Fitzroy and Sir Woodbine Parish. Berghaus also engraved our survey, and calls us "Two Gentlemen of the Potosi Mining Company"—read Arequipa for Potosi.

The province of Tarapacá lies between 19° and 21° 30' S., and 68° 15' and 70° 22' W. In 1628, it formed part of the province of Arica. It is divided into four curacies—viz., Tarapacá, Pica, Sibaya, and Camiña, with a mixed population of about 11,000, consisting of Spaniards, their descendants, Aymará Indians, and a few Negroes.

Those Indians who hold land pay an annual tribute or tax equal to £1 sterling; other Indians without land, 16s.; the white population, 12s; the latter also pay a property tax. The whole income of the province is under £3000.

CURACY OF TARAPACA.—The town of Tarapacá is 4,796 feet above the sea; 19° 56' S., 69° 35' W. is the seat of government, the chief of which is the Sub-Prefect. The ravine at the mouth of which it

---

[1] At this period, Don Roman Castilla was sub-prefect, now President of Peru.

is situated, rises in the Cordillera of Lirima. Seldom is there sufficient water to irrigate the land (which is carefully manured with guano) fit for cultivation in this quebrada, as well as in many others; but when thunderstorms with their heavy rains occur in the Andes, torrents or avenidas rush down the ravines, bringing with them masses of rock, trees, huts, cattle—indeed all that may be in their way, leaving, after one of these destructive floods, nothing but a bed of stones. The houses are built of adobe, and seldom of more than a ground floor, as a precaution against the frequently-occurring earthquakes. The produce of the land is maize, wheat, alfalfa (a medicago) or lucerne, fruit, and a few vegetables. Up the ravine are the Indian towns of Pachica, Laonsana, and Puchurca; in the vicinity are some gold, silver and lead mines.

On the road from Guantajaya to Tarapacá, is the Cerrito of Huara, a bramador or rumbling mountain. The sounds are generally heard at sun-rise. This hill is in a desert plain; during the day the country around is exposed to great heat; at night there is a considerable diminution of temperature: as the sun rises the air becomes heated, expansion takes place, rapid currents, and even gusts of wind are formed, which, striking upon the sides of the mountain, sets the sand in motion, and is most probably the cause of the rumbling sounds in question.

MAMINA, 20° 4' 48" S., is a large Indian town. The potato is here met with in perfection; this locality is supplied with water from clear boiling sulphur springs. Hereabout is much gypsum, magnesian alum, and carbonate of soda. Hamitca is in the vicinity, where there is a gold vein. To the east of Mamiña is the Indian town of Macaya, and then the high range of Yabricoya, abounding in copper, silver and gold. In the vicinity of Quipisca are many desert sandy ravines, and those unaccustomed to travel in such countries would be alarmed at the overhanging precipices, large masses from which have been thrown down by earthquakes. The track from Mamiña to Pica passes through many deep ravines without water. Pozo de Ramirez, is a well 210 feet deep, sunk in the Pampa for the use of travellers. In these regions, no one starts on a journey without a pair of bullock's horns (chifles) full of water slung in front of his saddle, provisions in the saddle-bags, and a thick poncho or two to serve as blankets, as at times one may be for days without falling in with water or a hut.

IQUIQUE, 20° 12' 47" S., 70° 14' W., is the principal port of the province, sheltered by an island (formerly thickly covered with guano), and situated at the north-west extremity of a low tract of ground, surrounded by high and barren mountains. Iquique stands in a stratum of broken shells, in all stages of degradation, in places several feet thick, intermixed with others similar to those now inhabiting the neighbouring seas, and have in all probability been elevated above the level of the ocean at no very distant date. The general opinion is, that there is a gradual upheaving of the whole line of coast, extending some distance inland; on this point Mr. Blake observes, that fragments of recent shells have been found in the Pampa of Tamarugal, 3000 to

3,500 feet above the sea, and distant thirty to forty miles.[1] Iquique owes its present importance as a port to the shipment of nitrate of soda from thence, and some silver from the mines of Huantajaya and Santa Rosa.

There is neither wood, water, nor vegetation here. Water was formerly brought from Pisagua, forty-five miles north; it is now distilled from sea-water. Provisions come from the interior, from other parts of the coast, and Chile. The population is employed in commerce, shipping the nitrate of soda, and fishing. During three years' residence at Iquique, I only once saw a slight shower of rain. Mean winter heat, 63° at 8 a.m., 67° at noon, 62° at 8 p.m.; summer heat, 72° at 8 a.m., 78° at noon, 74° at 8 p.m.

Of sea birds, there are immense flocks, including the cormorant, pelican, booby, gull, shag, &c.; to these birds is owing the existence of so much guano found on the coast and islands of Peru.

Of land birds, condors, vultures, hawks, and turkey-buzzards are very numerous. There are a few bats, rats, mice, fleas and mosquitos, the latter engendered by wet sea-weed; a vinchuca is occasionally seen; and there are several varieties of small lizards. Iquique is the only village on the coast of the province; the other places named on the charts are merely headlands, beaches, islands, &c., visited by fishermen in search of the fish called congrio, seals, and sea otters, in their ingeniously constructed balsas or floats, made of seal skins inflated with air. During their stay at such places, they live in caves or wretched cabins, built of whales' ribs covered with seal skins, and subsist on water, maize, and fish.

With the present steam navigation along the Pacific, facilitating the transport of merchandise and provisions, I am led to believe that this, perhaps the most barren coast in the world, will sooner or later be carefully examined for mines; and it would not surprise me to hear of important discoveries of precious and other metals, as, also, of valuable saline matters; then, although large cities may not rise up, places of great commercial importance will line the coast. I will mention a few spots worthy of further examination.

Alcaparosa, north of Pisagua, for gold. North and south of Pisagua are silver veins. Chanabaya, 20° 40' S. is an important locality, and, if water and provisions could be placed there at a reasonable rate, it is the general opinion that another Guantajaya would arise out of the desert; here both gold and silver veins have been partially worked. Chuchulai, in 21° 8' S., contains silver veins. At Paiquina and Chipana, north of Loa, gold has been met with. To the south of Loa, there is much guano, particularly at Paquique, in 21° 56' S. Ten miles south are the rich copper veins of Duendes and Tocopillo.

GUANTAJAYA.—These celebrated silver mines are about seven miles from the port of Iquique, and in 20° 14' S., 70° 7' W.,[2] 2,877 feet above

---

[1] During my residence, in early times, I never noticed any recent shells in the Pampa, neither during my last visit.

[2] In map, this spot is placed two or three miles too much south. Santa Rosa the same.

the sea. They are reached from the port by a track over a plain through which runs an immense ridge of sand. The road is then along the slope of the mountains to the caracol, or steep zig-zag road, the summit of which is 1760 feet. At the summit, the ground is loose, sandy, and thickly covered with angular pieces of rock, some in an advanced state of degradation, to which ages of solar heat have given a calcined appearance, some having crumbled into powder. Here is much salt, looking as if it had oozed out of the earth and crystallized by the sun's heat; at a distance, it has the appearance of a collection of bones, and the scene is one of absolute sterility. The mountains of Guantajaya, Santa Rosa, and others, are seen towering above the surrounding country. Everything is of a dull brown colour, except the bluish ranges of the Cordillera, in the distance, covered with snow.

The mines of Guantajaya have rendered the province of Tarapacá so celebrated in Peru, that it has sometimes been called the Potosi of the south. They were discovered, about 1556, by Spaniards from Arica, who worked at a spot called the Chiflones, but who after a time abandoned them. The mines were re-discovered by an Indian named Cucumate, during one of his journeys to the coast for guano, who made them known to Juan de Loyaza, who commenced working, but died without reaping much benefit. In 1718, Loyaza's son, Don Bartolomeo, found rich ore in the vein of San Simon, and, in 1727, the Paniso or unconsolidated rock (composed principally of argillaceous limestone containing fossil shells), at the foot of the mountain, was discovered, in which were found the papas or insulated masses of silver; one, met with in 1729, weighed 800 lbs., another in 1794, 400 lbs. In 1746, the paniso having been bored through, the principal vein was found, which led to the discovery of many others. The ores are native, chloride, chloro-bromide, and sulphuret of silver, and their combinations with copper, lead, &c.; the matrix is of carbonate of lime.

It was computed in 1826 that the mean annual amount of silver extracted up to that time, since 1726, was 750,000 dollars, which would give a total of about £15,000,000 sterling. Since 1826, the produce of the mines has been very irregular, not averaging more than 30,000 dollars a year.

There are about fifty mines; and in one only has a little water been met with, so impregnated with saline and metallic matters, as to be unfit for drinking.

In such a desert spot labour is very expensive, and the mining operations are generally carried on in the veins only, not working by shafts and adits, the system there being to extract little or no loose rock, and, as new works are opened, to throw the loose stuff into older ones; this has caused the mines to be called aterrada, or filled up. Periods elapse when but little silver is extracted; then a boya, or rich discovery is made; one amongst these was a mass of nearly pure silver, fifteen yards long and in places a yard thick. I might indicate positions where rich veins could be cut at other levels, and other boyas discovered; this, however, belongs to the mineralogy of the province, and is only locally interesting.

In flourishing times as many as 4000 persons have been employed at these mines: I have seen as few as 150. The habitations are generally built of caliche, that is, sand and salt, some few of wood, the material brought from Chile. The water for drinking is conveyed from the wells of Almonte (s. g. 100,105, temp. 70° F.). distant twenty-one miles, in llama skins containing fourteen gallons, selling for four shillings; when scarce, for much more. For a live sheep £10 has been paid, and £20 for a live bullock from Atacama.

At times it is distressing to see the miners returning from the sultry mine, the temperature of which is often 100° F. (highest exterior temperature in the shade 78°), and obliged to go on foot to Almonte for water.

Mean winter heat 8 a.m., 53°; noon, 64°; 8 p.m., 56°. Summer heat, 8 a.m., 73°; noon, 76°; 8 p.m., 64°.

Mines of Santa Rosa and El Carmen, discovered about 1778, are distant from Guantajaya five miles. Independently of yielding the class of ores similar to those of Guantajaya, there is much sulphuret of silver and copper (cochiso). From 1815 to 1825, one mine gave £600,000; and a boya in the Arcos mine, three yards long and twenty in height, gave £100,000.

PINTADOS, south of Santa Rosa, is a curious spot. Las Rayas, so called from some rude Indian work scraped out on the surface of a mountain (see p. 158, and plate at p. 159).

SALINAS DE CEBEMENO, or salt deposits, fifteen miles south of Iquique. Here salt is found on a plain fifteen to twenty feet above the level of the sea, and 1500 yards from the rocky shore. How has this been formed? Can it have been formed near to the edge of the ocean and then uplifted? or is it from saline waters of percolation from the interior? The salt is friable and crystalline, sometimes taking a curved appearance. It is met with in mounds, and a little below the surface, from one-eighth of an inch to two feet thick, and free from earthy matter. It is in layers between irregular strata of rock, in which are perpendicular splits also filled with salt, one layer communicating with another. When the layers are thick, they are made up of five or six smaller ones. They have an inclination towards the sea of 2° to 3°, and contain abundance of sulphates. Ship loads are occasionally taken to Chile.

The existence and origin of salt near the ocean is not difficult to understand; but when it is met with on the mountain range of the coast, in and near the Pampa of Tamarugal, in company with nitrate, sulphate, carbonate of soda, &c., also borate of soda and lime, as well as high up in the Andes at 15,000 and 16,000 feet, and perhaps higher, with, as I presume, no saliferous rocks, is a curious matter of speculation, and tempts one to surmise that so much salt in such elevated positions may derive its origin from other sources than the ocean, viz., from volcanic and the gradual decomposition of rocks containing the bases of saline materials in their composition.

Mr. Smith wrote me in 1850: "The large salares appear to be drawn from the earth by a powerful sun acting on a surface moistened by heavy dew; I think we nearly bared the mountains about Santa Rosa, when I sold a quantity of salt to Captain Bowers, in 1827; *there is now a very fair crop upon them.*" This is nearly a pure chloride of sodium.

CURACY OF PICA.—Pica 4,290 feet above the sea, 20° 30' 8" S., 69° 24' W. (the church), is on the eastern margin of the Pampa, on very sandy soil, at the base of Arid mountains; above which is an elevated tract, where the humidity of the air and occasional rain produce the ichu, iru and sajana pastures; upon which feed the domestic llama and alpaca and sheep, and, in the more retired parts, the wild vicuña and guanaco.

The land at Pica under cultivation is limited, the chief supply of water being from inconsiderable thermal and other springs, varying from 55° to 98° Fht.; the water is collected in cochas, or reservoirs, and carefully distributed to the vineyards and farms; some of which are supplied with water by means of socabones or adits driven on a slight incline; some of these adits are more than two thousand yards long, and were probably commenced by the Indians before the arrival of the Spaniards. The estates at Pica consist of small vineyards, orchards, vegetable gardens, and plots of alfalfa. Among the fruits are the grape, from which wine and brandy are made, figs, guavas, melons, chirimoyas, pears, peaches, quinces, small but very sour lemons, pomegranates; tuna, the fruit of the opuntia; date, pacay (prosopis dulcis), the largest tree of the country, and the favourite aji or capsicum, which the Peruvians use in almost every dish. Olives are also cultivated, canes for thatching, a little cotton, sweet potatoes, the castor oil plant, chañar, capulies, and a few other plants.

The principal houses are of adobes, but only of one floor in consequence of the earthquakes; the majority of the dwellings are merely bamboo huts plastered with mud, and have flat roofs. The streets are deep with loose sand, which, in the day time, during summer, becomes very hot and most painful to walk on, so much so, that the inhabitants keep a horse or mule saddled at the door to ride from house to house. This spot suffers from ague, a bad sort known as tabardilla, chuicchuic, and even peste (plague).

Locusts at times do great damage, and the vinchuca is common. The Cerro de Chuchulai is, famed for its buenos panisos, or as showing favourable indications of gold and silver.

MATILLA.—20° 31' 22" S.W. of Pica. Its farms are supplied with water from the valley of Quisma or Chintaguay, as well as from Adits. This spot was comparatively populous before the conquest, as there are many ancient tombs hereabouts. In the vicinity, are the warm baths of Culco, with shade under a barranco or cliff. There is also much sulphate of soda hereabouts.

PAMPA DE TARMARUGAL.—This interesting table-land takes its name from the tamarugo or tamarisk tree; another tree of this family is the algarobo, called carob and espino: these trees afford the principal fuel of the country, and grow wherever water may reach the pampa from the ravines to the east. Here is also buried underneath the soil large collections of dead wood of the above trees, sometimes called fossil wood. Mr. Smith wrote to me, in 1850: "Forests of fossil wood have been dug up in the pampa; and, singular to relate, the whole trees were found lying in the same direction, as if swept down at the same instant either by a hurricane or a torrent of water from the mountain ravines." The pampa extends throughout the whole length of the province, appearing to be elevated in the north: its height above the sea is from 3000 to 3500 feet; it is a continuation of the desert of Atacama. Its surface is strewed here and there with pebbles, patches of sand, salt, nitrate of soda, borate of soda and lime, and other saline bodies; much marly land, fit for cultivation if there were water, this reposes on rounded stones; and, lastly, porphyritic rock is met with.

By sinking wells, water is obtained at various depths; near the east margin it is not far from the surface, but towards the west it is deeper; still among the hollows, further west, as at La Noria, Cocina, &c., it is in places near the surface; this is owing to difference of level.

A curious point about much of the water in the Pampa is that, although there is so much saline material covering the plain, there is not much in the water. On the east a few ravines descend into the plain from the Andes, whilst there are other ravines quite dry. Only three of these quebradas reach the sea, viz., Loa, Pisagua and Camarones.

The view of the Cordillera from the western border of the Pampa is very fine. The sky is generally cloudless, and the heat of the day is intense; but the nights are cool even in summer, thanks to radiation and the land breeze. Shooting stars or meteors are seen to perfection at night darting into and across the plain; and the deceptive mirage sadly tantalizes the thirsty traveller.

Although a level plain, still, when rain has been abundant in the Andes and has escaped by the ravines into the Pampa, watercourses are formed, producing irregularities. About noon, in summer, it sometimes blows strongly from south-west, when the sand and dry earth (carauso) is carried before it in large quantities, and is very annoying to the traveller. Whirlwinds of this sand, and even land spouts are seen in the plain. In 1830, there was a terrible sand storm, the hurricane blowing from the south; the sand was lifted more than a hundred yards in the air; the sun was obscured; the people in the villages were greatly alarmed, they hurried to the chapels to embrace the statues of the saints, and pray to them for protection.

OBSERVATIONS ON THE DESERT COAST OF PERU. — Taking as the bases, first, the existence of the prevailing south to south-south-east winds on the coast during the greater part of the year; secondly, that the line of coast runs about north to south; thirdly, the northerly winds in winter.

The great south-south-east wind having been deprived of its humidity (contracted from the South Atlantic) in traversing the eastern portion of the continent of South America) ere it reaches the east base of the Andes, has already passed over much sterile country it has assisted to render so, arrives in the frozen regions of the Andes so dry as not to be in a position to deposit moisture of consequence (thus in a measure accounting for so little snow and ice in the Cordillera of South Peru from this source); then this dry south-south-east wind, blowing across the lands on the western coast, would I conceive be the main cause of its deserts.

Were the winds from the west, they would arrive charged with moisture absorbed from the Pacific; there would be periodic rains, and the now desert tracks would be fertile, but this probably at the expense (the more particularly on account of the Andean barrier) of there being deserts from east to west across South America; and the now prolific soil of Brazil would be like the desert of Atacama.

The reason of the inconsiderable streams on the west coast may be accounted for by the rather small quantity of snow in the Peruvian Cordilleras; and, as the rain in and near them is limited, and principally when the northerly winds blow during the winter months towards the Andes, meeting them with the cold atmosphere in south-south-east winds, atmospheric conflicts take place, when storms with rain, lightning and thunder occur.

In winter, the light north and north-north-west winds deposit some of their moisture (which from late observation is saline) on the summits of the mountains of the coast, giving rise to spare vegetation; but the lower portions of these mountains, as well as the more elevated tracks, as the Pampa de Tamarugal and desert of Atacama, absorb and hold so much heat as to prevent any moisture falling.

Onward goes the north and north-north-west winds, passing the arid mountains, to the east of the Pampa and desert, depositing there moisture in the shape of rain at considerable elevations near the base of the Andes; and, lastly, the remaining portion as snow and glacier.

From Pica to the Noria or well of Ramirez, the track goes through patches of espino trees. As there is some land here free from saline matter, but containing no humus or mould, experiments were made in 1820 to render these barren spots fit for cultivation; wells were sunk, the water extracted by pumps, and by irrigating the pure marl and sand, wheat, alfalfa, maize, and vegetables were produced. In 1850, another form of farming was resorted to, called "chacra sin riego," or a farm not requiring irrigation. About two feet of the very saline earth was cleared off the surface, thus approaching the water below the Pampa to within two or three feet, when sufficient moisture was obtained to grow maize, wheat and vegetables.

LA TIRANA.—20° 21′ S., 60° 43′ W. Good water is met with a few feet below the surface (s. g. 1·00255, temp. 70°); when heavy rain falls in the Cordillera, a small stream reaches here. It is rather a considerable place, and where the principal Buitrones or amalgamating works are established for reducing the silver ores, particularly of Huantajaya and Santa Rosa.

WELLS OF ALMONTE.—Here water is at the depth of thirty yards (s. g. 1°00165, temp. 70°). The mines are supplied with water from these wells. Here is a buitron.

NITRATE OF SODA.—At page 153, I refer to the more recent information regarding this valuable substance. Its existence in Tarapacá has been known in Europe about a century. In 1820 some was sent to England; but, the duty being high, it was thrown overboard. In 1827, efforts were unsuccessfully made by an English house to export it. In 1830, a cargo was sent to the United States, and found to be unsaleable: a part was taken to Liverpool, but did not sell. A cargo was taken to France, and, in 1831, another to England, when it sold for thirty and forty shillings the ton. The price has varied, in 1851 it was at fifteen shillings. Since 1830 to 1850, 239,860 tons had been exported.

The principal deposits of nitrate of soda yet known are in the western margin of the Pampa, on the sides of some of the ravines, and in some of the hollows of the mountains of the coast, La Noria being the principal oficina. The nitrate has not been found nearer to the coast than eighteen miles, and it seems as if salt was gradually transformed into nitrate. There are about 100 oficinas or refining works.

The nitrate deposits, or caliche, commence about Tiliviche, extending south to Quilliagua, with interruptions of deposits of common salt, borate of soda and lime, &c. The nitrate or caliche grounds vary in breadth, the average being about 500 yards, and in places seven to eight feet thick, sometimes quite pure. In the ravines and hollows, the nitrate is found on the shelving sides: the bottom of the hollows look like dried up lakes and are covered with salt two to three feet thick, and on the margins there is the nitrate—at times there is a hard earthy crust on it.

There are several varieties of nitrate: 1. White and compact, containing 64 per cent. II. Yellow, occasioned by salts of chrome, 70 per cent. III. Grey, compact, 46 per cent. IV. Grey crystalline, 20 to 25 per cent. V. White crystalline, resembling refined nitrate. All these contain iodine, as well as salt, sulphate and carbonate of soda, and murate of lime.

Recently, in connection with the nitrate deposits, borate of soda and lime has been found.

The rough nitrate is broken into pieces, put into boilers, water introduced, and the whole boiled; the nitrate is held in solution, whilst the earthy matter, salt, sulphates, &c., are separated and fall down. The saturated solution of nitrate is run off into shallow troughs to crystallize, now containing from 2 to 3 per cent of impurities, and is then conveyed to the coast for exportation. The province of Tarapacá contains nitrate for the world's consumption for ages; the Desert of Atacama yields it, and it is said to have been met with in the Andes and in the eastern plains.

Passing El Pugio (pucyu, a well) a small farm on the road from Pica to Guatacondo, and the Rio Salada, the route leads by Cuevas, Tambo,

Ramada, and Chipani, halting places without water. Having ascended the Cuesta de Chelis, and descended into the deep ravine of Guatacondo, a few trees are seen amongst masses of rock. In ascending the ravine, it becomes very narrow, and at one place it is taken up by a chajagua or waterfall. In order to pass this angostura, or narrow, a path has been cut out of the overhanging rocks, a few miles from which is the Indian village of

GUATACONDO (in Aymará, the Devil bound) 20° 57′ 51″ S. Here, granite, porphyries, clay-slate and their debris are seen in perfection. High up the ravine, in the Cordillera, are the mines of Ugina at 16,000 feet, and where gold, silver and copper are found in the same vein; also a white copper, called pampua; here, are gold washings also. The produce of the valley is maize, fruit and vegetables; a few sheep are reared. Impejza, Tigua and Yareta, are silver mines in the vicinity.

From the heights of Guatacondo, there is an extensive view into the desert of Atacama. The mountains of Conche, famed for their gold and copper mines, may also be seen. It is from that part of the country where large quantities of green sand or atacamite comes, for sanding letters instead of using blotting-paper.

QUEBRADA DE LOS PINTADOS, or the pictured ravine. Here are representations of Indians, llamas, dogs and other forms, on the sides of the dell; as well as at Quebrada Onda; the figures are, twenty to thirty feet high, scraped out in the marly sand, the lines being from 12 to 18 inches broad and 6 to 8 deep.

MANI, 21° 10′ S. in the ravine of Capana, takes its name from the earthapple, Mani (Arachis hypogæa); it is the most southern inhabited spot of the province. Near to this are some old gold works, as well as those of Catigna, in the Quebrada onda.

QUILLIAGUA is in the valley of Loa, where reside a few Indians. The stream, which is regarded as the south boundary of Peru, with Bolivia, is generally five feet wide and five feet deep, and brackish; during the rainy season in the Andes, its volume of water is augmented. It is in contemplation to open a canal above the village, so as to irrigate the neighbouring plain. Earthquakes are severely felt here.

LOA, on the coast, in 21° 30′ S., is the abode of a few fishermen. To the north, are the deserted gold mines of Chipani, and Marejo, also the silver mines of Paiquina. To the south are the gold mines of Guachan, Mr. Peacock informs me that some ore he obtained, yielded 50 ozs. the ton.

PAVELLON DE PICA is a hillock on the coast from whence large quantities of guano are taken.

MINES OF CHANABAYA. These are of gold and silver. It takes three days to transport water and provisions to them from the interior There are a dozen mines. From what I have been able to learn, I am inclined to think, now that there are such facilities afforded by steam-navigation, that this spot deserves further notice, and might be got at easily from the coast.

CURACY OF SIBAYA.—SIBAYA, 19° 47′ 33″ S. is an Indian town. Maize is grown, and sheep and llamas bred. In the vicinity is

Limacsiña, Guaviña, and the ruined village of Manca-Guaviña, prostrated by one of those rushes of water (avenidas) from the Andes. There is a route from Sibaya to Potosi, across the Andes, which takes an Indian 12 to 15 days. From Sibaya to Mocha there are two tracks, one by the mountains, used when the valley is impassable by reason of the sudden rushes of water through the Angostura, or narrow, which is two miles long, 800 feet deep, and two or three yards in width, in some places excluding the light of day. These augosturas appear to me to have been formed by earthquakes—they are called rajas, splits or fissures. This pass, although originally such a fissure, has been worn down by torrents 20 to 30 feet more, the latter distance being very smooth.

Mocha produces wheat and maize. Here resides an Indian family named Quispe-Sugso, descended from the Incas, paying no tribute. In 1850, I was informed that Juan Quispe-Sugso followed the calling of a muleteer. One of the Incas conferred the title of Quispe or resplendent in this family. At Mocha there is much gypsum, and in its mountains indications of gold.

Usmagama, Chusmisa and Guasquina are Indian hamlets where llamas are reared, and wheat, maize and potatoes grown. Gigantic cacti are hereabouts seen twenty feet or more high, the stems a foot thick, which, when split, serves for doors and rafters.

Usmagama is at the bottom of a deep ravine, prettily surrounded with trees, and has a picturesque appearance from the mountain road to Zipisa. The track is steep and dangerous, along a precipice in a zigzag course, some of the steps being cut out of the solid rock, and at great distances from each other, so that a mule in descending is obliged to drop both the fore feet at once, which is not pleasant to the rider.

At Guasquiña there is gypsum, and on the heights are abundant debris from the higher country, containing much sulphuret of iron, supposed to be a favourable indication of lavadero gold. At Chusmisa are hot sulphur springs.

On leaving Guasquiña for Zipisa, the track leads up the north side of the ravine: it is cut out of the mountain and looks almost perpendicular. The road is firm, but so narrow that there is much danger when travellers or troops of animals meet. From the summit of this road the track is most mountainous, until a dry quebrada is attained, which is entered by an escalera, or ladder path, a flight of steps at an angle of 45°, cut out of the rock, a sort of road the Indians of old knew so well how to construct. Here, travellers are obliged to dismount and lead their animals.

Zipisa, 19° 38′ 0″ S., at 10,250 feet, is in a very rugged country, supplied with water, from springs, conveyed by a long acqueduct made to wind round the mountains, a system used in Incarial times. Here, is a sanctuary, the resort of the pious in the month of June. It is a pretty spot, and where a few paraquets, wood-pigeons and small birds are seen.

Sotoca, 19° 36′ 18″ S., is reached by a mountainous up and down track, and half way between it and Zipisa, both villages are seen beneath the traveller, apparently at only a stone's throw. In the mountain of Yaracagua is a silver mine, and there is much sulphuret of iron in the debris that covers these mountains. It is supposed that the existence of this substance here will lead some day to the discovery of gold washings.

Curacy of Camiña.—At the mouth of the quebrada of Camiña, is the Port of Pisagua, from whence Iquique is supplied with water: the stream seldom reaches the beach. The mountains about Pisigua have veins of gold, silver, antimony and copper. From this place Huayna-Pisagua and Mejillones nitrate is shipped.

Tana.—Alfalfa is grown, and there are large deposits of salt in the vicinity. This ravine of Camina, like the other two of Loa and Camarones, cut straight through the Pampa; they are wide in parts, narrow in others; their structure is alluvial, and imbedded in them are rounded masses of rock, resulting from mountains to the east. I looked for fossil bones in this district, but found none: Garcilaso mentions the existence of bones of giants on the borders of the Desert of Atacama.

Quimpasa, Yalamanta, Moquella, Quistagama, Cuisama and Chapiquilta are native hamlets before reaching the large Indian town of Camiña (anciently Carvisa, one of the names of the llama,). Much of the cultivated land is far above the level of the stream, formed into terraces, and watered from above by means of an acqueduct running from some distance up the valley. Here we see the domestic llama and alpaca, and a little higher up in the mountains the wild huanaco and vicuña.

The track to Isluga leads up the ravine through trees and shrubs, leaving which to the N., by a long ascent, you arrive at the Cuesta of Parasuya without any road being distinguishable from the tracks made by the herds of llamas and sheep that graze on the mountains; these tracks continue nearly to the pile of stones known as the Pass or Pascana of Pacheta, 14,430 feet above the sea.

Maymaga has a marsh, the waters of which issue out of springs. Now and then a chinchilla and biscacha are seen,—also condors, eagles, and wild geese. These solitary and dreary spots are called estancias, where reside a few Indian families, tending the llama and jerking (or drying) its meat. From the N.E. the land is contracted by the mountains; a cuesta is ascended, when after passing the estancia of Mauqui, the track is very bad, over rising barren ground, without vegetation, until a high pass in the Andes is reached, known as the Abra de Pichuta, with its pile of stones. I have estimated this pass to be at least 15,000 feet above the sea. Much inconvenience was experienced in traversing this pass by the violence of the cold-piercing wind from S.E. From here the volcano of Isluga is well seen, giving out volumes of vapour, as well as the view of many snow-capped ridges. Ascending through a ravine, the coals and stream of Pasirugo, 14,079 feet are attained—this is a resting place of the Indian when tending his llamas. Anguaje is on a lake and is a llama farm. From here five small craters of the volcano of Isluga are seen—two near the summit—three some distance down the south side.

The VOLCANO of Isluga is not very conical. It was winter when I was there, and then it was covered with snow to its base. During the summer, sulphur is collected from the craters. Loud rumbling noises are heard in its vicinity and earthquakes frequently occur.

From the character of the rocks and debris of this region I should say that the Cordilleras in these latitudes, and far north and south, is one mass of volcanic matter. Passing the Estancia of Enquelca, on the border of a lake, the high Andean town of ISLUGA is reached. This is the largest village in this part of the Cordillera, on a good-sized stream which comes from the mountain of Carabaya and running into the lake of Isluga. In these elevated inland waters I saw an ugly-looking fish—the suchi—eight to ten inches long. I am inclined to give 14,000 to 15,000 feet of elevation to this town. In the hollows, a few potatoes and millet is with difficulty grown, and there are some scanty pastures. The severity of the climate freezes the potato readily, and in this state it is called chuño—the starchy part of the potato being changed into saccharine by freezing. Near here are water-fowl, a few ostriches, plovers and biscachas: the puma is sometimes seen, its prey the young llamas: the condor is also dreaded. Of fuel there is a little turf; the tola, a resinous shrub, and the more resinous yareta, of a globular appearance, the resin exuding in winter.

PAMPA DE SAL.—To the east of Isluga begins an extensive salt-plain, said to extend to Challapato and the insulated Cordillera del Frayle 40 leagues off and near to Potosi, varying in breadth from three to eight leagues; the salt being five to ten inches thick. From near Enquelca this Andean salt-plain is seen as far as the eye can reach, forming a regular white horizon, and in striking contrast with the dark bases of the Cordilleras. The elevation of this plain is at least 14,000 feet.

Caraquima is an estancia at the western base of the mountain of Mama-Huanapa. There are other estancias, as Xiquima, Turini, Chivullani, &c.

MAUQUI, 14,342 feet, is a small village, with a chapel larger than the whole place put together, and dedicated to N. S. de Guadalupe, who, it is said, appeared to an Indian woman on a hill north of the village, at which spot a large cross is erected.

LAKE OF THE PARINAS, or of the Andean Flamingos—This bird has some red on the breast and is a new variety. I have deposited in the British Museum a specimen. This lake is 13,567 feet in length, and has much wild-fowl.

PUCHULTISA.—Here are a few huts for the accommodation of Indian shepherds. A small stream runs by it, augmented by others from the boiling springs, water volcanos, or

VOLCANITOS DE AGUA DE PUCHULTISA: These are in a hollow, the surface of which is composed of a thick white crust. There are a dozen or more of these geysers, from three to five feet in diameter, with water boiling at various levels, some throwing the water to two feet in height. The water as it cools leaves a sediment which increases the size of the cones. There are more than 500 smaller ones dispersed over the hollow, emitting a sulphurous odour, whilst a rumbling subterranean noise is continually heard, like distant firing. May not the surface of this hollow be the covering to a comparatively quiescent crater, which, as the water runs into it from the mountains, gets heated, expands and forms these Andean geysers. The specimen of the white crust was lost, but I should not be surprised to hear when it is examined, that it contains salts of borax.

By the Quebrada of Biscachas, and a mountainous route by Ulmaga, round the base of Tata Jachura, (see p. 164 for ascent of this mountain) I came to the large Indian town of

CHIAPA, 19° 32′ S., 63° 30′ W.. 10,452 feet. Here wheat, maize, potatoes and vegetables are cultivated. In the month of June it freezes at night. The water used in the irrigation of the land is brought by aqueducts of some extent. Here grows the cactus, tola, culen, jarillo, aracache or wild celery, valerian and a few flowers.

Soga is between Chiapa and Camiña, by so mountainous and broken a track as to be called the Devil's Road.

QUEBRADA OF CAMARONES.— The boundary with Arica is a few miles north of the ravine. The water is brackish, and ague prevails in that part near the coast. Much black oxide of arsenic is found in the ravine. Chisa is a small vineyard in the valley of the same name, in which is also Miñimiñi, an Indian town, producing wheat and fruit.

INDIANS OF TARAPACA.—They are of the Aymará race. At pp. 166, 167, I have mentioned these Indians. I may here add, that they have been so subdued that they pass for an inoffensive and quiet race. They marry young and appear to lead a virtuous life. The Indian is slow in his movements, but most patient and persevering, performing long journeys with troops of mules and asses, laden with the produce of his land, for sale, whilst the women remain behind, assisting in the cultivation of the soil and tending the herds of llamas, alpacas and sheep. Their habitations are of rough stone, seldom more than one apartment—without windows; at the end is an elevated part, on which they sleep, on llama and sheep-skins. Their cooking utensils consist of a few earthen pots and dishes, and they manufacture the material for their clothing from the wool of llama, alpaca, sheep, and cotton.

At their homes they fare pretty well, living on llama meat, &c. Some have flour and vegetables, but their principal grain is maize, from which they make their bread and favorite chicha; but, with a little toasted maize and coca, they will travel for days over the most desert tracks. The coca is masticated with llipta, an alkaline ash mixed with boiled potato.

The dress of the men is a coarse cotton shirt, woollen breeches and jacket, stockings without feet, a large hat, and hide sandals. A long strip of cotton hangs loosely round the neck, and sometimes round the head and face, to protect those parts from the cold, or the intense heat of the sun. A waistband, of various colours, in which is the pouch containing the coca; this, with a coarse blue and red poncho, completes his attire.

The women wear a long cotton garment, over which is a woollen dress; then a long mantle fastened by tupus or pins of silver, sometimes these have a spoon at one end; a long waistband: then the lliclia or female poncho, in which they carry their children behind them. They wear sandals, but seldom any covering to the head; they are adorned with the gargantilla, or necklace of coloured beads, little crosses and small spoons. Occasionally a few Chirihuanos Indians of the Yungas visit Tarapacá. They are called the travelling doctors of Peru, in consequence of their ambulatory pharmacy being composed of remedies for all diseases: herbs, gums, resins, roots, charms of various sorts, including the loadstone; but the only useful one is the quinquina or peruvian bark.

SECTION I.—At Pisagua much black granite is seen, traversed by veins of quartz. The deep ravines of Tiliviche and Camiña are composed of sand, silicious pebbles, rounded and angular masses of granite, volcanic rocks and much gypsum. From Yalamanta the section goes through the arid range of Cahuisa to a broken undulating region where there is pasture. The Volcano of Isluga succeeds, then touching the great Salt Plain we get to the Volcano of Carangas.

SECTION II. commences at Iquique with granite, then porphyries. At the silver mines of Guantajaya, (the Chiflones) and near the summit of the mountain, I examined a superficial layer called Manto, which is composed entirely of a fossil shelly deposit, principally of broken valves of gryphæ. Beneath the Manto argillaceous limestone is met with; and at the base of the mountain of Guantajaya, the Paniso, a peculiar unconsolidated mass is found, which contains the papas, or insulated masses of silver, as well as fossil shells. Darwin has figured three, viz.: Terebratula Inca, T. ænigma and Lucina Americana.

My friend, Professor Morris, on examining the fossil shells I obtained from the Paniso, names them as follows: Lucina excentrica; a Venus; Trigonia (a cast); and a new Lucina which he calls L. Bollaerti. The worn fragments of ammonites, probably A. plicatiles. Professor Forbes found one fragment of ammonite undistinguishable from A. biplex; others either biplex or nearly allied. Cast of a Trigonia near Costata; an Astarte and a Venus.

Having passed through the Paniso, argillaceous limestones are met with: then a hard basaltic formation: also a silicious rock.

The coast range being traversed, we reach the Saline Pampa de Tamarugal. There rise out of it some isolated silicious mountains; the principal ones are Challacollo and Challacollcito. In the former I visited some abandoned silver mines. In the arid range on the eastern border of the Pampa, there is much sand and detritus, underneath which, in all probability, the rocks are similar to those of the coast range. Next is an elevated country, broken by ravines, with much debris from the Cordilleras, with volcanic matters, then the Andes.

EARTHQUAKES.—A severe one is expected every six or seven years; but few days pass without a shock being felt, coming generally from the East. In 1795, as many as forty shocks were experienced in one day. In 1818 a series of heavy shocks continued for fifteen days, when the people left the town of Guantajaya; the ground opened and clouds of dust were raised in the streets by the violence of the concussions. On one occasion I was at the bottom of a deep mine here, when I heard a faint rumbling, which rapidly increased, sounding like distant thunder, and then it passed onwards; next followed a horizontal, undulating motion, which shook down part of the slanting road of the mines. The rest of the paper contains my route from Cobija to Coquimbo, by the coast of the Desert of Atacama, with observations on the meteoric iron of Atacama.

Abstract of Second Series of Observations on the Geography of Southern Peru; and on the Salt, Nitrate of Soda and Borax deposits in the Province of Tarapacá. By W. Bollaert, F.R.G.S., Corr. Mem. Univ. Chile. Read at British Association, Aberdeen, 1859.

In November, 1853, the steamer "Magdalena" took me to the West Indies in 16 days, and another steamer across the Carribean sea to New Granada; then by rail and the river Chagres across the Isthmus of Darien to Panamá. In a few days another steamer conveyed me to Guayaquil, and having left this port I bade adieu for some time to the sight of vegetation. The deserts of the Coast of Peru became the scene of my wanderings until I got to Chile, and revelled once more in the beautiful forests of Arauco.

PAITA.—Here we first got sight of the arid shores of Peru. The sandy cliffs are three to four hundred feet high, composed of horizontal layers, containing recent shells. I was informed, that as far as eight leagues inland, shells were found and of a species now existing in these seas. The impression one has in viewing these shores, is that they have not long since been uplifted from the sea, or that the ocean has retired. Water and provisions are brought from Piura, seven leagues off. It had not rained for the last eight years. The exports of the country are straw hats, hides and wool. Near here is much gypsum; and I found two Italians — political refugees and friends of Garibaldi—turning it, by burning, into plaster of Paris, and manufacturing images.

PIURA is on a river of the same name. Coal (probably tertiary) exists at Mal Paso on the estate of Mancorn. Coasting along the desert of Sechura I passed the Lobos Guano Islands, so called from the number of seals found there.

LAMBAYEQUE.—In this region are seen immense flights of huanaes, or guano-producing birds, some so gorged with fish as to find it difficult to get out of the way of our steamer. The balsas, or floats of wood used here, are wonderful things for a surf, and the way cargo and passengers are thrown on and lugged off, is amusing.

HUANCHACO, the port of Trujillo—the land of the ancient Chimus. Here we took in silver bars and much cochineal.

HUACHO.—In this vicinity much salt is collected, originating from the sea. The general appearance of these coast towns, including Huacho, when viewed from the sea, is that they are built in hollows. The houses are of one story high, giving to the town the aspect of having been razed, driven down, or swallowed up. It is impossible in a view of this kind, and recollecting something of its geological history, to divest oneself of the feelings attached to earthquakes.

Another peculiarity is the clay colour which pervades everything. Stone and wood are scarce, hence sun-dried brick is the building material. The sauce or willow (salix humboldtiana and falcata) is prolific where water may run, and protects the inhabitants from the tropical sun.

The only fertile soil of the Pacific slopes is formed by valleys, which seem to be a continuation of mountain passes. They are filled with small streams which descend from mountain snows and afford means of irrigation. They vary in dimensions, that in which Lima is situated is fifty miles in length.

The "Mercurio Peruano," I. 98, 116, states that in January, 1791, this district was visited by rains. On the 15th "heavy rain;" 16th, "mountain torrents;" 17th, "thick mist," temp. 75° F. In February, on the 10th and 14th, avenidas or mountain torrents came down the river, from rain, covering a space of from sixty to seventy leagues. This was a most extraordinary rain for the great quantity of it; for, after only two hours duration, it had formed new rivers and ruined many villages. 1746 is the date of the last heavy rains about Lima.

The following is also from the "Mercurio," being the account of an extraordinary meteor seen at Cañete on the evening of the 25th December, 1790, with the observers reflections thereon.

"The sun set at 6.12, a dusky meteor running north and south illuminated the valley. Its figure the segment of a circle, about 115° in circumference, the two extremities of which, perpendicular to the horizon, were accurately defined, and suspended in the air. Its equal aspect in every part denoted its thickness to be about half a yard. It was embellished, or rather rendered terrific by a mixture of black and ash colours, which resembled an overshadowed iris. It remained fixed and motionless in its primitive situation until 10.30, P.M., when it began to be dispersed by the rays of light emitted by the moon.

"While the people with uplifted hands implored the deity to suspend the calamities which this sinister token, as they thought it, announced to them, my mind was wholly occupied by reflections on the nature of meteors. The knowledge, such as it is, which I possess on that subject impelled me to make a philosophical exhortation to the spectators to combat their vain terrors; but I was deterred by the recollection of the austral aurora which appeared at Cuzco in the year 1742, and did not wish to bring down mischief on my head. The inhabitants of Cuzco, struck with awe at so rare a phenomenon, vented their curses on the learned Marquis of Valle-Umbrosa, who formed the hazardous resolution to attack their prejudices."

Remaining a few days in Lima, visiting the Chincha Islands, famed for the guano deposits, I found the whole coast to be arid and desert, with trachytic rocks, with here and there much indurated sand.

ISLAY.—This is now a large well-built place. It has two fountains and an iron mole. It is the port for the large inland city of Arequipa. The following occurred between two Frenchmen on landing here: one exclaimed—"Dans quel horrible desert nous sommes! c'est affreux! Pas un abre, pas de verdure, rien que du sable noir et aride, Mon Dieu! Mon Dieu! The reply of his friend was —"Nous venons ici pour chercher de l'or, et non de lieux champetres."

Dr. Hamilton says, on the road through the desert from Tacna to Arequipa, between Locumba and Moquegua, numerous marine shells are seen in the sand at a distance from and above the sea. They are similar to those at present found on that coast within the tide limits, thus indicating that at no very remote epoch there has been in that locality either an elevation of the land or a subsidence of the sea.

Mr. Hill states, on the road from Arequipa to the baths of Yura there is a narrow plain between high lands where the ground is covered with salt, which appears to issue everywhere from the ground in small patches, after the falling of the dew in the evening, and is gathered and purified.

ARICA is on a plain, a ribbon of alluvium, extending into the interior. The original formation of the whole is doubtless due to torrents during the early geological history of the western slope of the Cordillera. Here grow oranges, paltas, pomegranates, fine figs and much aji. There is ague caused by the decomposition of vegetation. This is the sea-port to Tacna, distant forty-one miles, and there is now a railway over the desert between the two places.

Señor Carrasco, in a representation he made to the government in 1853 about Arica, says: it has suffered from barbarous invasions, overflowing of rivers, terrible earthquakes, and hurricanes from the south; and that, from good data, it can be shown that forty years since the margin of the sea was 150 yards further inland; and that, in consequence of this retirement of the sea by upheaval of the land, it has been found necessary to lengthen the mole.

The water of Arica is so saline and earthy, that, before it can be used on the boilers of the locomotives, it has to be distilled, as also the water of Tacna for this purpose. The water used for the locomotives on the Copiapo Railway, is distilled from the sea, that of the wells being earthy as well as saline.

Mayen describes the vegetation of the Peru-Bolivian Andes thus— On ascending from Arica, you have to traverse many miles, a steppe of gravel and sand, a desert without plants or animals. At Tacna some trees and bushes make their appearance: beyond this, olives, pomegranates and figs occasionally are seen. You next come to the region of the cactus, 5000 to 7500 feet. Higher up the vegetation is extremely beautiful; but at the pass of Guallilas (14,750) all vegetation has again ceased, and the whole broad mountain crest is a desolate waste till you descend to the table-land of the Lake Titicaca. Few trees are met with in this table-land, which consists chiefly of extensive pastures and fields of grain. The road from Chuiquito to Puno is like a flower garden. Maize at 12,900, viscachas 15,000, flamingos 13,000, condor's nest 15,000—its flight to 23,000. Snow limit of west chain 18,500, east ditto 15,900.

PROVINCE OF TARAPACA.

IQUIQUE is the principal port in the province of Tarapacá, for the export of nitrate of soda. In 1825, when I first went to Peru, it was the landing place for the silver mines of Huantajaya and Santa Rosa. The mines having been badly worked, and as labour was most expensive, they were almost abandoned. The existence of nitrate of soda in this region, attracted attention; its extraction and refining was found to require but little capital and to be more profitable than mining, and Iquique, from a mere collection of fishermen's huts, now has a poulation of about 5,000 people.

I was rather astonished, when in Valparaiso, to hear German female street-singers; but more so, in Iquique, to hear an Italian boy playing on the organ. Iquique now has its newspaper, the "Mercurio de Tarapacá."

This now considerable town, with well-built habitations and warehouses, an amalgamating establishment for silver ores from one mine in Huantajaya, as also for the Desmontes or refuse of the mines, is in a complete desert, and water for drinking is distilled from the sea. In former times water was brought in boats from Pisagua. Two wells have been sunk towards the mountains in Iquique; but only a little, very saline and sour water obtained. No artesian boring has been effected, and, from the geological character of the rocks, granites and porphyries, and the very little quantity of water of percolation there may be, and this probably saline, offers but little inducement, although an artesian well, producing good water, would give £10,000 a year. Provisions and coal are principally supplied from Chile; however, much English coal is used at the refineries. The luxury of ice comes from the United States.

My old friend, Mr. George Smith, was one of the first nitrate refiners, and mainly to his perseverance and untiring exertions, the exports of nitrate, which were only 18,700 cwt. in 1830, in 1858 amounted to 61,000 tons. Mr. Smith may be called the discoverer of the new boracic acid mineral found in the Pampa de Tamarugal; and I may claim some part in instigating and making extensive examinations of the Borate district, and giving it more publicity in Europe. Up to the present time (1860) the Peruvian Government does not allow its extraction, probably with a view at some future period of making it a State monopoly, like the guano.

HUMBOLDT'S CURRENT, in September, 1854, off the port of Iquique. —During a calm of 12 hours, the "Guise" was drifted 15 miles to N.W.: thus, when sailing vessels get to leeward of a port in these latitudes, they may be several days fetching in to their destination.

On my voyage to Europe in a sailing vessel, on a W.S.W. course, on the third day from Arica, we got out of the cool water of this current, into warmer.

The 21st of April, 1854, at Iquique, the temperature was, 8 A.M., 66° F. Bar.: $30\frac{1}{8}$; noon 67° $30\frac{1}{16}$ $\frac{4}{5}$, 9 p.m., $30\frac{1}{16}$ $\frac{4}{5}$, with same regularity through the month: indeed, throughout the year, the barometer has but little change.

About this period much dew falls at night; even a few drops of light rain with winds from the North. The gigantic cactus now thrives on the Lomas or mountain heights: a few bulbous plants and flowers appear in May, and this is the "Tiempo de Flores," for the inhabitants of these desert shores, who ascend the mountains to pic-nic, gather flowers, and an oxalis, which makes a good salad.

As the nitrate shipped at Iquique is brought from the refineries by mules and asses, the number of dead, dying and skeletons, in and around the town, is something considerable. The dying animals, covered with sores, are persecuted by flies and mosquitos; and, when dead, their flesh is soon consumed by condors, eagles and gallinazos.

When I first knew Iquique, in 1826, there was seldom more than a hundred people there; it was very healthy all the year round; but at Pica and Tarapacá in the interior, and where there was water, and consequently decomposing vegetation, terciana or intermittent fever of a bad sort, was generated. In those times, all foreigners were looked upon as doctors, and when one was in possession of a medicine-chest, such was a sufficient diploma. I had a medicine-chest and was sent for to Pica; my patient was soon relieved, but I took a terciana, which was followed by a bad dysentery. I had to go to Arica in search of a medical man, there was none there; however, after a time, H.B.M. ship, "Volage," visited the port, I was taken out to sea for a cruize, and with the help of calomel and opium, I soon recovered under the kind superintendence of Dr. Hammet. The native treatment for terciana is as follows: first a dose of sulphate of soda, then a spoonful of powdered Peruvian bark, in a glass of wine; then a glass of lemonade, generally repeated twice or thrice; this averts the fever or cuts it.

For some years past, about the month of June, Iquique—where there is no vegetation—is terribly scourged with what is called peste, and very much like yellow fever. It has been thought that this fever was brought from Panamá by the steamers; but I think this peste is engendered at Iquique. There is now an increased population. The soil is sandy, but there is no drainage whatever; to this must be added the ordure of thousands of animals that bring the nitrate down from the refineries; then a hot sun, pouring on the soil-impregnated ground, the greater portion of the year, is I think, sufficient to cause peste at Iquique, and which at times is fatal; 100 died of it in 1854. When coming from the interior and entering Iquique about sun-rise, the stench at times is most fetid, and known as the "barber." The Callao "barber," is described as a nauseous smell in May and June, and ascribed to vast numbers of small dead fish washed in by the swell and deposited in the sand.

MOLLE is six miles S.E. of Iquique. I had occasion to visit this spot many times in company with Mr. George Smith, who had been induced to put up two parallel iron-wire ropes from the summit of the mountain 1800 feet high, to the shore, so as to send down, in a running suspended car, nitrate of soda, and by its weight in the descent to cause a similar car to ascend, laden with coal and provisions. The principle of this may be correct, but the very great length of wire required, viz., 3735 feet of $3\frac{1}{2}$-inch circumference, of 10lbs. per fathom, breaking strain said to be 20 tons—working, 60 cwt.,—so strained and weakened the more central portion of the wire rope, that on trial they broke. They were spliced several times, but the same breaking occurred; when the costly idea of a "Flying Railway" was abandoned.

At this spot there is no water, yet there were flies, mosquitos, vinchucas lizards, rats, mice, scorpions, centipedes and large fleas. Here formerly were amalgamated some of the silver ores of Huantajaya with sea water. The sargasso, a gigantic sea-weed of interminable length, is in great abundance; at certain times of the year is seen floating about a beautiful polypus, large and round, called "Agua Viva," or live water. It is asserted, that should it come into contact with the body when bathing, by a sucking action causes inflammation.

There is a tradition that this spot is called after a molle tree that once grew here—if so, water comparatively fresh must have found its way to the vicinity of the tree, most probably originating in the garuas, or a very slight rain, more frequent formerly than at present. An adit was driven a few yards at the foot of the mountain, when, it is said, traces of water (probably of percolation) made its appearance, but too salt to drink. A well 30 yards deep was sunk by M. Digoy, at the foot of the mountains of Guantaca (Iquique): water, rather warm was obtained, but it was very brackish; some said it might be drank. The ground went through was sand, rounded stones, a sort of clay with rounded stones, to the rock. Another well, sunk hereabouts, by Mr. Smith, at 40 feet, came to a little salt, bitter, and sour water.

I will now allude to the fact that at Huantajaya, 10 miles N.E. and about 2,300 feet above the sea, there is a silver mine known as the Quebrada, and at 648 feet depth, a small portion of saline water is found, s. g. 1010,16, temp. 78°, containing chlorides and sulphates, a little alumina and iron. Similar water is met with at 700 feet in same mine. Can this water percolate towards Molle and Iquique, through hard porphyries, and cause so much surface salt? or rather, is it the saline vapours from the ocean, which have been wafted to the mountains of the coast for ages, and coated them with salt, and there being no rain to wash the salt back into the sea, accumulates and remains on the land.

Two leagues S.E. from Santa Rosa, is the Pozo de los Ingleses, a well sunk in 1826, by an English Mining Company, they got to damp ground, but did not proceed further, as the company broke up.

Accurate levellings through the coast range and deep hollows would be interesting in connection with this subject of percolation. The pampa of Tamarugal is, say 3,500 feet above the sea; saline waters are ever coming into that plain from the Cordillera, run and percolate into the hollows on the east border of the coast mountains, and some saline matters may be blown by the wind on to the sides of the said mountains, and account in some measure for the surface salt there.

At Molle, sea-cliffs are seen, containing thick layers of recent shells and saline matters from the sea: these mix and decompose each other, forming sulphate and muriate of lime.

The mountain of Molle is very steep, much of it covered with very large quantities of disintegrated porphyritic rock, caused by solar action and dews: this at times gives way in the upper part and runs down to the base, there forming something like the Paniso of Hantajaya.[1]

In August, 1853, half a league north of Mejillones, 19° 50' S., there was a great fall of disintegrated rock from the upper part of the mountain into the sea, which lasted nine days; the noise was heard at Mejillones, and volumes of dust seen in the air.

The rock of the coast is porphyry, with indications of copper: indeed a copper mine has been opened near Iquique. Old sea-beaches are seen with recent shells, 50 feet or more above the sea. Broken shells are met with further up to the foot of the mountains. I suppose this would be called the uplifting of the coast, rather than the retiring of the sea.

Mr. Smith wrote me in 1850, that the coast certainly appeared to have risen since he had lived there, since 1822, but that it was very gradual.

---

[1] See observations by Mocsta on the expansion and contraction by solar heat of the hill of Santa Lucia, on which stands the observatory of Santiago do Chile, translated by me for the Astronomical Society, 1854. Also change of level by action of water on the rock, on which is the Armagh observatory.—Timb's Curiosities of Science, 1857.

SALT.—Sea water at Molle, s. g. 1,026,3, 71° F.—From the shore at Molle and its vicinity, to 100 feet or even more, may be seen patches of salt mixed with sand, from a few inches to a foot thick. This salt I do not think is formed by water of percolation, neither has it flown over in a liquid form from above ; it is a recent superficial deposit, not from sea-spray, but in all probability risen in vapour from the Pacific and deposited as saline dew on the land. Continuing my researches I found this sort of salt all the way up the mountain of Molle, and also on higher ones. At the spot where the upper works of the Flying Railway were fixed, it was requisite to cut away the rock, when solid salt was found filling crevices. It was heavy, transparent, and soluble in water; this salt must have been deposited at higher elevations and then by dews brought downwards.

The rock of the country about here is porphyry; there are no salt-bearing rocks, and I do not see how salt could have got here by percolation from the interior—the sea has not left it—and I see no other way to account for these surface accumulations, from much above sea-level on the slopes of mountains; on the plains and hollows in the mountains[1] of the coast (until we descend, say to Cocina and the Noria, 3277 feet and some 30 miles from the sea) than that the great Pacific ocean by a burning sun in a cloudless sky becomes a cauldron, gives off saline vapours, some being wafted landwards and leaving salt on the surface of the country.

There are land-winds, but these are generally bone-dry, otherwise there would be rain and the saline matters washed back into the ocean; had there been rain the salt would have acted as a fertilizer and we should have had the beauty of vegetation; but, under existing circumstances, terrible deserts only meet the eye; but man is satisfied with the existence of rich metallic and other valuable substances.

I subsequently put up pieces of cloth at various elevations, particularly at Molle, at 1800 feet, having first washed them in distilled water; in a few days, they had become slightly coated with salt. I also did the same on the road from Iquique to the Noria, and at the Noria, when—after a few day's exposure to the atmosphere, they gave abundant traces of chlorides, thus showing the existence of saline matters in the air.

Ulloa says, "the houses of Carthagena have balconies of wood, as more durable than iron,—the latter being so corroded and destroyed by the moisture and acrimonious quality of the nitrous air." It is not the nitrous air exactly, but rather the larger quantity of saline matter taken up in vapour from the sea of that hot region.

In the winter season, from October to March, N.W. winds prevail, the air is cooled; at times, thick damp saline clouds roll off the Pacific upon the land, sometimes depositing a very light rain or garua. When

---

[1] The Paniso of Huantajaya, is a great collection of disintegrated rock, in which the nodules (papas) of silver are found, resulting from veins; at a little distance from the surface there is no trace of salt. I mention this to show the superficial character of the salt here.

travelling through this garua my poncho has become salt to the taste; and on testing the dews at Iquique I have found them saline. As such a system of things has been going on for ages, this may in some measure account for the surface salt in the positions I have mentioned.

This garua envelopes the mountains of the coast for 18 to 20 hours at a time. I have been lost more than once in a dense garua. Once in the month of September, 1827, I was lost all night, it was very cold and raw; this sort of weather continued some weeks, when the people at the mines of Huantajaya and Santa Rosa had most violent colds, and some died after a few hours illness; dysenteries and cholics were common.

There is the probability that some of the patches of salt on the lower part of the mountain of Molle, may be formed by the sand of the sea having been blown up there; this sand would be covered with salt, and accumulating would soon give indications, and ultimate layers and nodules of salt would be seen.

If we now go to the Noria and Pampa de Tamarugal, 3500 feet, and ascend into the Andes to 15,000, we find thick surface salt, this may result from some ancient and peculiar saliferous formation, but my impression is, that it is volcanic and comparatively recent, for nearly all the mountain peaks are volcanic. What I call, in the survey of the Province, the great Andean salt-plain, Mr. Cable informs me is known also as the Laguna de Sal, and it stretches from Conchas Blancas (white shells) to Oruro, being 150 miles long by 90 wide; the salt is thick in places; the rock of the country is principally of micaceous shists, and fossil shells are found at 12,000 feet. Indeed, there is the Andean province of Salinas in this region, so named from the very large quantities of salt found there.

CEREMEÑO.—The salt deposits at this spot I have referred to in first Series.

PATILLOS, 20 miles south of Ceremeño. Mr. Williamson informs me that half-a-league south are several salt deposits, thirty to forty feet above the sea, and from whence cargoes have been taken; that a quebrada in the cuesta of Patillos leads up to the Salar Grande, (one league distant), which is a large collection of salt, and it is believed there is nitrate there also. This Salar is sixteen leagues long, north and south, and in parts two wide. My informant thinks that the salt found at Patillos has its origin from the Salar Grande by means of subterraneous channels.

I may state, that a long way east of Ceremeño is the Salar del Carmen, but I do not think that the salt found at Ceremeño, has other origin than the present ocean.

To the west of the Salar Grande, Mr. Smith has explored the Hundimientos or natural wells; they are from four to eight yards deep. In some places the water is found a foot from the surface, two yards deep, and good. These wells are narrow at surface, widening below.

Morro Grande de Tarapaca is 5780 feet above the sea. I made the ascent, which was most fatiguing; the summit is a scene of the most desert character.

The Garuas in the winter months produce spare pastures on the slopes of such mountain masses. A little water is occasionally found in rocky hollows at the top. At this season of the desert pastures, an Indian may be seen tending his asses and mules, who regale on fresh provend. Then a few Huanacos may be observed feeding; a fox occasionally prowling about and a few slate-coloured and greenish birds. There are several species of plants, (including some blue and white bulbous ones,) the principal being an oxalis. I sent a collection from here to the Linnean Society. A few cardones, or gigantic cactus, thirty to forty feet high and fifteen in girth, are also met with. I found three specimens of Bulimi, which I gave to Mr. Cuming.

Ansuelo Rocks at Iquique & Pampa—The rocks are hornblend and sienitic granites, the latter containing sulphuret of iron. Here the sea spray is rapidly exfoliating the granite. This rock rises hereabouts to two thousand feet or more, and is seen in the upper part in junction with porphyry. During the winter months a slight vegetation appears, including much oxalis. It is stated that the oxalic acid in the oxalis is in combination with potash, which it gets from the granite. I may state that the cacti grow on the granitic debris, but not on the adjoining porphyry.

The Ansuelo pampa has the appearance of rising shelly beaches (at Iquique is a rocky eminence called the morro, on which stood the ruins of a fort until 1854,—it is reported that formerly the sea flowed round it; the lower part is now many feet above the sea—I think I could make out an increase in the elevation of this part of the coast since 1825), and behind them the ground is depressed, where sea water, by filtration, comes in, which, mixing with dead shells, decomposition takes place, when large quantities of a well crystallised salt is formed, mainly of sulphate of lime.

Iquique Island.—Was once thickly covered with guano. It is the burial place for foreigners. It is two miles round; its highest part fifty feet. It appears originally to have been merely a collection of rocks (porphyry), the channels are now filled with shells. The island is covered with sea-rounded stones. Does this not show that elevation has been going on? There is one shelly locality twenty to twenty-five feet above the sea at the west end. Of sea birds there are many pelicans, gulls, divers, and an occasional penguin.

Seals are met with about the rocks: from their skins the useful balsa is made. The number of sea birds are diminishing since they have been disturbed by civilization; and they do not lay their eggs in such quantities on these shores as formerly.

Mines of Huantajaya.—I had the pleasure of taking Professors Raimundi and Mariani to the mines. These gentlemen had just returned from an official exploration of the borax deposits, for the Peruvian government. Only one mine was working, the Lecaros, belonging to Don M. B. de la Fuente, yielding ores of native, chloride, and sulphuret. Near the surface a silver ore called lechendor is often met with; this, according to Domeyko is a chloro-bromide. The ores of Lecaros were giving three to four marcs the aroba, equal to twenty-four to twenty-five ounces the twenty-five pounds of ore. Only thirty miners were at work, and these Chinese. The shell, Conchalepas Peruanis, is the lamp used by the miners.

The works in the mines of Huantajaya afford a good opportunity of examining the interior of the earth. On the summit of the mountain there is surface salt. At the Chiflones is seen a thick superficial layer called manto, composed of a fossil shelly deposit of broken valves of Gryphæ, principally G. Darwinii. The Chiflones are about 2,500 feet above the sea. Raimundi made out that the layer of manto was three to four yards thick, composed of terebratula, mactra, &c., difficult to separate; also a new gryphæ. About here, also, are silicious rocks, and the appearance of great disturbance, also many cross courses.

If we now go to the base of the mountain we have, first, Caliche or surface salt, with earthy matter; second, Paniso, a thick debris of angular pieces of rock, none of them water-worn, neither are there indications of saline matters. This Paniso, I conceive, results from the breaking up, by long continued solar action, assisted by dews, of the argillaceous limestone principally, and where fossil shells of this formation are found; third, argillaceous limestone; fourth, porphyries. I could not trace any saline matters in these rocks; but at 648 and 700 feet in the Quebrada mine (1,600 feet above the sea) saline water is met with. I may state that twenty miles to the east, is the saline hollow of Cocina, 3,000 feet above the sea, with water near the surface. Thus, then, we have, at Cocina and its meridian, saline waters which may have percolated to and are found in this mine. There are periods when rain is somewhat abundant in the Andes; then these waters of percolation would rise higher than 1600 feet above the level of the sea. I have already given some particulars as to the extraordinary richness of the ores of Huantajaya. The most recent information is in a paper by Don. M. B. de la Fuente, translated by me in the 26th Vol. of Geographical Soc. Trans.; wherein it is stated that the mines of Huantajaya, Santa Rosa, and some few others, produce in a century £30,000,000. In the museum, at Madrid, exists a mass of native silver from the mines of Huantajaya, presented by Don F. de la Fuente, weighing two hundred and sixty five-pounds.

The projectors of a company to work the Desmontes, or refuse of Huantajaya, say, and truly, that there are millions of tons of valuable Desmonte, or refuse ore, inside and outside the mines.

Average of fifty samples gave them $39\frac{1}{2}$ ounces of silver per ton. From picked heaps, $71\frac{1}{2}$ ounces.

Mr. Smith and myself have always thought the average would be about eighty ounces the cajon of 6400 pounds, which is below the above estimate.

It is probable that with economical amalgamating machines, say at Iquique, or in England, the reduction of the Desmontes would be remunerative.

Mr. Williamson, of Iquique, observes that there exists in the mines of Huantajaya and Copiapo an exact analogy; there is found the same stratification of "Caja Piedra" which divides the "Criaderos." In Huantajaya, only the upper portions of the veins have been worked. Mr. Williamson recommends to do as they did in Copiapo, to pierce the "Caja Piedra" by shafts and adits. I may observe that this Caja Piedra was pierced in the Piqueños and some other mines, and native silver was found in masses or pockets, but this system was not fully carried out. Mr. Williamson adds that one mine, La Vieja, has employed five hundred people; two-thirds of these were Apires, who took an hour to bring up three to four arobas of ore or rubbish (Desmonte).

With regard to the interior heat of the earth, 1° F. is given for every fifteen yards of depth. In 1826, whilst superintending mining operations at Huantajaya in descending dry mines of a hundred and fifty to two hundred yards in depth, and in which work had not been carried on for years, I was repeatedly struck with the effect of the elevation of temperature as I descended, the rock of the mine feeling comparatively warm, and now attribute it to the internal heat of the earth.

The following is told of a young girl of Huantajaya (where there is no water) who, on going to Tarapacá, where there is a stream, on seeing it, exclaimed "O what heretics these Tarapaqueños must be, to let so much blessed water run to waste—pray save it, save it!

A cura, who had come from Arequipa to Huantajaya, on seeing a troop of asses laden with Odries or skins filled, enquired what they contained; "water" was the reply, "water in bags; no, that I cannot believe." However, on examination, he found such to be the case. The Cura soon returned to Arequipa.

I proceeded with Professors Raimundi and Mariani to the abandoned mines of Santa Rosa. Our track was over Caliche (here of salt, with calcarious and siliceous matters) patches of salt, much of it nodular, being nearly a pure chloride of sodium, containing no sulphates, and only with a trace of lime, this sort reaching high up the mountain of Santa Rosa. We looked intently at this salt formation, and were puzzled to account how it got there, viz., on the slope of a mountain and in such quantities. By percolation, here seemed improbable; I ventured to suggest that it might be deposited by saline dews from the ocean. It is superficial, in lumps, ridges, patches, and in some of the hollows, as if a foaming sea had been suddenly stopped. Then follow sand, disintegrated rock, argillaceous limestones and porphyries.

Has saline waters from the interior ever got into these hollows? If so, perhaps saline dust may have been blown up the sides of the mountains, and the damp air and dews fixed the salt there.

We returned by the mines of El Carmen and the Cañada; how I wished that I had been accompanying a Murchison or a Lyell: they would have examined and explained the effects produced by upheavals, depressions, disintegrations, and other disturbances in this earthquake region. They, I think, would have been struck at the rapidity with which the hardest rock disintegrate, and the amazing collection of loose pieces of rock and dust continually falling from the upper parts of mountains, forming panisos at their bases.

Rarely, for the last was in 1819, heavy rains fell in the Andes; and even in the Pampa of Tamarugal, and as there is so much saline matter at 15,000 feet, saline streams came down, shallow lakes were formed, and streams poured into the ravines west of the Pampa. The quebrada, of Pasos, near the Noria, was inundated, trees grew, some remaining to this day.

Well, we find the saline matters on the mountains of the coast to be nearly pure chloride of sodium; but, to the east, in the region of saline waters, we find salt, nitrate and sulphate of soda, salts of lime, borate of soda and lime, and salts of iodine, chrome and traces of bromine.

In 1852, some water came into the Pampa from the Andes: since then I have no account of such an occurrence.

From Iquique to La Noria—January.—Iquique may be said to be built on a plain of elevation, composed of dead shells, conchuelo (not fossil), in places ten feet thick. They are burnt, with sea weed, into lime for building purposes. Near to the sea, the shells are perfect, of Trochusater, Mytilus Orbignyanus, Venus Per, Mesodesma, Concholepas, &c. Inland, thirty to forty feet above the ocean, and where they must have lain for ages, with a little sea salt, they are finely divided and chemically changed. Sometimes whales' bones are found in this Conchuelo. If this shelly deposit is raked about on a dark night, phosphorescence is observed. A long ascending track is journeyed over, with high porphyritic mountains on the left, and the Medano de la Ballena, a huge sand mountain, on the left. A friend of mine once went up on the east side: and, descending on the other, was nearly buried in loose sand; his horse was imbedded for a while: it appears to be on the increase. A very steep rocky zigzag cuesta is ascended 1761 feet. The track is now over plain and undulating ground to the top of the Cañada or ravine, 2475 feet, then a descent, ascent, long descent to a spot called La Fonda Inglesa, 2830 feet—a collection of rocks, which is made a half-way house of, and the saddle bags searched for refreshment. After which, there is a long ascent; here I once found the fragment of an ammonite. The rocks about here are porphyritic and argillaceous limestones, in a rapid state of degredation. On descending, you come to the Salar, salt and nitrate of soda basin of Cocina 3000 feet above the sea. Here we see the bottom of a hollow thickly covered with clinker-looking salt, water being found in the wells at four feet (s. g. 1005) with scarcely a trace of nitrate. On the sides and elevations in the hollow is found the caliche, or native nitrate of soda. Passing the nitrate works of Yungay, 3230 feet, we arrive at the principal nitrate quarries of

La Nueva Noria, 3,227 feet above the sea. Water boils at 206° F.

Here are two towns built of salt, from the Salares, one called the Noria, the other the Salar.

Numberless quarries of nitrate are observed at the rising bases of hills and undulating ground from 50 to 150 feet above the Salares, and evidently of an older date than the salt in the Salares. There is no nitrate in the Salares. The chimneys of the boilers are seen smoking; the Norias,[1] for extracting water from the wells. The scene is of absolute sterility, with heaps of skeletons of mules and asses around the various Oficinas, or nitrate refineries. The water here has to be distilled for drinking, but the animals drink from the wells. When nitrate has been accidently or purposely put into the drinking troughs, the animals are poisoned, swell up and die. S. G. of the water 1004,9, temp. 78°, containing no nitrate. There is a well known as that of Isidoro Marquez, (s. g. 1005,88, temp. 75°): nitrate is found in it.

La Noria is pestered with a green fly, and the bed bug swarms. As if to welcome my arrival, there was met with a large nodule of borate, weighing fifty pounds, and where I saw, for the first time, this interesting mineral in situ; this specimen is now in the Museum of Practical Geology, in London.

In the superficial saline crust here, are angular fragments of granite, porphyry, siliceous and argillaceous rocks, and underneath they are in situ.

Mr. Blake has stated the existence of fragments of marine shells to have been found in the nitrate beds. I looked most carefully for such but found none.

Darwin, in speaking of the Pampa de Tamarugal, a few miles east of the Noria, supposes that it was formerly an inland sea, and from the sea got its salt. I suppose that the saline matters have been washed down from the Andes; and, as to the iodic salts, we need not look to the sea for them, as iodine and bromine exists in the minerals of these regions.

TEMPERATURE, January 21st:

5 a.m.	Cool land breeze, Terrel	64° F.
1 p.m.	Strong breeze from S.W., clear sky	83° ,,
,, ,,	In the sun	92° ,,
,, ,,	On a heap of sand	128° ,,
10 p.m.	Calm and clear sky	53° ,,
	Water in a well eight yards deep	72° ,,

In the month of October the greatest variation of the aneroid was from 26.44 to 26.53. On the 17th October, 1854, aneroid and thermometer stood as follows:—9 a.m., 76° F. 26.48. Noon, 78° 26:48; 6 p.m. 57° 26.46. On the 23rd November, at same hours, 64° 26.34 74° 26.36; 74° 26.36.

In summer, when iron work is exposed to the sun, it becomes too hot to be handled, and dark rocks are at about same temperature. This great and bright solar heat causes rocks to expand considerably during

---

[1] From the Arabic word Naora, a well, and the rude machinery of a moveable cross piece of wood, at one end a bucket, the other a weight.

the day, and, in cooling at night, to crack and their surfaces break away. Aqueous vapours from the sea and the Andes, wintry mists, and slight rain, the air in peculiar states, as when with much ozone, (this last in particular) may play an important part in the formation of nitrates from chlorides.

CLIMATE AT THE NORIA.—In winter, during the morning, light easterly winds. Noon, sea-breeze south-east to south-west, blows strong occasionally from north-west, with much mist. In summer, but little north wind; principally from the south with clear weather, and extreme barometric regularity. In the month of June, ice has been seen one-eighth of an inch thick. March 29, 1854, during the night rained a little, the dusty ground was covered with spots; 6 a.m. misty, wind south-east veering to south, blowing all day from south-west. As the sun went down, light airs from west, then a calm. During the night the Terral, or land breeze, from east to south-east.

FORMATION OF CALICHE OR NITRATE OF SODA, AND ITS MANUFACTURE INTO REFINED.—Section of Nitrate ground at La Noria, descending, I. Costra, or crust, composed of earthy matters, angular pieces of rock, salt, and other saline matters, about two feet thick.

II. Caliche, granular layers of Nitrate of Soda, containing salt, other saline and earthy substances, and angular pieces of stone, to five feet thick, often accompanied with much Glauberite, (Sulphate of Soda) some Pickeringite (magnesian alum) mixed with earthy matters, as silica, alumina, carbonate and sulphate of lime; also, Iodine, Bromine, Chrome and Boracic acid mineral. III. Coba is the general loose earthy covering to the Silico-calcareous and porphyritic rocks, and here at the Noria the Borate is found in nodules, from the size of a pea, to two feet in diameter. In some parts of the Coba the borate is seen in thin striæ with sulphate of lime.

In this region, it appears to me, that salt and other saline matters, including boracic salts, have been formed in the Andes, and brought down by streams and percolation. (The almost pure chloride of sodium on the mountains of the coast, I have supposed to be mainly indebted to the salt-vapours of the ocean) There is scarcely a trace of organic matter in the soil, to afford nitrogen to change the salt into nitrate. Ought we not rather look to the atmosphere for nitrogen, and the various chemical changes resulting from solar heat, dews, and occasional slight rains.

The salt of the Salares is a mixture of various saline substances; and, as there is abundance of calcareous minerals, the nitrogen of the air may give rise to nitrate of lime, then the change will be as follows:

```
              Nitrate of Soda.
       ┌─────────────────────────────────┐
       │ Nit. Acid.  ─────   Sodium      │
       │                     Oxygen.     │
       │                                 │
Nitrate of Lima.                          Chloride of
       │                                  Sodium.
       │                                 │
       │                                  Water.
       │                                 │
       │                     Chlorine.   │
       │ Lime.       ─────   Hydrogen.   │
       └─────────────────────────────────┘
       Chloride of Calcium, or Muriate of Lime.
```

The Saliteros say that one may almost see the salt of the Salares transformed into nitrate. A Salitero observed to me that he could not tell where the salt came from, but he believed the nitrate was formed by light rains trickling through saline and earthy matters, turning the salt into nitrate. Some caliches when quarried are called green, and on exposure to the air ripens, yielding the nitrate more easily. Sometimes the salt and caliche has a yellow, pink or green colour, caused, I think, from chrome, iodine and bromine.

MANUFACTURE OF NITRATE FROM CALICHE.—The nitrate grounds are known to be on the edges of the salares and rising ground: at the Noria water is within a foot of the salar. There are some nitrate grounds without any apparent salar, and where water is now thirty to forty yards deep, and even deeper; but salt has been there to form the nitrate.

Having Cateado, hunted for, and found the nitrate ground, habitations are built of salt from the salar, wells are dug, the water being extracted by Norias; paradas or iron boilers in pairs are fixed; depositos or settling tubs; bateas of iron or wood as crystallizers; tubs for mother liquor; provisions for the people and food for animals. The salitero or refiner can now commence operations, having, however, previously obtained legally his estacas of 200 square yards. Some manage to become possessors of very large tracks of nitrate grounds.

The Salitero now directs his barretero or quarryman to make openings with a heavy iron bar, increasing in width at bottom, through the costra and caliche to the coba; this is the tasa or cup into which is put from one to fifteen hundred weight of very rough powder (made from nitrate of soda, and sulphur from the volcano of Isluga), the upper part being well rammed with loose earth; these are called Bombones, and are exploded, which loosens the earth and turns it up. The irregular masses of caliche are broken into large lumps, collected out of the loose mass and conveyed in panniers by asses to the oficina or refinery; here the large pieces are broken into smaller by the Asendrador and thrown into the boiler, to which, when nearly full, water is added, and the boiling commences, more caliche being added at intervals. In about seven or eight hours the saturated boiling point of the liquid has attained a temperature of 240° F., when the mother-waters are added. The boiler-man now removes with a shovel the borra or salt that has been precipitated, and earthy matters separated and subsided to the bottom of the boiler. The solution is bucketed out into the deposito, where a further quantity of earthy matter, the Ripia, goes down, leaving a clear solution, which is then run into coolers, where crystallization takes place, producing salitre or refined nitrate of soda, which is shovelled out of the bateas, and the sun's heat soon dries it. It is now bagged and sent to the coast for shipment. The best refined nitrate was found to be composed of water, 0.11; salt, 1.84; sulphate of soda, 0.35; nitrate of soda, 97.70=100,00. This nitrate trade employs nearly all the people in the province, about 12,000, exclusive of foreigners and Chinese labourers. The exports are now 61,000 tons annually, and could be increased to any extent, as the nitrate grounds are inexhaustible.

Messrs. George Smith and Co. have been using large boilers, and of more scientific construction, with advantage, they also have commenced boiling by steam. The fuel used is the tamarugo and algarobo trees, these are getting very scarce, thus much English and Chile coal is also resorted to.

This nitrate of soda has been known about a century. It was discovered by a woodcutter, named Negreros, in the Pampa de Tamarugal, by his having made a fire at the spot that still preserves his name, the ground began to melt and run like a stream, the melted substance was examined and found to be nitrate of soda.

About 1794, the German mineralogist, Haenke, was sent to the province to teach the method of its extraction and turn it into nitrate of potash for gunpowder, which it is said he did, by adding to it a solution or ley prepared from burnt cactus, which contains 8 per cent. of potash. Caliche was subsequently sent to Concepcion, in Chile, to be turned into nitre, but with little success. In my first series I have given some particulars as to the history of nitrate and its varieties, also that it contained chrome and iodine. Of chrome it is in very small quantities, but as to the iodine, Ulex, of Hamburg, got six-tenths per cent. out of a mixture of caliches. Hayes, of New York, the same. Ulex obtained one-half to one per cent. from the mother-waters. I suspect that in some varieties the per centage of iodine is greater than given by Ulex. Sea-water only contains one-millionth part of iodine; that found in the nitrate has its origin, I conceive, from mineral iodides and iodates. When the caliche has a yellow or orange colour, it is called azufrado and canario. The mother-waters at Negreros are sometimes blood red. I once supposed that this colour was owing to iodine, I now think it is from Chrome. Bromine has been found in the caliches.

About 1853, several vessels were sent to the west coast of Africa, in the hope of being able to ship nitrate of soda, but the saline matter met with there proved to be salt. The vicinity of the Dead Sea has been examined for nitrates, but none as yet found.

Nitrate of soda is well known as a fertilizer, and is used extensively in the arts. It has been converted into nitrate of potash for the gunpowder makers, but its employment has not been patronised in consequence, it is said, of its deliquescence. I am informed that pure nitrate of soda is not deliquescent—is it that such property is owing to chloride of calcium, the imported nitrate always contains ?

TEST FOR NITRATE OF SODA.—The cateador or caliche-hunter easily distinguishes nitrate by the taste, which is bitter and cooling; salt is merely saline. A delicate test is the following, which will show if there be only 2 per cent. :—Add sulphuric acid to a portion in a tube, when, if nitrate be present, red fumes will appear. Salts of soda are distinguished from salts of potash, the soda giving no precipitate with muriate of platina. Hofstetter is said to have found 0.43 nitrate of potash in a sample of refined nitrate from Tarapacá.

NITRATE OF POTASH. ECUADOR OR QUITO.—In the province of Imbaburá, at Ibarra, thirty leagues from the port of Pailon, I examined from this locality saline matters extracted from surface soil containing much nitrate of potash. I am not prepared to say if this nitrate of potash exists in great quantities; and, until a road is made from Ibarra to the Pailon, it could not be exported.

Salts of potash, it would seem are rare in South America; and the principal reason why nitrate of potash is not found in any quantity, as in India, is the scarcity, I suppose, of potash-yielding rocks.

It is a practical remark, that the production of nitrate of potash is greatest during the prevalence of hot winds. There are continual scorching winds blowing over the great nitrate of soda region in Peru.; and, without entering into the question of nitrification, I may observe, that salts of lime are generally present in the surface formations of nitrate of potash in India, and in the nitrate of soda of Peru.

Near Lima, a small portion of nitrate of potash is procured, by washing the earth from ancient Indian graves.

NEW BORACIC ACID MINERAL.—I have already said, that Mr. George Smith may be called the discoverer of this valuable substance. I give further on a resumé of Professor Raimundi's report, with his analysis of several varieties. I will now give some details of my own examination of the Pampa de Tamarugal, where it principally exists, and in large quantities. At page 159 of this work, I make general reference to the borate.

VISIT TO THE BORATE TOWNS.—Mr. Girdwood, formerly a pupil of Dr. Percy, and chemist to Mr. Smith's establishment, accompanied me on this trip, and to whom I am indebted for valuable suggestions and assistance.

Leaving the Noria and ascending the steep side of its hollow, our course lay east by south, over undulating country, between high mountains, some giving off very large quantities of detritus; descending a ravine, and approaching the Pampa de Tamarugal, we came upon nitrate caliches at the Rinconada, and descending a little lower, an extensive salar is entered, having on its west margin considerable tracts of nitrate caliches. A few tamarugo[1] and algarbo[2] trees are seen; but, excepting these, a salt desert and arid plain occupies the fore ground, and far away to the east are the mighty Andes.

On the eastern margin of the Salar in particular, as well as in it, and where the ground is free from salt, there the borate is first met with, in some places, from the surface to three feet below it. We progressed along an old dry watercourse (free from salt) into the Tisas or borate towns, at 3,200 feet; the sky was very clear and blue, and the sun intensely hot. We visited the two small villages, built of salt; around them excavating and collecting the borate was going on to some extent, although against the orders of government, and conveyed by unfrequented tracks to the coast, and smuggled off.

Some few persons have been allowed occasionally to ship small parcels, but up to the present time (1860), the extraction of the borate has not been permitted, although its exportation would be beneficial to the province, and the substance of great use in the Arts in Europe.

The borate ground is generally flat, and the surface free from salt, the mineral making its appearance in uneven nodules of all sizes, but generally that of a large potato (one was found at the Noria weighing fifty pounds). The nodules are sparely or plentifully imbedded in a now dry saline mud; however, in some places, this saline mud is damp and even wet, from its proximity to the water of percolation of the Pampa. This water doubtless plays an important part in the formation of the borate. Much glauberite, in large and small crystals, is found at times combined with the borate, as well as separate.[3] Sometimes the ground or strata is made up entirely of borate. This is the general position of the mineral, having water not far off below; and I cannot help thinking that surface waters in particular have brought saline matters from the Andes into the Pampa, and with boracic salts; in the Pampa they have found lime and soda, which has given rise to the present borate of lime and soda formation.

Independently of the surface water, brought down from the Andes through the numberless ravines that run into the Pampa, there is always some portion percolating into and through the Pampa, as seen in the hollows of the mountains of the coast, near the surface at Cocina, and found at 700 feet deep in the mines of Huantajaya.

---

[1] Raimundi says it is a Prosopis, or it may be a new genus.

[2] Prosopis dulcis. Seemann calls the algarobo of Panamá, Hymenaea splendida; that of Peru, Prosopis horrida; that of Chile, P. siliquastrum.

In Tarapacá the Tamarugo is sometimes called Algarobilla; its pods are round, one to two inches long. The pods of the Algarobo are eight to nine inches long, and contain saccharine matter. The Tara is of the family of Mimosa, it yields much tannin, the pods are flat.

[3] Millo or Pickeringite, (magnesian alum,) is found in the mountains of the Pintados, in veins traversing the rocks there, the veins from three to five feet thick, white and some pale yellow (probably from chrome).

In working the borate grounds, the boratero has merely to open a hole in the soft surface of the ground, and commence immediately picking out the nodules of borate and bag them, the substance being ready for transit to the coast and exportation. This requires little or no capital, whereas quarrying and refining nitrate of soda is a serious matter on the score of outlay. Up to March, 1854, some 10,000 quintals had been extracted, selling in England for about £30 per ton.

Dr. Philippi, during his investigations in the desert of Atacama, in 1853, did not observe any borate, but much salt and a little carbonate of soda; a friend of mine gave me a specimen said to have come from near Calama, in the northern part of the desert. I have examined several saline materials from that region, but salt and sulphate of lime have predominated: no nitrate of soda has yet been brought from there, although it is said by some to exist.

ABSTRACT OF PROFESSORS RAIMUNDI AND MARIANI'S REPORT TO THE PERUVIAN GOVERNMENT.—The result of our labours is, that the pure borate of lime is found in only few places, as in the Rinconada, Cabreria, Tronco, and between the oficinas of Independencia and Colombia. The borate found under the salitres is accompanied by glauberite. The white pasty substance found in many places, particularly at the Pascana del Tronco, as also in nearly all the spots covered with grama grass, is not borate, but a mixture of sulphates of lime and soda and salt..

The substance collected near the Aguada del Sur, has no value.

Borate from Cabreria and Rinconada, gave 42.20 per cent. boracic acid. From the Pascana of Pedro Castro, 21.25, is of a yellowish colour (probably from chrome); a white matter from Tronco, Challapozo, and Challapozito, borate of lime, 5 per cent.

White matter from Aguada del Sur, no borate, principally sulphate of lime; but, one league distant, good borate is met with.

At the Puquios of Quilliagua is a Polyhalite, composed of sulphates of lime, magnesia and potash, with salt. The salt found near Matilla, called San Sebastian, is Thenardite.

Under the calichales of Challa, there is much glauberite. In Zapiga, under the nitrate, borate is met with, containing borate of lime, 35.17; borate of soda, 20.21. Borate, between Independencia and Colombia, contains 43.130 boracic acid. At page 159 I give Mr. Dick's analysis of a fine specimen of borate. Mr. George Smith made borax from it in Iquique. He sent borate to the United States, where it was examined by Hayes, and obtained the name of Hayescine.

TEST FOR BORATE:—When in small quantities, macerate in alcohol, adding a little sulphuric acid; evaporate the solution, in firing it, and, if there be the merest trace of boracic acid, it will colour the flame green.

NOTES of journey from La Noria, in the months of January and February, to the mines of Yabricoya, in the Andes.

Towards the east-north-east, in the mountains of the Noria, are some small water-courses, caused by garuas, which play a part in forming nitrate from salts.

There is an old silver mine at summit of ravine of Los Pasos.

An algarobo was planted in the amalgamating works of Rivero, at La Tirana, about 1828. It is now a fine tree, 25 feet high and 1½ yards in circumference, and has its pods. I took some resin from it. (In the patio of Dr. Bokenham's house, in Tarapacá, is a very old algarobo, 60 to 70 feet high, measuring 6 feet in girth; a light pinkish juice exudes, which, on exposure, becomes black; this is a gum, bitter and wholly soluble in water; sulphate of iron discolours the solution, showing it to contain tannin.) La Tirana is pestered with the vinchuca (Conorhinus, sex turburculatus), or black bug of the Pampas. Not long since, an Indian was laid out for dead and put into a yard, during the night, the vinchucas sucked a large quantity of blood out of the body, he revived, and was living in 1854.

In 1827, I found the water of the wells at La Tirana to be s.g. 1,00165 temperature 70°; in 1854, 1000,92, temperature 76°. February 6th, the air at 6 a.m., 47°, exposed in the belfry of the church to the cold terral from the east; in the village, 52°: water in the wells, 68°: soil alluvial and in layers.

Three leagues east-south-east from La Tirana, is Digoy's farm of Challa; the track is through trees and salt calichales; the salt looks as if a foaming saturated sea had been suddenly stopped. This appearance has been produced by capillary action, as water is near the surface. The water at present is but slightly saline, but increases in saltness to the west. Juri and Santana are similar farms in this salt desert; they are known as Chacras sin riego, and the manner of bringing them into cultivation is curious. The saline matters, two feet thick, are removed and used as walls, this brings the soil down to within a foot or so of water, when maize, wheat, vegetables, &c. are grown.

MACAYA, 6270 feet—Here is much pink and white mesotype. 6 a.m., air, 50°; 7 p.m., 59°. Hot springs, 100°. Chuca, or carbonate of soda on the margin of streams. Gypsum abundant, but no salt.

Passed the silver mines of Jauja,[1] on the way to the mines of Yabricoya. 5 a.m., February 1, air, 42°; 6 a.m., 41°; noon, 55°. In the sun, 70°; 1 p.m. in the sun, 75°. These mines were first worked for silver, but at present only copper is sought for. The ores consist of oxides, arsenurets and sulphurets. The arsenuret gave copper, 20.70. The summit of the mountain of Yabricoya is 13,480 feet.

MAMIÑA, 5,980 feet; the hot springs, 130° to 131°, containing much sulphureted hydrogen, s. g. 999·95, temp. 78°. Visited copper mines of the Inca, they are about 11,000 feet above the sea.

From Mamiña are seen the silver mines of Quinquina.

JOURNEY FROM IQUIQUE TO TARAPACA, IN FEBRUARY.—At the La Peña Oficina, 3452 feet, some of the nitrate grounds are free from salt.

Tarapacá, February 26th, 6 a.m., 58°; 9 a.m., 73°; noon 77°; in

[1] The name of this mine has inadvertently been placed in the large Map (Geogr. Soc. Journal, 1851,) in the valley of Mani.

the sun, 98°; 4 p.m., 80° in a room, with strong breeze blowing from S.W.; midnight, 71°, and calm. Tarapacá is 4796 feet above the sea, and up to the top of the ravine, 3000 feet more; the latter part hopelessly barren, and where, perhaps, vegetation has never existed; the rock is porphyritic.

March 9.—Rebellion in the town. The Outs turned the Ins out; two killed, some wounded, many imprisoned; others fled. In the midst of the firing and killing at 5.27 p.m., severe shock of an earthquake, continued at intervals seven minutes. Some days afterwards, the party in power entered Iquique, when there was a repetition of killing, wounding, imprisoning and running away. The earthquake above mentioned was felt all over the province. And the fight in Tarapacá was called "La Batalla del Temblor;" that of Iquique, "Batalla de los Asesinos," when a fellow, named Legay, shot the Governor, Don Isidro Marquez, and took command of the place.

CHILE.—When I first wrote on matters connected with Peru and Chile, I intimated that when readier means of transit presented themselves, the desert coast of Peru and the northern portion of the coasts of Chile would be carefully examined, valuable mines, &c. discovered. We see what a considerable trade the nitrate of soda is, and that of borax must soon be important; old mines will be re-worked and new ones opened.

The coast of Bolivia begins to share in this march of progress, it has its copper mines. Continuing south we come to the Bay of Mejillones, to which of late the Chilenos assert their right of territory.

Here is a locality known as the Chimba, in the centre of the Peninsula, formed by Morro Mejillones and Morro Moreno, worthy of a visit by the Cateadores for gold in particular. Since I journied along this coast in 1828-9, important copper mines have been discovered and worked; at that period I was benighted and lost with a tired mule, and had to lay myself down on a sandy solitary plain till day-light; that desolate spot now boasts of the flourishing port and town of

CALDERA in 27° 20′ S. The port is secure and almost land-locked. It has a mole, to which steamers and vessels come alongside. The town is built on sandy ridges; there is no water except that produced by distillation from the ocean or brought by rail from Copiapo. The river is but a small stream (anciently called Mamoas) used for irrigation, which consumes all the water at about ten miles from the town of Copiapo; the whole stream could be contained in a channel five or six yards wide to two deep.

A railway connects Copiapo with the port of Caldera, its length is 50 miles, and an electric telegraph is forming; beyond Copiapo it extends 25 miles further to Pabellon; another railway is in course of construction to the mines of Tres Puntas, about 75 miles in length;

and Mr. Wheelwright is now projecting a railway from Copiapo across the Andes into the pampas of Buenos Ayres.

COPIAPO, the capital of the Province of Atacama, in Chile, is 1213 feet above the sea. In the town, its vicinity, and valley, there are fifteen large amalgamating establishments worked by water power, each extracting silver from five tons of ore every twenty-four hours. At Copiapo and within a distance of twelve miles above it, there are four copper smelting works, with fourteen furnaces; and in the port of Caldera there are four works, with twenty-six furnaces. These smelt with English coal principally.

There is a German establishment at Copiapo, with five furnaces for smelting silver Relaves, or the earthy matter remaining from the silver ores after amalgamation; this refuse always contains a portion of silver which has escaped amalgamation, particularly the sulphuret.

Copiapo has four churches, a hospital and theatre. The town is lighted with gas. The Protestants have a cemetery adjoining the Catholic burial-place, in the latter are some good marble monuments, executed in Europe. In the principal square is a fountain, with a statue of Juan Godoy, the discoverer of the great mineral wealth of Chañarcillo, in 1832, which produced, in ten years, twelve millions of dollars. The town is situated in a narrow valley, surrounded by arid mountains, in which abound mines of gold, silver and copper; lead, iron, bismuth, antimony, cobalt, arsenic and quicksilver are also met with. There are 235 mines of silver, 14 of copper and 6 of gold in this department.

There is a promenade near the town, planted with sauces, (willow) and where a band of Italian musicians occasionally perform.

Earthquakes are of common occurrence; the town has been destroyed several times, and the inhabitants are always prepared to witness a similar visitation. October 5th, 1859, at 8 a.m., commenced a series of violent shocks, continuing for some days; there were 116 shocks in twenty-four hours, and the sea receded twenty-three feet at Caldera.

The valley of Copiapo has rather an inconvenient neighbour, viz.: the valley of Paypote, which comes direct from the Cordillera; in its run of sixty leagues, it takes in the waters of many ravines, and, were rain at all continuous, Copiapo would be washed away; in 1832, the water of Avenidas reached the sea.

Copiapo is healthy; in summer it is very hot during the day, but cool after sun-set; in winter there is a dry bracing air, and a slight frost has been seen early in the morning.

Rain falls once or twice a-year in the winter, but for a few hours only. The want of rain prevents the growth of vegetation, and, except on lands watered by the river, not a tree, bush, or blade of grass is to be seen. The hills are bare rocks, having occasional patches of fine sand. The atmosphere is clear and the sky cloudless the greater part of the year. A planet has been seen shining brightly at 1 p.m.

The houses are mostly built of adobe; (mud and straw sun-dried) the roofs of same material.

The Intendente La Fuente, in his "Memoria," 1854, says, the Province of Atacama in Chile is composed of the departments of Copiapo and Huasco.

HUASCO has the city of same name and district of Ballinary,[1] and the town of Freirina; the former is divided into eight sub-delegations, with 15,000 inhabitants. Freirina has six sub-delegations and 10,000 inhabitants. Copiapo has seventeen sub-delegations, and 40,000 inhabitants. In 1828, there were 4000 souls in the valley of Copiapo. In 1712, only 900 souls.

Copiapo and Huasco exported from 1851 to 1853, or two years and four months, 14,120,548 dollars in silver and copper. The mine of Buena Esperanza, in Tres Puntas, produced in six months, (in 1852), 495,151 dollars.

The establishment at Piedra Colgada that had been in operation since November, 1852, to October, 1853, had operated on 8422 quintals of relaves, the lowest ley being 14 marcs; the highest, 70 marcs, the cajon.

Exports of Metal and Mineral from the Port of Caldera in 1853:

Marcs of gold	560¾ at 25 dols.	m.	70,094 09
" silver	328,197 " 9 dols. 75c.	„	3,199,920 75
Quintals of sulphuret of silver	116,961¼ " 15 dols.	qu.	1,754,427 00
Quintals of copper in bar	894⅓ " 16 dols.	„	14,316,800 00
Copper ore, quintals	144,546¾ " 2 dols. 50	„	361,367 00
		Dollars	5,400,125 64c.
	= £1,080,025		

Colonel Lloyd says: that 10,000,000 dollars worth of metals were exported in 1853: if this was so, then nearly one-half was smuggled off into Bolivia and across the Andes.

COQUIMBO shipped, in the months of June, July and August of 1859, from the copper mines of Tortoralillo, Coquimbo, Guayacan, Herradura and Tongoy, value 758,358 dollars. The silver mines of Arqueros, Higuera, Brillador, Tambillos, Tamaya, Laja, &c., doing but little.

---

[1] Don Demetrio O'Higgins, now in London, gives me the substance of the following note: Ballenary was founded by his grandfather, the Captain-General of Chile, Don Ambrosio O'Higgins, after his native place in Ireland. Don Ambrosio became Viceroy of Peru, and his son, the gallant and patriotic Don Bernardo, was the first President of Chile. Ballenary is a well-built city, its streets are at right angles, and it is a thriving place.

Chile exported in 1857, value　　19,778,150 dollars.
" imported " "　　20,196,968 "
" exported in 1858 "　　18,335,422 "
" imported " "　　18,186,292 "

England imported in 1858, 6,418,751 dollars, and exports to, were 9,460,966.

The principal Chilian exports are, copper in regulus, bars and ore; silver in bar and ores; guano; coal; wool; gold; gold and silver coin; and plata piña.[1]

LONGITUDE OF VALPARAISO.—In Geographical Society's Journal, 1858, are the Observations relative to the Geographical position of the West Coast of South America, by Carlos Mocsta, Director of the National Observatory of Chile.

The longitudes of Callao and Valparaiso served to determine intermediate points between these two ports, also the coast of Equador and Panamá.

During the last few years, the port of Valparaiso has been in contact with Santiago, by means of the Electric telegraph, which has given the most correct means of knowing the difference of meridian of the two places. Thus, it has been proved, that the difference of longitude between Santiago and Valparaiso, is 3 m. 56.5 s.

From various results, the longitude of Santiago de Chile is deduced to be West of Greenwich 4 h. 42 m. 32.4 s., and that of Valparaiso, 4.46.28.9, and compared with Paris, 4.55.49.5.

This value differs 17 s. 1, from that adopted by the English expeditions for the longitude of Valparaiso; *and by this said quantity, in nearly all the maps, the whole of the West Coast of South America is placed too far to the West.*

THE SEVERAL LONGITUDES, COMPARED WITH THAT OF GREENWICH.

	H.	M.	S.
Santiago	4.	42.	32,4
Valparaiso	4.	46.	28,9
Callao	5.	8.	37,3
Lima	5.	8.	8,6

Humboldt gave for Callao, 5.18.18; Fitzroy, 5.18.15

At p. 257 I mention that accurate levellings through the coast ranges would be interesting. I am informed, whilst the last sheet of this work is going through the press, that a line of railway is projected from Iquique to the principal Nitrate works: thus we may soon expect to get a section through the coast range.

---

[1] Mr. Griffin, in his Prospectus of a line-of-screw Steamers from Europe to Chile, says, during 1855, upwards of 5000 tons of valuable silver ore was shipped to Europe; of Bar Silver a Million sterling.

REGISTER OF EARTHQUAKES, BAROMETER AND THERMOMETER, KEPT AT THE BOLSA, VALPARAISO, 1853.

		8 A.M.		NOON.		4 P.M.	
January	1st	62°	29.83	64°	29.90	65°	29.86
"	15th	65	29.86	67	29.90	68	29.86
"	30th	64	29.88	65	29.90	66	29.91
February	1st	64	29.83	67	29.85	69	29.83
"	15th	68	29.58	67	29.87	72	29.83
"	28th	66	29.85	66	29.88	69	29.88
March	1st	64	29.85	66	29.87	66	29.83
"	15th	65	29.95	71	29.93	73	29.90
"	30th	62	30.00	64	30.01	63	30.01
April	1st	62	30.02	69	30.05	70	30.07
"	15th	60	30.06	61	30.08	64	30.07
"	30th	68	30.18	62	30.18	67	30.16
May	1st	68	30.09	62	30.10	64	30.08
"	15th	58	30.05	56	30.05	64	30.06
June	1st	60	30.09	62	30.10	64	30.08
"	15th	59	29.94	61	29.96	62	29.94
July	1st	56	30.06	60	30.04	63	30.97
"	15th	56	29.95	58	29.97	62	29.96
August	1st	58	29.88	58	29.26	60	29.95
"	15th	52	30.05	58	29.97	62	29.96
September	1st	58	30.08	64	30.10	66	30.06
"	15th	58	29.80	62	29.92	64	29.91
October	1st	63	29.90	66	29.97	70	29.93
"	15th	64	29.94	66	29.97	70	29.93
November	1st	62	29.88	70	29.91	72	29.91
"	15th	64	29.85	68	29.85	70	29.81
December	1st	68	29.92	74	29.92	76	29.91
"	15th	70	29.84	74	29.82	74	29.84
"	31st	63	29.72	66	29.70	70	29.70

May 6th, 1854. Very strong Norther, with rain; many vessels driven on shore; at 4 p.m., 29.62; temp., 60°.

There is but little variation in the climate. During what is called the winter, the thermometer occasionally falls for a few hours to 52°; but the mean throughout the year, at noon, is about 65°. In the evening and morning it is 60°.

EARTHQUAKES OBSERVED AT VALPARAISO IN 1853:—

January	6 .	2.29	p.m.,	strong earthquake.
February	28 .	7.38	"	earthquake.
March	18 .	1.42	"	"
April	4 .	5.40	"	"
May	16 .	11.20	"	"
June	19 .	2.48	"	"
July	5 .			lightning, thunder and hail.
"	18 .	5.20	"	earthquake.
"	22 .	12.48	"	"
September	18 .	5.00	"	"
October	15 .	10.15	"	"
December	10 .	2.15	"	very strong.
"	22	1.30	a.m.	"

It is worthy of remark that only one shock is noted as occurring at a.m.—all the rest p.m.

I am told, that during the Spanish rule in Chile, a postman, named Molina, going across the Cordillera to Uspallata, an earthquake caused a large mass of rock to fall on him, and he and his mule were flattened under it. There is now an inscription on the stone: "Aqui está aplastado el correo Molina."

CURRENT BOTTLES.

In November, 1853, on my way to South America, I had as a fellow-passenger, Lieutenant Hooper, R.N., lately returned from the Arctic region; his constitution was broken, but it was hoped that a trip to the West Indies might re-establish him. This did occur, and I heard that he died shortly afterwards.

On his voyage from Southampton to St. Thomas's, he threw over sealed bottles containing the Admiralty papers, with the view of furthering our knowledge of oceanic currents.

During my passage across the Carribean Sea, along the Pacific, and round Cape Horn to Europe, I followed his example.

1853.	Mark.	Lat.	Long.		
Dec. 5	I.	15° 48' N.	67° 55' W.,	on board Steamer, "Teviot,"	Capt. Sawyer.
6	II.	13.45	70.51	,,	,,
23	III.	5.50	79.50	,,	"Lima,"
				,,	Capt. Bloomfield.
24	IV.	2.31	80.45	,,	,,
25	V.	0.40 S.	81.05	,,	,,
1854					
Dec. 22	A	26.50	82.00	,, bark "Pickwick,"	Capt. Graves.
1855.					
Jan. 1	B	29.52	80.00	,,	
4	C	32.40	76.20	,,	
23	D	33.26	79.40	running between Juan Fernandez and Mas Afuera.	
26	E	36.52	84.05	,,	
29	F	41.08	79.55	,,	
31	G	44.17	79.16	,,	
Feb. 2	H	47.00		,,	
3	I	49.39	80.25	,,	
5	J	54.23	79.17	,,	
7	K	57.02	72.13	,,	
8	L	57.30	68.00	,, off Cape Horn.	
9	M	56.31	63.04	,,	
10	N	56.02	60.00	,,	
11	O	54.53	59.00	,,	
12	P	52.51	56.00	,,	
13	Q	51.10	52.45	,,	
14	R	49.10	52.30	,,	
16	S	47.38	48 40	,,	
18	T	45.23	43.39	,,	

1853.	Mark.	Lat.	Long.	
20	U	41. 21, N.	43. 15, W.	on board bark "Pickwick"
22	V	38. 41	41. 15	,,
24	W	36. 22	37. 19	,,
26	X	34. 54	31. 44	,,
28	Y	33. 50	26. 36	,,
Mar. 2	Z	33. 20	22. 48	,,
4	Z^1	31. 45	21. 40	,,
6	Z^2	29. 50	19. 20	,,
8	Z^3	28. 30	19. 10	,,
10	Z^4	26. 37	16. 45	,,
12	Z^5	25. 49	18. 19	,,
14	Z^6	20. 13	18. 30	,,
16	Z^7	14. 10	22. 00	,,
18	Z^8	8 43	23. 00	,,
20	Z^9	3 37	23. 51	,,
22	Z^{10}	0 03	24. 28	On the Equator.
24	Z^{12}	3 52 N.	24. 33	,,
26	Z^{12}	6 08	25. 50	,,
28	Z^{13}	9 16	28. 39	,,
30	Z^{14}	13. 07	31. 43	,,
April 1	Z^{15}	17. 25	34. 30	,,
3	Z^{16}	21. 27	35. 44	,,
6	Z^{17}	24. 11	36. 50	,,
8	Z^{18}	29. 40	37. 06	,,
10	Z^{19}	34. 03	37. 00	,,
13	Z^{20}	36. 38	36. 48	,,
14	Z^{21}	40. 54	31. 24	,,
16	Z^{22}	42. 32	28. 00	,,
19	Z^{23}	42. 29	25. 30	,,
22	Z^{24}	42. 34	21. 30	,,
24	Z^{25}	44. 15	19. 30	,,
28	Z^{26}	44. 28	15. 26	,,

The following is communicated by the Admiralty:—

Z 7.—Bottle thrown over-board, March 16, 1855, in latitude 14° 10′ S.; longitude 22° W., from "Pickwick," from Valparaiso to Liverpool, T. Graves, Comr., in strong S.E. trades, course N. Found about 25th November, 1855, at Inhambupe, 60 miles N. of Bahia, Brazil.

Z 21.—Bottle thrown over-board, April 14th, 1855, in latitude 40°, 54′ N.; longitude 31°, 24′ W., from "Pickwick," from Valparaiso to Liverpool, T. Graves, Comr., in S. & S.S.W. breezes. Found 26th May, 1855, 1¼ leagues W. of St. Matthew's, in Terceira. Influenced by a N.W. wind, which had thrown it in a S. direction 200 miles in 42 days, or nearly 5 miles per day.

www.ingramcontent.com/pod-product-compliance
Lightning Source LLC
Chambersburg PA
CBHW031332230426
43670CB00006B/326